The History of

Mauchline

Village & Parish

Other books by Dane Love:

Scottish Kirkyards	Robert Hale
The History of Auchinleck – Village & Parish	Carn Publishing
Pictorial History of Cumnock	Alloway Publishing
Pictorial History of Ayr	Alloway Publishing
Scottish Ghosts	Robert Hale
Scottish Ghosts	Barnes & Noble
The Auld Inns of Scotland	Robert Hale
Guide to Scottish Castles	Lomond Books
Tales of the Clan Chiefs	Robert Hale
Scottish Covenanter Stories	Neil Wilson
Ayr Stories	Fort Publishing
Ayrshire Coast	Fort Publishing
Scottish Spectres	Robert Hale
Scottish Spectres	Ulverston Large Print
Ayrshire: Discovering a County	Fort Publishing
Ayr Past and Present	Sutton Publishing
Lost Ayrshire	Birlinn
The River Ayr Way	Carn Publishing
Ayr – the Way We Were	Fort Publishing
The Man Who Sold Nelson's Column	Birlinn
Jacobite Stories	Neil Wilson
The History of Sorn – Village & Parish	Carn Publishing
Legendary Ayrshire	Carn Publishing
The Covenanter Encyclopaedia	Fort Publishing
Scottish Ghosts	Amberley Publishing
Scottish Kirkyards	Amberley Publishing
A Look Back at Cumnock	Carn Publishing
A Look Back at Girvan	Carn Publishing
A Look Back at Ayrshire Farming	Carn Publishing
Ayr Then and Now	The History Press
Ayrshire Then and Now	The History Press

www.dane-love.co.uk

THE HISTORY OF

MAUCHLINE

VILLAGE & PARISH

DANE LOVE

CARN PUBLISHING

© Dane Love, 2012.
First Published in Great Britain, 2012.

ISBN - 978 0 9567550 3 2

Published by Carn Publishing,
Lochnoran House,
Auchinleck, Ayrshire, KA18 3JW.

Printed by Bell & Bain Ltd,
Glasgow, G46 7UQ.

Contents

List of Illustrations

Introduction

Writing this history of Mauchline parish is one that I have been working at for a number of years. There is much that has been written on certain aspects of the district, especially the connection with Robert Burns, but there is so much more that is not readily available to the interested reader. Hopefully this volume will help to fill a considerable need in the general history of the parish.

Published histories of Mauchline are either dated or brief, and it is hoped that this volume will fill a void in the knowledge of the various aspects of village and parish history. Much of what is written has not appeared in print before, the result of research in numerous locations, from original notes and accounts, to information gleaned from gravestones and family history research. Even that which has appeared in print before may not be generally accessible, or readily discovered, and by collating as many of these references as possible has resulted in a book that I hope Mauchlinites will find not only of interest, but useful too.

The way I write and research for books like this one results in numerous people being asked questions about places, people and all aspects of Mauchline history. Often this information may have been gleaned many years ago, and held either on file or in my head, for future use. To list everyone whose contribution has resulted in this book would be impossible, if only due to a short memory, as in many cases the contribution may have been for some other project, or else supplied for no project in particular. However, the following people are due some recognition for their help in specific aspects of the book: Rev David Albon; Ayrshire Archives; Brian Bogle; Burns Monument Centre; Jim Davidson, Ballochmyle Golf Club; Bob Forrest; Hugh Hodge; Alison Holliday of Mauchline Castle; Stroma Leith; Lloyds Banking Group Archives; Jimmy McGhee; Lynne McLean, Mauchline Primary School; John McPheators; Janette Paterson; Mauchline Bowling Club; Mauchline Scouts; Royal Bank of Scotland Archives; Rev Alan Telfer; Lord Weir; James Wilson, Auchmillan; and James Wyllie of Andrew Kay Ltd. Special thanks are due to my wife, Hazel, who has assisted in many ways with this book. To those I have missed out I extend my apologies.

Dane Love
Auchinleck, 2012.

CHAPTER ONE

EARLY TIMES (to 1510)

DESCRIPTION OF PARISH

The parish of Mauchline lies in the central part of Ayrshire, called Kyle, and within that half of Kyle named Kyle Stewart. This gets its name from having been under the jurisdiction of a steward, as opposed to the southern half of the province (beyond the River Ayr), called King's Kyle, which came under the direct jurisdiction of the crown. The parish extends to 8,988 acres, and is approximately eight miles in length from north to south, varying from two to four miles in breadth from east to west. The parish has no real natural boundaries in most places, for it crosses the River Ayr to the south, to bring in part of the north end of Auchinleck estate, and in most places is marked only by fences and field boundaries, other than a stretch to the south, where it is marked by the Dippol Burn, Lugar Water and River Ayr, and to the north, where a section is bounded by the Cessnock Water. Most other boundaries are fairly indistinct and unnatural in style, and in many cases have been defaced or removed in modern times.

The parish is surrounded by seven other parishes – Craigie, Riccarton and Galston to the north, Sorn to the east, Auchinleck and Ochiltree to the south, and

1.1 The early history of Mauchline is lost in the mists of time – Mauchline from the hilltop *(Derrick Phillips)*

Stair and Tarbolton to the west. The parishes of Sorn and Muirkirk were originally part of a much greater Mauchline parish, but these were separated to form ecclesiastical units of their own – Muirkirk in 1631 and Sorn in 1656. The remainder, Mauchline parish, was only one fifth of the size of the original parish.

Most of the parish is reasonable agricultural ground, suitable for ploughing in most places, but often left for growing a grass crop or for grazing. In 1846 it was reckoned that all of the parish apart from 300 acres of woodland and a small stretch of moss comprised arable ground. Of the parish acreage, it was reckoned in 1950 that around 5,400 acres were under cultivation. The soil is light and sandy near the village, in some places it comprises a rich loam, but in general it is clayey. Some areas of the parish are well-wooded, usually around estate policies.

The highest point of the parish is located at March House, where Mauchline parish meets the parishes of Sorn and Galston. At that place the ground is only a few feet higher than the summit of Mauchline Hill, at 656 feet above sea level. The lowest point in the parish is located where the Mauchline Burn meets the River Ayr, just upstream from the Burnfoot Bridge – there the land is around 188 feet above sea level.

The village or town of Mauchline is located approximately 470 feet above sea level, though this of course varies across the community. Mauchline Cross, being the centre of the town, is 467 feet above sea level. The Ordnance Survey benchmark on the wall of the church is 470.7 feet above sea level. The summit of Mauchline Hill, which is of course outwith the built up area, is 642 feet above sea level, the highest point within a radius of 2¾ miles. This height is attained to the east, at Weitshaw, in Sorn parish. To the south, the next place of a comparable height is located at Darntaggart, Ochiltree parish, a distance of 6½ miles. To the north we have to travel 7½ miles, to the moors of Loudoun parish, before attaining the same height, whereas to the immediate west, the next point of a comparable height can be found on the Island of Arran, 30 miles distant.

The name Mauchline has been spelled a variety of ways over the centuries. Early versions include Machlein, Machlene, Machlin and Maghline. In the *Statistical Account*, Rev William Auld noted that the spelling becoming more common at that time (i.e. 1791) is Machlin. He stated that the name derives from Gaelic, and that it means 'field of flax', from magh, meaning field, meadow or plain, and lion, meaning flax or lint. Writing in the *New Statistical Account*, in 1837, Rev John Tod noted that 'of late it is more commonly spelled Mauchline', implying that the other variants had been used until fairly recent times.

The name meaning 'field of flax' is not that commonly accepted today. Writing in *Prehistoric Man in Ayrshire*, published in 1895, John Smith states that the name means 'the field of the lake'. The derivation of the name is thought to come from the Gaelic words *magh*, and *linne* or *linn*, which means pool, or lake. The second element is harder to appreciate for the district – there are meadows aplenty around the village, but few lakes. The meaning has often been widened to include springs, of which there are plenty in the immediate vicinity of the town, or pools, there being small pools in the Mauchline Burn at various locations.

THE BRONZE AGE

Mauchline is noted for a particularly good example of Bronze Age rock art surviving in the parish. Located south of Kingencleugh, in the Ballochmyle gorge, two main vertical cliffs of sandstone have at sometime around 2000-1500 BC been decorated by Bronze Age man. The rock art had been hidden by trees for many years, and it was only when these were cut down in 1986 that local man, Bert Liddell of Catrine, recognised their significance. In 1987 the site was then partially excavated by members of Catrine, Sorn and District Local History Group, under the guidance of Dr Noel Fojut, an Inspector of Ancient Monuments. At the same time a drawn and photographic survey of the carvings was undertaken. Although some new markings were discovered, no artefacts were found.

1.2 Bronze Age cup and ring markings *(Dane Love)*

It is reckoned that the carvings were made over a long period of time, from the Neolithic period, which is represented by cups, cup-and-rings, cups in squares, channels and ringed stars. These carvings constitute the largest collection on the slabs. There are also three rough carvings indicating what may be deer, and it is thought that these may be contemporary with the main carvings. Speculation also hints that the carvings were made by a variety of artists, rather than just one, as some are well executed, whereas others are rough and ill-laid out.

A second phase of carving was suggested by one of the surveyors, Ian Scott, who felt that some of the carvings were perhaps lettering in the Lombardic style, carved onto the rocks in the mediaeval period. A few letters were too difficult to read, but those which he felt were decipherable read 'ASAID'. What this could possibly mean was not worked out.

1.3 Bronze Age cup and ring markings *(Dane Love)*

A third phase of carving was the inclusion of the numbers 1751 carved on the south-western cliff. This, it was agreed, represented the year and it was felt that it was in no doubt carved onto the rock in that year. Why there was no record of any of these cup-and-ring carvings from the eighteenth century remains a mystery, their existence being forgotten about until 1986.

The carvings at Ballochmyle are reckoned to be one of the largest such groupings in the British Isles. They are also quite unusual, but not unique, in that they are found on a vertical surface. Also, there is a pattern that appears to be found only on this face, a cup or dash surrounded by a square or rectangle, of which there are many examples. Another strange feature is the inclusion of carved deer, perhaps does or hinds, a pair together and one on its own.

A few Bronze Age artefacts have been discovered across the parish. Near to Mauchline Mains farm a Middle Bronze Age flanged axe head was discovered in 1994 by a metal detectorist. The axe head was declared treasure trove, and was allocated by the authorities to Glasgow Museums.

IRON AGE

There are few relics of the Iron Age in Mauchline parish. This period of history is generally ascribed to around 500 BC to around 500 AD. On Ballochmyle golf course, on a bluff overlooking the new Howford Bridge, a possible Iron Age settlement of some sort was discovered during an aerial survey undertaken in 1981. From the air crop-marks revealed a large circular feature on the ground. The site has not been excavated, but there is a possibility that the circular shape is the ploughed-out remains of a circular 'mount' or round wood, forming part of the policies of Ballochmyle estate.

ROMAN PERIOD

The Romans occupied much of southern Scotland from 80 AD to 200 AD. Whether or not they were in the Mauchline area is not known, but there has been speculation that a Roman road made its way through the parish. The theory behind this is that there was a Roman Road up through Nithsdale, heading for Loudoun Hill Roman fort. More recent aerial surveys have indicated that the long-looked for road more likely went by way of Sanquhar and Muirkirk, crossing the moorland uplands.

In the past, excavations were made at various places throughout the parish where old roads were known to have existed, in the hope that they would provide evidence of Roman road-building. At each of the digs evidence of an ancient roadway was found, but nothing to confirm anything as old as from the Roman period.

DARK AGES

In AD 681 there is said to have been a battle at or near to Mauchline. A group known as the Cruithne, or Cruithni, came over from Ireland with the intention of conquering much of south west Scotland. The ancient British or occupants of the ancient Strathclyde (Alcluydensians) who lived in this area managed to gather themselves together and came to meet them as a force. A bloody battle ensued, and the Cruithne are said to have been soundly defeated. The site of the battle is often reported as Mauchline Muir. It is also said that the same struggle resulted in further battles in AD 702 and 703.

EARLY LANDOWNERS

In the eleventh century the whole of what was known as Kyle Stewart (that part of Ayrshire between the River Irvine and the River Ayr/Lugar Water boundary, was owned by the Stewart family, which held the position of High Steward of Scotland. The lands were sparsely populated at the time, there probably being nothing resembling a village in the parish, only sparse 'ferm-touns' – small communities of farmers grazing cattle and tilling small areas of soil.

King David I of Scotland, who reigned from 1124 to 1153, may have been the first person to introduce the monks of Melrose Abbey to Mauchline. The monks were Cistercian in their order, and were noted for their belief in self-sufficiency, being active farmers and brewers. They are also credited with spreading the technology of the water wheel, building mills and improving dams and lades to increase power. Again, at Mauchline, the Haugh Mill may have roots as far back as the time of the Cistercian monks, for the earliest reference to it dates from 1527, thirty years or so before the Reformation.

The lands of Mauchline were granted sometime between 1165 and 1178 by Walter, High Steward of Scotland, son of Alan (or FitzAlan), to the monks of Melrose Abbey. The extent of the grant covered 58,573 acres, forming the present parishes of Mauchline, Sorn and Muirkirk, and comprised the Barony of Kylesmure. At the time the land was fairly uncultivated, being classed as forest, though there were considerable extents of pasture within it. The Stewarts also granted the monks of Melrose a carracute of land to improve where it was most convenient to do so. The grant by Walter Stewart was confirmed at his request by King William.

The monks erected a cell here, and over the following centuries greatly extended their possessions. A home for the monks who preached at Mauchline was erected, known as a grange, as well as associated offices, barns, granaries, and a hospice. At the same time a chapel was erected, though exactly when this took place is not known.

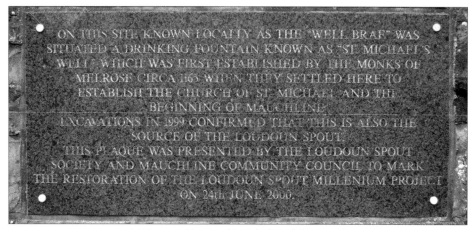

1.4 Plaque marking site of St Michael's Well *(Dane Love)*

The church at Mauchline was dedicated to St Michael, who was one of the principal angels, mentioned in Daniel, who fought against Satan and who rescued souls near to death. His feast day was 29 September. He is also attributed with miracles creating springs, perhaps one of the reasons why he was chosen as Mauchline's saint. Near to the church, at the lane known as the Burgher Road, was St Michael's Well, dedicated to the saint. Some called the well the Burgher Well. This well was the main supply of fresh water for the village that grew around it. The well became covered over the years, and latterly was more or less lost. However, in 1999, excavations at its site uncovered the well, and on the wall by the path a granite stone was affixed, bearing the inscription:

> On this site known locally as the 'Well Brae' was situated a drinking fountain known as 'St Michael's Well' which was first established by the monks of Melrose circa 1165 when they settled here to establish the church of St Michael and the beginning of Mauchline. Excavations in 1999 confirmed that this is also the source of the Loudoun Spout. This plaque was presented by the Loudoun Spout Society and

Mauchline Community Council to mark the restoration of the
Loudoun Spout Millenium *[sic]* Project on 24th June 2000.

The monks extended their estates in Ayrshire, and in addition to Mauchline
acquired the lands of Kylesmure and Barmure. These estates were formed into a
regality, with the centre of control, or court, being located at Mauchline.

It has been claimed that in, or about, the year 1165, there was also founded St
Mary's Cistercian Priory of Mauchline. This was a cell of Melrose Abbey. However,
some think that this was an error, and that no priory was ever established in
Mauchline. According to the *Fasti Ecclesiae Scoticanae*, written in 1920, ruined
portions of the Cistercian priory remained. Writing in a note in a subsequent
volume, Rev Dr D. E. Easson states that 'there was no monastery at Mauchline, and
the frequently repeated statement that there was (it goes back at least to Habakkuk
Bisset) rests on nothing better than conjecture.'

A charter of 8 January 1430 issued by King James I to the monks of the church
of St Mary, Melrose, lists the lands which belonged to the abbey at time. In it
reference is made to Mauchline:

> ... ac omnes eorum terras de Machlyne quas habuerent in puram
> elemosinam ex concessione senescallorum Scotie, - liberas et
> immunes ab omnibus prisis, captionibus, cariagiis, martis, et aliis
> talliagiis quibuscunque, ad opus regis, et desuper prohibuit ne quis
> contra dictam concessionem, ipsos religiosis aut terras suas predictas,
> vel corum homines predictas terras inhabitants, vexare, etc.,
> presumeret.

The church of Mauchline has often been described as being 'barn-like' – the
Ordnance Gazetteer of Scotland, published in 1892, describes it thus. What type of
barn is the question that is not answered, was it the small Scots single-storey barn
still typical of the local farms, or else the large barn to be found all over England,
with their stout walls, heavy timber roof and extensive interior. The only illustration
of the old church appears to be an engraving found on a Mauchline box, and
replicated in John Taylor Gibb's *Mauchline Town and District*, published in 1911.
This shows the church to have been basically a single-storey structure, built of
random rubble. There are few windows, and these are merely small rectangular
openings, not the lancet windows or traceried openings we would associate with
churches. The two gables were unadorned, not even with corbie-steps, the slate roof
covering over the wall-heads. On the northern gable an exterior stairway is shown,
leading to a doorway about eight feet or so above ground level. Above this doorway
is a strange belfry, perhaps built of timber, reaching to the apex of the roof. There,
in a small open bellcote, hung the kirk bell. Also on the northern wall was a

doorway at ground level.

The west wall of the kirk had perhaps two or more doorways in it, one of which appears to have been arched and which may have been adorned by a carved stone surround. Adjoining it was a simple rectangular doorway. Centrally placed on the south front was a large archway, the interior of which had been built up.

If this old kirk incorporated remnants of Mauchline's ancient priory, then the only two parts of it identifiable as being of some antiquity were the arched doorway and large arch. No doubt it was not bricked up originally, and perhaps another wing or aisle adjoined the building at this point.

Dr Edgar, in his book on *Old Church Life in Scotland*, describes what the building was like:

> The church was a long, narrow, low-walled building, with a high, steep roof. For many a day previous to its demolition the ground outside the wall was in some places several feet above the level of the floor inside, and at the door on the south wall there was a flight of descending steps that led down into the area of the church. It was buttressed all round too with unsightly stair-cases, one in the centre of each gable and two against the north wall, all leading to separate galleries within...

1.5 Mauchline Castle in 1791 by Francis Grose *(Author's Collection)*

1.6 Mauchline Castle in 1889 by MacGibbon and Ross *(Author's Collection)*

In the sixteenth century a hospitium, or spital, was established at Mauchline, also belonging to the monks of Melrose Abbey.

During the time of the crusades, which took place in the thirteenth century, some local knights may have taken part, for there is a tradition that one of the oldest stones in the kirkyard was a Knight Templar's stone. This was a large heavy narrow slab of stone, lying prostate on the ground. There is no inscription on the stone, but there was at one time a sword or perhaps two carved along its length.

Robert Wishart, Bishop of Glasgow, granted the church of Mauchline to Melrose Abbey on 30 June 1315, for himself and his successors. The grant allowed the abbey to hold the church in the barony of Kylesmure, and gave permission for the church to have the insignia of a parish church. The church was to hold all the teinds both great and small, and be equipped with its own cemetery, etc. This grant was later confirmed by John Lindsay, Bishop of Glasgow, in 1326.

Mauchline Castle was probably built sometime in the middle part of the fifteenth century. The old tower, which still stands in the centre of the village, was erected as a fortified dwelling for ecclesiastics employed in managing the extensive church lands. The tower is built of the local sandstone, ashlar in style, and rises

1.7 Interior of Great Hall, Mauchline Castle
(Author's Collection)

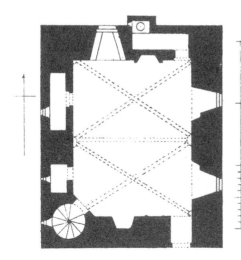

1.8 Plan of principal floor of Mauchline Castle
(Author's Collection)

through three storeys. The ground floor has two barrel-vaulted chambers located side by side. They are interconnected, but do not have any fireplaces within them. These vaults are reached through an ancient doorway. On the east wall are two windows, the carved stone arches being of considerable antiquity.

In the south-west corner of the tower is a spiral staircase built within the thickness of the walls. This leads up to the first floor. This storey is occupied by a large hall, measuring 25 feet by 20 feet. It is vaulted, the stonework divided into two bays with groined arches springing from carved corbels. On the east side of this room are two sets of square windows. On the north wall is a garderobe built within the thickness of the wall, the latrine chute protruding on the exterior face of the wall. On the west side of the hall are two small chambers (one measures 9 feet by 3 feet, the other 5 feet by 3 feet), both of which have tiny openings to the exterior. Another large window, which has benches within the splays, existed on the north wall, but this has been built up. The large fireplace is located on the south wall. A second fireplace is located on the north side of the room, perhaps indicating that this room was at one time divided.

The third floor is incorporated partly within the roof space of the tower. A series of corbels at the wallheads at one time supported a parapet, within which was a pitched roof and corbie-stepped gables.

1.9 Mauchline Castle in 2012 *(Dane Love)*

On the vaulted ceiling of the main hall of the castle is a boss, on which is carved the arms of Abbot Andrew Hunter of Melrose Abbey (*c.* 1444-71). This probably gives a fair indication of the age of the tower, which was probably erected to replace an earlier structure. The erection of fortified tower-houses by abbeys was not uncommon at the time, for there appears to have been some unrest in the district, and the tower was erected to protect the money and charters of the district, as well as for the safety of its abbots. A similar tower house, though larger in size, was built alongside Crossraguel Abbey in Carrick, in the early sixteenth century.

A number of other old charters associated with Melrose Abbey give us tantalising information concerning places in the parish. There was a charter issued by Peter de Curry to the Abbey of Melrose of the lands of 'Dalhengen', or Dalsangan, and Bargour. These lands were bounded by the burn that flowed from Loch Brown (then known as the Duve Loch) and the Cessnock Water. The charter notes this as 'qui jacent inter rivulem cadentem de Duveloch et Saxnoc.'

Other early references to Mauchline locations include a charter that was issued by Robert, Lord Boyd, in favour of Robert Campbell of Kingencleugh in 1474, granting him the lands of Kingencleugh.

CHAPTER TWO

SIXTEENTH CENTURY

On 30 October 1510 Mauchline was created a free Burgh of Barony by charter issued by King James IV from Edinburgh. The superior of the burgh was the abbot of Melrose Abbey. The charter, in Latin, reads as follows:

> Apud Edinburgh, 30 October.
> Rex, - pro specialibus favoribus erga Rob. abbatem monasterii de Melros, et conventum ejusdem, ac pro edificatione et pollitia fiend. in villa de Mauchlin et apud ecclesiam esjudem pro asiamento et hospitatione ligeorum, - infeodavit et creavit Villam de Mauchlin, cum domibus, etc. ejusdem, in dominio de Kilis-mure, vic. Are – liberum Burgum in baronia; - cumfacultate inhabitantibus emendi et vendeni, etc. necnon ut essent burgenses et potestatem haberent eligendi ballivos, etc. necnon ut haberent crucem foralem et forum die Mercuri singulis ebdomadis, et liberas nundinas annuatim in die St Francisci in mense Octobris et per octavas ejusdem; cum theoloneis, etc. – et cum potestate dictis abbati et conventui terras dicte ville in rodis burgalibus hereditary assedandi.

In 1521 Hew Campbell of Loudoun made a contract with the abbot of Melrose, Robert Beaton, whereby he was appointed the Bailie of the Regality of Mauchline. Campbell was astute and, aware of the religious and political troubles of the period, could see that the rich lands of the monastic houses were likely to be broken up. The deed reads as follows:

> Be it ken be thir presents, &c. bundin and oblist, on ye faith and treuth of my bodie lelely and treulie, and heirs-mail to be gotten of my bodie, myn and their executours, with gudes whatsoever and gear movabbil and immoveabil, to ane Rev. fader in God, Robert, Abbot of Melrose. That forasmeikle as ye said Rev. fader, in Convent with haill and full assent, has made me and my hears foresaid bailzie to all and syndrie,

ye lands of Kylesmuir and Barmuir, lying within ye Bailzerie of Kyle-Stewart and Sheriffdom of Air, I sall, with friends and allyes mainteen and defend said Rev. fader and Convent in ye said lands against all whatsoever, ye sovereign alane excepted.

The deed was signed by Hew Campbell, and witnessed by John Campbell of Little Cessnock, John Hamilton of Macnairston, John Duncanson, Chancellor of Glasgow, Matho Crawford, Hew Crauford of Heateth, and others.

Campbell promised that he would not tax any of the Kylesmure tenants, ask for carriage service from them, or take the fines charged in the barony court. He was also unable to appoint a deputy without permission from the abbot, and was banned from hunting or hawking over the lands held by the farmers. Tenants who were in default of their rent or for whatever other reason, he was obliged to evict, even although that tenant was a friend or there was a bond of manrent between them.

As part of the agreement, Campbell had to pledge his rents, lands and moveable estate for the honouring of the agreement.

During the 1550s, Melrose Abbey decided to feu out the lands of Kylesmure, the barony in which Mauchline was located. The farms were taken on by numerous tenants who had previously held their lands by quasi-heritable life leases.

In 1583 the residents of Mauchline decided to establish the village as a free burgh. This caused some considerable strife in Ayr, where the magistrates, council and community made their feelings known. Accordingly, the Ayr Council noted in their minutes that they had been greatly hurt as the Mauchline folk had:

2.1 Kingencleugh Castle around 1900 *(Author's Collection)*

24

Taking vpoun thaim and presuming to be ane fre burch to tak vp custumes, mak lawis & constitutionis within thaim self to the dirogatioun of the liberties of this burch as gif thai wer fre.

The council sought legal advice concerning the problem, with an intention 'to the vtter depriuatioun of the pretendit liberties.'

LANDOWNERS

As explained, Hew or Sir Hugh Campbell of Loudoun acquired much of Mauchline parish, and settled his family here. He was created a Lord of Parliament on 30 June 1601, taking as his title, Lord Campbell of Loudoun. He died on 15 December 1622 and, as his son predeceased him, he was succeeded by his granddaughter, Margaret, Baroness Loudoun. She married Sir John Campbell of Lawers, and when he was raised in the peerage on 12 May 1633 as Earl of Loudoun, he took as a subsidiary title the Lordship of Mauchline. The honorary title of Baron, or Lord Mauchline is maintained to the present time by the heir of the Earl of Loudoun. The main branch in the parish was the Campbells of Kingencleugh, or Kinzeancleuch as it was also spelled.

On 30 January 1566 Sir Matthew Campbell, Sheriff of Ayr, obtained a charter of the dominical lands and lordship of Mauchline, as well as others in Ayrshire, from Michael, Commendator of Melrose Abbey. This was confirmed by the Great Seal on 1 February 1567. Campbell's lands included the forty pound lands of Mauchline, with tower and fortalice, Blairkip, Blairmulloch and Haugh Mill.

The first Campbell of Kingencleugh who is recorded is thought to be Hew Campbell, who lived in the latter part of the fifteenth and early sixteenth centuries. He was a younger son of Sir George Campbell of Loudoun, who died around 1484/5. This Sir George was the father of another Sir George, father in turn of George Campbell, father of Sir Hugh Campbell of Loudoun.

Hugh, or Hew, Campbell of Kingencleugh was mentioned by Rev John Knox as being offended by those who barred the kirk of Mauchline against the entrance of Rev George Wishart in 1544. According to Knox's *History of the Reformation*:

> that they should debar them from entreing the kirk, and concluded by force to enter; but the said Mr George [Wishart] withdrew the said Hugh, and said unto him, 'Brother, Christ Jesus is as potent in the fields as in the kirk'.

Accordingly the minister and the barred congregation left the churchyard and made their way to a dike by the side of the muir, located on the south west of Mauchline, where they held their service.

Hew Campbell was succeeded by his son, Robert Campbell, who was to marry a distant cousin, Elizabeth Campbell, daughter of the Campbells of Cessnock Castle. His name is listed as one of the absentees in the assize on the lairds of Lochnorris Castle (Old Cumnock) and Eccles (Penpont, Dumfriesshire), which was held on 14 November 1554. These lairds were to be tried for intercommoning, or having dealings, with Hunter of Ballagan, who was a rebel at the horn. The lairds, however, came in the King's will. In 1559 Robert Campbell is noted as being cautioner for John Willock, a converted Scottish Franciscan friar, who was denounced as a rebel for usurping the right of the church, and for preaching within the burgh of Ayr. Robert Campbell was amerciated, or fined for him.

At the start of 1566 John Lockhart of Barr (d. 1575) and Robert Campbell conducted Rev John Knox on a tour through Kyle, taking him to houses where his reformed doctrine would be welcome. In this trip Knox preached at Kingencleugh, as well as at Barr Castle (Galston), Carnell Castle, Ochiltree, Gadgirth Castle and Ayr. At some of these meetings Knox is known to have dispensed the Lord's Supper.

Robert's support for the church is seen in his decision to give up half the teinds that he was due from the parish of Ochiltree to support the protestant minister there.

Again, in 1566, according to Pitcairn's *Criminal Trials*, he acted as surety for William Johnstone, bower, burgess of Edinburgh, 'for his entry at the next Justice Aire of Edinburgh, to underlie the law for art and part counselling and devising the death of Senzeour Dauid Riccio.' The murder of David Rizzio in the Palace of Holyroodhouse in Edinburgh brought forth suspicion of many people across Scotland, so high were the feelings at the time. Those who had actively promoted the Reformation were uppermost in this list, which even included Rev John Knox, and thus Campbell was suspected of having taken part in some way.

On 17 May 1569 a further charter issued under the Great Seal of Scotland was issued to Robert Campbell of Kingencleugh, which listed his properties at that time. These included Over Haugh, Kingencleugh, MacNaughtscroft, Shield, Nether Haugh, Willockston, Bridgend, MacLanachanston, Aird, Darnford, Clews, Bruntshiels, and Haughholm.

There is a tale concerning Robert Campbell in Wodrow's *Analecta*. Apparently, prior to the Battle of Langside, which took place on 13 May 1568, Campbell went to the Regent Moray, whom he supported, and asked of him that, should the Queen be defeated, which he thought was likely, then if the estates of her supporters were to be divided up, could he have the estate of the Sheriff of Ayr (Sir Matthew Campbell, died *c.* 1593), as he was a friend of his. Regent Moray replied that it would be time enough to divide up estates once the victory had taken place. Campbell, however, persisted, and eventually was promised that if the Queen lost the battle, then the estate of the sheriff would indeed be given to him. Campbell then told the Regent that the Sheriff of Ayr was also a Campbell, chieftain of his clan, but that he was still a youth, bred in ignorance and influenced by bad company. However, he explained that he had an excellent disposition, and that he still hoped that he would do great things in the west of the country, supporting the Reformation.

Mary Queen of Scots was indeed defeated at Langside, and the Sheriff of Ayr was one that was taken prisoner. Accordingly, he was forfeited of his estates, and these were granted to Campbell of Kingencleugh as promised. Campbell of Loudoun remained in prison for a period, and once he was set free Robert Campbell returned his estates to him. Campbell of Loudoun did become a strong supporter of the Reformation and, in thanks for what Kingencleugh had done for him, presented him with a mill and some lands near to Kingencleugh.

A poem entitled 'A Memorial of the Life and Death of two worthye Christians, Robert Campbell of the Kinyeancleugh and his wife, Lady Kinyeancleugh', written by John Davidson, Regent in St Leonard's College and afterwards minister of Salt Preston, commemorates Robert Campbell and his wife:

> But to be plainer is nae skaith,
> Of surnames, they were Campbells baith;
> Of ancient blood of the countrie,
> They were baith of genealogie;
> He of the Sheriff's house of Air,
> Long noble, famous and preclair;
> She of a gude and godly stock,
> Come of the old house of Cessnock,
> Quais lord of mony years bygane
> Professed Christ's religion plaine;
> Yea, eighty years sinsyne and mair,
> As I heard aged men declare.
>
> Some preachers did till him resort
> Where mutuallie they got comfort;
> The treuth on their part was declared,
> No temporal benefits he spared;
> They lacked not gude intreatment
> In daylie food and nourishment;
> Gif there was mair necessitie
> They needed not to crave supplie;
> So privatelie in his lodgeing,
> He had baith prayers and preaching,
> To tell his friends he no whit dred;
> How they had lang been blindlins led.
> Then Robert, like a busy Bie,

Did ride the post in all countrie;
Baith North and South, baith East and West,
To all that the gude cause profest,
Through Angus, Fyfe and Lowthian,
Late journies had he mony ane;
By night he would pass forth of Kyle,
And slip in shortly to Argyle;
Syne to Strathearne and to all parts,
Where he know Godly, zealous hearts;
Exhorting them for to be stout,
And of the matter have no doubt.

He also wrote regarding Lady Elizabeth Campbell:

Never man heard her complain
As many wives in the countrie,
I trow I luked angerlie
On her gudeman who at all tide
Was aye so reddy for to ryde;
For so oft ryding could not miss
But to procure great expence,
He might look, as they tell the tale,
When he came home for well cooled kail!

Robert Campbell was friendly with Rev John Knox. When the great Reformer was ill and dying, Campbell attended him regularly, and their friendship grew even more. He was one of the few people who were allowed into Knox's chamber when he was in his dying days. An account of Knox noted that 'besides his wife and Bannatyne, Campbell of Kinyeancleugh, Johnstone of Elphinstone and Dr Preston sat by turns at his bedside.' It is recorded that Campbell was one of the last men to whom Knox spoke, commending his wife and children into his care.

Robert Campbell died in 1574, leaving an only child, Elizabeth. She was born around 1524 and was married about 1553 to John or Robert Campbell (born c. 1520 - died after 1602). They had four children, Robert (born c. 1554 – died after 1613), John (born c. 1558 – died after 1636), Charles (born c. 1562) and George (born c. 1566). Elizabeth Campbell succeeded to Kingencleugh fully in 1586. In 1613 the Loudoun deed of entail was drawn up, in which she is listed.

The south-west part of the parish formed part of Barskimming estate, which was on 12 October 1375 granted to William Rede (or Reid), son of John Rede. William was married to a woman named Katherine and was succeeded by their son, John Rede of Barskimming. He was one of a number of *nobiles viri* who took part in an inquisition held in Ayr on 10 May 1399. From him was descended Adame Rede of Barskimming, also known as Adam Rede of Starquit, or Stair-White. He was one of the Lollards of Kyle who disputed with Bishop Blackadder before King James IV. He was granted a charter of the lands and castle of Ardcarden in Kintyre on 15 September 1498, along with the duty of maintaining six archers, who were to fight on behalf of the king should they be required, against the inhabitants of the Western Isles. He was married to Jonet Campbell of Thirdpart.

Other small lairdships included Auchmillan, which became the property of the Gibbs. According to the Chartulary of Melrose, these lands were granted to James Gibb on 20 February 1555. The document notes that money was required to rebuild their house, or 'place' as it was styled (representing a sizeable building), which had been burnt by the attacking foes of England during the border wars. The charter continued, noting that the monks:

> give, grant, etc., all and hail the six shilling and eight penny land of old extent of Auchmilling, hitherto subject to the payment, according to rental, of three pennies, in *arreagiis et careagiis*, and in lie bondage silver, to the amount of nine pennies of the usual money of Scotland, with all the houses, places, valleys, moors, lakes, mills, multures and thair accompaniments, huntings, fishings, peturies, charcoal, rabbit warrens, dovecots, orchards, brazures, breweries, woods, stones and lime, with mines and carts, *herezeldo et mercheta mulierum*, and with common pasture, and all the usual liberties named or unnamed, and all privileges and accommodations, paying a feu-duty of 6s 8d in *areagiis et careagiss*, and thirty pennies in silver, to our well beloved James Gib in Auchmilling.

CHURCH

The church in Mauchline formed part of the vast lands belonging to the Abbey at Melrose. As a result, much of the teinds that were gathered were sent to the abbey, to keep the monks and pay for the upkeep of the large monastical buildings. The route taken by the carts loaded with grain went by way of the River Ayr and thence by way of Priesthill, north of Muirkirk, before crossing the hills to Lanark and thence to Carnwath. At that point the loads were passed on to the carriage men from Melrose, who had come to collect it.

In a similar way, much of the rent payable by the feuars of Kylesmure was taken eastwards by the same route to Lesmahagow, where a priory existed, maintained by the abbots of Kelso. The chamberlain from Kelso and his officials collected the rents and feus at Lesmahagow Priory, on behalf of the joint commendator of Kelso and Melrose, James Stewart.

Sometime in the sixteenth century the monks of Melrose Abbey established a *hospitium* at Mauchline. Little more is known about this facility.

Of priests who served in the chapel at Mauchline the list is incomplete. At one point the curate of the parish, James Mitchell, paid William Aird to serve as the chaplain in the parish. In 1562 Rev Andrew Mitchell is recorded as being the chaplain and curate.

Ministers in parishes were entitled to employ parish clerks, or assistant ministers, who were usually presented to the bishop by a patron. These positions were in most cases foregone conclusions, the patrons usually selecting someone they knew and voting him in. It was often the case that these parish clerks were gentry family members,

2.2 Old Parish Church around 1800 *(Author's Collection)*

perhaps younger sons. A few cases of disputes have been recorded where the election of these clerks has not gone smoothly. Mauchline in 1524 was one such case.

On 1 and 2 November 1524 Hugh Campbell, Sheriff of Ayr and Baillie of the lands of Mauchline since 1521, arranged an election in Mauchline parish for the appointment of a new clerk. He had put forward Adam Reid, his servant, who was probably one of the Reids of Barskimming. He was to succeed William Lame. In total 173 landholding householders in the parish made their way to the manse to record their support for Reid and he was duly elected.

On Sunday 6 November 1524 Campbell stood up within the church and asked the congregation if they wished to object to the election of Reid. Campbell's presence was intended to make sure that there was no objection, and Reid was duly inducted by the assistant chaplain. Campbell then handed Reid the holy water stoup as a symbol of his office.

Two folk did protest at Reid's appointment, however. One was David Lundy, who had been nominated by the monks of Melrose Abbey, they of course being patron of the church, and John Liddell, who was one of the monks who supported Lundy, claiming that he had been prevented from being elected by force, and that Reid had simply been elected as he was a servant to Sir Hugh Campbell.

The outcome of the dispute is not fully known, however, but it is known that in April 1529 John Lundy was inducted to the clerkship, having produced a letter of provision from Melrose Abbey. Prior to Lundy's appointment there is no reference to a popular election, perhaps the monks of Melrose using their power to appoint him. It is known, however, that the parishioners were instructed to answer to Lundy for all of the fruits of office. Five parishioners, including three Reids, were witnesses to the instrument recording Reid's induction.

The names of some other parish clerks in Mauchline are known. In 1507 the clerk was

2.3 Rev John Knox *(Author's Collection)*

Alexander Hervi, who is noted in papers at the Vatican in Rome. In 1524 William Lame was noted – he died that year, resulting in the disputed election. John Lundy followed Adam Reid. In 1555 and 1557 reference is made to Mungo Campbell as clerk, no doubt a member of the Netherplace family.

In 1544-5 George Wishart began preaching across Ayrshire. He was a reformer, and questioned much of the Roman Catholic faith. He was invited to preach in Mauchline, but word of this reached Sir Matthew Campbell of Loudoun, Sheriff of Ayr, who, with four others went to the kirk and barred the door. Their aim was 'for [the] preservation of a tabernacle that was there, beautiful to the eye.' It is thought that this tabernacle was some form of shrine, presented to the church by the monks of Melrose, and thus valuable to them. It was feared that Wishart and his reformers would see it as a symbol of the Romish church, and would destroy it as part of their zeal. With Campbell that day were two other Campbells, dependents of the Loudoun family, and also George Reid of Daldilling, in Sorn parish.

Hugh Campbell of Kingencleugh was a supporter of Wishart, and was there when the doorway was barred. He was keen to have the door forced open, but others dissuaded him from carrying this out. Indeed, Wishart addressed the crowd, saying, 'Brethren, it is the word of peace I preach unto you, the blood of no man

2.4 Rev George Wishart *(Author's Collection)*

shall be shed for it this day. Jesus Christ is as mighty in the fields as in the church; and He Himself, while He lived in the flesh, preached oftener in the desert, and by the seaside, than in the Temple of Jerusalem. It is the word of peace that God sends by me, - the blood of no man shall be shed this day for the preaching of it.'

Instead, Wishart held an open-air service on the edge of Mauchline Muir, south-west of the village. He stood on a turf dike to address the congregation, who seem to have come from far and wide to hear him. It was a hot and pleasant day, the congregation sitting and standing around Wishart in considerable numbers. The sermon appears to have lasted for three hours. It is noted that 'one of the most wicked men that was in that country, named Laurence Rankin,' was present on the day of the service, and having listened to Wishart was converted to his way of thinking. In his conversion, the tears ran freely down his face, much to the wonder of those present, and it was noted that he was a changed man for the remainder of his lifetime.

Wishart is reckoned to have stayed in the neighbourhood for a further month, and it is thought that he spent most of this time staying at Kingencleugh. During this period he also preached at Galston (in the Barr Tower) and at other places.

A tradition claims that whilst Wishart stayed at Kingencleugh he planted a tree in the woods near to the house. When it was mature it was cut down and used to make the communion table for Mauchline kirk.

2.5 Primrose Stone *(Dane Love)*

REFORMATION

The protestant Reformation took a number of years to spread over much of southern Scotland. The first major event in the change from Roman Catholicism to Protestantism took place in December 1557, when the 'First Bond' of Protestant lords was determined to take a stand to overthrow the Roman Catholic church, but it was not until August 1560 that some parishes had been converted. One of the main acts of the reformers was to destroy almost all of the Roman Catholic imagery located within churches, so that Scotland lost thousands of historical treasures in this period of history. Mauchline church had an important tabernacle within the parish church, and it was probably destroyed at this time.

One of the zealous reformers was Charles Campbell of Bargour, who is known to have involved himself in destroying Catholic imagery within churches, including 'Eucharistic chalices, altars, breaking up choir stalls and breaking church windows in Cunninghame, Kyle and Carrick, as well as in Renfrewshire and Lanarkshire.' No doubt he would have been heavily involved in destroying anything that resembled Catholic imagery in his own parish.

When the reformers took over Mauchline kirk, they cleansed it of items that were regarded as belonging to the old form of worship. Thus many ancient pictures, artefacts and screens were destroyed, leaving the church building more open. The altar was destroyed and in its place a new pulpit was erected, facing north.

It has also been speculated that the buildings of the ancient priory or church at Mauchline were removed at this time, leaving only Mauchline Castle and the main church building standing. What the other ecclesiastical buildings were has been the subject of much speculation over the centuries, and only extensive archaeological digs will today reveal the secret.

As part of the 'new way', the reformers converted the choir of the old kirk into a school room, for the education of the children of the village.

In 1562 the minister was Rev Robert Hamilton, who also served in the church at Ochiltree. He seems to have been a student at St Andrews in the 1550s. He had been appointed to preach in the unplanted kirks of Carrick. In December 1562 Rev Hamilton was appointed to a small committee that was to preside over the Act of Admission of Superintendents, a short-lived group that temporarily replaced the bishops. That he was held in high regard is obvious from the reference to this committee, which noted that it comprised, 'The Superintendent of Glasgow, Mr Knox, minister of Edinburgh, Mr Robert Hamilton, Minister of Uchiltree and Mauchline, and other learned men.' Rev Hamilton was translated to Irvine Parish Church in 1566. He was still an important minister, for in 1567 he was one of seven men who making up a committee appointed by the General Assembly of Scotland 'to decide questions'.

In 1567 the minister and kirk session complained to the General Assembly that one of their elders, Sir William Hamilton of Sanquhar, was still offering hospitality to another of the church's elders, John Spottiswood, who had been excommunicated by the kirk for adultery. The church was supported in its stance by the assembly, issuing a warning to Hamilton that if he did not desist from meeting with Spottiswood as demanded by the church, then he too would be excommunicated.

The next minister in Mauchline was Rev Peter Primrose, who seems to have been appointed in 1567. He was the son of Duncan Primrose, a bailie in Culross in Fife, and Helen Smith, or Smyth. He attended the Leith Convention in 1572 and in 1574 also served as minister in Galston. He is noted in 1573 as having a lease of part of Mauchline mill. In 1582 he subscribed a local testament, and in 1587 he was a witness to a charter of Lockhart of Bar. He was one of the members of a committee appointed in 1586 to deal with irregularities amongst ministers in Ayrshire. Again he served in a committee in 1589 concerning the preservation of the Reformed religion in Kyle. In the same year Rev Peter Primrose had a joint minister serving with him at Mauchline. This was Rev John Inglis, but of him little is known. Rev Primrose was married, but to whom is not known. One of his sons, Rev Peter Primrose, became minister of Crossmichael in Ayrshire. His daughter, Margaret, married William Spottiswood of Foular. Another son, Henry Primrose, became a notary in Mauchline, and was also ordained as a reader in the church. It is also thought that Duncan Primrose, the King's physician, may have been another of his sons.

In 1576 it was noted that the Readership in Mauchline was vacant. After this it was covered by Henry Primrose, serving from 1578-91.

It is possible that a new manse was erected for Rev Primrose, for an old date stone was formerly located on an outbuilding of the old manse in Mansefield Road, inscribed MPP 1594, referring to 'Magister' Peter Primrose. This stone was reproduced in sandstone on the gable of the new terrace of cottages built in Mansefield Road.

CHAPTER THREE

SEVENTEENTH CENTURY

VILLAGE LIFE

In 1606 Hugh Campbell, Lord Loudoun became possessed of the lands of Mauchline as a temporal lordship. Following the Reformation, the lordship and barony of Kylesmure were granted by the Crown to Hugh Campbell, Lord Loudoun. The grant included the patronage of the church. The act was passed in 1606 and reads:

> All and haill the landis, lordship, and baroneis of Kylismure, and Barmure, with castellis, touris, fortalices, maner-places, zairdis, orchardis, houss biggingis, mylnis, multuris, woddis, fischeingis, tennentis, tennandreis, seruice of frie tennentis, fewfermes, annexis, connexis, dependences, pairtis, pendiclis, and pertinentis of the samin quhatsumeuir, lyand within the baillerie of Kyle-Stewart and schirefdome of Air, ffra the act of annexatioun maid vpoun the tuentie-nynt day of Julij, the zeir of God Jm. vc. fourscoir sevin zeiris, annexand the temporalitie of all benefices within this realme to the patrimonie of his Hienes croune; togidder with the paroch kirk of Machline, personage and vicarage thairof, with all and sindrie teynd scheves, vtheris teyndis, fruittis, rentis, emolumentis, and duetes perteining and belanging thairto, lyand within the baillerie and schirefdome foirsaidis, ffra the Abbacie of Melros and benefice thairof, quhairunto the samin pertenis and pertenit of auld, as ane pairt of the patrimonie thairof: To the effect that his Maiestie may gif, grant, and dispone to the said Hew lord of Lowdoun, and his airis-maill, &c. . . . and als to the effect the toune of Mauchline may be erected in ane frie burgh of baronie, to be callit in all tyme cuming the burgh of Mauchlene, with ane ouklie marcat day vpoun Setterday, and tua frie fairis zeirlie . . . . . To be holdin of oure souerane lord and his successouris in frie blenche, frie heretage, frie lordschip, and frie baronie, for euir; payand thairfoir zeirlie, the said Hew lord of

Lowdoun, and his airis-maill foirsaidis, to oure said souerane lord and his successouris, the seruice of ane frie lord and baroun in parliament, with the soume of ane hundreth merkis vsuale money of this realme, at the feist of Witsonday, in name of blenche ferme; and als payand zeirlie to the minister serveing the cure at the said kirk of Machlene fourtie bollis aitmeill and thrie hundred merkis money foirsaid, at the termes vseit and wont, and furneschand bread and wyne zeirlie to the celebratioun of the communioun within the samyn kirk, &c. [The pension granted to Sir William Seyton, brother-german to Alexander of Dunfermaling, Chancellar, furth of the saids lands of Kylismure, and Barmure, and teyndis thairof, not to be prejudged by this act.]

This charter re-established Mauchline as a free burgh of barony, and the village was given the right to hold a weekly market and two annual fairs. The charter granting this right was destroyed when the Register Office in Edinburgh went on fire at the beginning of the eighteenth century. The people of Mauchline did not bother asking for a new charter, and Mauchline did not reacquire the power to elect its own magistrates. The affairs of the parish were managed by justices of the peace.

In 1631 it was decided that the large parish of Mauchline should be reduced in size, and thus the parish of Muirkirk was removed from it. At a spot known as Garan, a new church was established to serve the new parish, initially known as the Moor Kirk of Kyle, soon becoming Muirkirk.

In 1647 the General Assembly passed an act that was intended to establish a second charge in the parish. However, the act was carried out such that instead of Mauchline becoming a collegiate charge, the parish was separated into two halves. The removed part was established as the parish of Sorn. The Presbytery approved the division of the parish of Mauchline on 15 August 1649. On 7 November 1649 the Presbytery made arrangements and decided upon a site for a new church, manse, kirkyard and glebe. This was located somewhere on the estate of Gilmilnscroft, to the south of Sorn, but investigations earlier last century by the factor of Gilmilnscroft estate to locate the chosen site (probably nothing was erected) came to nought.

In 1656 a second large chunk of Mauchline parish was removed, to create the parish of Sorn. This left the final third of the parish remaining, which continues as Mauchline parish. The creation of the parish of Sorn seems to have been more troublesome than that of Muirkirk, for it is noted that the church building in the village was not erected until 1658. The unsettled religious times of the Covenanters played a part in the slow formation of Sorn parish, and it was noted that the parish was not fully completed until 1692. With Muirkirk and Sorn parish removed from Mauchline, the remaining parish was little more than one fifth of its former extent, though the fifth remaining was the most productive agriculturally.

Rev John Blair was admitted to the charge of New Mauchline in 1649. He was educated at the University of Glasgow. In 1662 Blair was deprived from his charge as a result of the Act of the Privy Council which removed ministers who failed to declare their adherence to the king as head of the church. He was one of a number of men who were accused of seditious conduct on 14 July 1663. Captured, he confessed to the charge and on 18 August 1662 he was banned from being a minister and was ordered to remove to somewhere north of the River Ness 'under the highest peril' before 1 October that year. Banning ministers north of the River Ness was a common punishment during the time of the Covenanting struggle as this area was strongly Episcopal at the time. Rev John Blair may not have adhered to the banishment, for he is noted as having preached at a conventicle held at Inverkeithing in Fife during the winter of 1679-1680.

One of the first detailed maps of Scotland was published in 1654 by Joan Blaeu of Amsterdam. The sheet covering *Coila Provincia* or the Province of Kyle, gives a fairly accurate description of the layout of the watercourses in the district, along with locations of castles, estates, and significant farms. Mauchline is depicted with the symbol for a church and castle. The name is spelled 'Mauchlyne', and across the Mauchline Burn is a symbol indicating that it was bridged near to the church at that time. Estates in the parish are 'Bhellachmyl', with its tower and enclosed woodlands; 'Kinzankleug', also with its tower and woods, but unenclosed; and 'Mosgauil', shown with a tower in enclosed policies. At 'Mongairswood' the symbol for a church is shown, something that is not known to have existed otherwise. Farm names in the parish, as shown on the map, are: Weltoun, Hauch, Coufoldshaw, Boigwood, Garfell (Garfield), Foular, Killoch, Auchenbrain, Freendleshead, Lawesbridge, Dykfeeld, Over, Mid and Nether Bargaur, Bridgehous, Barwhillen, Drufork, Braehead, Meklewood, Willockshill, Hol, Tournourhil and Herin. The map also shows Loch Broun as a considerably-sized loch, the only one in the parish.

In 1690-1 a single one-off tax payment of fourteen shillings per hearth, or fireplace, was payable by everyone in Scotland, apart from paupers, in order to pay back funds used by the army. In Mauchline parish there were 335 hearths accounted for, and payment collected. There were a further 27 hearths where the occupier of the house failed to pay, and 30 hearths belonging to the poor, and thus did not need to pay.

The mid seventeenth century was a hotbed of religious struggle, and one aspect of this that occurred across Scotland was witch-hunting. Rev Thomas Wyllie was noted as being particular strong in his anti-witch actions, having been a witch-hunter before coming to Mauchline, and continuing the practice on his return to the Stewartry of Kirkcudbright. One can only assume that he continued this hunt whilst serving at Mauchline, though no evidence as yet connects him with any local witches.

3.1 Mauchline parish area from Blaeu's Map of 1654 (*Author's Collection*)

It is likely that Rev Wyllie was responsible for at least some witch-hunting in the local parish, being involved in witch-hunting in Galloway before being appointed to Mauchline, and on his return to Kirkcudbright he was involved again, resulting in Janet Miller, Katherine Clacherty and others being executed in 1658. In 1670 Wyllie moved to Coleraine in Ireland where he served for a number of years before returning to Fenwick, where he died on 20 July 1676.

Witch-hunting did take place in Mauchline, however, for in 1671 Marion MacCall was tried for witchcraft. She was found guilty of some degree of witchcraft, but not enough to have her executed. She was punished by other means.

In the later seventeenth century one John Reid called the farmer's wife at Drumfork a witch during a quarrel in which they resorted to fighting with fists.

The brawl was called before the Kirk Session, the accusation of being a witch being something that was seriously contemplated. Realising how serious his accusations were being taken by the kirk session, and what the likely outcome for Drumfork's wife could be, he changed his story to say that he had said that she lied like a witch.

In the same way, a number of old records make reference to people and events in Mauchline. On 14 February 1606 Hew Campbell in Mauchline was involved in the slaughter of John Glencorse of that Ilk. He was charged before the courts for this later in the year.

Glimpses of parish life can be found in a variety of places. The Kirk Session minutes make reference to a variety of things happening in the parish over the years. In 1693 reference is made to eight shillings being awarded to 'blue-gowns', or official licensed beggars who travelled around the country.

A few people from the time are noted in early records. In the mid seventeenth century James Marshall is recorded as a merchant in the village.

In the seventeenth century the school in Mauchline was still being held in the church, usually in a disused chancel. This proved to be unsuitable, and in 1677 reference is made to the school being located in 'Matthew Hunter's chamber', for which a rent was paid. From the minute books we get a few references to schoolmasters and education in the parish during the seventeenth century.

On 16 May 1642 it was recorded that George Young, Reader and schoolmaster, had demitted his office. The session appointed John Greg in his place. He was the son of Rev James Greg of Newmilns. On 17 January 1644 reference is made to John Greg, schoolmaster in 'Machlyng', that he is 'appoynted to have ane privat exercise the nixt day, Text John 10 ch. 27 v.' Greg appears to have been reluctant to carry out this appointment, for he is described as being 'expectant' at subsequent meetings. On 8 May 1644 he must have appeared, for he sustained his 'Theses de judice controversiarium'.

In 1695 the school appears to have had no schoolmaster, for the session minutes refer to the fact that 'they want a schoolmaster, their Minister and they are to lay forth themselves to get one.' This took a few months to achieve, but by 20 November 1695 it is recorded that 'the presbytrie having taken accompt … of one Mr Patrick Johnstoun schoolmr, his qualification for teaching, & having found him qualified, & his testimonialls being satisfying, they allow his to teach a school att Machlyne to qch [which] place he is invited by those concerned.' Mention is made on 24 August 1698 that Mauchline 'had a school Mr & salary for him conform to law.'

Patrick Johnston must have left around 1699 for on 5 July 1699 it is noted that 'Mr Gavin Houstoun schoolmr invited to teach a school at Machlyne, produced sufficient testimonials form the mini[ste]r of Lochquhinoch & other of good credit signifying his Christian behaviour & capacity to teach a grammar school; & the Mod[erato]r & some of the presb[ytery] having certain knowledge of the same, he is allowed to teach in the place fors[ai]d; he declared his willingness to sign the Confession of Faith when he should be required.'

CHURCHES

With the arrival of the new century, Rev Peter Primrose still served as the minister. He has been described as 'the most Presbyterian of Presbyterians.' In 1610 he made his name when he stood for his beliefs at the General Assembly. King James VI had decided to introduce Episcopacy to the Scottish church that year, and at the General Assembly the moderator and business committee were very much in agreeance with the king. Most of the other ministers across the country appear to have accepted the demands of the king, apart from Rev Primrose. He stood up and addressed the assembly on his Presbyterian beliefs. Rev Primrose appears to have demitted office prior to 13 December 1617 and was dead before 15 November 1621.

In 1621 Rev John Rose MA was appointed as minister in Mauchline. He had graduated with his arts degree from Glasgow University in 1606. He was on the excise at Glasgow on 2 May 1621. On 15 November 1621 he was presented to Mauchline by King James VI. He married Elizabeth Bell, daughter of John Bell, Senior, and they had a son, Rev John Rose, who was to become the minister of Monkland in Lanarkshire. Rev John Rose Senior died in January 1634, aged about 48. His wife was to marry a second time, to Rev George Young, who was to become minister of Mauchline also.

There may have been a short ministry in Mauchline in 1634, for at that time Rev Thomas Peebles is noted as being minister within the Glasgow Com. Decisions of 25 February 1637.

In 1635, sometime before 29 June, Rev George Young MA became the minister. He had previously been the Regent at Glasgow University. He was translated to St Mungo's Parish in Glasgow in 1644, but he ministered to the Tron Church. The congregation in Mauchline were unwilling to let their minister go and made remonstrances to the presbytery to try to keep him, but they were unsuccessful.

In 1638, Rev George Young was one of those who signed the National Covenant in Edinburgh. He is noted as having been a man of tolerance and moderation, and it is noted that he suggested one very small alteration to the wording on the Covenant, which was to prevent some internal wranglings among the Covenanters at a later date. Rev Young also subscribed to the Solemn League and Covenant in 1643 and was active in opposing Roman Catholic rituals in the church. However, he did speak out against those more puritanical Covenanters who were against ministers kneeling in the pulpit for private devotion, to the repeating of the Lord's Prayer in public worship, and to the custom of concluding the singing of Psalms with a doxology.

In June 1646 Rev Thomas Wyllie MA was inducted as minister. He had previously served at Borgue in Kirkcudbrightshire (appointed in 1642) but was presented to the parish by John Campbell, Earl of Loudoun and Lord Chancellor. He was admitted as a burgess of Ayr on 23 April 1649. Wyllie was a friend of Rev Samuel Rutherford, one of the most renowned Covenanting ministers. Rev Wyllie was translated to Kirkcudbright around the year 1655.

Rev Wyllie was later to be ejected from Kirkcudbright church in 1662, after the restoration of Charles II. He was prevented from preaching for ten years, but in 1672 he was granted permission to become the minister of Fenwick Church. He died in 1672.

The next minister was Rev James Veitch MA. He was the son of Rev John Veitch, minister of the upland parish of Roberton in Lanarkshire. He was Regent in the University of Glasgow from 1649 until 1656, when he was admitted to the charge in Mauchline. He became involved in the Covenanting struggle, and on 28 May 1662 he refused to take the Oath of Allegiance, which placed the king as head of the church, without any reasonable explanation. He, with other ministers, claimed that they would sign the Oath so long as the king's authority did not extend to spiritual matters. He was compeared to appear before parliament in Edinburgh, his act being regarded as treasonable. For this he was imprisoned for several weeks, from the end of May until the middle of September. On 16 September 1662 he was deprived of his charge by the Privy Council and the charge was declared vacant. Veitch was forbidden to return to Mauchline.

Rev Veitch was a strong Covenanting minister and spent some time preaching in the fields at conventicles. In March 1669 he was accused of preaching irregularly, as well as of carrying out baptisms, by the authorities. His treatment was so harsh that even the Privy Council regarded his sufferings as being beyond the norm and he was awarded compensation of 300 merks for the losses sustained by him.

Whilst Veitch was banished from the parish church, the pulpit was filled by a number of ministers who had accepted the indulgence, or were willing to come and go a bit with the authorities over their beliefs. The first minister was Rev William Dalgarno MA, who was translated to Mauchline from Kirkmahoe in Dumfriesshire around the year 1665. He remained at Mauchline for about four years before being translated once more to Dunsyre in Lanarkshire in 1669.

When Rev Dalgarno left Mauchline the pulpit was filled once again by Rev James Veitch. He was granted an indulgence by the Privy Council on 9 December 1669 which allowed him to return. Things did not settle for Veitch, for on October 1674 he was accused of contravening the terms of his indulgence, and a second case against him was made on 3 November 1681. When this case was brought before the Privy Council they threw it out on 24 November. Further charges were put to Veitch. On 2 August 1683 he was charged with breaking his confinement to the parish. Veitch admitted this on 3 January 1684. He was removed from the church once more, and was deprived of his licence to preach. He was also ordered to leave Scotland and refrain from carrying out services in the fields, unless he was able to pay a caution of 5,000 merks. Veitch crossed the border to Northumberland, where he stayed with his brother at Stanton Hall. Things continued to go against him, and eventually the Veitch brothers left England and spent three years in Holland.

During Veitch's ministry, in 1671, the bell in the tower of the church had to be repaired. What specifically was wrong with it is not known. The public clock was also repaired, the wooden face, or 'brod' as it is called in the minutes, was repainted in 1667.

At Mauchline the pulpit was to be filled by another indulged minister. Rev Robert Archibald had formerly been the minister at Dunscore, but was deprived of his charge. He was admitted to Mauchline, jointly with Rev Veitch to start with, on 3 September 1672, but it is doubted whether he ever took up the post.

On 29 August 1684 Rev David Meldrum MA was admitted to Mauchline. He was an Episcopal minister, or 'curate' as the Covenanters unkindly called them. Nevertheless, he remained at Mauchline until he was deprived of the charge by the Act of Parliament of 25 April 1690 which restored Presbyterianism as the established Church of Scotland. Unlike many local parishes, such as Sorn or Old Cumnock, Rev Meldrum does not appear to have been rabbled by the villagers. He seems to have been quite moderate in his beliefs, and on 2 September 1691 he was received into the communion of the Church of Scotland by the Presbytery of Irvine. On 22 August 1694 he was inducted as the minister of Tibbermore in Perthshire.

During the ministry of Rev Meldrum, Rev James Veitch made a return to Mauchline once more. He was admitted under the Act of Toleration on 30 October 1687. The Kirk session minutes record that on 30 October 1687, 'The qlk day Mr James Vetch, minister of this parish of Mauchlein (being returned from Holland, the place of his banishment, legall restraints being taken off) preached publicly heair againe.'

During his time as minister Veitch compiled a manuscript entitled *Ane Sober Inquirie into the Lawfulness of the Presbyterian Ministers, their Acceptance of a Libertie to Preach the Gospel upon the Indulgence, and the people's dutie to hear them.* This was never published. Rev James Veitch was married to Jean Dunbar. Veitch died sometime before 28 July 1694, his wife surviving him.

The next minister was Rev William Maitland. He was born in 1671, the son of Rev William Maitland, minister at Beith. He was called in April 1695 and ordained on 25 September that year. He was the first minister of Mauchline to be selected by the members of the congregation, previously the minister being appointed by the patrons of the parish. Maitland was married in September 1690 to Mary, eldest daughter of James Stewart of Lumloch. She was the niece of Sir Archibald Stewart of Blackhall, 1st Baronet. Maitland's marriage to Mary Stewart brought with it a tocher or dowry of 8,000 merks. They had at least two sons, William Maitland, who set up as a surgeon in Mauchline, and James Maitland of Barcaple, also a surgeon.

During the seventeenth century the kirk session was basically the police for the parish. There are numerous references in the kirk session minutes of people in the parish being reprimanded publicly or punished for their actions. A number of examples will give an idea of the power of the Kirk Session at the time, and what punishments they could inflict. The minutes also give a few tantalising names of Mauchline residents from times past:

March 26 1672 – Intimation was appointed to be made the next Sabbath day that people vaig not abroad on the Sabbath, and that they tak care that their children vaig not.

October 13 1672 – The qlk day compeiring Jean Edward, and partly by her own confession, and partly by witnesses yat were sworn, was convit. of frequent scolding, cursing, swearing, and fighting with her husband, Hew Smyth, and beating of him; qrupon she was ordained to be rebuked publickly and suspended from the sacrament of the Lord's Supper.

February 22 1676 – It was decided 'that the two elders who collect on the Sabbath shall goe through the town and search who are in the houses the tyme of sermon.'

May 13 1673 – There is intimation to be made the next Saboth that people ly not in yairds, nor in the field, or wander on the Saboths.

August 15 1680 – Scandalous carriage on the Sabbath-day, such a flocks of children playing on the streets and in the churchyard, bearing of water, and the like, ordained to be reproved and forbidden after this by the minister.

September 7 1690 – Two elders reported 'George Miller in Mauchline and his [wife] to the Session for their selling aill and drinking it in their house with incomeres, which they did find with them in the tyme of the forenoon sermon.'

BATTLE OF MAUCHLINE MOOR

The political and religious troubles of the mid seventeenth century saw the Covenanters at odds with the king. Charles I was beheaded and his place as ruler was taken over by Oliver Cromwell, who ran the country under the Protectorate. The Scots were in many cases against this, and there was still sufficient support for King Charles. The Scots Commissioners met with Charles at Carisbrooke Castle on the Isle of Wight and on 26 December 1647 they signed what was known as 'The

Engagement', binding the king to obtain authority for Presbyterianism in Scotland for three years, amongst other deals.

The supporters of the king, Duke of Hamilton, Earl of Callander, Major General John Middleton and Lieutenant-General William Baillie, led the royalist army against the Protectorate, and the first skirmish or battle was to take place on the outskirts of Mauchline, at what was known as Mauchline Muir.

In Ayrshire a number of ministers had opposed the new engagement, and built up a considerable following. In addition to standing against the Engagement, they also were very much against the protectorate's levy on the people to pay for the war. They made arrangements for a communion service to be held in Mauchline on 11 June and large numbers came to take part. Many of these were armed, though it is not known if this was planned, encouraged by the ministers, or whether it was a spontaneous rising. The supporters were without a leader, however, for they had met in Kilmarnock the day before and decided against rising against the authorities.

Seven ministers were present that day, Rev William Adair (Ayr), Rev Alexander Blair (Galston), Rev William Guthrie (Irvine), Rev Gabriel Maxwell (Dundonald), Rev Matthew Mowat (Kilmarnock), Rev John Nevay (Loudoun), and Rev Thomas Wyllie (Mauchline). They gathered together a force of two thousand supporters, who made their way to Mauchline. The number had gathered from far and wide, though most of the opponents were from Ayrshire and Lanarkshire.

At Mauchline, the vast numbers under the minister held a communion service out in the open muir on Sunday 11 June 1648. The service was bad enough, as far as the authorities at the time were concerned, but they were particularly disturbed at the fact that the communicants were armed with swords.

The Covenanters were anticipating further support to come from Argyll and Fife, where their number was strong, but this failed to materialise. Disappointed at the failure of the support to turn up, the Covenanters on the muir decided to disperse and make their way home.

Just as this was about to happen, the Commonwealth soldiers attacked. The troops under the Earl of Middleton and Colonel James Turner had made their way to Mauchline to investigate the large numbers meeting there, anticipating some form of revolt. They had six troops of horse and a further troop was following on behind, led by the Earl of Callendar.

The ministers on the Covenanting side advised the two thousand supporters to scatter, for their own safety. They also negotiated with Middleton for an hour before the attack came. Although his force was six hundred cavalry strong, he only ordered part of his men forward. These men were forced back by the 2,000 Covenanters lined up against them, of which 1,200 were horsemen. Callendar's men joined those who had been repelled, adding to their number, and making them more able to face the Covenanters. A second attack was more forceful and had more success. A short battle ensued, with casualties on both sides. The Covenanters now turned around and fled. At first Middleton ordered his men not to kill, but some claim that this was only shouted for the benefit of the ministers' hearing, and not for his soldiers.

The Earl of Middleton was injured in the affray. He received a wound to the head, and it is also reported that he was injured on his back as he fled the field, pursued by a blacksmith.

Another important figure who received wounds from the Mauchline Covenanters was Sir John Hurry, or Urry. He was originally a supporter of the Covenanters but changed sides, supporting Montrose and the Royalists. He was captured after the Battle of Carbisdale and beheaded in 1650. Like Middleton, he was wounded to the head. With Middleton and Hurry injured, Callendar's reinforcements arrived, adding to the soldiers already there, decisively repelling the Covenanters.

One account, written by Rev Thomas Wyllie, tells of the soldiers pursuing the Covenanters as they fled south towards Barskimming. As the Covenanters came towards the River Ayr, at the large crook in the river at Airds Holm, they found themselves trapped by the water – they would have to either turn and fight or drown. Apparently, they turned and forced their pursuers back a mile and a half towards Mauchline yard dikes, that is the walls at the back of the gardens in the village.

Wyllie also relates a story whereby one of the soldiers pursed a Covenanter towards Barskimming Bridge. The Covenanter, probably a local, did not cross the bridge but fled to the steep rocky bank on the north side of the river, downstream from the bridge. There he climbed down and hid himself on a rock shelf, hanging onto a tree root to prevent him from falling into the river. The trooper in pursuit was less lucky, for he was riding so fast that he fell headlong over the precipice into the river below, drowning in the water.

The battle did not last long, both sides making a tactical retreat. The number of dead is reckoned to be around 30-40, even on both sides. Turner claims that only ten or so Covenanters were killed. It is reckoned that most of the Covenanters fled to the hills of southern Ayrshire and into Galloway.

About sixty of the Covenanting rebels and five officers were taken prisoner on the field and transported to Ayr. They were imprisoned in the tolbooth and council house, indeed, so many were held prisoner that the council of Ayr had to meet in the provost's house. A court martial was arranged for their trial, Turner being the president. The sixty 'country people' were pardoned and allowed to go free. The officers were tried, found guilty, and sentenced to death, but they were eventually pardoned, the authorities reckoning that leniency would prevent further revolt. These officers were expected to sign a confession and oath supporting the parliament in implementing the Engagement on 19 June 1648.

The ministers present at the battle were also captured, but they were to be released the following day. The General Assembly summoned the ministers who were active at Mauchline to appear before it in July 1648, but only four turned up. They informed that Assembly that 'under their hand protested that directly nor indirectly they had not persuaded the people to meet there that day.' They were examined for some time, eventually being sent away after some weeks.

James Turner compiled his Memoirs, which were published at a later date. In them he gives his account of the battle:

> Whill I lay at Paislay, a communion, as thay call it, is to be given at Machlin church, to pertake wherof all good people are permitted to come; bot because the tie were, forsooth, dangerous, it was thought fit all the men could come armed. Nixt Monday, which was their thanksgiveing day, there were few lesse to be seene about the church then tuo thousand armed men, horse and foot. I had got some intelligence of the designe before, and had acquainted the Duke with it; who ordered me expreslie not to sturre till Calander and Muddletones coming; who accordinglie on the Saturday before the communion came to Glasgow, where I met them, and then went straight forward to Paslay. A rendezvous is appointed by Calander to be of horse and foot at Steuarton hill nixt Monday. From thence Lieut. General Middleton is sent with six troopes of horse to Machlin moore, where the armed communicants were faid to be. I intreated my Lord Calander (bot to no purpose) not to divide, bot rather march with all his forces, then hazard the overthrow of a few, which might endanger the whole. We advanced with the rest, as the foot could marche; bot it was not long before we heard that the communicants had refused to goe to their houses; and having ressaved a briske charge of Middletons forlorne hope, had worsted it; and that himselfe and Colonell Urrey comeing up to the rescue, were both wounded in the heade; which so appalld their troopees, that if they lossd no ground, they were glad to keepe what they had, and looke upon the saincts. These unexpected news made Calander leave my refiment at Kilmarnock, and take his horse with him up to Middletone. In intreated him to march at least at a great tropt, if not at a gallope; bot he would be more orderlie, and therefor marchd more sloulie. We met numbers of boys and bedees weeping and crying all was lost; bot at our appearance the slashing communicants left the field, the horse trulie untouched, because not fiercelie pursued. About sixtie of their foot were taken, and five officers. The ministers that came in our power, who had occasioned the mischief, were nixt day dismisd. Nixt day we marchd into Aire, where a court of warre is appointed to be

keepd about the prisoners. The country fellows of them are pardone; the officers sentenced to be hanged or shot; bot thereafter were pardond; to which I was very instrumentall, thogh I had bene president in the court of warre. Lieutenant Generall Middletons wound, and Colonel Urreys sufferd them to ride abroad within four or five days.

In 1649 an Act of the Scottish Parliament noted that the ministers were 'charged and processed befor the Committee of Estates as traytors for being airt and part of that opposition made at Mauchline Muir.' As time and politics changed, 'now the estates having found the said late engagement against England unlawful, and having approven all the opposition that was made thairto as lawful and such as the opposers were bound unto by the Covenant, thairfore finds and declares that the rising in arms at Mauchline Muir by the good and wel affected people there assembled, and what was done there by them and by the said ministers in opposition were not onlie lawfull bot a zealous and loyall testimony to the Truth and Covenant and that which became faithful ministers of the Gospel and people zealous for the truth to do.'

It is said that the government side's military chest had been hidden prior to the battle, and that it was discovered some years later.

The Covenanting difficulties continued, though Charles I was beheaded on 30 January 1649. It was not until the Restoration of Charles II as monarch in May 1662 that the Covenanting struggle was to return to Mauchline.

COVENANTERS

One of the outed ministers, Rev James Blair of Cathcart parish in Renfrewshire, was summoned before the Privy Council in 1663. He admitted that he had carried out the functions of ministers by preaching, baptising and marrying since being deposed in 1662. The Privy Council prohibited him from carrying out any form of ministry without warrant from his ordinary. He was warned that he should remove himself from Mauchline, where he seems to have been based at the time, and where he last preached, to north of the River Ness. Should he escape from where he was confined then this would be at the highest peril.

In 1666, what became known as the Pentland Rising started in the village of St John's Town of Galloway in the Stewartry of Kirkcudbright. The Covenanters had risen against the soldiers who were intent on punishing an elderly man, forcing them to give up their intentions. Not knowing what to do next, these Covenanters decided to march on Dumfries, where they kidnapped Sir James Turner, commander of the soldiers in south-west Scotland. They returned westwards, making their way back to Dalry and thence north through Dalmellington to Ayr.

At Ayr the Covenanters were organised by Colonel James Wallace of Auchans and it was decided to march on Edinburgh, where the intention was to lay their petitions to the authorities. The Covenanters made their way eastward, passing through Ochiltree and Cumnock before heading through Lanarkshire towards the capital. On the outskirts of the city they camped, but they were soon overtaken by the soldiers of the king and were defeated at the Battle of Rullion Green, which took place on the edge of the Pentland Hills, on 28 November 1666.

As the Covenanters were making their way through central Kyle, from Ochiltree towards Cumnock, a detachment comprising a few members was sent north towards Mauchline, to reconnoitre the district. This party was led by John Ross, who is thought to have been a Mauchline man. Unfortunately, word was delivered by John Millar to the Covenanters as they camped overnight at Cumnock on Friday 23 November, that the Royalist soldiers were at Kilmarnock and that Ross and his men had been captured.

Ross and his men had headed north, separating themselves from the main party of Covenanters. As they crossed country, they were spotted by soldiers under the command of the Duke of Hamilton. Also in the party was John Shields, who is known to have been the tenant of the farm of Titwood, located in the parish of Mearns, Renfrewshire. The two men were taken by the soldiers to Edinburgh where they were held in the gaol.

John Ross and John Shields were tried at court in Edinburgh and both were found guilty of rising against authority. They were sentenced to be hanged, which was carried out at the Grassmarket in the capital on 7 December 1666. Once the bodies were lifeless, they were cut from the scaffold and lowered to the ground. To emphasise to the people of Ayrshire what would happen if they rose against authority, the heads of the two Covenanting martyrs were cut from their bodies. The heads were placed in a sack and carried back to the county. In Kilmarnock they were to be placed on spikes on the Watergate, left there as a warning to others. Ross and Shields' hands were also cut from their bodies and these were sent to Lanark for public display on the town ports, or gateways, for at Lanark the Covenanters had re-sworn their allegiance to the Covenant.

When the period of killing had passed, the people of Kilmarnock had the heads of Ross and Shields removed from the Watergate and decently interred in the Laigh Kirkyard. A headstone was erected over the grave, bearing the inscription:

> Here lie the heads of John Ross and John Shields who suffered at
> Edinburgh Dec 7th 1666 and had their heads set up at Kilmarnock.
> Our Persecutors mad with wrath & ire;
> In Edinh members some do lie, some here.
> Yet instantly united they shall be,
> & witness 'gainst this nation's perjury.
> See Cloud of Witnesses.

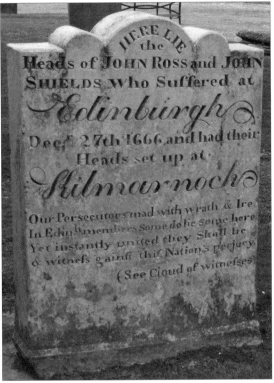

3.2 Ross & Shields grave, Kilmarnock *(Dane Love)*

A number of Mauchline Covenanters were active at the Battle of Drumclog, near Strathaven, and subsequently at the Battle of Bothwell Bridge, near Hamilton, both in 1679. At the latter battle many Covenanters were taken prisoner and transported to Edinburgh. After some time in gaols across the city, many were banished to America as slaves. One of the slave ships, the *Crown of London*, was shipwrecked at the Mull Head of Deerness in the Orkney Islands on 10 December 1679. There were 209 Covenanters drowned on that occasion, two of them belonging to Mauchline parish. These were William Drips and William Reid.

In 1684 a list of rebels was compiled by the Scottish authorities. This details numerous Covenanters who were wanted by the authorities for their religious adherence. The list is broken down into parishes, but at the time it was drawn up, Sorn was included within the parish of Mauchline, making it more difficult to separate the Mauchline names from the whole parish. However, in Mauchline and Sorn there were 39 names listed. Those known to belong to Mauchline parish were as follows:

Adam Reid in Mauchline
John MacGavin, tenant to 'Kinzeancleugh'
James Fisher, Kingencleugh
William MacGavin, smith in the Haugh.
John Mitchell of Breichead, or Bogwood.
John Law, son of John Law, portioner of Barneight.
John Mitchell of Bogwood (listed twice)
John Semple, factor to Barskimming estate.
John Marshall, feuar in Mauchline.
James Millar in Haugh.
James Mitchell in the Aird.

John Graham of Claverhouse (1648-89), the arch-enemy of the Covenanters, is known to have passed through Mauchline on at least one occasion. In a letter written to his superior, General Thomas Dalyell of the Binns, from East Kilbride on 15 June 1684, he details his movements in the area:

> May it please your Excellency: I parted on Friday [13th] at twelve o'clock from Paisley, went by Kilmarnock and Mauchlin, but could hear nothing of these rebels. So, hearing Colonel Buchan was at the old castle of Cumnock, I took by Ochiltree, who sent an express to a tenant's house of his, near Airdmoss, and he brought certain notice that they had been at a meadow near his house the night before, to the number of fifty-nine, all armed.
>
> Upon which I sent immediately to the Glenkens, to Captain Strachan, to march to Dalmellington, and to the Sorn, and to leave Mauchlin on the left hand, and Newmilns and Loudon-hill on the right, and so to this place, scouring all the suspected places as he came along.

The letter indicates just how thoroughly the dragoons scoured the area in search of the Covenanters.

On 6 May 1685 Sir William Drummond of Cromlix (1617-88), commissioner, ordered that four men and one youth should be executed in Mauchline. These men were Covenanters, and had been gathered from various places throughout Scotland. A party of Highland soldiers had been marching to the south west in order to supply reinforcements to Drummond when they captured the men – Peter Gillies, John Bryce, William Fiddison, Thomas Young and John Bruning.

Peter Gillies is thought to have been a waulker (or bleacher of cloth) from the village of Skirling in Peeblesshire. It is known that in 1674 a Presbyterian minister held a conventicle at his house, notification of which was sent to the local laird, who owned the waulk-mill. The curate, or Episcopal minister, of Skirling also became aware of the conventicle, and Gillies was thrown out of his home by the laird. He then moved north and lived in Muiravonside, which is a rural parish to the west of Linlithgow, in the county of Stirling. Gillies seems to have taken over the Waulkmill of Woodside in Muiravonside and continued working. It is known that he was a married man. However, in 1682 the curate of Muiravonside noted Gillies's non-conformity and sent word to the soldiers that he was a wanted Covenanter. The soldiers came to his home, but he had escaped and they left empty-handed. Gillies was able to return home, but he was still listed as a fugitive.

On 30 April 1685 the party of Highland soldiers left their base at Falkirk and marched to Muiravonside, where they found Gillies at home. It is recorded that Gillies's wife had only given birth to a child a few days previously and was still considerably weakened. She watched in terror as the soldiers whisked Gillies away, not allowing him to speak with her or to change his clothes. Within an hour some of the soldiers returned, claiming that Gillies had told them that he had some firearms, and they told her that his life would be spared if she told them where they were hidden. The wife replied that her husband had no arms of which she was aware, and if they were to take his life, she would try to say, 'Good is the will of the Lord, and He who did all things well, could not wrong her or hers.' The soldiers were incensed at her remarks and threatened to burn her home. As they left, they plundered the house of all that they could carry away.

John Bryce, a weaver from West Calder, in West Lothian, was unfortunate in that he was visiting Gillies on a business deal when the soldiers arrived at Gillies's home. Bryce had come to collect some cloth which Gillies had been dressing for him. Both were taken captive, and forced to march westwards. The pair were tied together and driven in front of the soldiers. A few miles onward they stopped, and the soldiers blindfolded Gillies and forced him to his knees. They aimed their muskets at him, and terrorised him thus for half an hour. At length, they recommenced their march.

The soldiers made their way to Carluke in Lanarkshire, where they apprehended two other Covenanters, William Finneson, or Fiddieson, and Thomas Young. It is claimed that these two were captured with the assistance of footmen employed by Cromwell Lockhart of the Lee, a notorious persecutor of Covenanters in Lanarkshire. These two Covenanters are not mentioned in Rev Robert Wodrow's *History of the Sufferings of the Church of Scotland*. The party appears to have reached Middle Wellwood, west of Muirkirk, on 4 May 1685. Peter Gillies was given time to write a letter to his wife. In it he sends his love to her and their five children, and places their care in the Lord. He wanted them not to think that he was about to die, but that he would soon be beyond the reach of his enemy.

The party of soldiers continued their march westwards, and between Sorn and Mauchline picked up a young man, John Bruning, who was reportedly herding some cattle. It was noted that he had neither stocking nor shoe upon his feet.

On 5 May 1685 the five men were examined by Lieutenant-General Drummond, Master General of the Ordnance. It is said that a jury of fifteen soldiers was arranged, but this trial was illegal, and the jury was corrupt. A copy of the indictment against the men was placed in their hands, in which it was claimed that they refused to pray for the king, as well as other crimes. It was recommended that they should suffer death, and that their lands and goods should be forfeited. The men were found guilty, and the sentence of death was passed, to be carried out on the following day. The indictment reads:

Peter Gillies in Muirend-side, John Bryce in West Calder, [William Fiddison, Thomas Young and John Brouning,] you and ilk one of you are indicted, that, contrary the laws both divine and human, the laws and practices of this realm, and several acts of parliament, ordaining an humble submission, by all persons, to kingly power and authority, and an acknowledgment of their just power and greatness, and of their full consent to the laws and acts in their jurisdictions, and giving sufficient demonstrations of their loyalty and adherence to their prince, as their head and sovereign, in all things and cases, when required; and the opposers thereof and refusers, to give sufficient testimony of their loyalty and consent, as aforesaid, being justly to be reputed enemies, and not friends, rebels and not subjects, and, by the same laws and ordinations, are to be cut off from other loyal, obedient, true, conforming subjects. Yet true it is and of verity, that you, in a manifest contempt of those laws, though living under a gracious prince and sovereign, having cast off all fear of God, duty and allegiance to the king, have not only, contrary to the word of God, and all law and equity, most traitorously and impiously shaken off all love and obedience to kingly power, by a long time homologating with the principles of those rebellious traitors, and blasphemers of God and the king, joining with them in their wicked courses and practices, wanting nothing but an opportunity to murder and assassinate his majesty's subjects of the contrary opinion; but also openly and avowedly disowned the king, his just authority and government, adhered to the covenant, owning and approving rising in arms against the king, and those commissionate by him, and refuse to pray for the king, whereof, and of the other crimes specified, you being found guilty by an assize, you and ilk one of you ought to be punished with forfeiture of life, lands, and goods, to the terror of others to commit the like hereafter. You are summoned to compear before Lieutenant-General Drummond, commissioner of justiciary, within the tolbooth or court place of Mauchlin, this fifth of May, to answer to your indictment.

Held overnight in Mauchline Castle, the Covenanters were led out to the Loan Green on the following morning. They were not allowed to read from the Bible prior to their death, and the soldiers prevented them from saying any prayers. Once they had been executed, their bodies were buried on the spot, in a grave hastily dug by the soldiers and two country people. No coffins were allowed, nor grave clothes to wrap the bodies.

According to the *Short Memorial* by Rev Alexander Shields, John Graham of Claverhouse, George Douglas, 1st Earl of Dumbarton (*c.* 1636-1692), and Colonel James Douglas were also involved in the executions at Mauchline. John Graham of

Claverhouse had been appointed by Charles II as commander of the regiments of horse that had been raised against the Covenanters. In 1684 he had been appointed captain of the king's new regiment of horse. The Earl of Dumbarton was the third son of William, 1st Marquis of Douglas, and had only recently been appointed as commander-in-chief following the accession of James VII, but he was still in London at the time of the executions (assuming the date of 6 May to be correct). He returned to Edinburgh on 13 May, and unless the date of the hangings in Mauchline is incorrect (perhaps they took place on the 16 May?), why Dumbarton is traditionally associated with them is unknown. Colonel James Douglas (d. 1691), was the

3.3 Mauchline Martyrs' Memorial *(Dane Love)*

second son of the 2nd Earl of Queensberry and brother of the 1st Duke of Queensberry. He was involved in the martyrdom of many Covenanters, particularly in Galloway and Dumfriesshire. At the time of the Mauchline martyrdoms, Douglas was headquartered in the village.

An account in the records of the Privy Council of 8 November 1688 makes reference to the gallows at Mauchline and their removal at this time:

> As for that bussines at Mauchline anent the taking doun of the gallowes and that their sould have bein fourscore of armed men at the doing of it, I have spoken with verie honest men who was in Machline at that time and declares that their was noe armed men their, and that the gallowes was sawen doune in the night time with a saw when noe bodie knew of it an it is believit that it was some of thes peoplls friends who was hangit upon it that did saw it doun.

Over the grave of the five Covenanting martyrs a flat gravestone was later erected, measuring approximately twelve feet by six feet. It bears the inscription:

> Here lies the Bodies of Peter
> Gillies, John Bryce, Thomas
> Young, William Fiddison & John
> Bruning, Who Were Apprehen
> ded and Hanged Without Trial
> at Mauchline, Anno 1685, acc
> ording to the then Wicked's
> Laws for their Adhereance to
> the Covenanted Work of
> Reformation. Rev xii II.

> Bloody Dumbarton, Douglas & Dundee
> Moved by the Devil & the Laird of Lee
> Dragged these five men to Death with gun and sword
> Not suffering them to Pray nor Read God's Word.
> Ouning the Work of God was all their Crime.
> The Eighty Five was a Saint Killing Time.

It is said by some that Robert Paterson, the 'Old Mortality' of Sir Walter Scott, was responsible for the verse.

In 1830 the old stone was becoming too worn and it was decided to erect a new gravestone over it, copying the original inscription. In turn a third stone was erected over the second stone, an obelisk of red Ballochmyle sandstone. This was unveiled on Saturday 19 September 1885 and bears the inscription:

> IN MEMORY
> OF
> PETER GILLIES,
> JOHN BRYCE, THOMAS YOUNG,
> WILLIAM FIDDISON,
> AND
> JOHN BRUNING,
> BURIED HERE, ON THE SPOT WHERE
> THEY WERE HANGED
> ON THE 6TH MAY 1685,
> FOR ADHERANCE
> TO THE
> COVENANTED WORK OF REFORMATION.

THIS OBELISK IS THE THIRD MEMORIAL STONE ERECTED ON THIS
SITE IN MEMORY OF THE FIVE MARTYRS BURIED BENEATH. THE
ORIGINAL STONE, WITH INSCRIPTION INTACT, IS NOW INSERTED A
FEW YARDS OFF, IN THE WALL FACING THIS SIDE OF THE MONUMENT,
THE SECOND STONE, BEARING THE DATE 1830,
WAS A COPY OF THE ORIGINAL.

'SLAIN FOR THE WORD OF GOD AND THE TESTIMONY
WHICH THEY HELD'

ERECTED IN THE YEAR 1885 BY PAROCHIAL SUBSCRIPTION AFTER A
BICENTENARY SERVICE, CONDUCTED JOINTLY BY ALL THE MINISTERS
IN MAUCHLINE, WITHIN THE PARISH CHURCH ON 3RD MAY 1885.

3.4 Mauchline Martyrs' Obelisk *(Dane Love)*

The obelisk, designed by Matthew Muir, sculptor of Kilmarnock, was surrounded by railings. The original stone was taken from the site and built into the wall of an outbuilding associated with Mauchline Public School in 1885.

In 1993 the original inscription from the old stone was incorporated on a new Creetown granite slab, also built into the wall adjacent to the old stone, paid for by the Scottish Covenanter Memorials Association and sculpted by Aubrey Jones of Coylton. In 2006, when work commenced on the building of a new extension to Mauchline Primary School, both these slabs were removed from the outbuilding, which was to be demolished, and were instead incorporated in a new entrance portico to the grounds of the school. Built of sandstone coloured concrete, the portico incorporates the two memorials facing each other and was unveiled in 2007.

A local tradition associates the building at the corner of Kilmarnock Road and Castle Street, adjoining Dr Mackenzie's and Burns' houses, with the execution at the Loan. At the time, Sir William Drummond of Cromlix lodged at the inn, run by a Mr Fisher. The locals refused to supply Drummond with ropes with which to carry out the hangings, but he was able to get them from Mr Fisher. Accordingly, it was always said that a curse rested on the house. Over the doorway, facing Kilmarnock Road, is a stone lintel, its inscription much worn, but which has a later date of 1748.

In the old kirkyard is a small headstone marking the grave of James Smith, another Covenanter. The inscription gives a few details of his story:

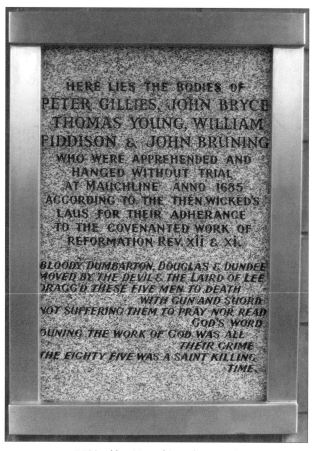

3.5 Mauchline Martyrs' Stone *(Dane Love)*

HERE LIES
Intered the corpse of JAMES
SMITH, who was wounded by
Captain Ingles, and his Dragoons, at the Burn of Ann in Kyle,
and there after died of his wounds
in Mauchline prison, for his adhe
arance to the word of GOD and
Scotland's Covenanted Work
of reformation, A. D. 1684.

The story of Smith is difficult to unravel, for in the old kirkyard at Galston another memorial stone to the Covenanters commemorates, among others, 'James Smith, East Threepwood, who was Shot near Bank of Burn Ann by Captain Inglis and his dragoons and buried there.' The two stories are too similar to refer to different incidents, and yet they claim that he was buried in two different places.

Of James Smith's life little is known. He was recorded on a list of fugitives published in 1684. It is thought that he was implicated in the storming of Newmilns Tower by the Covenanters in April 1685, when they broke into the castle and released a number of Covenanters who were held prisoner there. In the affray one of them, John Law, was killed and he was buried in the castle garden. The soldiers spent time searching for the Covenanters

3.6 James Smith's Gravestone *(Dane Love)*

responsible for the attack on the garrison, and probably came upon James Smith near to the Burn Anne, or Burn Awn, south of Galston. He was accused of giving food to those who had escaped from the tower. The spot where he was captured is located to the north-east of Threepwood farm, on the site of East, or Wee Threepwood farm, long since demolished. Captain Peter Inglis, who was the leader of the garrison at Newmilns, arrived at the door and when Smith answered Inglis shot at him. He had been shot at his own front door, the bullet causing wounds.

The two tales differ now. The Galston story claims that the shot killed him, and that his body was left to rot where it fell. Some locals took it and buried it at the location, and tradition claims that a small headstone marked the grave for many years.

The Mauchline tale claims that Smith, once he was wounded, was captured and taken by the dragoons back to the garrison at Mauchline Castle. He was held there for a time, awaiting trial, but he suffered from his injuries and died in the castle. The soldiers accordingly removed the body and buried it in the kirkyard.

3.7 Covenanter's Flag, Mauchline Parish Church *(Dane Love)*

The date on the Mauchline stone appears to be an error, for instead of 1684 it should read 1685. The attack on Newmilns Tower took place in April 1685, so Smith could not have died in Mauchline prior to this. The headstone was erected in 1727 and was re-erected in 1806.

Rev Alexander Peden spent his last few days at his brother's home, Tenshillingside, in the parish of Mauchline. This farm was located within Auchinleck estate, owned by the Boswells. When Peden died his family took his corpse under the cover of darkness and interred it in the Peden burial ground in the old kirkyard at Auchinleck. The story that he was buried in the Boswell vault is erroneous. However, after six weeks, the soldiers discovered that Peden had died before they had been able to capture him. Undeterred, they decided to dig up his body and carry it to Cumnock where it was the intention to hang the lifeless corpse from the gallows tree on the Barr Hill. However, in Cumnock the spectacle of the soldiers carrying Peden's body was spotted by the local lady, the Countess of Dumfries, whose protestations to her husband, Lord Dumfries, resulted in him forbidding them from hanging the body on the tree. Instead, the soldiers dug a hole at the foot of the gallows tree and there interred him, 'out of contempt', according to the gravestone. An old flat stone commemorates Peden, replaced by a later headstone, and in turn replaced by an Aberdeen granite monument, erected in 1891. This had been designed by Robert Ingram.

Another tale from the Covenanting period has been connected with the parish of Mauchline. It is said that Rev William Guthrie (1620-65), minister of Fenwick, and Captain John Paton (1614-84), met with a group of Covenanters at a small conventicle held somewhere within the parish. The Lord's Supper was being celebrated at a spot so secluded that the Covenanters thought that they would not be found. However, the soldiers under General Middleton and the Earl of Loudoun came upon them and surrounded them. It is recounted that Lord Loudoun knew Guthrie, for the minister had previously been employed as a tutor to his eldest son, Lord Mauchline, and that he had

3.8 Gilbert Macadam's gravestone, Kirkmichael *(Author's Collection)*

lived with him for a number of years. Loudoun pleaded with Middleton to allow them to go, which he reluctantly relented to.

In addition to the Covenanters' graves and memorials, there survives in Mauchline Parish Church the Mauchline parish Covenanters' banner. This now hangs on the wall inside the church building. It is claimed that the flag was carried at the Battle of Mauchline Muir (1648) and later at the battles of Drumclog and Bothwell Bridge (1679). The flag bears the motto *For God, Covenanted Reformation, Presbytery, Government and Crown*, and in the hoist is a St Andrew's saltire with the word Machlin. The flag was handed over to the Kirk Session of Mauchline in 1955 for safe custody by the trustees of the late Colonel M. C. Hamilton-Campbell of Netherplace. In 1980 the flag was officially gifted to the congregation.

LANDOWNERS

With the Reformation past, the lands of the abbeys were broken up and passed over to secular owners. Much of Mauchline parish was thus acquired by Sir Hugh Campbell, Lord Loudoun, whose principal seat was Loudoun Castle, in Loudoun parish, near Galston. He took over most of the parish at that time, using Mauchline

Castle as the local estate headquarters. He died on 15 December 1622.

Mauchline Castle was extended sometime in the second half of the seventeenth century. This wing has a ground floor which is vaulted, and thus the wing may have incorporated part of an outbuilding of the original castle complex. The extension was built in the Scots Georgian style, with large sash windows, corbie-stepped gables and rendered walls.

During the time of the Covenant, the Loudoun estates, and thus the bulk of Mauchline parish, were transferred between various owners, depending on who was in favour, either with the king, or else the Commonwealth under Cromwell. In 1652 the lands were apprised from John, Earl of Loudoun and granted to James Livingston of London. Livingston sold the lands to James Dunlop of that Ilk, who sold them in 1663 to Hugh Montgomerie of Bridgend. The charter, which was written in English, is extensive, detailing the Loudoun properties at that time, but the following extract gives details of Loudoun properties in Mauchline parish:

> …the lands of Mungerswood, Cultersland; with manor-place and buildings; the mill called Hauchmilne, and mill-lands; the lands of Mosgavill, Dykfeild … the £10 lands of Mauchlane, with tower, fortalice, and manor-place of Mauchlen, with town and burgh of Mauchlane, with a weekly market and three fairs yearly; the lands of Mauchlen-Mayns, Machlinschaells-Bowers, Cowfald-shawe, and moor thereof called Cowfaldshaw-mure; Fowlar, Cranisland, Grasmallies, Wolton alias Little Fardell, Netherplace, and Knockshare; the tenement in Machlan once belonging to David Dunbar; …the mains of Bargour, including the lands of Roddingo and Faulds, Bargour called Garrouch, and Saltrae … Overhaugh, called Kinzeancleauch; McNochts-Crofts, Sheills, Netherhauch in Kingencleugh; Willockston, Bridgend and meadow of McLonachanstoune; Netherhauch, with salmon and other fishing in the river of Air; the lands of Bruntcheill and salmon fishing; the field and walk-mill of Hauch, lying between the wood of Kinzeancleugh on the east, the haugh-holme on the south, the grain mills of Hauch on the west, and the mill acres on the north … Killihaugh and Auchinbraine, Bornachthill, Hoilous …

In 1668 the lands were again transferred to Hugh Montgomerie of Bridgend, and a charter to these lands was issued from Edinburgh on 3 July. They were later returned to the Loudoun family.

These lands were returned to Sir Hugh Campbell of Loudoun in 1668. A new charter was issued, with one interesting difference – Sir Hugh had the right of trying wrong-doers within the baronies of Kylesmuir and Barrmuir, 'the market cross of

Machlin to be the place of distraint or apprising.' This is one of the few references to the fact that Mauchline, being a burgh, had a market cross of its own.

Ballochmyle house and estate appears to have been acquired by the Reid family, either late in the sixteenth century, or else early in the seventeenth. It was probably the Reids who acquired the estate when the monks of Melrose Abbey gave up their lands at Mauchline. The Reids were a significant family in Kyle at one time, the earliest references to them perhaps being that of 10 May 1399 when an inquisition was held at Ayr. In that document are listed 'Johannes Reid de Dalrumpill' and 'Johannes Reid de Barscemyng'. It is thought that the various Reids who established families in the Mauchline district were all descended from the Barskimming family.

The first known Reid of Ballochmyle is mentioned in a testament of Robert Harper of Barleith, dated 1613. His Christian name is not known, but Paterson, in his *History of Ayrshire*, thinks that he may have been the first lay owner of Ballochmyle. He also speculates that there was a mill there, resulting in the name 'Ballochmyln', and that this would be one of the last properties that the monks would give up. Where the mill may have been located is not known.

John Reid of Ballochmyle is noted in 1615, being mentioned in a testament of Alexander Reid, a merchant burgess of Glasgow, and again in 1618, noted in a testament of John Reid, burgess of Glasgow. No doubt the two Glasgow merchants were close relations. He was married to Jonet Crawfuird of Lochnorris (Old Cumnock parish) and they had at least two children – John who succeeded, and Helen, who was married to Adam Ayrd (or Aird), portioner of part of the lands of Catrine.

On 15 March 1634 a crown charter confirming the lands of Ballochmyle to John Reid, 'junior of Ballochmyle' was granted. His own testament was recorded in 1661, having been lodged by his son, also John, who succeeded. He was married to Margaret, daughter of Rev James Greig, minister of Loudoun.

The third John Reid is known to have been a Commissioner of Supply for Ayrshire. He and his son, again named John, are often named in the Kirk Session minutes of Mauchline. They were zealous elders in the church following the Revolution. However, prior to that time, John Reid was a keen supporter of the government, and as a result was a persecutor of the Covenanters.

Reid's most infamous part in the hunting down of the Covenanters took place in July 1685. A minor laird, Gilbert MacAdam of Waterhead in Carsphairn parish, had been banished to America where he was to be kept as a slave. However, MacAdam had contacts and money, and he was able to buy his freedom from slavery. He returned to Scotland, and settled back in the district. One Saturday night he was in attendance at a conventicle at the home of Hugh Campbell at Kirkmichael when they found themselves surrounded by a group of militia, under the command of John Reid of Ballochmyle and Sir Alexander Kennedy of Culzean. The Covenanters tried to make an escape, but as MacAdam was leaving by way of a window, he was shot by one of the soldiers. In later years a small gravestone was erected in Kirkmichael kirkyard, on which it records that he was shot 'by the laird of Colzean and Ballochmyl'. Either Reid or Kennedy did not want their name associated with this shooting, and had their names obliterated on the stone. However, soon after, a mason, perhaps the 'Old Mortality' of Sir Walter Scott, returned and re-cut their names on the stone, deeper than ever. The tampering on the stone is still visible to this day.

John Reid of Ballochmyle seems to have died around 1697. He had been married to Margaret, daughter of Mungo Campbell of Netherplace, and had at least one son and a daughter. The daughter, Margaret, was married in 1681 to John Mitchell of Turnerhill. The son, another John Reid, succeeded.

This fourth John Reid appears to have taken possession of Ballochmyle prior to the death of his father. He was made a burgess of Ayr on 3 October 1681. On 1 February 1688 he obtained a charter under the Great Seal of the lands of Ballochmyle. He had married Sarah, the daughter of a nearby laird, Robert Farquhar of Gilmilnscroft (d. 1698), on 22 June 1677. They appear to have had six children – John, Robert, Charles, James, Margaret and Sarah. It is thought that Sarah Reid was married on 1732 to John Dick of Glaisnock.

Kingencleugh Castle was erected sometime around 1600 by the Campbell family. Some accounts claim that the date of erection was earlier, on the basis that John Knox visited, but it is more likely that he came to an earlier building, of which

3.9 Kingencleugh Castle in 2012 *(Dane Love)*

nothing survives. The style of the tower is more in keeping with the late sixteenth century or early seventeenth. The castle comprised of a main block, measuring a minimum of 33 feet (its full length is not known due to the ruins having been removed) by 20 feet wide, to which a tower adjoins at the south-western end, measuring 11 feet by 8 feet.

The entrance doorway to the castle is rather small, originally having a round Saxon arch over it, but this has fallen. In the re-entrant angle between the main block and the wing are signs of a corner turret, the lower part of which is corbelled

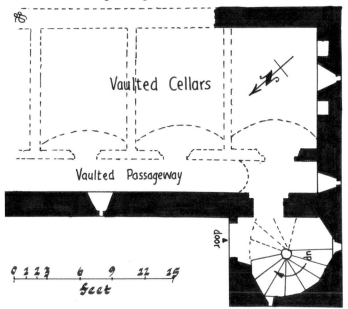

3.10 Plan of Kingencleugh Castle *(Dane Love)*

from nothing. The door wing contained a spiral staircase, which rose up to the first floor, giving access to the great hall. It also wound further up to the second floor, and the third floor may have been accessed by a small spiral stair located within the turret in the re-entrant angle.

The wing rises through four floors, the small gable having corbie-steps on it, in total reaching around 23 feet. The uppermost floor appears to have had a small chamber within it, containing a small fireplace, the flue of which led through a chimney on the gable.

The main block may have been a similar height, though most of it has disappeared, leaving little to confirm this. The walls are constructed with rubble blocks of sandstone, the corner stones, or quoins, being dressed. Much of the castle is built of red sandstone, but there is also a fair percentage of the masonry being blonde sandstone or freestone. The walls that survive are around thirty inches thick, and the lower floors appear only to have had narrow slit windows. The ground floor of the main block appears to have been barrel-vaulted, there probably being three or more vaults lying side by side below the great hall. A passageway around three feet wide was also vaulted, running alongside the vaults. On the ground floor, in the south-western vault, are two square aumbries, located either side of a window.

Although the location of the castle near to the glen is quite defensive, and the lower floors of the building had only slit windows, Kingencleugh was not a major defensive structure. It was built when lairds were keener on comfort, but there was still a need for a strong-built defensive house.

Elizabeth Campbell was still the lady laird at the opening of the seventeenth century. It is known that she had four sons, by her husband, John or Robert Campbell (*c.* 1520-*c.* 1602).

On Elizabeth's death in 1627 the estate passed to her son, John Campbell. He is mentioned in various documents from 1602 onwards. In 1636 John Campbell also succeeded to the estates of his grandfather, probably in the paternal line. A charter under the Great Seal of Scotland was issued on 19 July 1634 to John Campbell of Kingencleugh of the four pound lands of Ballochbrock, Drumlamford, Corriedow, Corrieban and Arnimean in Carrick.

John Campbell was succeeded by his son, also John Campbell. He was to be one of the Committee of War in 1648. John Campbell of Kingencleugh was admitted as a burgess and guild brother of Ayr on 30 October 1681; at the same time his servant, Adam Miller, was admitted as a burgess.

John Campbell was succeeded by his son Hugh

3.11 Campbell of Netherplace armorial bearings *(Dane Love)*

Campbell. He married a kinswoman, the daughter of Sir Hew Campbell of Cessnock.

Kingencleugh Castle appears to have been abandoned as a residence in the early to mid-eighteenth century. The old tower house was left to crumble to the ground, aided by local farmers who used its walls as a ready source of building material. The castle was gradually covered in ivy, and thus it remained for some time. Around 1890 or so, the laird decided that the farmers should no longer use the tower for stone, and decided to have the remains repointed and the walls replastered, leaving the tower to stand as a folly within the grounds of the later house.

Netherplace House was erected in 1620 by Mungo Campbell of Cowfauldshaw, who was given sasine of the lands of Cowfauldshaw, Netherplace and others. The original mansion was probably a Scots tower house, L-shaped in plan. The style was typical of Scots lairds' houses – L-shaped, three storeys in height, with Georgian paned windows. At a later date the wing was extended to the east, and a second wing, almost unconnected with the main block, was added to form a courtyard, the eastern opening of which was closed off by a tall wall and gateway.

Mungo Campbell was married to Janet Craufurd, daughter of John Craufurd of Craufurdland Castle and Margaret Wallace, daughter of Hew Wallace of Carnell Castle. Margaret had previously been married to George Campbell of Ducathall.

Hew Campbell succeeded to Netherplace. He is thought to have been the son of Mungo, though this is not confirmed. Hew Campbell appears to have been the first to use the term 'of Netherplace', in place of Cowfauldshaw. Some say that these two names are of the same place, and that Netherplace replaced the quainter Cowfauldshaw, but it is more likely that the new mansion was named Netherplace, and that Cowfauldshaw was located elsewhere, and was gradually superseded as the main seat on the estate.

Hew Campbell appears to have been married twice. His first wife was Margaret Petheine, or Peden. She was probably a daughter of the Pedens of Auchenlongford, in the parish of Sorn. The name of his second wife is not known. Hew Campbell's will was recorded in 1640. In it reference is made to his eldest son, Mungo, who succeeded, but also to John, Margaret and Mary, children of his first marriage, and George and Marion, children of the second marriage. His second wife also seems to have predeceased him.

The Mungo Campbell who inherited Netherplace appears to have been something of a rogue and character. He was married around the year 1650 to Elizabeth Dalrymple, daughter of Dalrymple of Langlands. They had one son, also Mungo, and two daughters, Elizabeth, who was married in 1681 to William Mure of Bruntwood, and Margaret, who married William Duncan of Heilar, Sorn parish.

Mungo Campbell was involved in a family dispute. What the difficulty was is not known, but the feud ended up with Mungo killing his full cousin, John Campbell in Mossgiel, in Mauchline in 1642. That the local laird was involved in such an event would have resulted in much gossip and taking of sides in the parish, but it was not unknown for feuds to occur in Ayrshire at that time, and there are other examples of lairds murdering others across the county. This was a rather late example, however.

On 15 June 1642 Rev George Young, the parish minister, was ordained by the presbytery of the church to 'summon from the pulpit Mungow Campbell, son to Hew Campbell in Netherplace, to compeir before the Presbiterie, to be halden in Ayr the 20th of July nixtocum, to answer before them for the cruel and unnatural murthering and killing, in the town of Mauchline, of John Campbell in Mossgaviel [Mossgiel] as was gravlie related.' What happened is not related, but almost one year later, on 12 April 1643, a supplication was presented to the Presbytery from Mungo Campbell of Netherplace by his brother-in-law, Alexander Pedan or Peden, expressing his willingness to give obedience and satisfaction to the Presbytery, so that his life should not be in danger. The presbytery responded stating that they conceded in the terms noted. The process against Mungo Campbell continued for a number of years thereafter, until on 16 September 1646 the church:

> …compeired Mungo Campbell of Netherplace, in the habit of sackcloth, and in all humilitie confessed the unnatural murther of and killing of John Campbell, his cousin-german. As also he confessed his frequent falls in fornication sinsyne. The Presbyterie considering heirof, ordane the said Mungo to compeir in the habit of sackcloth in the kirk of Mauchline, in the place of public repentance, two Lord's days, till the Presbyterie advyse at thair next meiting what further shall be enjoyned to him.

Mungo Campbell appears to have spent his time in the place of repentance at Mauchline, but the presbytery was still not finished with him. On 18 November 1646 he was ordained by the presbytery to give further signs of his repentance within the kirks of Galston, Ochiltree and Tarbolton. On the following December he again had to face the presbytery, dressed in sackcloth, which referred his case to the minister and session of the parish church of Mauchline. What they did with him is not known, but it is thought that the punishment meted to him was now complete.

3.12 Netherplace House around 1900 *(Stroma Leith)*

Mungo was succeeded by his eldest son, also named Mungo, sometime in the second half of the century. This Mungo was a more upright citizen, for he became the Sheriff-Depute of Ayrshire, and served as an elder in the parish kirk from at least 1672 until 1700. He was married in 1698 to Jean Menzies, daughter of Sir Alexander Menzies of that Ilk, chief of the clan Menzies. They had a son, also named Mungo, and two daughters. One of these, Sarah, was baptised on 15 September 1699, but may have died in infancy, as no further reference to her is noted. The other daughter, Susannah, never married, and died in 1719.

Perhaps influenced by his wife's connections with clan chiefs, Mungo Campbell of Netherplace matriculated his own coat of arms with the Lord Lyon in Edinburgh on 24 July 1694. The blazon reads, 'A gyronny of eight pieces, ermine and gules, on each of the last four gyrones a besant, Or.' The crest is a right hand issuing erect from a cloud holding a signet letter. The motto, *Optime Quod Opportune* translates as 'seize your opportunity'.

INDUSTRY

There was little industry in Mauchline of any scale in the seventeenth century. Agriculture was the main source of employment, and most other trades were in some way connected with it. There existed mills in various places in the parish, such as at Haugh and Dalsangan. Little is known about the mills at the time. Similarly, smithies existed at various places across the parish, such as Mauchline itself and the Haugh. The smith at the Haugh in 1684 was William MacGavin.

Coal mining did take place, mainly to the north end of the parish. Many of the old workings became forgotten about, and only by chance were to be discovered later. For example, in 1926 an old shaft was discovered at Friendlesshead farm. The farmer had noticed part of the field subsiding, and miners from the village, who were on strike at the time, came and reopened it. The wooden timbers supporting the shaft were rotten, but the miners cleared the shaft out, inserting new timbers, as they worked down to find out what was at the bottom. On Wednesday 15 December 1926 the miners struck a four feet thick seam at 37 fathoms. It was expected that a further 10 fathoms would reach the next seam.

LEISURE

The first reference to Mauchline Races appears in the first half of the seventeenth century. However, it was stated in the *Kilmarnock Weekly Press* of 8 May 1858 that the traditional race was claimed to be between five or six hundred years old. This would take its origins back to the middle of the thirteenth or fourteenth centuries. What basis the paper had for claiming the race to be as old is not known, but the race may simply have been a regular feature of a 'play day' or religious fair, which may have been as old as was claimed.

Mauchline Races was traditionally held on 30 April each year, which was St Catherine of Siena's feast day. The race saw men on horseback ride furiously from the Cross up the road towards Mossgiel. At a spot almost in line with East Mossgiel, or thereabouts, the horses had to be turned around and raced back down to the village centre once more. In distance, this would be around two miles.

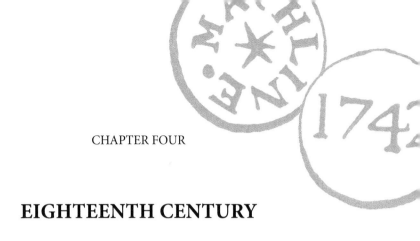

CHAPTER FOUR

EIGHTEENTH CENTURY

VILLAGE LIFE

The parish of Mauchline had grown in size to 1,169 inhabitants by 1755, according to Dr Webster's survey. By 1791, when the *Statistical Account* was compiled by Rev William Auld, the parish population had increased to 1,800. It was reckoned that around 1,000 of this number lived in the village of Mauchline itself. Of the 1,800, 870 were thought to be males, and there were 930 females. The number of parents was 700, and there were 829 children. A total of 270 servants or lodgers were also in existence.

Over the five years prior to 1790, there were an average 87 births per annum, 18 marriages and 42 deaths.

Writing in 1791, Rev Auld gives a short description of the average person within the parish which will entertain the present resident:

> In such a number there must be some exceptions; but, in general, they are a sober industrious people, charitably disposed: careful and even punctual in attending the church on Sundays, and on sacramental occasions; and their practice in the main is agreeable to their possession. The inhabitants are of a middle size, from 5 feet, 4 inches, to 6 feet, 2 inches, and make a decent appearance, particularly at public meetings. It is a great disadvantage to them that no manufacture is carried on: But they are willing to encourage any plan that may tend to promote the improvement of agriculture, commerce and manufacture; in all which they are making some progress. The manner of living and dress is much altered from what it was about 50 years ago. At that period, and for some time after, there were only two or three families in this parish, who made use of tea daily, now it is done by, at least, one half of the parish, and almost the whole use it occasionally. At that period good two-penny, strong-ale, and home-spirits were in vogue: but now even people in the middling and lower stations of life, deal much in foreign spirits, rum-punch and wine. In

former times, the gentlemen of the county entered into a resolution to encourage the consumption of their own grain, and for that purpose, to drink no foreign spirits: But, in consequence of the prevalence of smuggling, and the heavy taxes laid on the home-made liquors, this patriotic resolution was either forgotten or abandoned. As to dress, about 50 years ago, there were few females who wore scarlet or silks. But now, nothing is more common, than silk caps and silk cloaks; and women, in a middling station, are as fine as ladies of quality as were formerly. The like change may be observed in the dress of the male sex, though, perhaps, not in the same degree.

In the first half of the eighteenth century William Maitland, son of the parish minister, was a surgeon in Mauchline. At the end of the century it was noted that some of the residents were being inoculated against small pox with some success.

In 1791 it was reckoned by Rev William Auld that the parish rental value was £5,410 Scots, or about £450 Sterling. However, the real rental figure was £3,510 Sterling in 1790, a rise since 1750 when it was £1,260.

The *Statistical Account* gives a run-down of the number of various professions and trades. There was only one clergyman, obviously Rev Auld himself. There were two writers to the signet, or attorneys, and only one surgeon. There was one student studying at university. In the parish there were ten merchants, twenty weavers,

4.1 77 Loudoun Street, around 1900 *(Brian Bogle)*

70

twenty masons and twelve carpenters or wrights. There were only two tanners in the parish, but twelve shoemakers used the leather in the production of footwear. Ten tailors and four hosiers produced clothing. There were two butchers in the village, one saddler, and six smiths. In the parish there were two messengers at arms, or king's bailiffs, and three sheriff officers. By far the largest number of men were farmers, numbering 73. These farmers had a total of 240 horses and 1,080 black cattle.

At the end of the eighteenth century the parish had between £80-100 for the relief of the poor. It was reckoned that there were around thirty poor families, or 'weekly pensioners', in the parish. To raise money for poor relief, mortcloths were hired out for covering coffins at funerals. Other funds were raised by hiring out

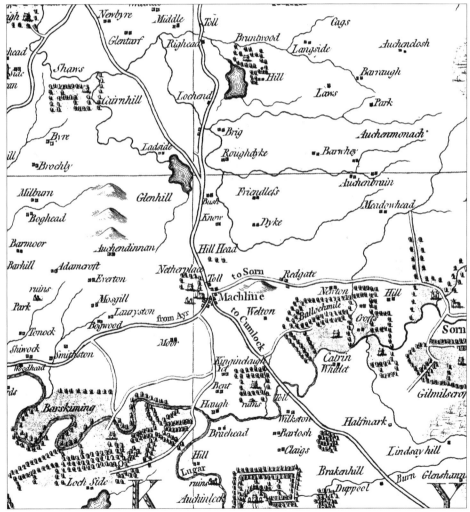

4.2 Mauchline parish area on Capt. Andrew Armstrong's map of 1775 (*Author's Collection*)

seats in the church and from collections, raising a total of £50 per annum. The difference was paid by the local heritors. In 1771 the heritors had met and agreed to make up an assessment of £22 10s 10d per annum towards the cost of looking after the poor. One half of this amount was payable by the tenants. As the century passed, this sum decreased in real value, resulting in Rev Auld recording that it was unlikely to keep up with the demands of an increasing number of poor in the parish. Rev Auld noted, 'It must be obvious to every body, that according to the present mode, the burden of maintaining the poor, is most unequally divided. It falls almost entirely on tenants, tradesmen, servants, and charitable persons attending the church; while other people, however rich, particularly non-residing heritors, whatever their income may be, contribute little or nothing to the charitable funds of the parish.'

Around 1710 it is claimed that Mauchline had a charter setting it up as a burgh, with the right to choose magistrates to run the community. This charter had become lost by the time of the *Statistical Account*, much to the regret of Rev William Auld, who felt that by having magistrates and officials, the village would have been run better, as they would 'promote good order, peace and happiness'. Writing in 1791 he stated that at that time 'riots and disorders' were too frequent.

Around 1780 Mauchline Friendly Society was established 'for the relief of distressed brethren'. The society invited members to join for a fee of one guinea, and in 1791 there were £300 in the funds. From this, those members who were unable to work were granted two shillings per week as an allowance. If the person was confined to bed then they were given three shillings per week.

Various events in the life of the villagers were notable throughout the eighteenth century. One that caught the attention of the people and no doubt was a talking point for many months, was when, on Friday 27 August 1790, William Carswell, a paper maker in the village, was sent to prison in Glasgow on suspicion of having forged a guinea note of the Glasgow Arms Bank. On the Monday after, Robert Stevenson of Kilmarnock was also arrested on suspicion of being involved in the forgery.

A murder was committed in the village on 19 March 1793. Mungo Miller, a tanner, was found dead in the street at five o'clock in the morning. John Thomson, who was an innkeeper in Mauchline, his ale-house located in the Cowgate, facing Horwood Place, was charged with the murder, along with his wife, Elizabeth Finlay, and their children, Hugh and Janet. They were tried at the High Court of Justiciary at Ayr in the autumn of 1795 by the Rt Hon Lord Justice Clerk, but the case against them was found not proven. David Thomson, formerly a baker in the village, and then a soldier in the Elgin Fencible Regiment was indicted as well, but did not appear. He was outlawed for this. He returned to Mauchline later, when his regiment returned from Ireland, and was apprehended. Whilst in jail he managed to get the sentence of outlawry recalled, serving abroad at the time. However, he denied all knowledge of the murder, but accused James Harkness, clerk to Gavin Hamilton. On hearing that he was wanted, he handed himself in at Ayr. At his trial on 3 April that year he was found not guilty, in fact the only material able to incriminate him was the testimony of David Thomson.

David Thomson claimed that:

> … on the night between the 18th and 19th of March 1793, he had been called out of his house by Janet Thomson, daughter of John Thomson, the innkeeper, who had been formerly tried; and that, on following her to her father's house, he was taken by her into a low room, where he found her father, mother, and her brother, alongst with James Harkness, standing by the dead body of Mungo Miller. That Harkness confessed himself to have been the murderer, and offered the Witness money, to assist in carrying the body to the place where it was found next morning, which he refusing, the persons present, with the assistance of another man then in the house, carried out the body themselves.
>
> In this story, he was directly contradicted by the family of John Thomson, and the other person, whom he alledged to have been employed in carrying out the body. His account of the wounds was also not consistent with the fact, as proved by the surgeons examined, and others; and there were several improbabilities in his narrative, — indeed, several of the witnesses gave very contradictory evidence.

The murderer appears never to have been found.

Another incident took place in May 1794 when a traveller with a dancing bear visited the village. The man found lodgings for himself but of course no-one was able to take in a bear. Accordingly, the man took the bear one mile out of the village and tied it to a tree in the middle of a wood, with the expectation that he would get it there the next day. However, a villager was up before him, and as he was walking through the wood found the bear, loose. He made his way back to the village in haste, and gathered together a small party of men, armed with scythes, cudgels and other make-shift weapons, with the plan of capturing the animal. Fortunately for the bear, its keeper had returned to the wood and was able to rescue it and contain it before the hunt party found it.

Mauchline Conversation Society was founded on 30 October 1786 and it survived for eleven years or so. The last entry in the surviving minute book dates from 20 November that year. The club existed to improve discussion and education amongst local men, David Sillar being the first listed. Other members included Burns' brother, Gilbert, who attended most meetings. Robert Burns was not a member. The subjects discussed were diverse, including current political subjects, as well as hypothetical questions such as 'should a man marry for love or money? Under the rules, should any member not attend then they were fined, the income used to purchase books for the society's library. Some of those known to have been acquired included Sir Henry MacKenzie's *Man of Feeling*, Rousseau's *Emile*, Voltaire's *Peter the Great*, as well as sets of *The Mirror* and *The Lounger*.

Other groups existing in the village in the eighteenth century include the Royal Mauchline Volunteers, which existed in 1799. Mauchline's Masonic Lodge, was founded in 1791.

In the few hours of leisure that the villagers had, the sport of cock-fighting appears to have been quite common. Rev William Auld, who was minister from 1742-1791, campaigned against 'the cruel and inhuman action of cock-fighting at Fasten-e'en,' or Shrove Tuesday.

Developments in the village were being made in the latter part of the eighteenth century. The old High Street, which extended from the Cross westwards towards the castle gates, was extended further to the west by the erection of cottages on either side. These were, in the main, single storey thatched dwellings, mostly occupied by weavers. Indeed, it is reckoned that the last hand-loom weaver still working in Mauchline occupied one of the last houses on the south side of the street.

This development was originally named New Street, but in later years was renamed Loudoun Street. At the western end, on the north side of the road, stands Campbell House, a double-storey red sandstone dwelling. When originally built around 1783 this was a single-storey cottage.

James Boswell (1740-1795), the noted diarist and author who lived at Auchinleck House, often paid a visit to Mauchline. From his journals we know that he came to the Castle, Netherplace, Ballochmyle and to Rev Auld's manse to visit and socialise with the occupants. He probably also paid a visit to the farms on Auchinleck estate that were within the parish of Mauchline, located on the south side of the River Ayr.

BURNS AND MAUCHLINE

The second half of the eighteenth century was when Robert Burns (1759-1796) lived in and around Mauchline. Much has been written about the poet's associations with the village, especially the people and places known to him. Many of these have been preserved as places of historical interest, whereas numerous others have been lost over the years. Burnsians will find more detailed accounts of Mauchline's associations with the poet in other works, in particular the *Burns Chronicle*, which has many articles on these connections.

Robert Burns was born at Alloway on 25 January 1759, the son of William Burness and Agnes Broun. On 11 November (Martinmas) 1776, at the age of six, Robert and his family moved to Mount Oliphant, a small farm near to Ayr. In 1777 the family moved to Lochlea farm, in nearby Tarbolton parish, but within a short distance of Mauchline. It was probably from this time onward that Burns' association with the village started. William was to have some difficulty in paying his rent at Lochlea, resulting in litigation, but he eventually won the case. He died in 1784 and was buried at Alloway.

At Martinmas (11 November) 1783 Robert and his brother Gilbert took on the lease of the farm of East Mossgiel and he remained there for four years. The farm, which extended to 118 acres, was sublet from Gavin Hamilton, writer in Mauchline, who was the factor to the Earl of Loudoun. For a number of years there were a number of old artefacts associated with the poet kept at the farm, within part of the old building. The Burns brothers' first year at Mossgiel was something of a disaster. The soil was poor clay, and the weather was difficult. Together with poor seed used on the ground, the results were not very successful.

It was whilst staying at Mossgiel that Burns wrote some of his better known works, including *The Cottar's Saturday Night,* and *To a Mountain Daisy.* The field in

which the poet traditionally upturned the daisy whilst ploughing is located to the rear of the farmhouse. In an adjacent field he spotted a field mouse, resulting in his To a Mouse.

Burns' Kilmarnock *edition of Poems, Chiefly in the Scottish Dialect*, was published in July 1786. The book was an instant success, selling out within a very short period. Originally he had made plans to emigrate to Jamaica, where he was to become book-keeper on a plantation, employed by Charles Douglas, manager on behalf of his brother, Dr Patrick Douglas of Garrallan (d. 1819). However, with the success of his book and the prospect of further fame, he cancelled these plans and remained in Scotland.

Robert wooed and won Jean Armour, the daughter of a

4.3 Robert Burns *(Lord Weir)*

prosperous local mason, James Armour. Jean was born on 25 February 1765, six years after Burns. They agreed to be married, perhaps even carried out an irregular marriage, but Jean's father was unhappy with her choice and destroyed their marriage contract. Jean, however, was pregnant, and Armour sent her to live with relatives in Paisley. She was to return from Paisley in September 1786, whereupon she gave birth to twins, named Robert and Jean. Jean was to die in infancy, and was buried in the Armour burial plot within Mauchline kirkyard. A second set of twins (daughters) were born on 3 March 1788, but they too died in infancy and were buried in Mauchline.

A gravestone was erected over the burial ground of the infants, restored in 1924 by the Carlton Burns Club of Glasgow. At the same time a new granite slab was placed on it, unveiled on 7 June 1924 by Thomas Killin of Glasgow. It reads:

> In memory of the infant children of the poet Robert Burns and Jean Armour; Jean, born 3rd Sept. 1786, died at the age of 14 months; Twin daughters, born 3rd March 1788, died a few days later; Elizabeth Riddell Burns, born 21st Nov 1792, died Sep 1795. Restored by the Carlton Burns Club, Glasgow, 1924.

Elizabeth Riddell Burns, who was born in Dumfries, died at Mossgiel. The stone was again restored and repaired by James T. Picken of Melbourne, Australia, in 1949, and again in 1983 by Glasgow and District Burns Association.

Robert and Jean were formally married in the writing office of Gavin Hamilton by John Farquhar of Gilmilnscroft JP and they moved into a house in Castle Street, rented from Dr MacKenzie. Burns, however, had by this time leased Ellisland farm from Patrick Miller of Dalswinton in Dumfriesshire. Whilst he was rebuilding the steading, he travelled between Mauchline and Dumfries, but eventually in the summer of 1789 he took his wife to Ellisland, where they lived until November 1791. They then moved into Dumfries, where Burns died on 21 July 1796. He was buried in St Michael's kirkyard. Jean lived for another 38 years, dying on 26 March 1834. She was buried alongside him, in a new mausoleum, erected in 1815.

Also buried in Mauchline kirkyard, but in a grave that cannot be identified, was John Burns, the youngest of Burns' brothers. He died in 1785 at the age of sixteen years.

With the success of his poetry, Burns was invited to meet the Edinburgh literati in November 1786. The second, or Edinburgh edition of his poems was published on 21 April 1787, and once more was a success. Many editions followed, raising the poet's fame across the country.

The grave of Gavin Hamilton was indicated by a marker erected by Partick Burns Club in 1919. It is located between the church door and the entrance gateway to the kirkyard. Gavin Hamilton was a writer in Mauchline, living in the Castle. He was also employed as factor of the Loudoun estates in the district, and it was Hamilton who had leased then sub-let East Mossgiel to the poet.

Like Burns, Hamilton was liberal in his thinking, and both men had much in common. They both joined the Freemasons. When Burns' first edition of poems was published, it was dedicated to Hamilton. Gavin Hamilton died on 5 February 1805.

4.4 Mossgiel around 1890 *(Author's Collection)*

One of Burns' first acquaintances in Mauchline was John Richmond (1765-1846), who worked in the office of Gavin Hamilton as his clerk. Burns and he were founder members of the Bachelors' Club in Tarbolton. Richmond moved from Mauchline to Edinburgh in 1785, where he became an apprentice to William Wilson, Writer to the Signet. When Burns went to Edinburgh in 1786 he lodged with Richmond for a time, contributing towards Richmond's rent. The friendship seems to have died sometime after 1787, for at that time Burns' letters to him dry up. In 1789 Richmond returned to Mauchline, having qualified as a solicitor. He ran the business until his death in 1846 at the age of 81. He was buried in the north-west corner of the kirkyard.

John Richmond's house still stands at 3 High Street, though when he occupied it, it was known as New House of the Kilnknowes (the Old House of the Kilnknowes is the present Ballochmyle Inn). A fine double-storey building, it is distinguished by its stone pilasters at the front doorway. The house was thatched up until the early twentieth century; John Taylor Gibb, writing in 1911, stated that it was 'recently slated'.

One of Burns' friends in Mauchline was James Smith, who lived in a house at the Cross. This was demolished in 1820 to allow the construction of New Road. Smith was described by Burns as 'the sleest pawky thief'. He left Mauchline in 1786 to live at Avon, near Linlithgow, where he began working in the calico printing trade. At the time of Mauchline Races in April 1788, Smith sent a printed shawl by the carrier John Ronald, to Burns, which he gifted to his wife. Smith's works at Avon proved to be unsuccessful, resulting in his emigration to the West Indies.

Jean Smith (1768-1854), sister of James, was one of Burns' 'Mauchline Belles', described in his poem as having 'wit'. Around 1788 she moved to Edinburgh where she lived for many years. She married James Candlish (1759-1806), lecturer in medicine at Edinburgh, who was 'the earliest friend except my only brother that I have on earth, and one of the worthiest fellows that ever any man called by the name of Friend,' according to Burns. At the time his surname was MacCandlish, but this was later shortened. On her death Jean was buried in the Old Calton kirkyard. A memorial there was erected by her son, Rev Dr R. S. Candlish, a Free Church theologian.

James Armour was a mason in Mauchline who seems to have been quite a successful businessman. He was to become Burns' father-in-law. Of Armour's work, there are references to a number of known contracts which he completed. He is said to have worked on Dumfries House, near Cumnock, and Skeldon House near Dalrymple. The old Howford Bridge across the River Ayr, on the south-eastern boundary of the parish, is known to have been at least one place where he worked in the parish, being paid in 1781 to make repairs to it. Whether or not he built the original bridge a few years beforehand is not known. Armour was employed by John Brown (1729-1802) of Lanfine (Galston parish) in 1772 to build a new mansion for him on the estate. Armour may also have been the architect of the new building, and he was paid at the rate of 33 shillings per rood of mason work.

James married Mary Smith on 7 December 1761 and they had eleven children, some of whom are interred in the kirkyard. These include three sons named Robert who died in infancy, two Marys who died as infants and Jean Armour. The latter was married to a Mr Lees and lived for many years in a cottage in the rows of houses at the top of Barskimming Road known as Glenlee. Mrs Lees died around 1865 at the age of 85 or so.

Burns' associations with Rev William Auld have been written about many times over the years. The poet's first mention in the kirk session minute books occurs on 10 June 1786, when it is noted that a letter was received by Mr Auld from Jean Armour. This reads:

Rev Sir,
I am heartily sorry that I have given and must give your Session trouble on my account. I acknowledge that I am with child, and Robert Burns in Mossgiel is the father. I am, with great respect,
    Your most humble servant,
    Signed Jean Armour.

Burns was called before the kirk session on 25 June and he admitted that he was responsible for his 'irregularity in conduct', in making Jean pregnant. For a further three times through July and August that year, both Burns and Jean appeared in the kirk to receive public reproof. Rev Auld was quite charitable towards them, for he allowed them to remain seated on their own chairs, rather than have to sit on the cutty stool.

On 6 August 1786 Burns was to receive a certificate from Rev Auld confirming him as a single man.

4.5 Jean Armour Statue *(Dane Love)*

Burns and Jean appeared before the kirk session again on 5 August 1788. The couple had partaken of a traditional marriage, and they were to admit 'their irregular marriage and their sorrow for that irregularity' before the session. Further, they intimated their desire 'that the Session will take such steps as may seem to them proper in order to the solemn confirmation of the said marriage.' The session rebuked the pair for their part in having an irregular marriage, but it was decided that the pair should 'be taken solemnly engaged to adhere to faithfully to one another as husband and wife, all the days of their life.' When this had been completed, Burns gifted the church with a guinea note which he wanted to be used for the benefit of the poor.

'Daddy Auld' is how Burns referred to Rev Auld in some of his verses. He is mentioned as 'Daddy

Auld' in 'The Kirk's Alarm', 'Apostle Auld' in 'The Twa Herds', and as 'Father Auld' in 'Holy Willie's Prayer'.

Poosie Nansie is the name given by Burns to Agnes Gibson. She and her husband, 'Black' George Gibson kept a house on the opposite side of Loudoun Street to the kirkyard gate, a building that has for many years been known as Poosie Nansie's inn. The date on the gable claims it was erected in 1700. George and Agnes' daughter, Janet Gibson, was known to Burns as 'Racer Jess'. She was mentally handicapped, but was very strong and gained her nickname from winning several races on which she had laid a wager. Burns refers to her as 'Racer Jess' in 'The Holy Fair', and as Jenny in 'Adam Armour's Prayer'.

One evening Burns was passing the inn when he looked through a window into a room in which some regulars were engaged in a carousel. This inspired the poet to write his poem, 'The Jolly Beggars'.

The inn kept by John Dow, or Johnnie Doo, was located on the corner of Cowgate with Loudoun Street. It was officially known as the Whitefoord Arms, after the owners of Ballochmyle estate. The building was a double storey structure, roofed in thatch, which by 1837 had been divided into two flats. The building was later to be demolished and in 1866 a new block was erected on the same site for the co-operative association. This inn was Burns' preferred public house in Mauchline.

Nanse Tinnock's Inn was located in Castle Street, almost opposite Burns' House itself. The inn is thought to date from 1712 and was also known as the Sma' Inn, from its diminutive size. The hostelry was taken over by Robert Weir in 1749 and his wife, Agnes Tannock, or 'Nanse Tinnock'. Robert died in 1782 and Nanse kept the inn going. Nanse was described by the poet as, 'A worthy old hostess of the author's in Mauchline, where he sometimes studied politics over a glass of guid auld Scotch drink.' Nanse, however, claimed that Burns was not a regular at her inn. However, Burns described her as 'a true ale-wife in the proverbial sense of the word, close, discreet, civil and no tale teller.' She is mentioned in Burns' 'The Author's Earnest Cry and Prayer.' Burns is also known to have written his poem, 'To Mr MacAdam of Craigengillan' within the ale-house. The Sma' Inn was unique in that it had a doorway facing Castle Street, but also one facing onto the kirkyard, making the inn popular at the time of the Holy Fair. Nanse Tinnock died on 22 December 1828 and was buried in the old kirkyard of Mauchline on the south side of the church.

Holy Willie is the name by which William Fisher was known to Burns. He was born in 1737, the son of a farmer. He was ordained as an elder in Mauchline kirk in July 1772, during the ministry of Rev William Auld. Although an elder, 'Holy Willie' lapsed into drunkenness on occasion, being rebuked by the session for this in 1790. He lived at Mid Montgarswood farm, in Sorn parish. Burns made Fisher the subject of 'Holy Willie's Prayer'. He also composed one of his epitaphs on him

4.6 Grave of Burns' Children *(Dane Love)*

– 'Epitaph on Holy Willie'. He describes him as 'a rather oddish bachelor Elder in the Parish Church of Mauchline, and much and justly famed for that polemical chattering which ends in tippling orthodoxy, and for that spiritualised bawdry which refines to liquorish devotion'. In 1809, during one of his drunken periods, he was walking home when he collapsed into a ditch, where his frozen body was later found. He was buried on the south side of the church.

Mary Morison is mentioned by Burns in various poems and songs. Who 'Bonnie Mary Morison' actually refers to has been disputed over the years. In Mauchline kirkyard is a gravestone to a Mary Morison who was for many years regarded as the person to whom the poet referred. Her grave is located by the side of the path on the south side of the church. The stone was only raised in 1825. However, in recent years, it has been claimed that the real Mary Morison was Alison Begbie, or Peggie Alison. Robert Chambers, in his biography of the poet, wrote that, 'Although Burns is not supposed to have had any particular person in view', it is widely thought that she was in fact Peggie Alison, referred to in the song, 'And I'll kiss thee yet, yet'.

Many accounts claim that Mary Morison lived at Mauchline Place, but an old Burnsian, Sandy Marshall, claimed that this was untrue, and that she did in fact live at a house known as Brownlea, which stood at the corner of Castle Street with the Knowe. In later years the Misses Tod occupied Brownlea – they were the grand-daughters of Gavin Hamilton.

James Hamilton was a young lad when Burns lived in Mauchline. He was to live until the age of eighty four, dying in 1862, retelling interested parties how he knew the bard when he was a child. His parents were friends of Burns, and young James often paid a visit to Mossgiel. It is said that he often 'ca'd the ploo to Robin'. On one occasion he was asked by Burns to take a letter and pass it to Jean Armour, on no account to give it to anyone else. Hamilton was later to become employed on the Netherplace estate, working for the Campbells for sixty years.

Many of the above people are commemorated by gravestones within the auld kirkyard, a plaque erected by the Burns Club indicating their whereabouts. Others associated with Burns who are buried in the kirkyard include Robert Wilson, buried on the south side of the church. When Burns and Jean Armour were estranged, Robert Wilson is said to have had a romantic relationship with Jean. Wilson was a native of the village, but had moved to Paisley for work, settling there as a weaver. When Jean's father sent her to the town, she met Wilson and they had a short romance. Burns was to refer to Wilson as the 'Gallant Weaver' in his song of that title.

4.7 Grave of Gavin Hamilton *(Dane Love)*

A watch and clockmaker in Mauchline at the time of Burns was John Brown. His grave is located in the north-west corner of the kirkyard. Burns refers to him as 'Clockie Brown' in his poem, 'The Court of Equity'.

James Bryen or Brydan was a farmer at Welton during the time of Burns. The poet mentioned him in his 'The Court of Equity'. In Burns' last letter to John Richmond, dated July 1786, Bryen was mentioned.

Laird MacGaun, or Master Tootie was a lad whom Burns recommended in verse to Gavin Hamilton. In later years, according to Burns' biographer, Robert Cromek, he was a 'knavish cattle dealer' in Mauchline. When he died he was buried on the east side of the church, against the kirkyard dike overlooking Loudoun Street. The name MacGaun or MacGaan was the local pronunciation of MacGavin.

James Humphrey was a local mason who did work around the Mauchline and

Tarbolton areas. He is thought to have worked on both Lochlea and Mossgiel. He was a keen arguer regarding church doctrine, and Burns satirised him in his 'Epitaph on a Noisy Polemic.' Years after Burns died, Humphrey appears to have become rather poor, and he often greeted strangers with the comment, 'Please Sir, I'm the bletherin' bitch, can you spare me a trifle?' in the hope that the tourist would give him a few pennies. Humphrey could no longer afford to keep his own house and his final years were spent in Failford poorhouse. He died in 1844 and was buried near the Armour graves in Mauchline kirkyard.

William Patrick was a young boy when Burns lived at Mossgiel and he was employed as a herd boy and general outdoor servant at the farm for around four years. In later years he was a great extoller of Burns and his family, and he collected his reminiscences in prose. He died at his home in Loudoun Street in 1864 aged 88, and was buried near the entrance gateway to Mauchline kirkyard. His recollections were gathered together and published as a booklet, entitled *Robert Burns at Mosgiel*, in 1881. He said that he often occupied the same sleeping area as Burns, and that he often heard him reciting his poems 'in the wee sma' oors ayont the twal.'

A lock of Burns' hair survives in the Otago Settlers Museum at Dunedin in New Zealand, which came from a former Mauchline owner. The lock is preserved in a photo-frame, complete with an old letter detailing its history. This reads: 'This genuine relic of the Poet, is a modicum of a larger lock, which belonged to Jean Armour. Of this she gave a portion to Jane Wilson, Mauchline, on her emigration to Bathurst, Victoria. At her death it was returned to her relatives in Scotland. Mr Edward McEwan of Mauchline became the possessor of it. And the half that he gave to my friend Mr John Stark of Glasgow, who again divided it with me at Glasgow in November 1865. J. Barr, Dunedin, 20th March 1872.'

LANDOWNERS

John Reid and his wife, Sarah Farquhar, remained in possession of Ballochmyle at the start of the eighteenth century. John appears to have died quite early into the new century, certainly by 1720, and he was succeeded in the estate by his eldest son, John Reid, probably the sixth laird of that name.

John Reid was educated for the Scottish bar, becoming an advocate by 1712. He was admitted as a burgess and member of the guild brethren of Ayr on 15 April 1712. He appears to have suffered financial difficulties. These problems were so bad that he was even imprisoned in Ayr, for the records of the gaol for 30 April 1720 make reference to 'John Reid of Ballochmyle, advocate, prisoner in the Tolbooth.' Few other references can be found to this last Reid of Ballochmyle, though he does appear in the parish records of Old Cumnock, where he was present at the baptism of Sarah, daughter of John Dick of Glaisnock, which took place in 1733.

John had at least one brother, Adam Reid, who was admitted as a burgess and member of the guild brethren in Ayr on 27 October 1720.

John Reid's pecuniary difficulties resulted in Ballochmyle estate being sold. It was purchased by Allan Whitefoord, probably around 1740. He was referred to in a list of heritors of Auchinleck church in 1760, but in 1743 mention is made of Allan Whitefoord of Ballochmyle, for on 19 April that year his servant, John Allet, was admitted as a burgess and freeman of Ayr. A later servant, John Blaw, was admitted as a burgess and freeman on 2 May 1748. Allan was the second son of Sir Adam Whitefoord, 1st Baronet, of Blairquhan Castle (d. 1727). He was a cashier with the Royal Bank of Scotland from 1725, and was appointed a Commissioner of Customs and Excise. He became the Receiver-General of the Land Tax for Scotland in 1733. Building up a considerable fortune, he was able to purchase Ballochmyle and make considerable improvements to the estate.

4.8 Ballochmyle House around 1880 *(Ballochmyle Archives)*

The old house was demolished and a new mansion house was erected for Allan Whitefoord. The new house is thought to have been erected around 1760, and it is believed that the Adam brothers were responsible for designing the elegant Palladian mansion. It is thought that John Adam (1721-1792) was the brother responsible for the design, though his father, William Adam (1689-1748) has also been suggested as supplying the original drawings.

The house comprised of a central block of three storeys, topped by a hipped roof. Arced corridors led from this block to two projecting wings, each of two storeys, though these were less decorative than the main house. The house was described as being a 'new house, very neatly fitted up and finished.'

Allan Whitefoord was never married and died on 26 March 1766. He was succeeded by his nephew, Sir John Whitefoord, 3rd Baronet of Blairquhan.

Sir John Whitefoord is referred to in the parish records in 1776. Sir John married Anne Cartwright of Ossington, Nottinghamshire. She died on 26 December 1801. They had at least one son, James, but he died in infancy and is buried in Mauchline kirkyard, west of the kirk. Sir John was a Major with the 11th Foot. He was also an investor with Douglas, Heron & Co., better known as the Ayr Bank. When this institution collapsed in 1772, Sir John was left with considerable debts, resulting in him having to sell off property. Ballochmyle was sold in December 1782 to the Alexander family, but the Whitefoords remained in residence in the mansion until 1784-5.

When Sir John died on 8 April 1803 the baronetcy became dormant, for there was no legal record of his uncle, Colonel Charles Whitefoord's marriage. Family tradition, however, claims that they contracted an irregular marriage under Scots law. If this is ever proved, the baronetcy could be revived.

Sir John was a contemporary of Robert Burns, and the bard wrote verses in his honour, 'Lines to Sir John Whitefoord'. They were both masons, and met through that organisation.

Sir John's daughter, Mary Anne Whitefoord, was the 'Maria' in 'The Braes o' Ballochmyle'. This song, which is also known as 'Farewell to Ballochmyle', was written by Robert Burns to mark the removal of the Whitefoords from Ballochmyle. On a copy of the poem Burns indicated that, 'I composed the verses on the amiable and excellent family of Whitefoord leaving Ballochmyle.' The family were apparently well-liked in the neighbourhood.

The Whitefoords had been at Ballochmyle for around forty years before they sold the estate. They remained at Blairquhan Castle, but again their financial state became poor and they sold Blairquhan to the Hunter-Blair family in 1798. Sir John eventually settled in Edinburgh.

In 1785 Ballochmyle House was occupied by Claud Alexander, son of Claud Alexander of Newton in Renfrewshire. The Alexanders were an old Renfrewshire family, tracing their descent from John Alexander, one of the tenants of the abbot of Paisley Abbey in 1472. In 1579 Robert and Janet Alexander purchased the property of the Paisley Tak. Their grandson, Robert Alexander, purchased Blackhouse, in the Renfrewshire parish of Mearns, and Boghall in Ayrshire, as well as Newton in Renfrewshire. He was born in 1604 and was a number of times elected as Baillie of Paisley. His son, Claud Alexander of Newton (born 1645, date of death unknown), was a noted Covenanter and suffered imprisonment in Edinburgh Castle and was fined £1,000 for his support for the Presbyterian church. His son, Robert (1681-1738), was succeeded by his son, Claud (1724-1772). Claud's heir, Robert, never married and had no children, hence the estate passed to the third son, Claud, who purchased Ballochmyle.

Claud Alexander was born in 1752, the third son of Claud of Newton and

Joanna, or Jean, Cuninghame of Craigends, who had married in 1746. Claud served in the Honourable East India Company's Service in India, becoming Auditor-General of the army accounts. He was also Paymaster General to the forces in India. Whilst he was abroad, his friends had purchased the estate of Ballochmyle for him. He returned to Scotland in 1786 and took up residence in the new Adam mansion. Claud married Helenora Maxwell in 1788. She was the eldest daughter of Sir William Maxwell, 2nd Baronet of Springkell in Dumfriesshire.

4.9 Alexander of Ballochmyle armorial bearings
(Dane Love)

To mark his new estate and marriage, Claud Alexander of Ballochmyle matriculated his coat of arms at the Lyon Office in Edinburgh on 23 July 1788. The arms are blazoned as, 'Parted per pale, Argent and Sable, a chevron, in base a crescent, in chief a flower de llys, all counter-changed within a bordure parted per pale Gules and Or.' The crest chosen was 'An elephant passant proper', indicative of their connections with India. The motto, *Perseverantio Vincit* translates as 'perseverance conquers'.

Claud and Helenora Alexander had eight children – three sons and five daughters. The eldest son, Claud, was born in 1789. William Maxwell Alexander was born in 1790, and succeeded his uncle, Boyd Alexander of Southbar, MP, to that estate. Boyd Alexander was born in 1796 and married a daughter of Sir John Hobhouse. The daughters were Margaret Maxwell Alexander, Joanna Alexander, Catherine Alexander (d. July 1834), Helen, who died in childhood, and Mary, who married Joseph Crampton of Yorkshire.

The house, though by far the largest in the parish, was still regarded as being too small, and in 1791 an extensive wing was added to the north of the main block. This contained the family nursery and other rooms, and it was erected for Claud Alexander.

Claud Alexander's sister, Wilhelmina (1756-1843), has been noted by posterity as 'The Lass o' Ballochmyle' by Burns. She was born in Paisley, the fourth daughter of Claud Alexander of Newton. She appears to have been at Ballochmyle on one occasion when Burns was in the vicinity and he spotted her walking in the wooded groves. On his return to Mossgiel he composed the song, 'The Bonny Lass of

Ballochmyle'. He sent Wilhelmina a copy of this on 18 November 1786 along with a letter asking permission to publish the song in a second edition of his works. Apparently the letter was ignored, however, she cherished it for the remainder of her life. Burns, scorned by the lack of a reply, included the letter in the Glenriddell Manuscript, noting that Wilhelmina was 'too fine a lady to notice so plain a compliment'. Wilhelmina Alexander never married, and died in Glasgow. At Ballochmyle a summer house, known as the Fog House, was erected in the grounds to mark the spot where the poet saw Wilhelmina. This was destroyed by fire in 1944.

4.10 Claud Alexander receiving word of his acquisition of Ballochmyle estate by Johann Zoffany *(Private Collection)*

The Campbells still owned Netherplace in the new century, Mungo Campbell being the laird at the opening of the eighteenth century. He died in 1720 and was succeeded by his son, also Mungo. This Mungo Campbell was married in 1720 to Magdalene, daughter of William Cuninghame of Craigends and his wife, Christian Colquhoun, daughter of Sir John Colquhoun of Luss, Baronet. They had one son, named William, and two daughters, Christian and Susannah. Mungo's wife, Christian, died in 1725. On 1 May 1728 Mungo's servant, Patrick Adam, was admitted a burgess in Ayr. Mungo is noted as a regular witness to various marriages that took place in the parish church. He died on 27 March 1771; his wife Magdalene on 24 August 1776.

A distant cousin of this laird was another Mungo Campbell, a son of Mungo Campbell, Provost of Ayr. His father died when he was an infant, and he was taken in by his godfather, Cornet Mungo Campbell. However, he died within a few years, and he left the young Mungo one thousands merks and a recommendation that he should be brought up by their kinsman, Mungo Campbell of Netherplace. This the laird did, raising and educating him as one of his own until he was eighteen years of age. He then entered the army, serving at Dettingen and other battles. He latterly became an officer of the excise at Saltcoats. However, Mungo Campbell became noted in local history for his part in the shooting of the 10th Earl of Eglinton. On Tuesday 24 October 1769 he and another were making their way through the lands of Eglinton's estate at the Ardrossan Parks, near Montfode, when the Earl spotted him. The earl was there with his carriage and four men to attend to him. Lord Eglinton accused him of trespassing, as well as of poaching on his lands twelve months earlier, but Mungo claimed that he had a right to be there, as an officer of the excise. Eglinton noticed that Campbell had a gun, and demanded that he hand it over, but Mungo refused. Lord Eglinton alighted from his horse, making his way towards Campbell. Campbell cocked his gun, but retired, keeping the gun aimed at the earl.

The four servants then rode up and a conversation was started. Lord Eglinton again accused Mungo of poaching in previous months, and demanded that he hand over the gun. Mungo replied that he would not part with the gun, and that he would sooner part with his life, telling Eglinton to back off if he regarded his own. Lord Eglinton ordered one of his servants to fetch his own gun from the carriage, and kept advancing at Campbell. Campbell kept walking backwards until he hit a stone and fell. As he rose the gun fired, hitting Eglinton on his left-hand side. The wound, though serious, did not kill the earl straight-off. He staggered to a knoll where he sat. He ordered that his servants should drive him back to Eglinton Castle, where they arrived at around two o'clock in the afternoon. A physician and a couple of surgeons were at the castle before he arrived, but they were unable to help. In his last few hours he managed to order much of his affairs, but he died next morning.

Mungo Campbell was captured and taken to prison in Ayr. He was then transferred to Edinburgh, for trial before the High Court of Justiciary on 27 February 1770. He was tried for the murder of the earl, but he claimed that it had been an accident. Nevertheless, he was found guilty and was sentenced to be hanged in the Grassmarket of Edinburgh on Wednesday, 11 April 1770. Prior to the execution taking place, Mungo Campbell hanged himself in his prison cell, using a silk handkerchief which he tied to an upended form on 28 February 1770. A note was found lying in his cell, which read:

Farewell, vain world, I've had enough of thee,
And now am careless what thou say'st of me,
Thy smiles I court not, nor thy frowns I fear,
My cares are past, my heart lies easy here,
What faults they find in me take care to shun,
And look at home, enough is to be done.

Campbell was secretly buried below the Salisbury Crags, but the interment becoming known, an Edinburgh rabble dug up the corpse, tossing it about until they were tired, reputedly kicking the head down the Royal Mile. To prevent further indecency Campbell's friends managed to get the body and had it buried at sea off the Bass Rock.

William Campbell succeeded to Netherplace in 1771. He was married to Lilias, daughter of John Neilson, who was a merchant in Glasgow, and his wife, Margaret Wallace, a daughter of Thomas Wallace of Carnell Castle. They had one son, William who succeeded, and two daughters, Margaret and Lilias. William Campbell died in 1786 and his wife, Margaret Campbell, in 1822. The daughter Lilias Campbell established a trust for the welfare of the old folk of the parish, bequeathing £500 for the old women and £300 for the old men.

William Campbell became the next laird of Netherplace.

The old castle of Kingencleugh was probably abandoned around the middle of the eighteenth century. A new house was erected slightly higher up in the same grounds, named Kingencleugh House, or Cottage. The exact date of erection is not known, but it has been speculated that it was around 1765, for within the garden there is a sundial bearing this date and the name Robert Gamble, perhaps an error for Campbell. However, this may also refer to Robert Campbell, born near the end of the seventeenth century, son of John Campbell and Elizabeth Adair, daughter of Rev William Adair (1614-1684), minister of Ayr. Robert was their second son and he died unmarried. He may have built Kingencleugh House, or cottage as it was also known, to live nearer his brother. In 1777 a single-bayed wing appears to have been added on the north-west side of the house.

The last of the Campbells of Kingencleugh appears to have been one Margaret Campbell. She was married to a man named MacGill. They both died at the start of the nineteenth century, leaving no children.

The estate was sold at this time, and the new owners were the Alexanders of Ballochmyle, after which the history of the estate becomes linked with that family. Kingencleugh was leased to various tenants, among these being James Smith, nephew of Archibald Buchanan of Catrinebank, or Daldorch, who worked at Catrine for a time before going on to Deanston Mill, and Archibald Buchanan, younger of Catrinebank (in 1847).

Mauchline Castle was extended in the late eighteenth century with the erection of a wing to the south of the seventeenth century block. This wing originally had one storey.

The castle was the residence of Gavin Hamilton WS, factor of the Loudoun estates. Gavin Hamilton was the son of John Hamilton of Kype (Avondale parish, Lanarkshire), who was the clerk to the regality of Kylesmure, or Mauchline parish, and his wife, Jacobina Young, daughter of a merchant in Lanark. John Hamilton of Kype was admitted as a burgess and guild brother of Ayr on 4 September 1756. Gavin was born on 27 December 1737. He became a lawyer, setting up his practice in Mauchline. He also acted as factor, or estate agent, to the Earl of Loudoun's estates around Mauchline, hence his association with Robert Burns.

Gavin Hamilton had taken on the lease of East Mossgiel from Earl of Loudoun and was using it as a summer residence. However, Burns' father, William Burnes, was at the same time in dispute with the owner of Lochlea farm. Robert and his brother Gilbert made secret arrangements to sub-lease Mossgiel from Gavin Hamilton, allowing them to leave Lochlea. When Robert Burns wrote his *Poems, Chiefly in the Scotch Dialect*, he dedicated the book to Hamilton.

In 1789 Francis Grose (c.1731-91), a noted antiquarian and artist, visited Ayrshire on his tour around Scotland looking at the antiquities. He sketched various buildings in Ayrshire, among these being Mauchline Castle. The drawing he produced was later included in his *Antiquities of Scotland*, published in 1791. The engraving produced by Grose shows the courtyard of the castle and adjoining house. A solid stone well-pump is located in the courtyard, in front of the old tower. Gavin Hamilton's house, which was built adjoining the tower, stands slightly apart from the castle, the gap between the two buildings occupied by an open stairway. The parapet that formerly existed around the tower is missing in this early drawing, the corners being occupied by short obelisks. Grose gives little of the history of the castle, other than noting that it was then the property, 'by purchase', of Gavin Hamilton Esq.

Within the castle is the room in which Robert Burns is thought to have married Jean Armour in May 1788. A room within the castle is also noted as being the place in which the poet wrote his parody-sermon, *The Calf*.

Mauchline House, or The Place, was erected in 1756, supposedly by the Earls of Eglinton. This seems unlikely, as an old date stone on the building bore the legend 'WG.ER.MDCCLVI', which would indicate that it was built by a man with the initials WG, and his wife ER. It is thought that a Mr Gibb had erected the house, probably one of the Gibbs of Auchmillan. It is said to have been a possible home of Mary Morrison, who was connected to Burns. For many years it was occupied by two sisters of the Montgomerie of Eglinton family.

Although The Place was erected in the middle of the eighteenth century, there is very little doubt that it replaced an older house which stood on the same site. Until it was demolished in 1935, there existed an old gatehouse that led into the rear courtyard of The Place from the Townhead. This gatehouse, which comprised of an archway through a narrow building, was decorated with ornate tall ogee-headed windows, circular porthole window over the arch, and a crenelated parapet. John Taylor Gibb reckoned that this archway dated from the sixteenth century.

On Barskimming Estate a new house was erected on the southern side of Barskimming Old Bridge, within Stair parish, for Sir Thomas Miller, Baronet, owner of the estate. On the Mauchline side of the river, the estate extended as far as the village. A new stable block was created on the Mauchline side of the river around 1774. This is a distinguished classical block, the pend passing under a square tower which is surmounted by an ogee slate roof, itself topped by a wooded belfry. James Boswell of Auchinleck visited Barskimming in 1780 and noted in his journal that he was 'much pleased with the beauties of nature and art at Barskimming.'

A new bridge across the River Ayr, linking Barskimming House with the Stable block, was erected in 1788 by Sir Thomas Miller. Barskimming Bridge, which has a span of one hundred feet, is built ninety feet above the river, which passes through a sandstone gorge below. It was noted by Rev Auld that this bridge 'excels all the bridges of the county in beauty and elegance, and is one of the greatest curiosities to be seen in [Ayrshire]. Even by 1837, when the *New Statistical Account* was written, Rev John Tod repeated the same description.

4.11 Mauchline House *(Author's Collection)*

Thomas Miller was the second son of William Miller, a Writer to the Signet, and Janet Hamilton. William Miller died in 1753. William and Janet Miller's eldest son, John, was a professor of law at Glasgow University, but died unmarried in 1780. The third son was Patrick Miller, who purchased Dalswinton estate in

4.12 Archway in High Street leading to Mauchline House courtyard
(Author's Collection)

Dumfriesshire, where Robert Burns visited and watched a steam boat launched by William Symington and Patrick Miller on 14 October 1788. Burns may have been a passenger. His son, also Patrick (1769-1845), was a Captain in the 11th Lancers, and M.P. for Dumfries from 1790-96. It was he whom Burns sent the original copy of 'Scots wha hae' to.

Thomas Miller was born on 3 November 1717 and on 16 April 1753 married Margaret Murdoch, the eldest daughter of John Murdoch of Rose Bank, Lord Provost of Glasgow. They had two children, William Miller and Jessy Miller, who was to marry John Dunlop. Thomas Miller married a second time, to Anne Lockhart, daughter of John Lockhart of Castle Hill, but there were no children by this marriage. Miller was educated at Glasgow, and was admitted to the Bar on 21 February 1742. In 1748 he was appointed as Sheriff of the Stewartry of Kirkcudbright, and later in the same year became joint principal clerk of the city of Glasgow. In 1755 he became solicitor to the excise in Scotland, and on 17 March 1759 became Solicitor General. In 1760 he became a lord advocate and in 1761 was elected as M.P. for Dumfries. He became rector of Glasgow University in November 1762. Thomas Miller became Lord Justice Clerk on 14 June 1766 and used the courtesy title, Lord Barskimming. He later changed this to Lord Glenlee. On 15 January 1788 he became the Lord President of the Court of Session, succeeding Sir Robert Dundas. He was created a Baronet (of Glenlee, in Kirkcudbrightshire) on 3 March 1788. However, he did not survive long after this, dying on Sunday 27 September 1789 at the age of 71, and was interred in the family vault at Stair. He was succeeded by his only son, Sir William Miller, 2nd Baronet of Glenlee.

Lord Barskimming was known to Burns, and in his poem, 'The Vision', he makes reference to him:

Thro' many a wild, romantic grove,
Near many a hermit-fancied cove,
(Fit haunts for friendship, or for love,
In musing mood),
An aged Judge, I saw him rove,
Dispensing good.

Sir William Miller, 2nd Baronet of Glenlee, was born on 12 August 1755 and on 5 November 1777 married his cousin, Grizel Chalmers, daughter of George Chalmers of Fife. They had three sons and two daughters, Thomas, William, John, Grizel and Martha. Sir William was also mentioned in Burns' works. In the 'Second Heron Election Ballad' he is noted as being 'Barskimming's guid knight'. He was admitted an advocate on 9 August 1777 and in 1780 was elected M.P. for Edinburgh, but was unseated on petition. On 23 May 1795 he was appointed a lord of session, taking the courtesy title, Lord Glenlee. He resigned in 1840. He died on 9 May 1846 and was buried in the north-east corner of the New Calton Burying Ground, Edinburgh.

Rodinghead House was the home of the factor of Loudoun and Cessnock estates, owned by the Campbells of Loudoun. The factor in the latter half of the eighteenth century was George Douglas, who was able to purchase Rodinghead from the guardians of the Countess of Loudoun. He married Isabella Dykes in 1794. In 1799 he made a 'voluntary contribution' of 30 guineas to the government, in addition to his taxable income.

In 1798 Captain MacDonald appears to be living at Rodinghead, for he was liable to pay Farm Horse Tax at that time.

Cessnock estate became the property of the trustees of Miss Henrietta Scott in 1787. She was the eldest daughter and co-heir of General John Scott of Balcomie (Fife). Henrietta fully inherited the estate in 1795 on her twenty-first birthday. Much of the northern half of Mauchline parish was part of the Cessnock estates, including the lands of Bargower, Rodinghead, Lawersbridge and Auchenbrain. Henrietta Scott was married on 4 August 1795 to William Henry Cavendish Bentinck, Marquis of Titchfield, who adopted the surname Scott-Bentinck at the time. He inherited the Portland dukedom on the death of his father in 1809, becoming 4th Duke of Portland. Lady Henrietta died on 28 April 1844.

In Mauchline, Beechgrove House was built sometime in the late eighteenth century for Dugald Stewart Hamilton, son of Gavin Hamilton of Mauchline Castle. A traditional Scots Georgian building, the house has two storeys. Hamilton was a surgeon, or doctor in the town, living here in the first half of the nineteenth century.

Adjoining Beechgrove House, within the Cowgate, stands Beechgrove Cottage. At the time of Burns this was occupied by Robert Morison, a cabinet-maker. Burns ordered some furniture from Morison when he took on the lease of Ellisland in

1788. An old tradition claims that Burns wrote his 'Address to a Haggis' in this cottage, but of this there is now no proof.

AGRICULTURE

Advances in agriculture were being made throughout the eighteenth century. From around 1750 all of the land in the parish had been improved, and most of it was enclosed by the construction of new stone dikes, fences or hedges. Not only were enclosures created around each farm, within the farms the ground was subdivided into smaller fields. During the second half of the century Mauchline Muir had been totally reclaimed, with enclosures created and planting of belts of trees carried out by Sir Thomas Miller. The muir had been improved and was now arable.

TRANSPORT

In the second half of the eighteenth century new roads and bridges were constructed all over Ayrshire. In 1767 the first Ayr Road Act was passed by parliament, which promoted the creation of turnpike roads through the county. The Mauchline and District Turnpike Trust was established at the same time.

One of the turnpike roads was the Edinburgh to Ayr turnpike. A route was delineated from Ayr as far as Mauchline by 1772, when the first toll-bar was constructed in the village. It is reckoned that within a few years of this the route was metalled. In 1772 James Smith, a merchant in Mauchline, was appointed collector of the composition for Mauchline parish at a salary of £1, 'for this season'. He seems to have been replaced by Gavin Hamilton, who is known to have been the collector from 1775 to 1791.

The 1767 act also established the road from Mauchline east towards Muirkirk and Edinburgh as a turnpike, but its creation took longer to materialise, passing as it does through wilder and more remote countryside.

The creation of the road through Mauchline required some demolition work, some narrow closes being opened up to form wider roadways, generally sixteen feet wide in the village. On 7 September 1768 the committee for the road from Ayr to Muirkirk noted that the road:

> Should run from the cross of Mauchline by the passage leading from the house on the east end of the town belonging to William Gibb to the high way that goes through the place where the public horse market is kept, opposite to which house belonging to William Gibb is a house belonging to John Peden. That so much of said Peden's house should be taken down as to make the high way at that place sixteen foot wide, and so much of the east end of Wm Gibb's house should also be taken down as make the high way between John Peden's office houses sixteen foot wide, and that the passage from that to the foresaid market place

be twenty foot wide from Wm Gibb's hedge along the south side of that passage by purchasing the ground or yards on the north side for the making of that passage.

In 1782 James Boswell (1740-95), a trustee on the committee for the road, walked the proposed route as far as Sorn. The route must have been erected soon after, but even as late as 1785 there were still a few bridges missing east of Muirkirk.

The new turnpike acts required the establishment of tolls or turnpike gates in order to collect monies from those who were using the new improved roads. The tolls were rouped to the highest bidder, and the holder of the toll could then collect the monies for themselves. The tollbar at Mauchline was rented by David Mitchell from 1783 to 1784, for which he paid £60. Originally this was located on Kilmarnock Road at the site of the old gatehouse leading to Netherplace. The tollhouse was situated on the east side of the road. This toll was later relocated further south-east, at the end of the cottages in New Road, next to the boxworks. This toll, known as Causeyhead Toll, stood where the present fire station now stands.

A second toll gate on the road from Kilmarnock to Cumnock was located at the Howford Bridge, which forms the southern extremity of Mauchline parish on the roadway. The toll house was situated on the southern side of the bridge, in Sorn parish, but virtually formed the southern boundary to the parish. The toll bar there was let to Alexander Jamieson from Whitsunday 1783 to Whitsunday 1784, for which he paid £35 15s.

The Howford Bridge on this roadway was erected when the new turnpike road was being laid out. The bridge seems to have been erected around 1780, but in March 1781 James Armour, the father in law of Robert Burns, was paid 7s 6d for repairs made to the bridge.

In 1774 a second Act of Parliament was passed which allowed for the repairing and widening of several roads in Ayrshire, which included the road from Mauchline to Millburn by way of Craigie Castle (Skeoch Road in the parish), and the road by Barskimming Bridge to Drongan (Barskimming Road).

Sir Thomas Miller of Barskimming was a noted supporter of road-building in the parish, as well as farther afield. He attended meetings of the Ayrshire Road Trustees from 1767 to 1780. When the new road from Kilmarnock to Cumnock, by way of Mauchline, was being planned, Miller was a subscriber. Personally, he was responsible for creating the road from Mauchline down Barskimming Road to Barskimming Old Bridge, and thence through Stair parish to Schaw, near Coalhall. This road was constructed from 1776 onwards. The road building acts of the time allowed a local landowner to take on the construction of turnpike roads, for which they would be due a percentage of the conversion money of each parish. Miller was keen for the road through the middle of his estate to be upgraded, for he noted that 'in its present state [it] is impassable for carriages.' For building the road Miller was due £9 17s 7d annually as his proportion of Mauchline parish's conversion money.

Others who supported the road building schemes included Rev William Auld, minister in the parish church, Robert Paterson, cashier to the Kilmarnock to Cumnock road committee, and Mr MacCrotchart, clerk to the road committee.

PARISH CHURCH

The old kirk was in poor condition by the eighteenth century, but it remained in use for the whole century. An old engraving of it gives us a picture of how it appeared at the time. On the southern wall the trace of a large arch is shown, indicating that there was probably an aisle on this side at one time, perhaps removed at the reformation. A public clock was on one side, its wooden face appearing to have been a source of difficulty regarding maintenance for some time. High on the steep roof was a small belfry, containing a bell, which could be rung from a rope which hung down the side of the building. To reach the belfry an external ladder was affixed to the wall, accessed from one of the numerous outside stairways which gave access to the lofts within the kirk.

These lofts were balconies which belonged to the heritors and were kept for private use, as well as for the use of certain tenants. The loft on the west side of the church belonged to the Boswells of Auchinleck. On the northern wall were two smaller lofts, separated by a window, which belonged to the Earl of Loudon (the patron of the parish) and the Reids then Whitefoords of Ballochmyle. A small loft, apparently added at a later date and uncomfortably fitted into the building, was located on the south side of the aisle, adjacent to the pulpit and precentor's desk. This belonged to the Millers of Barskimming. On the east side was another loft, known as the common loft, for the ordinary parishioners. This was located over the school-room.

The floor of the church had long communion tables running from east to west, with pews along the passages to either side. The pews were not affixed to the ground until 1775; prior to this date they were movable, or else parishioners would bring their own stools.

Rev William Maitland continued as minister of the parish church. At first he was noted as a kindly and friendly minister, but as the years passed his ministry became less effective. This may have been partially due to chronic ill-health. In 1723 the congregation wrote a letter of complaint to the presbytery, informing it that the minister was often absent from his charge, failed to carry out parish visitation, was ineffective in conducting the business of the kirk session and also failed to conduct worship regularly on Sundays. Whether the presbytery failed to respond, or whether they were ineffectual is unknown, but Rev Maitland remained as minister until his death.

In 1730 a new manse was erected for the minister, a date stone with 1730 and 'Mr WM' in a monogram being included. This was located on a road that linked the Cowgate with Welton Road, the present Mansefield Road. The manse comprised of an open courtyard of buildings, which included the manse itself, which had two low rooms and a cellar in the middle, with three bedrooms on the first floor and garrets. Adjoining were offices, consisting of a kitchen, brew house, byre, stable, barn and a shade [sic]. To the rear was a small garden of 1 rood and 18 falls. Water for the building was obtained from a pump-well in the garden. The open side of the courtyard faced south-east, over the fields that formed the glebe. Over the years the manse was repaired several times, perhaps including 1744, for an old stone with that date and 'Mr WA' existed, now copied on a stone in the gable of number one, Mansefield Road. In 1791 the minister's stipend comprised a mixture of cash and victual. The minister was paid around £100 annually, in addition to have the rights to the glebe, which measured around five to six acres.

4.13 Rev William Maitland's Stone *(Dane Love)*

Rev William Maitland served as minister in Mauchline for forty-four years. He died on 27 October 1739 at the age of 69. A memorial was erected in the kirkyard over his grave by his daughter, Mary Maitland, which notes that the minister had 'taught his flock with a sincere heart.'

There appears to have been a vacancy in the kirk for about two and a half years. Nevertheless, during this time the congregation arranged for new communion tokens to be minted. These are dated 1740.

On 29 April 1742 Rev William Auld was ordained and inducted to the church in Mauchline. He was to serve for almost fifty years, a much-loved and respected minister. Born in 1709, he was the second son of William Auld in Underwood (in the parish of Craigie) and Margaret Campbell, sister of Robert Campbell of Townhead of Newmilns. He was educated at the University of Edinburgh, from where he graduated Master of Arts on 6 May 1733, followed by the University of Glasgow and Leyden University. His first post was as chaplain to the laird of Shawfield, whose mansion was located in Virginia Street, Glasgow. He was licensed by the Presbytery of Hamilton on 27 November 1739 and received a call to Mauchline on 29 October 1741. In 1763, one of Rev Auld's sermons, *The Pastoral Duty Briefly Explained and Recommended*, was published in Glasgow. He also contributed the article on Mauchline parish to Sir John Sinclair's *Statistical Account*, in 1791.

Rev Auld was noted for being a rather dour disciplinarian, one who upheld the Calvinistic doctrine almost to the letter. And yet, he has also been described as a kindly and courteous pastor, who was fair and forgiving. During his term of office, the number of people attending his church increased from 450 in 1757 to around 1,400 in 1786. That he had considerable influence in making the parishioners attend church is obvious from the fact that membership dropped after his death to 500. In 1743 the presbytery instructed Rev Auld to hold weekday sermons, usually held on market days.

During the time of Auld's ministry, the Ayr Bank of Douglas, Heron and Company collapsed, in 1772. He had invested in the bank, which resulted in him becoming seriously financially insolvent.

In 1774, 'a complaint was formally given in by the session to the heritors against certain feuars for encroaching on the churchyard with new buildings and middensteads.' The kirkyard was at that time surrounded by more buildings than at present, and many had open stairs to the rear, leading to the kirkyard. In 1779 a decree was issued that all houses round the kirkyard should have their stairways removed, or else a stone wall would be built against them, preventing access to the kirkyard. This appears to have happened in most cases, apart from the stairway leading from Nanse Tinnock's. In the mid nineteenth century the caretaker of the inn used this stair to take washing into the kirkyard for bleaching amongst the tombstones. The new wall around the kirkyard was erected a few years after

4.14 Church Bell of 1742 *(Dane Love)*

1789, the year in which the school was removed from the church building to Mansefield Road.

Rev William Auld died on 12 December 1791 and was buried at the north-west corner of the kirkyard. He was never married.

A few relics that once belonged to Rev Auld still survive, mainly due to his associations with Robert Burns. Auld's writing slope, or portable desk, is preserved in the Otago Settlers Museum in Dunedin, New Zealand. Made from mahogany, the slope was taken to New Zealand by an emigrant and subsequently presented to the museum.

In 1742 a new bell for the church was provided. It is 21⅛ inches in diameter, and is plainly inscribed in Roman type, *FOR MACHLINE 1742*. The founder of the bell is not known, and it does not appear to be of a style used elsewhere in Ayrshire. In 1949 the bell was noted as being hung with wooden fittings, and is struck hourly by the clock. The clapper had struck in the same place since 1742, resulting in the soundbow being worn thinner. It was also noted that the tone was poor, and the bell had little 'breath', that is, when struck the sound does not remain and dies away quickly.

4.15 Communion Token of 1742
(Dane Love)

In 1777 new communion cups were presented to the church. These were inscribed, *For the Kirk of Machlin, AD 1777, the 35th year of Mr Wm Auld's ministry*. Who gifted them is not known, but it is known that they cost £9 10s. The lady of Ballochmyle gifted the baptismal bowl, in 1788. This is inscribed, *The gift of Dame Anne Cartwright, Lady Whitefoord, to the church of Mauchline, 1st July 1788*. In Lady Whitefoord's note to the minister at the time, she asked Rev Auld to accept the bowl as 'a small gift from me to the church of Machlin, as a grateful acknowledgement and lasting remembrance of the many happy years I past in that place, under your excellent instruction and ministry.'

Following Rev Auld's death, the pulpit at Mauchline was filled by Rev Archibald Reid. He was born in 1744, perhaps the third son of John Reid of

4.16 Baptismal vessel presented to church by Lady Whitefoord *(Dane Love)*

Tulliallan in Clackmannanshire. He received his education at the University of Glasgow and was licensed to preach by the Presbytery of Irvine on 3 March 1773. His first charge was at the chapel-of-ease in Greenock, Renfrewshire, where he was ordained on 21 June 1781. During his time in Greenock he compiled the chapter on Greenock for the *Statistical Account of Scotland*, published in 1791-99. He was presented to Mauchline by the tutors of Flora, Countess of Loudoun, in March 1792 and admitted on 28 June 1792.

In 1792-3 a new manse was erected for the minister of the parish church. This was built in the middle of the glebe, with an access road alongside the garden of Viewfield House. The new manse was a substantial building, and adjacent to it a separate block was erected to contain offices for the minister. The glebe extended to seven acres at this time. On Thursday 5 March 1795 the old manse was sold by public roup at Mrs Crooks' inn in Mauchline.

The hold of the kirk on the people as police and judge continued into the eighteenth century, and the kirk session continued to rebuke parishioners for their breaking of the rules. A further selection of these gives an indication of what was disallowed at the time, what the punishment was for the misdeeds, as well as a few names of people living in the parish:

> December 21 1734 – John Hamilton of Kype, clerk to the regality of Mauchline, confessed ane irregular marriage with Jacobina Young, daughter of James Young, merchant in Lanark, and had his son, Gavin [Hamilton – Burns' friend] baptized.

> March 8 1785 – Alexander Sim having committed a scandal by rising from his seat in the church while the congregation was singing the doxology, and with irreverent carriage going forth with his head covered, is to appear next lord's day to be rebukit in the place of repentance.

> March 8 1785 – It was decided that Jas. Miller and Margaret Tailer in Haughead, having entertained several people during service with meat and drink, should be rebukit before the congregation.

BURGHER CHURCH

Not all parishioners attended the parish church, some were seceders and others were Roman Catholic, amongst other groups. The Secession Movement began in 1733 in Stirling and quickly spread across much of Scotland. Ayrshire became quite a strong supporter of the church, and the church at Kilmaurs was one of the first in the county, established in 1740. Mauchline, although it had a number of seceders, had no church as early as this, for it was thought by these people that Rev William

Auld was a most saintly pastor and was held in esteem by them. The seceders met at various places in the parish or immediate vicinity, often in barns and sheds, much like the early Covenanters. A number of Prayer Unions were established, and two local ones met at Barrhill, midway between Mauchline and Tarbolton, and at Rottenrow, just outwith the parish one mile west of Crosshands.

However, once Rev Auld died in 1791, the seceders set about raising funds with which to build themselves a church of their own. The Burgher Congregation was established in 1793. The next parish minister, Rev Archibald Reid, was unpopular, and a number of members of the parish church left to join them. They were also joined by a number of members of the Secession congregations in Tarbolton and Old Cumnock.

The dissenters struggled to obtain a feu on which to build a church, the proprietors being against a dissenting chapel being erected in the parish. The local landowners refused to grant them any land, and it was not until a private bargain was struck with Ralph Sillars of Hillhead that ground for the building could be obtained. Stone for the church was also a problem, Claud Alexander of Ballochmyle, who owned the quarries, refusing to allow stone from his property to be sold to the dissenters. The members got around this by using second-hand stone from old farm buildings that were being taken down, or by carrying rounded stones from the river. Many of the first members belonged to Catrine. One adherent, an old widow from Catrine, donated the hearth stone from her home. This circular block was incorporated into the front of the church, facing Netherplace. Other stone for building was obtained when the foundations were being dug, rock being discovered under the ground.

By 1796 Mauchline Burgher Church was complete, services being held in what was better known as the 'Meeting House'. A simple 'box' kirk, it was located on what had been garden ground at the west end of the Back Causey, now known as Knowe. The building was plain but commodious, there being seating for 600 worshippers. Initially, having no minister of their own, ministers were supplied by the Associate (Burgher) Presbytery of Glasgow.

The church called a couple of prospective ministers, but both of them turned the congregation down. One was Rev William Irvine, who went to Stranraer instead, the other was Rev Dr James Laurie DD, who declined the call and emigrated to the United States. He died there in 1853 aged 76.

The first minister in the Burgher Church was Rev John Walker. Born in Linlithgow, he was ordained on 17 April 1799, having previously been the minister at Linlithgow West Church. The call to him was signed by 68 members and 20 adherents. When he was ordained a dinner was arranged in the Cross Keys Inn at a cost of £3 15s 1d. In 1799 the congregation had communion tokens struck for use by members.

EDUCATION

Gavin Houston appears only to have remained as schoolmaster at Mauchline for two years, for in November 1701 the session had to find a new teacher. On 26 November, the minutes note that 'Mr Greg, a schoolm[aste]r, being in terms of setling (as such) at Machlyne produced his testimonialls from the presb[ytery] of Arbroath qch [which] were sufficient: the Presb. Appoint Mr Gilchrist and Mr Cuming to take tryall of his fitness…'. The two men appointed to test James Greg reported back stating that 'he hath the Latine tongue, & think he may be usfull to teach a school if he be diligent, the presb. are to take cognition of him afterwards if he tarry in their bounds.'

James Greg was duly appointed, and on 14 July 1703 the minute book noted that the parish has a schoolmaster being paid the recognised salary according to the laws of the time. James Greg, however, appears not to have been the best example to his pupils. On 10 October 1704 he was removed from his position as session clerk and precentor in the church for he was found 'guilty of drunkenness with Mr John Reid at Galston.' Whether or not he was removed or suspended as schoolmaster as well is not specifically stated. On 2 November 1704 'Mr James Greg … confessed his sin of drunkenness & rush swearing by his faith … for which he professed his sorrow … & being rebuked … he was exhorted to live more circumspectly for the future qch [which] he s[ai]d he resolved through grace to doe which rebuke the presbytrie appoints to be intimate by the ministers of Galstoun and Machlyne from their pulpits … And the presbytrie considering that by a letter from Mr Maitland shewing that the s[ai]d Mr Greg's offensive cariage has been very afflicting to him since that tyme together with his sense th[e]r[e]of expressed befor th[e]mselves this day, they repone him to the exercise of his offices after the fors[ai]d intimation.'

Greg moved on in due course, and on 24 July 1706 the session minutes once again make reference to calling a new schoolmaster for the parish. On this occasion James Stewart was appointed, and again two men (James Gilchrist and Robert Cuming) were given the task of trying him to find out if he was suitably qualified. They reported back that they though him capable of teaching the grammar. Stewart, however, forgot to bring his testimonials, but Mr Maitland informed the presbytery that he has seen these from the minister of Kilmacolm in Renfrewshire, and from his regent. It was agreed therefore to appoint James Stewart, upon his signing the Confession of Faith.

The next schoolmaster was appointed in May 1710. Hugh Blackwood had previously taught at Muirkirk and had produced his testimonials before Mungo Lindsay and Samuel Lockhart, who thought him suitably qualified. On 24 May 1710, his testimonials shown to the presbytery and having signed the Confession of Faith, he was duly appointed. In 1719 there appears to have been a dispute between Mr Blackwood and the church, for he left the job and took with him the register, or minute book, and other minutes as surety over unpaid salary. The session was ordered to pursue the missing minutes, and settle their difference with Blackwood.

The next schoolmaster was Hugh Crawford, who was working in 1719. His fitness for the job was questioned, however, for he suffered from lameness, and James Laurie Jr. and Robert Miller were sent by the presbytery to find out if he was fit enough to continue. They were able to report back that he was 'very well qualified for that office; & that he has signed the Confession of Faith.' On 6 May 1724 Crawford's wife, Agnes Reid, was to be cited to appear before the kirk session on a charge of adultery with John Campbell, who lived for a time in Galston.

The next schoolmaster was probably Robert Gilchrist, who left in 1722. On 10 November 1725 there is a note concerning the lack of records in the session register. This may have been the task of the schoolmaster, who often also acted as session clerk, to complete. Mr Maitland 'told that Mr Blackwood has put it in a hand where he can command it at pleasure but that he has recovered none of the Minuts that are wanting & aledged to be in Mr Stewart & Mr Gilchrist, late schoolm[aste]rs there, their hands and qch [which] falls to be ingrossed in the register since the time he was ordained Minister at Machline: he is to seek them out, & fill them up in the book with what is in his own hand as was formerly enjoyned.'

Names of schoolmasters in the middle part of the eighteenth century are more difficult to identify. However, we know that James Baillie moved from Mauchline to Irvine where he began working as the third master at the school, 'to teach English after the modern way.' He moved on to Ayr within a year.

In 1779 it is noted in the kirk session minute book that 'by reason of the school kept in the church, by reason of many doors opening upon the churchyard and ready access to it from all quarters, it is altogether a thoroughfare and a place of rendezvous for all sorts of idle and disorderly persons, who break the windows of the church, break the tomb and grave stones, and deface the engravings theron, and the complainers are sorry to add, that the churchyard is now become a sort of dunghill and common office-house for the whole town, a receptacle of all filthiness, so that one can scarce walk to church with clean feet.'

Rev Auld campaigned for much of his ministry to get the school removed to another part of the town, out of the church building, pleading for an 'honourable regard to the house of God and the burial place of our fathers'. It took ten years from the above complaint before the new school was erected in 1789. It was built in half an acre of the glebe field, at the end of the roadway leading past the manse, linking the Cowgate with Welton Road. Located on the corner site of Welton Road with what became Mansefield Road, the school was a small building, but it was much improved from what the pupils had to endure previously. The new school building measured forty feet by 26 feet, and was over two storeys, and there was ground for the schoolmaster.

The schoolmaster in Mauchline at the time of Burns was Andrew Noble. He was also the session clerk to the church, and it was he who called Burns before the session for his philandering with Jean Armour. He was buried in the kirkyard, to the north of the parish church, where a Greek inscription translates as 'The best things are laid up in Heaven.' One of Burns' humorous epitaphs, 'lament him, Mauchline husbands a', is claimed in local tradition to refer to him, though most early editors of Burns' poems think it may refer to either James Smith (1765-c.1823) or 'Clockie' John Brown.

The schoolmaster was paid a salary of £10 per year for educating his pupils. It was noted that the Scots dialect was spoken in general at the end of the eighteenth century, but that this was generally improving, and becoming nearer to standard English.

The old schoolhouse was at one time located at the kirkyard, but this was demolished in 1789. A new schoolhouse was erected elsewhere at this time.

There were two private schools operating in the village during the eighteenth century, as well as a few elsewhere in the parish. In May 1798 a new schoolmaster was needed for one of these, and an advertisement was placed in the papers. This requested someone who could teach English, Writing, Arithmetic, Book-keeping and Latin. Church-music was desirable. At the time the school had between 40 to 60 pupils. The schoolmaster was paid 6 guineas per annum, the usual wages being 2 s per quarter for teaching English, 2s 6d for writing and arithmetic, and 3s for Latin. Fees for night schools and further training would be in addition. The previous teacher also received from 50s to £3 as an additional offering at New Year.

INDUSTRY

The mining of coal took place in the parish in the eighteenth century on a smallish scale. In 1787 a new pit was being sunk at Lawersbridgend, on the Cessnock estate of Miss Henrietta Scott. This pit was a new development for the time, for it was one of the first in the area to have a steam engine which was used for pumping out water, as well as for operating winding and hauling systems. Previously, pits on the Cessnock estate were operated without the use of steam engines, the shallower seams being less likely to fill with water. The cost of the new mine at Lawersbridge was carefully computed to discover whether or not the scheme was worth proceeding with. A letter from the Cessnock estate factor to D. Erskine WS in Edinburgh gives some fascinating facts as to the costs:

> Inclosed you have Mr Pope's letter to me giving his opinion of working the Coall at Lawsbridge. The expense of erecting the Fire engine he computes at £900 or £1000. The last sum in my opinion may be stated, as I have no doubt that the engine with the powers to work a ten inch bore will take from £700 to £800 to erect here and the Pitt Sinking and

other expenses may be estimated at £200. As to the profits that may arise on the coall Yearly, on giving up Nourishbank [Norrisbank, which was located further to the north-west] and Cessnock, I should … suppose the profits to be nearly £400 yearly.

By June 1788 the pit was progressing well, and the factor reported to his superiors that 'we are sinking the Engine pit at Lawersbridge, which is now about 16 fathoms down and looks well.' By September 1790 the pit had reached a depth of 40 fathoms (around 240 feet) and had found the main seam of coal. Sixteen colliers were employed in the mine, but conditions were described as being very cramped. Soon it was discovered that the steam engine was insufficient to cope with the amount of water that flowed into it. A fatality occurred at the pit in October 1790 when one of the miners was hit on the head by a dislodged boulder as he was descending the shaft. The factor reported: 'Circumstances still seem to be unlucky. About three weeks ago one of the Colliers lost his life in going down the shaft, by a loose stone falling upon his head. Since that time the colliers cannot be got to work regularly.… The Riccarton company, who always take every advantage, have on this account been bribing the workers and giving them large premiums to carry them off.'

The pit at Lawersbridge was completed, though the *Statistical Account* of 1792 names it as Bridgend, being an abbreviation of Lawersbridgend. Described there as a 'coal work with fire-engine' the pit may only have worked for a few years longer, being dogged by water ingress, and a number of geological faults. In June 1792 George Douglas wrote that the miners had 'met with nothing but one step and dykes crossing us at every three or four fathoms distance. There is no less than three downsteps the thickness of the coal in the distance of a few fathoms, which has almost put us into the old workings and out of the power of the engine.'

Douglas was starting to find that the coal-works manager, a Mr Pope, was also causing difficulties. He noted that he was a 'drunken monster' in one of his reports, and he had to be removed from his job. He was replaced by John Guthrie, described as 'a very intelligent, active, sober man.'

Quarrying was carried out at various places in the parish. Near to Mauchline the Ballochmyle sandstone was being excavated in what was described as a 'good' quarry.

Around 1791 the Barskimming Quarry was sunk to the south-west of the village. This worked the red sandstone on which the village was built. It was noted that the stone was soft to quarry, but that it became harder on exposure to the air, being a hard durable stone, ideal for building.

Stone of a different colour was quarried at Deaconbank, which lies about three miles to the north-west of Mauchline, near to the present Deaconhill farm. Two small quarries were established here, the stone being much in demand for its fine grain and white colour. Easy to work, the stone was popular for pavements and for making headstones.

Sandstone was probably quarried at Haughhead, for George Smith was a mason there until he died in 1769.

Limestone was quarried at Killoch farm, which in the latter half of the eighteenth century belonged to Miss Scott. Another limestone quarry existed at Auchmillan, located on the north side of the Auchmannoch Burn. This quarry was the property of Sir William Miller in 1791.

A small ironstone quarry was located at Killoch, the property of Miss Scott, but it probably did not produce much stone.

Tanning was a fairly important minor industry in the village. The tan yard occupied by John Miller was closed in 1795, and the yard and tenement of houses that he owned were sold off.

Milling continued on a small scale in the parish throughout the eighteenth century. At the Haugh Mill corn and other grain was milled.

At the Haugh a Lint Mill appears to have been erected around 1700. The mill lade that drove the Haugh Mill itself continued on and drove the mill wheel of the Lint Mill, which was located near the confluence of the lade with the River Ayr.

COMMERCE

During the eighteenth century Mauchline was a prominent market town, where cattle and horses were traded. A number of fairs were held throughout the year, on the first Wednesday after 18 May and on the Thursday after 4 November.

A number of inns existed in the town during the eighteenth century, some of them known to us only through their associations with Robert Burns. The more famous inn was Poosie Nansies, located in Loudoun Street, almost opposite the kirkyard gate. At the time of Burns this was tenanted by Agnes Gibson, alias Poosie Nancy, who was married to George Gibson, described by Burns in 'Adam Armour's Prayer' as 'black-bearded Geordie'. Burn celebrated the inn in his poem The Jolly Beggars. According to Allan Cunningham, in his biography of the poet, this inn was 'the favourite resort of lame sailors, maimed soldiers, wandering tinkers, travelling ballad-singers and all such loose companions that hang about the skirts of society.' Although Burns is known to have visited the inn, it was not his favourite hostelry in the town.

Burns favoured drinking place in Mauchline was probably the Whitefoord Arms, which was located across the Cowgate from Poosie Nansies, on the same side of Loudoun Street. A plain, thatched double-storey building, the landlord in Burns' day was John Dow, or Dove, hence it being known as 'Johnny Doo's'. Burns wrote one of his comic epitaphs in his honour:

Here lies Johnnie Pigeon;
What was his religion?
　　Whae'er desires to ken,
To some other warl
Maun follow the carl,
　　For here Johnny Pigeon had nane.

The Whiteford Arms had a few names over its time, such as the King's Arms and latterly as the Cross Keys. By 1789 it was occupied by Miss Crooks but owned by Ballochmyle Estate.

Another hostelry was the Black Horse Inn, which stood on the old road that linked Castle Street with the Castle. In the eighteenth century there was a square of houses here, the site now occupied by the church hall. At the time of Burns the inn was run by Hugh Morton. One of the local traditions associated with Burns claims that it was at the Black Horse that the poet stood with Jean Armour before a local Justice of the Peace, John Farquhar-Gray of Gilmilnscroft, and were officially declared man and wife. Morton's daughter, Christina was one of the 'Mauchline Belles'. She was married in 1788 to Robert Paterson, draper in Mauchline, with whom she had four sons and two daughters.

4.17 Poosie Nansie's Inn, around 1800 *(Brian Bogle)*

The Elbow Tavern was located at The Knowe, near to the gate leading into the grounds of Netherplace. It is said that Burns clandestinely met with 'Highland' Mary Campbell at this inn.

There is little record of those who ran businesses in the village during the eighteenth century. However, we do know that Andrew Brownlie was a butcher in the village, for on 22 March 1755 he was admitted as a burgess and freeman of Ayr. Similarly, Duncan MacFarlane was a gardener in Mauchline in 1758. He was admitted as a burgess and freeman on 8 May that year, at the request of Alexander Boswell of Auchinleck. Another gardener who was admitted as a burgess and guild brother on 5 June 1758 was John Mastertoun, at the request of Lady Waterhead and others. James Donald was a merchant in the mid eighteenth century.

SONS OF THE PARISH

Thomas Morton was born in Mauchline in 1783 but moved to Kilmarnock in 1786, after which he had little connection with the village. He was to become a noted astronomer and ingenious mechanic. Morton's father, who came from farming stock, was a brick-maker at Mauchline, indicating that trade was carried on in the district at the end of the eighteenth century. Young Morton was adept at making things, and as a child could manufacture pocket knives, small toys, whistles and equipment used on the farm. Apart from a spell working as a herd with an uncle on a farm near Stair, up to the age of ten, young Thomas was employed as a brick-maker with his father, by this time working at Gargieston, Kilmarnock. Young Morton was later apprenticed to Bryce Blair, a turner and wheelwright in Kilmarnock. Morton worked as a wheelwright for three or four years after his apprenticeship had finished. In 1806 he set up business on his own, and it was about this time his genius as a mechanic began to flower. He was in demand for repairing finely made instruments, each of which he took apart to discover how they worked. His workshop was powered by a windmill of his own making. Around 1817 he developed an interest in astronomy after being asked to repair a reflecting telescope, whereupon he began to make his own telescope. He noted that many telescopes produced by others were not as good as they could be, so he started designing better examples.

Morton's interest in astronomy also resulted in him erecting an observatory in Kilmarnock in 1818, at what became known as Morton's Place. This was a prominent landmark in the town for many years and was erected at a cost of £1,000. It rose 70 feet above the ground and afforded expansive views. Within it he had a 9 3/8 inch diameter Newtonian Telescope and a 7 inch Gregorian telescope. The tower also had a *camera obscura*, which projected views of the surroundings onto a flat surface.

As well as his development of astronomy, Morton was to be instrumental in improving the carpet manufacturing industry, which was a major employer in

Kilmarnock at that time. He invented the barrel, or carpet machine, which was used up until the Jacquard loom became the norm. He also made improvements to this loom. Morton is also credited with major developments to the three-ply loom, as well as the Brussels carpet machine, which operated with five colours using only four needles. In 1808 the Board of Trade, recognising his talents, gifted him with twenty pounds.

In 1826 Morton was honoured in Kilmarnock by a public dinner, at which he was presented with a silver punch-bowl, thanking him for bringing improvements to the trade of the town.

In 1835 he was elected as an Honorary Member of the Society of Arts for Scotland, which was to become the Royal Scottish Society of Arts in 1841. Also in 1835, he offered to make the telescope for the new observatory then being erected in Dumfries. He was invited to meet with the committee, but a letter to him from the secretary, John Jackson, comments of Morton's personal appearance – 'I give you this hint as a friend that you may brush up a little before making your appearance.' However, his enthusiasm and personality persuaded them, and he supplied an eight inch Gregorian telescope at a cost of £73 and a *camera obscura* at a cost of £27 10s. The telescope and associated instruments were sent to Dumfries by cart in July 1836 (just too late to view Halley's Comet, which had been the hope of the committee).

A number of Morton's telescopes still survive, and in 2005 a rare example of a 3½ inch reflecting telescope was sold at auction in the United States for over £3,000. Another of his telescopes is preserved in the National Museum of Scotland in Edinburgh.

Thomas Morton died at Kilmarnock in March 1862. He had a number of sons, including Charles and Alexander, both of whom made telescopes. Only one of Alexander's is known to exist, now in the United States. A report in the *Kilmarnock Standard* of 1 December 1866 mentions a Newtonian telescope made by Charles Morton. The observatory was passed to Morton's son-in-law, Thomas Lee FRAS (he married Agnes Morton), who was a teacher at Kilmarnock Academy. It was demolished in 1957. Agnes Morton was also to find some celebrity as a writer of poetry and hymns.

Dr Matthew Stewart was born in Rothesay in 1717, the son of Rev Dugald Stewart. He was educated at the grammar school, followed by Glasgow University. In 1746 he published his *General Theorems*, which were highly regarded and popular. He served as minister of Rosneath for a short time, before the mathematical chair at Edinburgh University became vacant. Not well known until his Theorems was published, he was not first choice for the post. However, he was appointed at the end of 1746. In 1761 he published *Tracts, Physical and Mathematical*. In 1763 he published *Distance of the Sun from the Earth*, where he calculated it to be 118,541,428 miles. He was found to be erroneous in this. His health declined soon after, and he retired to the country in 1772, leaving his classes to his son, Dugald Stewart, who was elected joint professor in 1775. He died on 23 January 1785 and his remains were buried in Mauchline, with a memorial on the kirkyard dyke, noting that he was a 'celebrated geometrician'.

Dr Matthew Stewart's son, Dugald Stewart, became the professor of Moral Philosophy at Edinburgh University. Dugald Stewart owned Catrine House, located at the east end of the Ayr Bridge in the village. In 1786 Robert Burns was invited to the Stewart house for a meal. Present on that occasion was Lord Daer, prompting Burns to refer to the day that he first 'dinnered wi' a Lord.'

CHAPTER FIVE

NINETEENTH CENTURY

VILLAGE LIFE

The population of Mauchline parish in 1800 was 1,746. By 1811 it had grown slightly to 1,871, of which 1,032 lived in the village. The parish and village populations grew as follows over the century:

		Parish	Village
1801	-	1,746	
1811	-	1,871	1,032
1821	-	2,057	1,174
1831	-	2,232	1,364
1841	-	2,156	1,327
1851	-	2,470	1,450
1861	-	2,303	1,414
1871	-	2,435	1,574
1881	-	2,504	1,616
1891	-	2,339	1,454

At the start of the nineteenth century, Mauchline was a notable centre for markets and fairs. According to William Aiton, writing in 1811, there were 'no less than twelve [fairs] in Mauchline every year.' He was not particularly enamoured of the village, for he wrote that the village was 'extremely irregular, the streets narrow, very crooked, ill-paved, often dirty, and their general aspect mean.' Of the kirk building he said that it was 'so extremely contemptible that I trust the heritors will soon get [it] replaced with buildings better suited to a living worship and their own opulence.'

The beginning of the nineteenth century was a time of civil unrest, when the Radical movement campaigned for universal suffrage. Mauchline appears to have been one of the hotbeds of the rising in Ayrshire, along with Kilmarnock, Ayr, Girvan and other communities with a high density of weavers. Radicals from Mauchline took part in various meetings and campaigns.

A report in the *Ayr & Wigtonshire Courier* of 21 October 1819, gives a typical example of one of the meetings held by the Radicals in Mauchline, on 16 October. Men and boys from Tarbolton, Newmilns, Kilmarnock, Galston, Cumnock, Auchinleck and Catrine joined the Radicals from Mauchline at a demonstration in the village, some of them carrying banners or flags. 'The meeting was attended by Mr Boswell, the Vice-Lieutenant, Mr Campbell of Nith's Place, Mr Logan of Knockshinnock, Mr Ferrier Hamilton of Westport, and other gentlemen. A number of special constables had been previously sworn, who were in readiness. It had been resolved, however, not to interfere with the meeting, the flags or music, and, in short, not to interfere at all, unless a positive breach of the peace was committed. But no disposition to riot was displayed.' The Mauchline Committee mounted a scaffold or platform that had been set up, and a Mr K---n gave the first speech. Around 700-800 people are reckoned to have been in Mauchline to hear the speeches, of which perhaps 500 are thought to have been supporters of the movement.

On Wednesday 12 April 1820 a troop of the Ayrshire Yeomanry Cavalry, under the command of Sir Alexander Boswell, Baronet of Auchinleck, surrounded Mauchline and arrested thirty Radicals in the village. These men were known as the 'Radical Committee of Ayr'. During the raid they also took a cache of arms and ammunition. The Sheriff Depute of Ayrshire, A. Bell, came to Mauchline from Ayr on the same day with soldiers of the 4th Royal Veteran Battalion. These men carried out extensive searches through the village and surrounding area, looking for more arms. They discovered a large number of pikes in a field near to the village the following morning.

In 1844 there is reference to three friendly societies in existence in Mauchline, their total membership being just under 300 people. These were for the 'relief of sick members and poor widows'. The number of societies had fallen, for around ten years earlier there appears to have been eight friendly societies. Two of the societies had been in existence for twenty years by that time, having funds of £240 and £160. To those unable to work, and members of the society, a payment of four shillings per week was made, rising to six shillings if they were confined to bed.

In 1837 there were around 40 parishioners in receipt of parochial aid. They received their payments monthly, on average five shillings each. The parochial fund got its money from collections at the church, as well as from hiring out the mortcloth for covering coffins at funerals. The income was around £50 per annum from these sources. A total of around £120 was paid out each year, the difference being made up by the heritors of the parish. It was noted that to receive money from the parochial fund was 'considered degrading' so that only those in dire need applied for it.

In the eighteenth century the village was served by Dr John MacKenzie, who lived in Castle Street, next door to Burns' House. He was trained in Edinburgh and brought to the village at the behest of Sir John Whitefoord of Ballochmyle. MacKenzie managed to acquire sufficient property to entitle him to vote in parliamentary elections. He was married to Helen Miller, daughter of the landlord of the Sun Inn, and one of Burns' 'belles'. In 1796, when Hugh Montgomerie of Coilsfield inherited the earldom of Eglinton, he persuaded Mackenzie to move to Irvine, severing links with Mauchline. MacKenzie was awarded a MD degree in 1824, became a member of the council in Irvine. He retired in 1828 to Edinburgh and on his death in 1837 he was buried in Irvine kirkyard.

Around 1820 major improvements were made to the village of Mauchline. The old and narrow streets of the village had become too cramped for the liking of the local laird, as well as increasing transport, and it was decided that new direct roads would be cut through the centre of the community. A number of houses had to be demolished at the Cross to allow this, as well as Back Causey. One of the buildings demolished on the north side of the Cross was the former home of James Smith, a friend of Robert Burns. On the south side the old Sun Inn was demolished, at the time occupied by John Miller.

5.1 New Road at the Cross *(Author's Collection)*

The new road was laid out approximately 35 feet wide (44 feet between the facades of the buildings), and apart from a slight deflection at the Cross, to suit existing buildings, was formed in three straight sections. When opened it was originally known as New Road, but in later years the northern part, from the Cross towards Causeyhead Toll, was named New Street, and the southern part, from the Cross to Beechgrove, was named Earl Grey Street.

New Road was lined with new buildings along much of its length. On what was to become Earl Grey Street a line of new buildings were erected on the east side of the street. Most of these buildings were erected to a standard specification, resulting in a terrace of similarly sized buildings. These stretched from the frontage of Mauchline House south for 66 yards to Manse Road. The Old Manse was still located behind the end of this terrace. One of the new buildings erected in what was to become Earl Grey Street was the Black Bull Inn, a modern coaching inn for its period, the stables reached through an arched pend. Another building was a branch of the Commercial Bank, located in the sandstone building with the ornamental pediment (now number 9 Earl Grey Street). On the west side of the street, similar double-storey buildings were erected, from the Cross to the dissected section of Manse Road.

North from the Cross, New Road did not have any new buildings erected on it for the first 60 yards, this still being back gardens of the houses in Castle Street and the High Street, as well as the route of Mauchline Burn. After the burn was crossed, new houses were erected on the east side of the road as far as the newly created toll gate, known as Causeyhead Toll Point. New houses were only erected on the west side of the road north of Back Causey (which has since been renamed the Knowe) to the lane known as the Burgher Road. The houses erected on this northern half of New Road were not as fine as those on the south of the Cross.

In the first half of the nineteenth century the road between Bargower and Rodinghead was realigned. This was carried out simultaneously with the creation of the new railway line in 1848. Originally the road took a route from Bargower farm direct up the slope to Rodinghead. However, the railway meant that the public road had to be redirected in order to cross the new railway bridge. The chance to remove the steep hill up to Rodinghead was taken, and the main road was rerouted by swinging it to the east, after crossing the railway, before swinging around to climb past Craighead farm to Rodinghead. At the time the owner of Rodinghead took the chance to have the road repositioned further east, and the old road past the house was destroyed and planted with trees.

In 1830 a new memorial to the Covenanters executed in Mauchline was erected at the Loan, paid for by public subscription. The epitaph from the original stone was copied onto the new one.

In the autumn of 1832 William Cobbett (1763-1835) visited Mauchline on one of his tours around Scotland. Member of Parliament for Oldham, Cobbett was a Radical politician and journalist who campaigned for improved conditions for agricultural workers. He described Mauchline as a 'little town'. He had travelled from Kilmarnock on the post chaise, and after visiting the boxworks and viewing 'the native place of Robert Burns', he caught the stagecoach to Cumnock and on towards Dumfries.

Other notable visitors came to the village in 1859 – Colonel James Glencairn Burns and William Nicol Burns, sons of Robert Burns. They toured the area visiting places associated with the bard, including the castle and Mossgiel.

The Third Report of the Inspectors appointed under the provisions of the Act 5 & 6 Will. IV c 38, to visit the Different Prisons of Great Britain (II Northern and Eastern District), published by HMSO in 1838, gives details on the prison and crime in Mauchline at that time:

Population about 1,400, or, including the landward part of the parish, about 2,300.

This burgh was formerly bound to uphold a prison of its own, but the charter which gave the burgh a constitution, and which bound the magistrates to maintain a prison, was destroyed in the burning of the Edinburgh Registry Office about 100 years ago. The present small prison was built about 15 years since by the heritors of the parish, the cost, including that of the land, was not more than about 50l-., but the place is not well adapted to its purposes. The building stands in a lane on the outskirts of the town, and consists of 2 cells, each 8 feet long, 7 feet broad, and 7 feet high, and containing, therefore, not more than about 400 cubic feet each. The place is insecure, owing partly to the weakness of the doors and to the means which exist for communicating with people on the outside. There was an instance of escape three or four months ago, on which occasion the prisoner picked the lock of the outer door with his fingers, the lock of the door being rusty and out of order. I found the prison clean, and it is tolerably ventilated, but it is sometimes very damp, and in winter it must be very cold. At the time of my visit the walls were quite wet, owing to its raining at the time, and to the roof not being slated or thatched, a brick arch covered with soil being the only protection against the weather. In consequence of the great dampness thus caused, the gaoler is often obliged to remove a prisoner to his own house during the night, putting him back again in the morning.

Those confined here are persons convicted of petty offences by the justices of the peace or the baron bailie, and offenders who have been apprehended and are about to be transmitted to Ayr. On an average, about 20 persons, I was told, are put in during the year. There appears to be no provision for feeding the prisoners or for supplying them with bedding. I do not, however, apprehend that they are ever allowed to remain without food or something to lie on; the baron bailie generally giving them some straw and a horse-cloth (as a matter of private charity), and the gaoler generally feeding them himself, and frequently, it appears, without being remunerated, the county, it is stated, refusing to pay any expense except that of conveyance to Ayr. A particular case was mentioned, in which the officer had lately had the trouble of apprehending a woman, and the cost of maintaining her for nearly two days (receiving her into his own house during the night, and getting another person to take turns with him in watching her), and all this, it was stated, without getting one farthing of remuneration. The consequence was, that on this woman appearing again in the village and committing some new offences, the officer refused to take her up, and she escaped with impunity. The man has no salary, and the baron bailie said that it was only by dim of persuasion that he was induced to act.

State of Crime at Mauchline. — There is very little serious crime here now, but there is a good deal of crime of a petty kind, consisting chiefly of out-door robberies, such as robbing orchards and turnip fields, stealing potatoes, linen left out to dry, &c. A month ago the whole of the wardrobe (including about 40 shirts) of a farmer's family in the neighbourhood, was taken off at once. Some vagrants, who had been seen lurking about, were probably the offenders; and the baron bailie said there was little doubt, that, had there been a well paid and active police officer at hand, these people would have been traced and caught. As it was, they all escaped.

Upon the whole, however, there appears to be less crime here than there was 30 years ago, and less particularly during the last 12 months. For about a year ago a very expert thief, who acted as leader to a gang, died, and since his death there have been few serious offences. While this man was alive, there were frequent cases of breaking into shops and houses, and carrying off large quantities of goods, money, &c. An efficient police, however, would probably soon have apprehended the men who composed this gang, including their leader. Among the offences formerly more common than at present were mentioned forgery and passing forged notes and base coin. There has lately been an increase in the number of out-door robberies, which is attributed to the recent badness of trade.

It is reported that there are about a dozen confirmed rogues in the village. One family is said to be particularly distinguished. As a class, the offenders are noted for habits of drunken-ness and for the want of education; and it is stated that the parents of the young offenders are for the most part of bad character themselves.

September, 1837.

A police station was established in the village by the mid nineteenth century. Only a few names of constables can be recalled, such as Mr Stewart in 1859, and James Morrison, who was later to serve at Darnconner and Cumnock.

In the 1840s a murder took place in the village when a group of Irish navvies working on the railway argued seriously, ending up with one of them being murdered. This event took place in the Cowgate, but the reason for the murder and who had carried it out remains a mystery to this day.

Similarly, there is an early reference to the need for a fire engine in the village. When Wilson & Amphlet's box works went on fire in 1870 the fire engines from Catrine and Kilmarnock were the nearest available. As a consequence of this fire a subscription was raised towards purchasing one for Mauchline, and it was noted that 'liberal subscriptions are being received.'

In 1855 the registration of births, marriages and deaths became compulsory by law, and registrars were appointed in villages and parishes across the country. In Mauchline the registrar in 1867 was Thomas Mitchell. He also had the position of Inspector of the Poor. The Inland Revenue opened up an office in Mauchline in the nineteenth century, and in 1867 the officer was Roderick Mathieson.

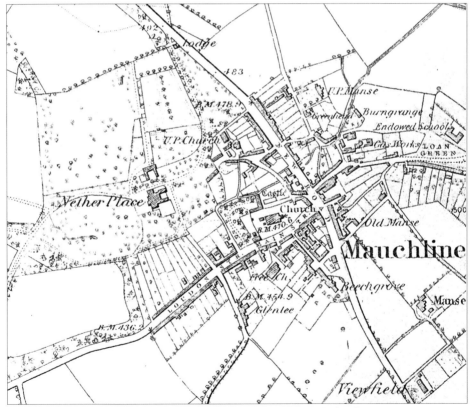

5.2 Mauchline from the Ordnance Survey Map of 1856 *(Author's Collection)*

On Thursday 25 January 1883 a newspaper was published in Mauchline entitled the *Mauchline & Catrine Advertiser & Tarbolton & Ochiltree Reporter*. Selling at 1d per copy, the newspaper did not last long. The paper was published by Mr Stevenson in Earl Grey Street, no doubt the same J. M. Stevenson who was chemist at the 'Cross Corner'.

Sons of Mauchline became involved in events beyond the parish and even the country. John Weir was killed at the Battle of Waterloo on 18 June 1815 and was interred in the old kirkyard.

A relation of the registrar and son of the parish, Thomas Mitchell, was killed in the First Battle of Bull Run. It was the first real major conflict of the American Civil War, taking place on 21 July 1861, and a victory for the Confederates. Mitchell was 27 years old.

A number of other residents of the parish were killed as a result of various accidents. Alexander Woodburn was killed at sea on 7 August 1853 at the age of 20. John Matheson was accidentally killed on 17 December 1879 at the age of 26.

The old kirkyard was becoming full and interments were becoming something of a problem. Accordingly, in 1882-3 the new cemetery was laid out alongside Barskimming Road. In 1922 an extension was added with a further 370 lairs.

In 1892 it was recorded that there were 367 occupied houses in the village, plus another 57 vacant homes. Many of the older properties were described as being in a very poor condition, many of which were still thatched, and local landowners commenced rebuilding parts of the village. In addition, businessmen were able to acquire feus and build homes for themselves or for their employees.

New buildings erected around this time include 5-15 Sorn Road, built around 1880 – these were named Jamieson Place by the developer, George Jamieson in Mosshead farm. The semi-detached houses numbered 1-3 Sorn Road were built in 1878, that nearest the Loan being Johnfield Villa. In 1870 a large villa was erected in the gusset of Welton Road with High Street, built facing up towards the Loan. Constructed of Ballochmyle sandstone, this building was for a time operated as a temperance hotel. Within the garden at the north-eastern end was a small summer house, a relic of the old Mauchline Place, originally forming an eye-catcher at the opposite end of the garden. Nearby, the semi-detached houses of Oakbank in Mansefield Road were built in 1895.

Mansefield Road was laid out with sandstone terraces on either side of the road in the late nineteenth century. One side of the road, where the old manse had been located, was owned by Andrew Pollock, of the Cowgate, and Andrew Smith, box manufacturer. The other side, on the manse field, was developed by Mauchline Co-operative Society, as were four semi-villas facing onto Cumnock Road.

In Loudoun Street, many of the old single-storey thatched houses were being demolished in the late nineteenth century and were replaced with new double-storey red sandstone houses, with slated roofs. Much of Loudoun Street was owned by Netherplace estate.

In Barskimming Road the old row of thatched cottages known as Glenlee was demolished and in its place a new terrace of six cottages was built, known as Wilson Place. Samuel Amphlet built nineteen houses in Barskimming Road, many of which were let to workers at the boxworks. Similarly, Brown Terrace in Barskimming Road was developed by Andrew Smith for workers at his boxworks.

5.3 Brown Terrace, Barskimming Road *(Author's Collection)*

A number of larger villas were erected along the side of Sorn Road. In the late nineteenth century Williamfield Villa was built, the home of William MacMillan (1844-1921), bank agent.

Similarly, in Cumnock Road, the large double villa of Estcourt and St Elmo was built before the end of the century, certainly by 1899. The owner was William Frederick Charles Howie, coalmaster, who let St Elmo to Edward Ettershank (d. 1929) in the early 1900s, a commercial traveller. Estcourt was sold in the mid-1920s to Frederick Fulton Wilson, printer and stationer, Howie having moved to Templetonburn, a large country house near Kilmarnock.

Transport to and from the village was readily available by a number of coaches which passed through the village in various directions. The 'Standard' left Kilmarnock's George Hotel every alternate morning and passed through Mauchline on its way to Carlisle. Other coaches, such as the 'Lass o' Ballochmyle' and the 'Marquis of Bute' also left Kilmarnock on alternate days (the former at 4:00 pm, the latter at 7:00 pm) en route to Cumnock.

In the last decade of the nineteenth century the village appeared as a rather prosperous little community to passing travellers. Writing in the *Ordnance Gazetteer of Scotland*, the contributor noted that Mauchline 'has a neat and pleasant appearance, and looks busy and prosperous in proportion to the number of its inhabitants.'

In 1891 the village had a population of 1,454, made up of 669 males and 785 females. The parish had a population of 2,339, of which 1,103 were males and 1,236 were female. Of this number eight parishioners were Gaelic speakers. There were 522 houses in the parish, of which 69 were vacant at the time of the census.

In 1891 the Boundary Commissioners for Scotland considered the extent of various parishes and 'tidied up' some anomalies in their boundaries. Thus, in that year, eleven acres of Sorn parish were added to that of Mauchline. These eleven acres were located on the farm of Garfield, and were little more than a couple of fields, located north-west of the farmhouse, and having no residence within them. Why they were originally part of the parish of Sorn is unclear.

Life in the village and district was subject to the usual minor disasters and troubles that have occurred over the years. Early in 1827, the winter was severe with deep drifts of snow, and several lives were lost locally. There were reports of drifts of snow fifteen feet deep and food was scarce. On 8 November 1899, a young Catherine Knox was drowned at the Haugh, at the age of fifteen months.

On Wednesday 20 July 1859 there was a major flood in Mauchline parish, which caused some considerable damage. A severe thunderstorm had struck, bringing down torrents of rain which resulted in a large flood, the likes of which had never been seen before, and which has probably never occurred since. At four o' clock in the afternoon, the rain and hail fell, accompanied by peals of thunder and lightning. The storm lasted for two hours, turning roads into rivers. Some of the streets in Mauchline were knee-deep in water, and the River Chalk filled to what was later calculated to be from fourteen to seventeen feet deep. It also expanded over the fields, forming a loch between New Road and Burnside House, from where Mrs Hamilton and her family had to escape.

Accounts of the damage and extent of the floods were later reported, and a local printer, H. S. Nisbet, produced a leaflet detailing some of these, which is worth repeating to indicate just how bad things were:

> In the thatched house on the other side of the burn, Mary Goldie, a young woman in a delicate state of health, was alone, and on the water reaching her bed, she managed to creep out upon the dresser, where she remained with her head at the ceiling, and the water up to her chin, till rescued from her perilous position by being drawn through a hole in the roof. In the adjoining house, Mr and Mrs Robert Smith fled to the attic and were rescued in a similar manner, by being taken through the roof.
>
> From the adjoining houses the inmates easily escaped, leaving all behind them, but, in the third, Mrs Hay, a frail old woman, lay till the water was up to her bed, and was then taken through a small window by Mr Stewart, our much respected police officer. At this place,

Burnside, the lowest house was submerged till up a good piece in the thatch, and in Mrs Hay's, the furthest up, the water was as high as the bed.

Opposite, on the expanse of water, were seen floating summer houses, boxes, barrels, pieces of furniture, etc., etc., and conspicuous among the debris, Burnside wooden bridge, which finally found a resting place near its more stable neighbour, the one at the Auld Kirn, as if the Two Mauchline Brigs were anxious to have a little chat on the strange turn of events which so unexpectedly brought them together.

As the increasing water could not get quickly enough away beneath the New Road, it flowed over on to the street till about knee deep, and then gushed round the Back Causeway with all the rapidity and appearance of a mountain torrent. What came boiling and foaming from beneath the road swept with relentless force through the broadside of the workshop at Gray's Bridge, which was lately occupied by Messrs Davidson, Wilson, Amphlet, who fortunately had removed from it nearly everything of value. Another workshop adjoining it was also torn down, and from the next dwelling-house, Mr Loudon's family, and other two children, were, with difficulty, rescued, also a pig at this place, and another on the north side of the New Road. Mrs Tannock, who lived above Mr Loudon, was caught in the passage when up to the neck in water, and both Mrs Tannock and the one who was trying to save her would have been carried off, had they not been rescued by another. All the houses from Gray's Bridge to the ones occupied by Miss Brown, Milliner and Dressmaker (formerly Nancy Tannock's), were flooded more or less, and the water, after passing through the broadside of the workshop, forced down about 25 yards of stone wall opposite, swept through some fine gardens, taking away bushes, vegetables, earth and everything in its course.

Next, it broke down the stone walls of the North West Vennel, and afterwards found for itself a more spacious channel through the policies of Netherplace. In the court at the back of the Mansion House and in the flower garden, the water stood as high as four feet, and the cellars were so completely filled that it came boiling out at the front. At several places on the lawns the water burst up from its covered channel. At the New Road it carried away about half the breadth of the street, and the other streets were more or less torn, and large holes scooped out in them, the worst of which was the Back Causeway.

After passing Netherplace the waters rushed on without meeting any impediment, till they came to the railway embankment, which forced them through the arch into the courtyard and around Bogwood houses, in which they stood as high as four feet in some places. The whole stock of cattle had been lately taken in to prevent injury from lightning, and they were now, in danger of drowning, had not all the doors been forced to make a passage for the rising waters, which carried off and destroyed a great deal of wheat, oatmeal and other property.

Great as was the havoc which the flood made in property, the greatest gloom cast over the town was the loss of one of Mr Drummond's family, an amiable girl about ten years of age. When the water rose high in the kitchen, all fled to the attics above, and when there they were in great fear of the flood sapping the foundations of the house. After engaging in prayer, and embracing each other, an aunt and a brother went out at a kitchen window and got to the adjoining fields. Mrs Drummond tried to keep the rest in, but Jeanie escaped

down stairs unobserved, passed out the window, and in attempting to reach her aunt was carried down the stream and drowned. The last words she was heard to utter were: 'We will look to Jesus and He will save us.' Her mother knew not that anything was wrong till the aunt gave a scream and cried out to those within, 'Keep well together for Jeanie's gone.' The dead body was shortly afterwards found caught in a hedge at Temple Bogwood.

Many gardens were completely destroyed, and, during the flood, there were seen floating down some of the streets pieces of furniture, cabbages and other vegetables, hay and large pieces of wood.

5.4 Gravestone to Janie Drummond *(Dane Love)*

As to the aggregate amount of loss sustained on the town and neighbourhood, no proper estimate can yet be given, and as great as the loss it is, we have reason to be thankful, for had the flood happened during the night there would have been a much greater loss of both life and property.

Janie Drummond, the girl who was drowned in the great flood, was later buried in the kirkyard and a red sandstone memorial was raised over her grave.

Similarly, on 27 February 1860, there was a severe storm in the district, causing considerable damage to some property. At this time a massive ash tree that grew in the old kirkyard was blown over, and when cut into slabs yielded 200 cubic feet of timber. Prior to being cut up, its girth was measured six feet from the ground and this was found to be fifteen feet.

LANDOWNERS

Ballochmyle House was still occupied by the Alexanders. Claud Alexander, who had purchased the estate in 1785, died in 1809.

His eldest son, Claud, who served as an officer in the 1st Regiment of Guards, succeeded him. He married Elizabeth Keatinge, daughter of Colonel and Lady Keatinge, and granddaughter of the 8th Earl of Meath. Claud Alexander and his wife never had any children, and when he died in 1845 the estate passed to his brother, William Maxwell Alexander.

Claud Alexander still felt that Ballochmyle House was too small for their needs, and in 1813 commissioned the Glasgow architect, David Hamilton (1768-1843) to provide plans for an extension. These were never executed.

William Maxwell Alexander was born in 1790. He gave up Southbar, near Paisley, on succeeding to Ballochmyle, Southbar being passed to his younger brother, Boyd. However, William owned Ballochmyle for just eight years, dying in 1853. He was never married, and again the estate passed to his brother, Boyd Alexander.

Boyd Alexander was born in 1796. On 17 January 1828 he married Sophia Elizabeth (died 19 October 1859), daughter of Sir Benjamin Hobhouse, 1st Baronet, and sister of the first Baron Broughton. They had a number of children, including Claud Alexander, who succeeded, and John Hobhouse Inglis Alexander (1832-1875). John Alexander was given the estate of Southbar, but through his wife became progenitor of the Alexander-Sinclairs of Freswick, in Caithness. Boyd Alexander died in 1861, being succeeded by his eldest son, Major General Claud Alexander.

Major General Claud Alexander was born on 15 January 1831. He married Eliza Speirs (born 12 May 1839), only daughter of Alexander Speirs MP, of Elderslie, on 12 February 1863. Eliza's mother was Eliza Stewart Hagart (1817-1910), daughter of Thomas Campbell Hagart of Bantaskine (1784-1863), from whom the Hagart name came into the family at a later date. Claud served in the Grenadier Guards, and was active at the siege of Sebastopol in the Crimean campaign. He stood for parliament and was elected as Conservative Member of Parliament for South Ayrshire in 1874 and served continuously until 1885. On 13 February 1886 he was created a Baronet, taking his title of Ballochmyle.

As if to celebrate his hereditary baronetage, in 1886 Claud Alexander commissioned the extension of Ballochmyle House. This was designed by the architect, Hew Montgomerie Wardrop, and the cost was just short of £40,000. The style of the building erected by Wardrop was unusual, and was an eclectic mix of Jacobean and Georgian styles. Unlike the Adam house, the new extension was constructed of Ballochmyle sandstone. Parts of the walls of the Adam buildings were removed, as well as the two wings, to allow the new block to knit with the old. The east elevation, overlooking Catrine, was left virtually untouched. Internally the new block had three joining corridor-halls, with staircases in each. The walls of the main halls were sumptuously panelled, and the ceilings were decorated in the neo-Jacobean style. Over the new front door was a spectacular carving of his baronial arms. At the same time as the Wardrop additions were being made to the mansion, a new West Lodge was erected.

5.5 Ballochmyle House *(Author's Collection)*

Sir Claud Alexander was a Deputy Lieutenant and Justice of the Peace for Ayrshire and Renfrewshire. Sir Claud Alexander died on 23 May 1899, where upon he was succeeded by his only child, also Claud, who became the second baronet. Sir Claud preferred to live in Sussex, so from that time onward the house of Ballochmyle was let out.

Now part of Ballochmyle estate, Kingencleugh House or cottage was let to various tenants, some of them being relatives of the Alexanders of Ballochmyle. One of the more picturesque and notable was Lady Cecilia Brabazon, who was at Kingencleugh from at least 1837. She was the aunt of Claud Alexander (d. 1845), and the fourth daughter of Anthony Brabazon, 8th Earl of Meath. Her two brothers were to succeed as 9th and 10th earls in due course. For many years a portrait of her hung in the dining room of the house. She was described as being 'a fairly stately

5.6 Ballochmyle House policies in 1848 *(Ballochmyle Estate Archives)*

dame, with a sweet, though imperious, expression.' Lady Cecilia spent some time improving the grounds around Kingencleugh, planting daffodils, London pride and Canterbury bells, in the glen below the house, making it very picturesque. This part of Kingencleugh Glen became known as the Lily Glen. A number of residents of Mauchline in the 1920s could still recall Lady Brabazon being taken in a magnificent carriage, her footmen standing to the rear, holding on for dear life to the leather straps as the carriage sped along. Lady Cecilia Brabazon died in 1849.

Later tenants of Kingencleugh included John Duncan Thomson, of Kelvinside,

Glasgow, who was in residence at the end of the nineteenth century, followed by his daughter, Miss Margaret Thomson.

At the start of the nineteenth century William Campbell owned Netherplace. He decided to enlarge the house considerably, the foundation stone being laid on 14 April 1827. A new Tudor-Gothic extension was added on the west side of the old baronial house. This had two principal floors, the main block having five bays, the central one depressed. Centrally placed was a gothic porte-cochere, with octagonal pillars at the corners. The masonry of this block was regular dressed stone, with angular hoodmoulds over the Georgian windows. At roof level there was a Tudoresque parapet with corner towers. To the north of this block, and perhaps contemporary with it, was a lower wing, also of two storeys, finished to match the main block. A stair window had a gothic arched window, and on the façade was a large stone bearing the Campbell arms.

The older seventeenth century house was partially recased at the time, tall Tudor chimney stalks being added and a corner turret with crenellated head, to match the new block. At second floor level, above the windows, ornamental pediments were added.

5.7 Netherplace House *(Author's Collection)*

William Campbell of Netherplace was never married, and he died on 25 December 1843, being buried on 2 January 1844. He was succeeded to the estate by his eldest sister, Margaret Campbell. She was unmarried also, and on her death on 5 July 1847 the estate passed to the younger sister, Lilias Campbell. She died on 20 April 1851 aged 73.

With no direct heirs, the settlement agreed by the last male laird, William Campbell, Lilias's brother, kicked into place. The estate was to pass to Lieutenant-

Colonel John Ferrier Hamilton of Carnell Castle and Westport, the last three siblings' second cousin. Although he was to inherit the estate in life-rent, it was to pass to his second son in fee.

This was Col. Charles Vereker Hamilton, second son of Ferrier Hamilton and his wife, the Hon. Georgina Vereker, daughter of 2nd Viscount Gort. Charles Vereker Hamilton adopted the surname Hamilton-Campbell at this time. He was married to Mary William Sancroft Randall, only daughter of Samuel Randall of Orford in Suffolk, and had five children, the eldest son, William Kentigern Hamilton-Campbell being born on 30 September 1865 at Carnell Castle. Other children were Georgina Julia (d. 1923), married on 10 January 1890 to George Douglas Findlay (1860-1940), later Findlay Campbell; John Ferrier Hamilton-Campbell (born Cairnhill (Carnell), 25 October 1868, died at Macedon, Australia, 15 August 1944), May, and Julia.

Charles Vereker Hamilton -Campbell was a major in the East India Army and a Colonel

5.8 Charles Vereker Hamilton-Campbell of Netherplace *(Stroma Leith)*

in the Ayrshire Yeomanry Cavalry. He was described as 'a splendid type of the country gentleman, and was held in the highest respect by rich and poor alike'. In 1872 his Netherplace Estate extended to 1,627 acres, with a valuation of £2,654. Col. Charles Vereker Hamilton-Campbell died on 5 May 1886, aged 67, after which his wife and young family moved elsewhere. His wife, Mary Hamilton-Campbell, died on 20 May 1872.

The archway over the drive leading to Netherplace House from Loudoun Street was built in 1873 by Charles Hamilton-Campbell. Previously the drive to the mansion from the street appears to have been open.

For much of the nineteenth century Netherplace was tenanted by various families. In the middle of the century the tenant was John Hope, Lord Justice Clerk of Scotland. He was the great-great grandson of Charles Hope, 1st Earl of Hopetoun. Born on 27 May 1794, he was married in August 1824 to Jessie Scott Irvine (died 31 October 1872), daughter of Thomas Irvine.

John and Jessie Hope had a son, William Hope, who was a Lieutenant commanding the 7th Regiment of Foot (later the Royal Fusiliers). Born on 12 April 1834, educated at Trinity College, Cambridge, he was married on 29 April 1857 to Margaret Jane Cunninghame-Graham, third daughter of Robert Cunninghame Cunninghame-Graham of Gartmore in Perthshire. She was the aunt of the politician and writer, Robert Bontine Cunninghame-Graham (1852-1936). They had a number of family – Adrian Charles Francis (1858-1904), John Archibald Graham (1864-1897), Charles Douglas (1867-1947), Laura Charlotte (1859-1936), Jesse Margaret (1870-1920) and Margaret Elizabeth Horatia (1873-1947). Margaret Hope died on 11 December 1909.

Lieutenant Hope was awarded the Victoria Cross for his bravery on 18 June 1855 at the battle of Sebastopol in the Redan area of Crimea. He was only twenty-one at the time, but he went over the front to assist the adjutant who was lying beyond the trenches, badly wounded. Despite getting the aid of a further four men, they were unable to move him, so Hope ran back across heavy fire to get a stretcher. He was to be one of the first recipients of the Victoria Cross, being presented it by the Queen in Hyde Park on 26 June 1857.

When he returned home from the front there was a considerable party at Netherplace, with a bonfire and fireworks. Three small cannon, acquired from Catrine for the event, were used to fire salutes.

Hope was promoted to Lieutenant Colonel and took a keen interest in the veteran movement, becoming commander of the 1st City of London Artillery Volunteers. He was to invent the shrapnel shell for use with rifled guns. Colonel Hope later leased Parsloes Manor from the Fanshawe family from 1867-78, and served as a military attaché to Lord Napier. Colonel Hope did not last long after his wife had died, for he passed away on 17 December 1909 at Chelsea. They are both buried in the Brompton Cemetery in London, the grave marked by a small cross. His Victoria Cross is on display in the Royal Fusiliers Museum within the Tower of London.

Another tenant was Mrs Middleton, the widow of the owner of a tea plantation. When she was at Netherplace her two boys were noted for their skill in playing cricket. One of them, Captain Bay Middleton, died when he fell from his horse during a steeplechase race. He had also served as an equerry to Elizabeth, Empress of Austria, when she went hunting at the Curragh.

The next tenant was James Baird Thorneycroft JP. Thorneycroft was a director with William Baird & Co. Ltd., being a grandson of Janet Baird, sister of James Baird (1802-1876). His mother, Jane Whitelaw (13 October 1824-29 September 1908), married Thomas Thorneycroft (10 December 1822-6 February 1903) of Hadley Park, Shropshire. James Baird Thorneycroft was one of eight children, born on 19 March 1851 at Crescent Cottage, Tettenhall Road, Wolverhampton. He married Annie Chalmers Nicoll on 29 June 1847 at Old Monkland, Glasgow.

Mauchline Castle was in 1837 the home of Alexander Hamilton, a Writer to the Signet, and son of Gavin Hamilton. By 1846 the castle was occupied by Mrs Hamilton. Sometime in the early nineteenth century the south wing was rebuilt with a second floor. In 1878 the castle was purchased by the Rt Hon Charles Frederick Clifton Abney Hastings (1822-1895), created Baron Donington in 1880. He was the husband of the 19th Countess of Loudoun, whom he married in 1853. On the death of Lord Donington, the castle had become the property of his trustees and it was let to William Wilson, Inspector of the Poor.

Mauchline House was abandoned as a small mansion by the early nineteenth century and by 1858 was being described as a 'disgrace to town'. It now served as shops and houses.

Barskimming estate was still the property of Sir William Miller, 2nd Baronet, Lord Glenlee. He resigned as Lord of Session in 1840 and died on 9 May 1846. His eldest son, Thomas, had died in 1827, so the title passed to his grandson, Sir William Miller, 3rd Baronet. Sir William was the eldest son of Thomas Miller and Edwina Gordon Cumming (who married in 1814). Thomas and Edwina Miller also had four other sons, Alexander Penrose Miller (1817-80), who became a Major in the 92nd Gordon Highlanders, George Cumming Miller (d. 1868), a Major in the 54th Regiment, Thomas Miller (1819-99), and Matthew Miller (d. 1860).

Sir William Miller, 3rd Baronet of Glenlee, was for a time a Lieutenant in the 12th Lancers. He was born on 12 September 1815. He married Emily MacMahon on 27 April 1839. She died on 8 August 1892. She was the second daughter of Lieutenant-General Sir Thomas MacMahon, 2nd Baronet. They had two sons, Thomas who succeeded and William Stewart Miller (born January 1853, died 29 August 1913) as well as two daughters, both of whom died unmarried. Sir William Miller died on 30 October 1861 and was succeeded by Sir Thomas Macdonald Miller, 4th Baronet of Glenlee.

Many of the farms in the northern part of the parish remained part of the Portland estates. William Henry Cavendish-Scott-Bentinck, 4th Duke of Portland, and his wife, Lady Henrietta, owned vast estates across Scotland and England, but rarely visited. The 4th Duke died on 27 March 1854 and was succeeded by his second son, William John Cavendish Cavendish-Scott-Bentinck, 5th Duke of Portland. He was born in 1800 and following a career in the military and politics became a recluse in his later life, spending most of his time at the family seat of

Welbeck Abbey in Nottinghamshire. He died unmarried on 6 December 1879.

The Portland estates passed to a distant cousin, who became 6th Duke of Portland. However, some local estates in Ayrshire were inherited by his sister, Lucy, who had on 8 November 1828 married the 6th Lord Howard de Walden. Thus, in 1879 the estates became the property of Lord and Lady Howard de Walden. Lucy, Lady Howard de Walden, died on 29 July 1899.

Rodinghead was the property of George Douglas, who had purchased the estate at the end of the eighteenth century from his employer, the guardians of the Countess of Loudoun. Around 1804-5 the house was extended. In February 1804 he insured Rodinghead House for £500 with the Sun Insurance Office, household goods, etc. for £500 and his farm steadings and stock for a further £500. George Douglas was one of five partners who founded the Kilmarnock Banking Company in 1802. This business survived until 1821, when it was taken over by Hunters & Company Bank of Ayr. Douglas was married in 1794 to Isabella Dykes (died March 1815) and they had at least one son, also George, and four daughters, of whom two died unmarried. George Douglas died on 26 January 1826.

5.9 Rodinghead House in 2012 *(Dane Love)*

George Douglas succeeded his father but appears to have lived elsewhere. He married a daughter of Hugh Campbell of Mayfield, but they had no children. In 1846 Rodinghead House was occupied by George Urie. George Douglas died on 5 February 1850. The estate passed to his sister, Elizabeth, who married Captain Francis Hay of the 34th Regiment. He was the brother of Hay Boyd of Townend of Symington. Captain Hay and Elizabeth were succeeded by their son, Colonel James George Hay Boyd (d. 1904), of the 20th Regiment, but he had succeeded to Townend and lived there.

Roughdyke formed a small property in 1837 owned by Captain Campbell.

A number of smaller houses with private owners existed in the immediate vicinity of Mauchline village.

5.10 Beechgrove House (Dane Love)

Beechgrove was a small mansion in private ownership at one time, owned in the mid nineteenth century by Dr Dugald Hamilton, a son of Gavin Hamilton, associated with Burns. Dugald Hamilton married a daughter of John Finlay of Glasgow, and they had two daughters, Mary and Norah. In addition to owning Beechgrove House, he owned Catrineholm farm, at Catrine, and Auchtitench, a hill farm at the eastern extremity of Auchinleck parish. Nora Hamilton was married to Major Wallace Adair, a relative of her own. The Adairs remained at Beechgrove until around 1880, when it was sold. By 1899 the house was the property of Mrs Margaret Ferguson or Reid. Beechgrove House was extended to the side in Victorian times, creating an elongated mansion. A larger Victorian wing was added to the side of the entrance front at a later date.

Viewfield House was built in the early eighteenth century on the Cumnock Road, next to the junction with Catrine Road. In the mid nineteenth century it was the home of Robert Wodrow (1758-1845), a descendant of the noted Scottish church historian Rev Robert Wodrow. The ancestry of the Wodrow family has been traced to Rev Patrick Wodrow, who was the vicar of Eaglesham and who converted from the Roman Catholic faith. His son, John Wodrow, was responsible for killing a man named Hamilton in Eaglesham kirkyard, on a Sunday. His son, Robert Wodrow, was chamberlain to the Earl of Eglinton over the Eaglesham estates from around 1640-60. He fought with the Covenanters at the Battle of Rullion Green in 1666 and was imprisoned thereafter. The next in line was James Wodrow, who became Professor of Divinity at the University of Glasgow in 1692. Born in Eaglesham on 2 January 1637, he married Margaret Hair, of Kilbarchan parish, Renfrewshire. He died in 1707. Their second son, Rev Robert Wodrow, was born in Glasgow in 1679 and studied theology, becoming university librarian. He left to become a tutor to Sir John Maxwell of Nether Pollok, before being licensed to preach by the Presbytery of Paisley in 1703. In 1704 he was ordained as minister at Eastwood Parish Church, Renfrewshire. He gathered many historical accounts of the sufferings of the Covenanters, his father having suffered for the cause, and published *The History and Sufferings of the Church of Scotland from the Restoration to the Reformation*, in two volumes, 1721-2. For his work in compiling this, he was granted one hundred guineas by the king. He married Margaret, daughter of Rev Patrick Warner of Ardeer, minister of Irvine, in 1708 and they had sixteen children, three sons of whom became ministers.

5.11 Viewfield House *(Dane Love)*

The eldest, Rev Robert Wodrow, succeeded as minister at Eastwood. However, he 'fell into dissipated habits' and resigned. The second son, Rev Patrick Wodrow (died 17 April 1793), was minister of Tarbolton from 1738-93. He served as Burns' minister for a time, and is mentioned by the poet in 'The Twa Herds'. He married Elizabeth Balfour, the youngest daughter of Mr Balfour of Pilrig House (Edinburgh), on 15 June 1755 at St Cuthbert's, Edinburgh, and had a son, Robert Wodrow of Viewfield. Another son was Rev William Maitland Wodrow, who is buried in Mauchline kirkyard. Rev Patrick Wodrow was buried in Tarbolton. The third son of Rev Robert Wodrow was Rev James Wodrow, minister at Stevenston.

Robert Wodrow of Viewfield was married twice, firstly, in 1783, to Elizabeth Paterson, and secondly, in 1789, to Martha Paterson. By Elizabeth he had four children, Robert, who must have died in infancy, two Elizabeths and Mary or Maria. By his second wife he had Patricia, Lilias Jane, William, Robert, and two Margarets. Their eldest son, Rev William Wodrow, was a very talented and popular minister at the Scots Kirk or Swallow Street Chapel in London. The second son, Robert Wodrow, established himself as a merchant in Glasgow, but was also known for his profound research into theological subjects. A daughter, Elizabeth, was married on 13 March 1815 to Rev John Thomson of Newbattle.

In 1797 Robert Wodrow was appointed as clerk and cashier to Mauchline and District Turnpike Trust, replacing Gavin Hamilton, who had been dismissed. This dismissal was challenged, but following a meeting on 30 April 1798 Wodrow's appointment was upheld, and Hamilton was ordered to hand over the relevant books and cash that he still held.

By the end of the nineteenth century, Viewfield was owned by Janet & Jean Guthrie Muir.

Associated with Mauchline was Sir Jeremiah Dickson KCB, who was buried in the old kirkyard where a fine sandstone memorial was raised over his grave. Dickson was to be the Governor of Nova Scotia, in Canada, for a short period, serving from 2 to 29 August 1846. He was a noted soldier, serving with distinction for many years. He was a Cornet with the 8th Dragoons from 1798-99. He was then raised to be a Lieutenant with the 2nd Dragoon Guards in 1799, and became a Captain with the same regiment in 1803. He served in Hanover in 1805. In 1806 he was appointed as a Major in the Quarter Master General's Department, and a Lieutenant Colonel by brevet on 1 August 1811, serving in Stralsund, Copenhagen and Walcheren. As a Lieutenant Colonel, Dickson was Assistant Quartermaster General to the army in Spain and Portugal, being appointed to that position in 1812. He was present at the battles of Vittoria, Pyrenees, Nivelle, Orthes and Toulouse. He was awarded the Peninsular Gold Cross with two bars for his service in the Pyrenees and Nivelle, although the latter award was unofficial, in 1812-13. He then served in Flanders and was active at the Battle of Waterloo, in 1815, and the capture of Paris. After peace in Europe, he served on the staff as Assistant Quartermaster General in

England and Ireland, becoming a Colonel in 1825, a Major General in 1837 and appointed Colonel of the 61st Foot (Gloucestershire) Regiment from 1844-1848, serving in Bengal. Sir Jeremiah Dickson married Jemima Langford-Brooke (b. 6 November 1791), daughter of Lt. Col. Thomas Langford Brooke of Meere (1769-1815). One of their sons, Charles Dickson, was killed by a fall from his horse at Onehunga, near Auckland in New Zealand, on Monday 6 October 1851. Sir Jeremiah's coat of arms comprised, *Argent, a chevron between three estoiles of six points wavy, Gules, on a chief of the Last as many pallets Or.* For a crest he had: *On a mural crown Or, a stag couchant guardant Proper, attired*

5.12 Sir Jeremiah Dickson memorial *(Dane Love)*

Or. Sir Jeremiah Dickson died on 17 March 1848, aged 73.

CHURCHES

The Rev Archibald Reid was still the minister in the parish church at the start of the nineteenth century. He continued in the pulpit for three years before he died unmarried on 5 April 1803. He was buried in the kirkyard, where his gravestone notes that he was 'a man beloved by all who had the pleasure of his acquaintance.'

The next minister at Mauchline was Rev John Tod. He was born around 1768 and was married on 3 March 1806 to Wilhelmina Kennedy Hamilton (d. 21 March 1858), the daughter of Gavin Hamilton, Burns' patron. Rev Tod was licensed by the Presbytery of Dalkeith on 4 June 1793. He is said to have been noticed as a volunteer by Lord President Hope and recommended by him to Flora, Countess of Loudoun, who presented him to Mauchline on 17 October 1803. He was ordained on 10 May 1804. Rev Tod and his wife had eleven children – six sons and five daughters – Gavin Hamilton Tod (6 December 1806-24 May 1813), Isabella (b. 10 December 1807), Helen Kennedy (b. 10 December 1807), George (14 December 1810-8 January 1812), Anna (8 August 1812-23 September 1835), Henry Hamilton (a daughter – b. 11 May 1814), Gavin George (6 April 1816-6 April 1821), John Agnes (b. 17 August 1817), John Alexander (b. 4 February 1819), who became a merchant in Glasgow, Agnes Finlay (3 October 1820-27 April 1828) and James (11 September 1822-31 July 1834). Rev Tod had an unnamed sermon published in Glasgow in 1826, and it was he who compiled the chapter on Mauchline parish for the *New Statistical Account of Scotland*, written in July 1837.

Tod was paid a stipend of 15 chalders of grain, half meal and half barley. The glebe of seven acres was also worth £24 per annum to the minister. He died in 1844 aged 76 at Brownlea, Castle Street.

5.13 Parish Church around 1900 *(Author's Collection)*

During Tod's ministry the old church had become too small and uncomfortable for the parishioners and it was decided to replace it with a new building. The old church of St Michael was demolished in 1827 and the new parish church was opened for worship on 2 August 1829. During the time the parishioners had no building in which to worship, they were given the use of the Secession Church, for which they made a donation of £40.

Built of local red freestone, the church is gothic in style, and incorporates a tower of around ninety feet in height, surmounted by spirelets of a further ten feet. The copestone of the building was laid at 3:30 pm on 14 October 1808 by R. W. M. Alexander Hamilton, Gavin Hamilton's son. The church was built to seat 1,100 worshippers.

The architect responsible for designing the church was James Dempster (1797-1867), who was to design a similar style church building in 1831 for the parishioners of Cathcart, south of Glasgow. The latter church no longer exists, being demolished in 1931, leaving only the tower surviving in the old kirkyard. Dempster's practice was based in Greenock, where he also operated as a land surveyor. Of his works, he is known for St Margaret's R. C. Church in Ayr (1826) and Gourock Old Parish Church (1832). He also designed manses at Rosneath (1838) and Inveraray (1842). Also associated with the design of the church at Mauchline is William Maxwell Alexander (1790-1853) of Southbar, Renfrewshire, an amateur architect. He was the brother of Claud Alexander of Ballochmyle, and thus may have been commissioned to design the new parish church. He actually inherited Ballochmyle and owned it for eight years from 1845 until his death.

The gargoyles over the entrance doorway were sculpted by James Thom (1799-1850), a local born sculptor, who is famous for carving the statues of Tam o' Shanter and Souter Johnnie, now preserved at Souter Johnnie's Cottage in Kirkoswald. James Thom was born at Skeoch farm, on the road to Tarbolton.

Over the doorway a plaque was inscribed with the following information:

This Edifice,
Opened for public worship, 2d August
1829
stands on the site of the old Church,
which was built in the 12th century,
and after having been in use for about
600 years,
was taken down in 1827.
'An House of Prayer for all People'
'Built upon the Foundation
of the Apostles and Prophets,
Jesus Christ himself being the
Chief Corner Stone.'

The next minister in the church was Rev James Fairlie. Born in 1805, the eldest son of John Fairlie, schoolmaster at Fenwick, he was educated at the University of Glasgow. After graduating with an arts degree in 1824, he was licensed by the Presbytery of Irvine on 8 June 1830. His first ministerial position was as an assistant to Rev John Tod in Mauchline church. Rev Fairlie was presented as minister by Flora, Countess of Loudoun and Marchioness of Hastings, on 23 August 1838 and was ordained as assistant and successor to Tod on 14 November 1838. He was a much-liked minister, noted for his courtesy and judgement. Fairlie had a few of his sermons published, three single sermons were published in Ayr in 1834, Kilmarnock in 1843 and in Glasgow in 1844. A book of *Five Sermons Addressed to Emigrants* was published in Glasgow in 1852. Rev James Fairlie was never married and died on 2 July 1874. He was buried in the old kirkyard, where a granite memorial marks his resting place. In the session book his elders noted that he has been 'an amiable and excellent man, an accomplished preacher, a ripe theologian, and a faithful pastor who has borne with him to the grave the regret and esteem of all who had an opportunity of appreciating his worth.'

When the new church was erected, the clock from the old church was at first proposed to be transferred to the new building. However, it proved to be rather ancient and worn, despite attempts at repairing it, so instead a new clock was acquired during Rev Fairlie's ministry. The clock was manufactured by Alexander Breckenridge & Son of Kilmarnock and is dated 1859.

On 27 February 1861 a severe gale blew down the ancient tree that had grown in the kirkyard for six centuries or so. Located at the west end of the church, it was known locally as the 'Kirk-end Tree' and prior to the new kirk being constructed, the church bell was hung from a branch. When it fell it caused some damage to the

5.14 Church clock *(Dane Love)*

large window on the gable of the church, but otherwise little else was affected. The girth of the tree was in excess of six feet, which caused some difficulty as no saw large enough in the district could cut through it.

Rev Dr Andrew Edgar DD was inducted at Mauchline in 1874. He was born in Catrine, the eldest son of Andrew Edgar, who practised as a solicitor in Mauchline, and who was factor of Ballochmyle estate. Edgar was educated at the University of Glasgow and was licensed by the Presbytery of Ayr on 4 July 1855. His first post was a missionary at Toward Chapel, near Dunoon in Argyll. He was ordained to Tongland Parish Church in Kirkcudbrightshire on 5 March 1863. He was presented to the charge at Mauchline on 26 November 1874 by Henry, Marquis of Hastings.

Rev Andrew Edgar wrote a book entitled *Old Church Life in Scotland: Lectures on Kirk-Session and Presbytery Records*, which was published in 1885. This book was based on talks delivered in Mauchline during the spring of 1884. They were part of a course of lectures on the history of Mauchline parish church and the parish records. The initial object of the lectures was to supply the parishioners with various scraps of information on the history of Mauchline gleaned from the kirk session records. Initially Edgar was persuaded to arrange his lectures into a format suitable for publishing, but he noted that 'after I had agreed to publish some of the lectures, it occurred to me that it would be desirable to recast them and widen their scope, so that interest in them might not be limited to people connected with Mauchline parish.' Around half the book is filled with examples of church discipline, but Edgar removed the names in case it offended any descendants still in the parish. However, in the case of Robert Burns he didn't, and supplied every reference to him from the records. It was for the research for this book that he was awarded an honorary Doctorate of Divinity from Glasgow University in 1886.

Other books from Edgar's pen were a *Catechism for Young Communicants*, published in Edinburgh in 1888, and *The Bibles of England*, published in Paisley in 1889.

In 1882, during Edgar's ministry, a new organ was acquired for the church, allowing music to accompany the singing of psalms and hymns. The 'Organ Movement' arranged for a petition of 105 signatures to be handed in to the Kirk Session in July 1881, requesting that an organ or other musical instrument be acquired to assist the congregation and choir in the singing of hymns and psalms. Many of the elders were against the movement, but it was decided that one should be installed, as 'the service of praise in public worship, being a service that pertains to the Congregation to render, is most fittingly and most profitably rendered by general congregational singing, and that the proper use of a musical instrument in public worship is to promote and help, but not to restrain or supersede congregational singing.' The organ acquired was made by an amateur, James Andrew of Barskimming Mill, originally for his personal use. He spent some considerable time in making it when he was not busy at the mill. Although he was a member of the Free Church, on his death the organ was acquired by the parish church and installed to accompany public singing. The cost of the organ was £50, to which was added repair costs of £73 1s 0d. In addition £80 19s 0d was spent in erecting the organ gallery.

Another innovation was introduced gradually in 1887. Several members of the church had approached Dr Edgar with the request that they be allowed to stand whilst singing and sit or kneel whilst praying. This was more or less the opposite as to what was normal, originally worshippers sitting to sing and standing during prayers. To allay possibilities of a rift in the congregation, Dr Edgar and the elders considered the matter for three months before allowing the proposal to go ahead, 'hoping that members of the congregation would be very tolerant of any difference of opinion or practice that might be found to exist in regard to this matter.'

Around the same time as when the organ was installed, the interior of the church was renovated and laid out differently. In the galleries pews were kept for the local heritors – owners of the estates of Netherplace, Barskimming, Ballochmyle, Auchinleck, Carnell, Catrine House and Rodinghead. Tenant farmers were allocated seats in the side of the kirk, the central block of pews being designated for the ordinary members of the church.

Rev Edgar was married to Mary Sybilla Cowan on 24 November 1865 – she was the daughter of Rev Samuel Cowan, minister of Kelton in Kirkcudbrightshire, and she died at St Andrews on 14 January 1928 aged 82. In 1929 the Edgar family gifted two silver patens to the church in her memory.

The children of the Edgars were successful in their own fields. Andrew Colville Edgar was born on 7 November 1866 and died on 2 April 1883. Mary Campbell Edgar (born 3 January 1869) was married on 12 September 1895 to George Smith MA, headmaster of the boys' residential school at Merchiston Castle, Colinton, Edinburgh, and afterwards master of Dulwich College, London. Mary Edgar was an accomplished poetess. Campbell Cowan Edgar D.Litt, was born on 26 December 1870, worked at the Department of Antiquities, Cairo, Egypt, and died on 10 May 1938. John Stewart Edgar was born on 26 October 1872 and died on 23 March 1916. Charles Samuel Edgar became the professor of Greek at Stellenbosch, South Africa He was born on 29 April 1874. Jean (or Jane) Violet (b. 24 November 1875) was married to Rev John Manisty Hardwick, assistant master at Rugby School. Sybil Frances Edgar was born on 27 July 1877. A third daughter, Magdalen Grace Edgar, was born on 22 July 1880 and died on 18 May 1943. Audrey Colville Edgar was born on 1 February 1884.

Doctor Edgar served at Mauchline for fifteen and a half years until his death in Ayr on 23 March 1890. The kirk session recorded 'the removal from their midst of an earnest preacher of the Gospel, a devoted servant of Jesus, and an accomplished scholar and author.' He is buried in Mauchline Cemetery.

In 1912 Dr Edgar's family presented two new silver communion cups to the church. These are inscribed, 'In memory of the Rev Andrew Edgar DD, minister of Mauchline 1874-1890, gifted by his children.'

Rev Dr Joseph Mitchell DD was ordained at Mauchline on 17 September 1890. He was born in the parish of Brechin, Angus, on 20 July 1859, the son of Joseph Mitchell and Janet Miller. He was educated at Craig Public School followed by the University of St Andrews, from where he graduated with a Master of Arts degree in 1885 and Bachelor of Divinity in 1887. He was licensed by the Presbytery of St Andrews on 5 May 1886 and at first served as an assistant minister at St Mary's Church, Dundee, before taking up the pulpit at Mauchline. The minister's stipend in 1892 was worth £237 per annum plus manse.

In 1887 two members of the congregation each donated £100 towards the cost of erecting a church hall. Plans for the new facility took time to come to fruition (the fund in 1890 stood at £633) for it was not until 4 April 1895 that the new church hall was opened, though the date stone indicates 1894. This was erected on open ground at the corner of Castle Street with the lane behind the kirkyard. Built of red sandstone, the hall was designed in the late Gothic style by the Glasgow architect, John B. Wilson. The hall was opened on the Friday by Rev Dr Story and a soiree was held on the Saturday. The main hall measures 66 feet by 36 feet, seating 600, with additional rooms and porch. The cost of construction is not known, but on 17 January 1896 the moderator recorded that he had 'insured the church hall for £1,000 – building £800, furniture £200 – and that the annual premium thereon was 16/-.' The mason work was carried out by H. Hyslop, the wright work by John Boyd and the slating by R. Millar. In 1894 the Session agreed to the purchased of Mr Blair's house in Castle Street at a cost of £310, to be demolished to improve the vicinity of the hall.

UNITED PRESBYTERIAN CHURCH

A number of parishioners did not attend the parish church and instead adhered to the Meeting House, or Secession Church. The first minister, Rev John Walker, remained in the pulpit for 38 years. He did much to settle the differences between the parish church and the Secession Church, allowing them to co-exist. During his ministry the number of members grew, and from 1836-7 a group of them decided to establish a new congregation for themselves in Catrine. Rev John Walker died on 8 August 1836 in his 75th year. His obituarist at the time described him as being 'of eminent piety and much gentleness.'

In 1837 the Secession Church, which linked itself with the Associate Synod, had 83 families associated with it, totalling 448 people, of which 226 were communicants.

The second minister was Rev David Thomas, who served for 38 years. He had been the minister of Glasgow's Wellington Street Church. Rev Thomas was originally ordained on 29 July 1835 as Mr Walker's colleague and successor, and he took over in 1836. David Thomas was born in Glasgow. He was appointed clerk of the Committee of Bills and Overtures of the United Associate Synod in 1846 and, following the establishment of the United Presbyterian Church, continued in the same office. He became a prominent figure in the United Presbyterian Synod following the union of the Secession Church with the Relief Church nationally in 1847. At that time the church in Mauchline became the Mauchline United Presbyterian Church. Thomas was the author of 'Congregational Finance in Non-Established Churches.' Rev Thomas died in 1874.

On 27 July 1875 Rev Wilson Baird was ordained at Mauchline United Presbyterian Church, and he served for fifty years. At the time of his induction the church had 247 members. Baird was born in Cumbernauld on 28 May 1847, the son of Rev Hugh Baird and Barbara Wilson. Educated in Cumbernauld, he went on to attend the University of Glasgow, the United Presbyterian College in Edinburgh, and was licensed by the United Presbyterian Presbytery of Falkirk in October 1874. For a short time he served as an assistant at Patrick Newton United Presbyterian Church, Newtyle United Presbyterian Church and Lochee United Presbyterian Church. He married Caroline Henderson Rollo (1849-1937), daughter of ex-Provost David Rollo of Dundee, on 16 December 1875. A son, Rev John Wilson Baird MA, was minister at Kirkgunzeon, Kirkcudbrightshire, followed by St Andrews Parish Church, Fife.

Rev Wilson Baird's son, Rev John Wilson Baird MA, was born in 1891. He was educated at Kilmarnock Academy and Glasgow University, from where he

5.15 North Church *(Author's Collection)*

graduated as a minister, serving at Kirkgunzeon in Kirkcudbrightshire, St Andrews, and Aberdeen.

The old church was beginning to cause some difficulties for the congregation. It had an exterior stairway that led to the gallery but, prior to its demolition, the gallery suffered from rot. On a number of occasion worshippers entering the gallery stood on the floor, bursting through both the floorboards and the plasterwork underneath. The church had a roof with a central gutter (the building was described as being like two long sheds built together) and water seeped through from the gutter into the building.

During the ministry of Rev Wilson Baird, the original Meeting House was demolished in 1884 and on the same site a new church building was erected. Instrumental in the campaign to have a new church erected were the minister, Rev Baird, and Thomas MacCall (1816-1889), a local artist, who is buried in the new cemetery. A committee of seventeen men oversaw the erection, which took a year to complete. The foundation stone was laid on 6 December 1884. The old hearthstone, taken from the house of a widow in Catrine that was built into the original building, was saved, and this was inscribed *Old Church 1796*. It was built into the walls of the new church, located high on the front wall, almost beneath the cross. The original proposed estimate for the church had been no more than £1800. However, the cost of building the church, in addition to buying a cottage for demolition and building a new cottage, was a little under £2,500. The cost was met by £1,000 promised by members, a grant of £200 from the Ferguson Bequest Fund, a second grant of £130 from the United Presbyterian Church Board, leaving just £250 to be paid for by the members. One member, an old widow from the Cowgate, had nothing to give, but volunteered to take in a lodger and save half a crown per week from his fee, eventually giving £2. The opening collection of £262 meant the church was built without the aid of a bazaar. The new place of worship was named the Walker Memorial Church after Rev John Walker. The architects of the new gothic building were Baldie & Tennant, of Glasgow, and Alexander Hyslop of Mauchline erected the building. The church was opened for worship on Friday 30 October 1885 by Rev Dr Mair of Morningside, a former member of Mauchline United Presbyterian Church.

FREE CHURCH

In 1843 the Church of Scotland split over the question of church government. Those ministers who refused to accept secular interference and patronage left the Church of Scotland and founded the Free Church of Scotland. In Mauchline around two hundred parishioners left the parish church and established a Free Church in the village. The two main leaders in Mauchline were Claud Alexander of Ballochmyle and William Templeton of Lochhill (1778-1850). It was to be part of the Presbytery of Ayr, but in 1860 petitioned to be transferred to that of Kilmarnock and Irvine. At first they worshipped in the United Secession Church, but in 1844 they were able to build a church and manse for themselves. Claud Alexander of Ballochmyle was very supportive of the church, and he gifted the site for the church to the congregation at no charge. This was located behind the houses of Loudoun Street, at the foot of Horwood Place, though access to the church was from Loudoun Street itself. The site for the manse was granted at a nominal feu duty of 1 penny per pole. The cost of building the church was reckoned to be as low as £40, the materials being supplied by members.

On the first page of the Free Church Session Minute Book a note was made about the formation of the Free Church in Mauchline:

> Previous to the Disruption in May 1843 a movement had been made in the parish of Mauchline in favour of Free Church principles. That movement was aided by the present Minister of the Establishment in this parish [i.e. Rev John Tod]. At the Disruption, however, the person referred to practically renounced the principles he had professed and remained in connection with the Established Church. But though the minister acted in this way, the people did not follow his miserable example. Many of them along with two of their Elders left the Establishment. The elders referred to were Claud Alexander Esquire of Ballochmyle and Mr William Templeton, Lochhill. Immediately after the Disruption, the adherents of the Free Church met for worship in the United Secession Church which was kindly granted for this purpose.

A pewter chalice, for communion purposes, was acquired by the church in 1844. This is inscribed 'Free Church Mauchline 1844' and can now be seen in the Baird Institute, Cumnock. In 1848 the Free Church had a congregation of 245.

The first minister of the Free Church was Rev Gilbert Johnstone, ordained on 14 March 1844. He was called by 207 members and 38 adherents. He remained at Mauchline for three years. Johnstone was born on 2 November 1817, the eldest son of William Johnstone, a schoolmaster in Glasgow. Educated at the University of Glasgow, Mauchline Free Church was his first charge. He moved to the Free Church in New Cumnock in 1847 and remained there for a further three years, before going to the Free Church in Govan in 1850. Johnstone decided to move from the Free Church and joined the Church of Scotland, being appointed minister of Shettleston, Glasgow, on 22 November 1864. He was married on 26 November 1850 to Jane Briggs Burns, daughter of Rev Dr George Burns DD, minister of Tweedsmuir in Peeblesshire. They had two sons and five daughters – William (31 May 1858-25 March 1859), George Burns (b. 9 December 1862), Esther Struthers (b. 1 December 1851 and married Rev Dr John Ferguson DD, minister of Linlithgow), Mary Shanks

(7 January 1853-20 August 1861), Jane Briggs Burns (26 August 1856-20 July 1872), Helen (b. 31 March 1860 and was married to Rev Dr John Smith DD, minister of Partick Church) and Williamina (born 1 March 1866 and was married to William Henry Henderson, controller of the General Post Office in Edinburgh). Rev Johnstone died on 25 August 1892 and was survived by his wife who died on 27 June 1911.

After a year-long vacancy, in 1848 Rev George Fairley was inducted to the charge. Membership had fallen gradually, being 245 when he was inducted. His ministry was a long and successful one, for he remained at Mauchline for thirty years, until his death on 4 March 1878.

He was replaced in the pulpit by Rev John J. W. Pollock MA, on 5 September 1878. During his ministry things changed in the service, such as in 1881 when it was decided to stand for praise and sit for praying. In 1882 the hymn-book was introduced. Pollock remained for nine years, until 1887, when he was translated to Arbroath High Church. He retired in 1896, moving to Ascog on Bute. He died at Rothesay on 9 December 1917.

During Pollock's ministry a new church was built on the site of the old one. The last service in the old church was held on 11 May 1884, and after communion that afternoon the church was closed, ready for demolition. Whilst work was progressing, the congregation worshipped in the parish school. The architect of the church was Alexander Petrie (d. 1905) of Glasgow, who was responsible for numerous buildings across the west of Scotland, including Free Churches at Barr and Colmonell in Ayrshire. It was built by George Reid of Catrine. Additional land was acquired behind the church in 1885. The new building was opened on 26 July 1885, Rev Professor Lindsay DD preaching. The cost of the new building was £1,800.

In 1887 Rev William Binnie MA was ordained and inducted to Mauchline. He was married on 23 November 1887 at Tradeston in Glasgow to Jessie Dougall Fletcher, by whom he had John Binnie, born at the Free Church manse in Mauchline in 1899. John Binnie became a Procurator-Fiscal in Dunbartonshire and elsewhere. Rev Binnie died in Ayr in 1924.

Membership of the church was 245 in 1848, dropping slightly to 233 in 1900. In 1896 the architect J. A. Morris carried out a site inspection of the Free Church.

OTHER RELIGIOUS GROUPS

Smaller religious groups also existed in Mauchline in the nineteenth century. Around 1847 there was a small group of Brethren worshippers, who adhered to the Bowesite principles, developed by John Bowes (1802-74). Around 1877 a second brethren group was established, and it seems to have survived to around 1903. In 1897 it is known to have worshipped in the Lesser Temperance Hall.

In 1837 the *New Statistical Account* recorded that there were only three Roman Catholics in the parish.

In 1815 a Bible and Missionary Society was established in the village, which was noted as being promoted with some success. It was still extant in 1837. At one time the society contributed £24 per annum towards missionary work, but on another occasion there was a dispute regarding 'pure circulation'. As a result, contributions dropped to around £14 per annum by 1837.

EDUCATION

In the nineteenth century there were four small schools in the village to cater for the pupils who could afford to pay for a simple education. Only one of these was a parochial school, the other three being unendowed. The Parochial School in the village had Thomas Mitchell as master in 1837, receiving the maximum salary, in addition to a garden and the sum of £9 for renting a house. At that time, the *New Statistical Account* noted that English, writing, arithmetic, practical mathematics, Latin, Greek and French were taught. Around £60 per annum of school fees were collected in 1837, the expenses for teaching being 10 shillings for English, 12 shillings for writing, 14 shillings for arithmetic, and 16 shillings for Latin, Greek and French. In 1841 Mitchell is noted as living at Burngrange.

In 1837 Hugh Smith ran another small school in the village. This was located within Burns' House, where he taught in one of the apartments on the ground floor. He died on 26 February 1847 aged 96 and his grave is in the old kirkyard. His son in law was Hugh Miller (1814-1876), an artist.

At one of the other private schools, English, writing, arithmetic, Latin and Greek were taught.

In 1847 the New Educational Institute was erected at the side of the Loan Green by James Stewart. When it opened it was a fee-paying school, though the third-born and any subsequent children in a family attended free. Thomas Mitchell was transferred to the new school from the old parochial school, remaining as headmaster for many years. He was also session clerk in the church. He died on 3 June 1875 aged 83. John Thomson was the schoolmaster at Mauchline until his death on 28 October 1885, aged 43 and was buried in the kirkyard. Hugh William Kilgour was for over forty years a teacher in Mauchline. He died on 15 May 1893 at the age of 74 and is buried in the Mauchline cemetery.

In 1866 the summary of Her Majesty's Inspector's report gives a good account of the school. 'The school is in a thoroughly efficient condition throughout – the younger children in charge of Miss MacLaren seem to be carefully and ably instructed. A beginning has been made with sewing and knitting.' At the time the head teacher was James Stewart and the other teacher was Jeanie MacLaren.

James Stewart was to leave the public school in 1867 to go to Edinburgh University. He was replaced by Thomas Reid, who had been trained at the Established Church Training College in Glasgow. Soon after Reid's arrival, it was noted that attendance at the school increased. However, by 1870, the inspectors were less satisfied with the work of the school

> In some respects the school is in a less satisfactory condition than formerly. Of the 83 scholars presented in the several standards, 12 failed in reading, 8 in spelling, and 21 in arithmetic, the percentage of passes being thus about 84, or 14 less than at my last visit. In the current year great attention might be directed to the reading of the 2nd Standard, to the spelling of the 5th and to the arithmetic of all above the 2nd. The P[upil] T[eacher] is expected to show improvement in Grammar, Spelling and Geography at his next examination.

Whether Thomas Reid was felt to be an unsuitable head teacher for the school or not, shortly after this report he moved to become the teacher at Crosshands Public School in the parish. In his place John Thomson of South Woodside Free Church School in Glasgow was appointed – he was 28 years of age at the time. The Inspectors were able to report in 1872 that 'the general efficiency of the Standards as measured by the percentage of passes obtained in the three subjects prescribed for examination is considerably higher than at my last visit and creditable on the whole.'

School Boards were established to govern and run schools in each parish, and the first election for members of the board in Mauchline parish took place on 15 March 1873.

Inspector's reports at the school began to decline thereafter, for in 1873 it was noted that 'the efficiency of last year is not maintained … the desks are inadequate and unsuitable.' It was also recorded that the former headmaster, Thomas Mitchell, was being brought into the school and teaching religious education out of kilter with the prescribed timetable: 'The retired teacher Mr Mitchell should be informed that, as a rule, no departure from the arrangements of the approved timetable can be allowed in the management of the school, and that least of all can he be permitted to introduce a Testament lesson during the hours set apart for secular instruction.' The pupil teacher, William Murray, was also failing in his work at the school, and the inspectors threatened to reduce the grant payable should Mr Murray fail to the same extent again.

In following years the inspector continued to be critical of the standard set by the school. In 1875 he 'regret[s] to report that the school shows great falling off since my last visit.' In 1876 things improved – 'the school is very efficiently taught in both departments.' In 1877, 'I have much pleasure in reporting that the school is in a very satisfactory condition.' The average attendance in 1883 was 170 pupils.

On 15 May 1884 a statement of income and expenditure for the School Board of the Parish of Mauchline gives a few details of educational costs at that time.

Income:

School Fees	£108	0s 8d
Educational Grants - Mauchline	£160	9s 2d
- Crosshands	£52	19s 0d
School rate collected 1½d per pound	£183	15s 1d

Expenditure:

Salaries: John Thomson	£219	14s 11d
Jane Connal	£98	18s 5d
Maggie Ramsay	£14	9s 2d
Mary Wyllie	£2	10s 0d
G. Johnstone (music)	£10	0s 0d
Robert Strathdee (Crosshands)	£91	18s 8d

In 1884 the school was described as being 'altogether one of the best in the district.' Its roll had increased to an average attendance of 175.

Following the death of John Thomson in 1885, the school was run in the interim by Robert Jenkins until a new headmaster was appointed. This was James Marshall MA. The inspector noted in 1888 that 'this school is worked in two groups, and almost with the minimum staff, which leaves no time for higher work.' The school was deemed insufficiently suitable for the parish and it was decided to construct a new school. On 31 May 1889 the headmaster recorded in the log book that 'Classes thin this week owing to approaching changes. Old Public school closed today.'

The Educational Institute was extended to take the larger number of pupils. The headmaster's old house was incorporated, being converted into classrooms.

The new school was opened on 3 June 1889 with accommodation for 474 children. The pupils gathered that day at ten o'clock in the morning on the Loan Green where they were allocated their teachers and taken to the new classrooms. The teaching staff had now increased to a head teacher, seven teachers, plus a teacher of sewing and cookery. In 1892 the school had 420 pupils on its roll, earning a grant of nearly £420.

In addition to the day school, there also operated Mauchline Public Evening School. In the Inspector's Report of July 1897, it was noted that 'this school is taught with fidelity and care. The scholars show interest in their work and their acquirement is in all respects proficient.' It gained a grant of £22 15s.

A second school existed in the parish at Crosshands, with room for 83 pupils. At the start of the nineteenth century this school had an endowment paid by the Duke of Portland, allowing the schoolmaster a house with garden. In 1892 the school had an average attendance of forty pupils, earning a grant of nearly £40. In July 1897 the Inspector's reported that 'this school is under vigorous and spirited management. The discipline is searching and the school habits regular. The pupils show good mastering of number and words. They also combine with accuracy and promptness. The composition is rounded in the fifth and sixth standards, but more finish is needed in the third and fourth. More attention should be given to mental arithmetic. The knowledge of things is suitable. Miss Wallace will shortly receive her certificate.' The school was granted £32 15s 6d as a result. Teachers at Crosshands school included Thomas Reid (from 1871), Robert Strathdee (1884), Mr Hastings (until 1895) and Jeanie Wallace (from 1895). Miss Wallace was paid £60 per annum, plus a free house and £5 each year for cleaning the school.

5.16 Public School and Loan Green *(Alison Young)*

HEALTH

A number of surgeons had practices in Mauchline to supply health services to residents who could afford to pay for them. Dr Mackenzie had a small consulting room in his house in Castle Street in the late eighteenth and early nineteenth century. When he died, the doctor's 'shop' was taken over by Dugald Stewart Hamilton, son of Gavin Hamilton. In the first half of the century Dr Dugald Hamilton is referred to as the 'town's doctor', by then based in the Cowgate.

In the 1830s and 1840s we have reference of James Nicholson (1796-1848), surgeon in Mauchline. John Mitchell was a surgeon in the village in the middle of the nineteenth century. He died at Kilmarnock on 14 February 1863, aged 45. His grave is in the old kirkyard.

Alexander Miller was a surgeon in the village and died on 14 January 1868 aged 32 years. Alexander M. Wilson operated as a surgeon in the village in 1867 and also had his own drug store.

Matthew Foulds was for 35 years a surgeon and general practitioner in Mauchline. He also had a chemists or drugstore in the village, located in Earl Grey Street. He died on 22 October 1883 aged 64 and was interred in the new cemetery.

In 1892 Mauchline Nursing Association was founded to assist in the care of patients suffering from various ailments or following accidents.

INDUSTRY

At the start of the nineteenth century, the principal industry in Mauchline was still hand-loom weaving. Most of the houses located along what became Loudoun Street probably had looms within them, the master of the house weaving various types of cloth, which were sold on to agents who took the cloth to the city markets. In the early 1840s the trade in hand-loom weaving slumped all over Scotland, and it has been calculated that this slump also caused other local industries to suffer. However, with the decline of this home-based industry, many of the workers were to find employment in the newer factories making wooden boxes and other examples of treen.

At the Haugh Mill James Hamilton is noted as being in possession in 1851. He was both the miller and a timber merchant – the Six Inch Ordnance Survey map of 1856 indicating that the mill was used for both milling corn and sawing timber. He also was the tenant of 33 acres of land. He left the mill sometime before 1868, for by then he was listed as being the proprietor of lands at Burnside, Mauchline. An old plan of 1828 shows that the lade, which drove the Haugh Mill at that time, worked a total of three wheels. These were arranged consecutively, the centre one being used to drive the corn mill. The lade took water from the weir across the River Ayr, around half a mile upstream, and at first the water passed through a tunnel cut through the natural rock before embouching into an open lade.

The internal workings of the Haugh Mill appear to have been removed either late in the nineteenth century, or else early in the twentieth. According to James Pearson Wilson, writing in 1944, 'all the machinery was cleared out long ago and after being used for other purposes, the water wheel was also removed.' He explains that the mill was used for grinding corn, and that the kiln loft had extended over the old kiln. The corn was taken in at the kiln loft and loaded onto the kilnhead over the breast, the traditional style of milling.

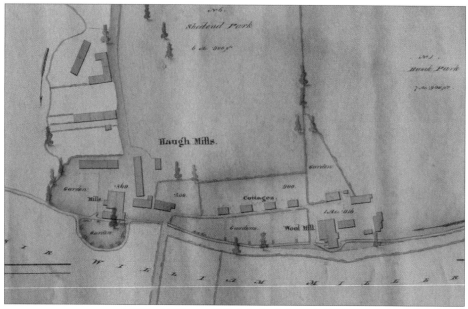

5.17 Haugh Mills map, 1847 *(Ballochmyle Estate Archives)*

The next operator of the Haugh sawmill was Adam Wilson (born in Minishant in 1823), who appears to have started in business there in 1856. The firm of Adam Wilson & Sons was established by him, then taken over by his son, William Wilson JP, who erected a large steam sawmill at Auchinleck in 1876. The firm opened another sawmill at Troon harbour in 1888, where it still operates. In 2011 the firm, sold to the Glennon Brothers of Ireland in 2008, made a profit of £4.5 million.

East of the Haugh Mill proper was another mill, shown as a 'Woollen Mill' on the old Ordnance Survey map of 1856. The woollen mill was established in 1845. This was powered by the same mill lade as the Haugh Mill. Between the two was a row of cottages, occupied by workers at the mill. The mill was for a number of years operated by William Holland (1797-1860), followed by Adam Ramsay (1899), though it was the property of Ballochmyle estate. In 1837 it was noted that upwards of thirty people were employed at the woollen mill, working eleven hours per day, five and a half days per week. The woollen mill produced yarn which in general was transported to Kilmarnock for the manufacture of carpets.

The Lint Mill at the Haugh became abandoned sometime in the first half of the nineteenth century, being shown in ruins on the Ordnance Survey map of 1856.

The village of Haugh was a hive of activity in the mid nineteenth century, for at that time there was also a smithy and malt kiln in operation, located between Haugh farm and Haughhead. In 1837 the village had a population of eighty people.

There were also other mills in the parish. Dalsangan Mill was located on the Garroch Burn, which flowed from Loch Brown, the miller in 1841 being Hugh

Morton. The burn never had any great head of water or flow in it, and the mill is known to have become disused by 1860.

In 1860 the Ballochmyle Creamery was erected by the side of the River Ayr at the Haugh. The site chosen was where the old Lint Mill had stood, near where the mill lade re-joins the River Ayr. Around 1890 the creamery was purchased by Robert J. MacCrone and he redeveloped the buildings in a Swiss cottage style of architecture between 1899 and 1900. The name of the architect is unknown, but the buildings had a dainty appearance, with gabled hip roofs.

5.18 Ballochmyle Creamery *(Author's Collection)*

In 1821 William and Andrew Smith's boxworks was opened in Mauchline, manufacturing snuff boxes with the secret hinge. This industry appears to have started locally in Cumnock, but soon separate box makers established works in neighbouring villages, such as Mauchline and Auchinleck. William Smith set up in business as a stone mason in the village, carving headstones, as well as producing hones, or 'Water of Ayr' stones, quarried at Stair. William was succeeded in the stone mason business by his two elder sons, James Smith (b. 1787) and John Smith (b. 1789). His two younger sons, William Smith (1795-1847) and Andrew Smith (1797-1869), established a boxworks in Mauchline, no doubt originally for holding the hones.

The factory in Mauchline was erected on land between what was still known as New Road (now Kilmarnock Road) and Greenhead. The works at Mauchline grew to become the most significant, producing 'Scotch' snuff-boxes, cigar-cases, card-cases, toothpick cases, lancet cases, needle cases, tea caddies, ladies' work boxes, ornaments and knick-knacks of various kinds. Most of these were produced from white varnished timber, such as sycamore, or were tartan-painted. Many of the original boxes were decorated by notable artists. Latterly the boxworks made whitewood articles in a vast variety of shapes and styles, often including the unique 'Scotch Joint'. Smith also produced the 'royal inimitable razor strop.'

In 1829 the firm opened a showroom and warehouse in Birmingham, supplying the considerable market in England. In 1832 Smith was granted the royal warrant of William IV. In the autumn of the same year William Cobbett MP visited the factory on one of his tours. It is quite interesting to read his comments on the business:

> … we set off in a post-chaise to Mauchline … and to see also, the most ingenious, the most interesting manufacture of snuff-boxes, made of the wood of the sycamore, and painted and finished, in all the various shapes and colours that the manufacture exhibits to the eye. Mr Smith, the proprietor, most obligingly conducted us through the several departments. Some of the work-people were hewing out the wood, which, from that rough state, we saw passing on from hand to hand, till it became an elegant piece of furniture for the pocket. Some were making drawings upon paper; others making the paintings upon the boxes; and all was so clean and so neat, and every person appearing to be so well off.

In 1837 there were around sixty people employed at the box works, working for ten hours each day, six days per week. They were paid according to their skill in either box-making or painting the finished boxes. According to the *New Statistical Account*, the 'works are so conducted as to be injurious neither to the health nor the morals of the individuals engaged in them.'

Andrew Smith also devised a scale copying machine which he called the Apograph. This was a metal frame which supported a drawing board and pens, and allowed the user to copy an illustration, redrawing it at a smaller scale, varying from ⅛ to ¾ in size. The Apograph can be seen in the National Museum of Scotland.

The firm also produced a number of patents for box-making equipment. In 1853 a 'ruling machine' was registered by William Smith. In 1856 Andrew and William patented a machine for 'ruling ornamental figures'. A variation of this was patented in 1861 by Andrew Smith for 'producing ornamental lines and figures on metal, etc.' In 1855 Andrew Smith patented a portable case for cigars, cards or spectacles. Numerous other patents followed, including a letter weighing balance (1862), which can still be obtained in various forms today

In 1843 the brothers split the business, having quarrelled, but William's death in 1847 left Andrew running the whole business once more. He took on his own son, also William (1827-1867), as well as his daughter, Jane. William (the third) died before his father, who died in 1869. The business was inherited by the fourth William Smith (1863-1949), but he was only six years of age at the time. Until he was able to take over, the business was run by his Aunt Jane and his mother.

The factory operated by Smith employed up to 300 men and women at its peak. In 1890 the factory suffered a major fire. The works were rebuilt after the fire, by this time expanding over the equivalent of three cottages and their gardens. These were the last three cottages on New Road, apart from the Toll Cottage which followed.

Facing Kilmarnock Road was a block of buildings of two storeys, that nearest the village centre having a showroom on the ground floor and an office above. Next door, in the middle cottage, was a store on the ground floor and a dwelling above. The third building, adjoining the Toll Cottage, had a workshop on the ground floor and a second dwelling above.

SCOTCH SNUFF BOXES.

WILLIAM & ANDREW SMITH,

BY SPECIAL APPOINTMENT,

MANUFACTURERS OF SCOTCH SNUFF BOXES

TO

HIS MAJESTY,

Warehouse—28, Great Hampton-street, Birmingham:

MANUFACTORY—MAUCHLINE, AYRSHIRE, SCOTLAND.

CIGAR, CARD, TOOTHPICK, LANCET, AND NEEDLE CASES.

Tea Caddies and Ladies' Work Boxes, with Scotch Joints.

MANUFACTURERS OF THE ROYAL INIMITABLE RAZOR STROP.

5.19 Smith's Boxworks advertisement *(Author's Collection)*

In the former gardens behind an extensive works were located. The main factory was located in a two storey building behind the showroom. In the middle was a yard, with a large saw bench for cutting sycamore or plane trees. Adjoining this was a machine shop and a boiler house. Behind the third building on Kilmarnock Road was a drying shed, where boards cut from trees were left to dry out. Beyond was a store and engine shed. A set of bogey rails from the yard crossed Loch Road to a former field where there was a large log yard and drying shed.

Smith's had a branch office in Birmingham, at 61 Charlotte Street, in 1867, and at other times had a warehouse in the city at 28 Great Hampton Street.

One of the managers of the boxworks for a time was David MacQueen JP, who lived at St David's, Loudoun Street. He died in 1905, aged 80, and was buried in the cemetery. MacQueen was also active in Mauchline School Board and a keen horticulturalist, being a member of Mauchline District Horticultural Society.

A number of important artists plied their craft at Smith's boxworks in the early years of their career. Amongst these was Sir Daniel MacNee (1806-1882), who was to become Scotland's leading portrait painter of his time. He painted snuff boxes at Cumnock, followed by Mauchline, before going on to become the president of the Royal Scottish Academy.

5.20 A collection of Mauchline Ware *(Dane Love)*

Another was William Leighton Leitch (1804-1883). He worked at Cumnock boxworks for a year before coming to Mauchline to work at the boxworks. He later moved on to London, becoming a celebrated water-colourist. He was honoured by being asked to give lessons to Queen Victoria for over twenty years, and Queen Alexandra in 1902. Among his works is a view of the 'Old Lint Mill' at the Haugh, the site of which was later occupied by Ballochmyle Creamery. Whilst living in Mauchline, William Leighton Leitch and his wife lost a daughter, Jean, who died in 1831 aged 3 years. She was buried in the old kirkyard.

There were other manufacturers of snuff boxes in the village at different times. In 1837 we have reference to Paterson & Lucas, manufacturers of snuff boxes.

Slater's Directory of 1867 gives us the information that there were four other box manufacturers in the village. These were Archibald Brown; John Davidson & Sons; Marr, Wilson & MacMillan and Wilson & Amphlet.

Messrs Davidson, Wilson & Amphlet had their original factory located near to Grey's Bridge in Castle Street. The company was owned by two Mauchline men –

John Davidson and Robert Wilson – and Samuel Amphlet of Birmingham. The factory at Grey's Bridge became too small for their production requirements, so on 1 April 1859 they acquired property in Barskimming Road. The title deeds for this ground noted that it was part of 'The £10 lands of the Mains of Mauchline, Parish thereof, Bailiary of Kyle Stewart and Sheriffdom of Ayr.' The lands had previously been part of a marriage contract to the Countess of Romney and others by the Earl of Loudoun. At the time the boxmakers acquired the ground, the lands were occupied by David Morrison, farmer, Primrosebank. The move to the new factory was completed just as the great Mauchline flood was taking place, meaning that they did not lose much of value.

On 16 October 1864 John Davidson gave up his one third share of the business and set up a factory of his own, back in the original factory in Castle Street. Wilson & Amphlet continued at their Barskimming Road works, and also had an outlet at 29 Graham Street in Birmingham. On 20 August 1867 Robert Wilson transferred his remaining share of the business to his nephew, Edward MacEwan, but the firm retained the name Wilson & Amphlet. Robert Wilson died in September 1871. On the day of his funeral, in October 1871, Wilson & Amphlet's factory in Mauchline was destroyed by fire, causing £1,000 worth of damage. Locals tried to dowse the flames with buckets of water passed along a chain from Mauchline Burn. The fire brigades from Catrine and Kilmarnock were sent for, but by the time they arrived the building was virtually destroyed. The factory was rebuilt in October 1871. On 8 January 1885 Wilson & Amphlet sold the factory to George, William Robert and William Smith of Smith's boxworks, who required further premises to cope with the demand for their wares.

5.21 Baker's Van made by Pollock of Mauchline *(Author's Collection)*

John Davidson was the son of a miner and was born in 1817 in the parish of Dailly, near Girvan. He moved to Cumnock in 1834 and joined the snuff box manufacturing trade there. He was married in 1837 and lived at Holmhead, in the parish of Auchinleck. Davidson and a friend, George Clarke, moved to Mauchline and started working with Messrs Smith. They set up their own factory but at a later date the partnership was dissolved. Davidson then joined Wilson and Amphlet in partnership for a few years before setting up on his own once more, back in Castle Street, bringing his son Joseph in as a partner. Davidson was also active in the campaign to build a town hall in Mauchline. He died on 2 February 1872 of typhoid fever.

Another old industry, which Mauchline was at one time noted for, was the manufacture of shoes, this, weaving and snuff-box making being the principal trades in the 1830s.

5.22 Contractor's Cart made by Pollock of Mauchline *(Author's Collection)*

In 1867 Andrew Pollock began making agricultural equipment in Mauchline, moving into the village from the smithy at Tarbolton. The business was originally located at the head of the Cowgate, the site developing into a sizeable complex. The business had grown over the years as he invented new machinery and improved on other existing machines. An example is the advertisement from the 19 September 1877 edition of the 'North British Agriculturist':

New Potato-Digging Machine. A. Pollock, Mauchline, begs to intimate to farmers, potato merchants, and others, that he is now able to supply this machine, and can with confidence recommend it for being the best machine for raising potatoes ever offered to the public.

Perfect in work, light and easy to draw. A. Pollock has invented a much lighter machine, with broad-rimmed wrought iron wheels, admirably adapted for moss land or light soil. The road wheels are all made of wrought iron this season. Carriage paid to all railway stations in Scotland. Price Lists and testimonials post free on application.

Mauchline, 5th September 1877.

A new patented version of the potato-digging machine was developed in 1881, available from agents in Glasgow, Edinburgh, Fife, Dumfries, Castle Douglas and Thornhill. An advertisement from the time reads:

This Season these Machines have undergone considerable improvement. The Gear has now been completely covered so that the largest-topped Potatoes cannot get entangled about the Machine.

A. Pollock has invented a much lighter Machine, with Broad-Rimmed Wrought-Iron Wheels, admirably adapted for Moss Land or Light Soil.

The Road Wheels may be had either of Wrought or Cast Iron. As there are three different weights of Machines, they can be supplied to suit any Soil. Carriage Paid to all Railway Stations in Scotland, England, and to the principal Sea-Ports in Ireland.

Mauchline, 26th Sept. 1881.

Andrew Pollock died suddenly on 1 October 1904 aged 63 and was buried in Mauchline Cemetery. His son, John Pollock MB ChB, DPH, was a doctor and surgeon, and died at Stoke-on-Trent in 1953 aged 59.

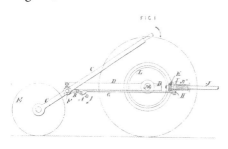

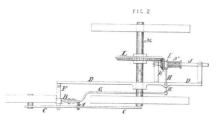

5.23 Patent drawing for Pollock's Potato Digger
(Jimmy McGhee)

A number of blacksmiths worked across the parish at various smithies. At Ballochmyle Gate Smithy William Anderson (1772-1880) was the smith, followed by William Ramsay – he died on 29 October 1906 aged 84 - and James MacCartney.

There was also a smithy at the Haugh, in 1841 William MacGavin being the smith there. The smithy at the Loan Green was in 1899 operated by Hugh Baillie.

Auchmillan Smithy was initially located at Auchmillan farm, but later moved to be near the Gorbals, across the water. The smith in the 1830s and 1840s was Robert Wilson. In the 1830s the village of Auchmillan had a population of 35.

At Crosshands, the smithy was the property of Portland estate, but it was leased by various occupants over the years. In 1841 the smith was James Paton, by 1851 it was William Elliot who remained until at least 1899, being succeeded by Thomas Elliot.

The Auchmillan Limeworks were located on the north side of the Auchmannoch Burn at Auchmillan. Operational in 1860, there was an extensive limestone quarry and associated limekilns. The manager for fifty years was James Gibb (born 1745), one of the Gibbs of Auchmillan. The works were part of Barskimming Estate. It is known that Robert Burns, when he farmed Mossgiel, came to Auchmillan for his lime, bringing two horses and carts for it. The quarry at Auchmillan was disused by 1897.

The limestone quarries at Killoch, in the north-east corner of the parish, were abandoned by 1856. A lime kiln associated with the workings was also disused. Further to the west, midway between Killoch and High Holehouse, was another limestone quarry, located on the north side of the road. This had been abandoned by 1856. The lime kiln associated with it was located by the side of Blacks Burn, north-east of Low Holehouse.

Smaller limekilns and workings were to be found all over the parish. In 1860 there were limekilns noted at Friendlesshead and Lawersbridge farms to the north of the parish.

The Ballochmyle Quarries appear to have commenced production near the end of the first half of the nineteenth century. The quarry produced bright red-coloured sandstone, which was fine-grained and ideal for building purposes. The sandstone had been formed from wind-blown sand, which had created dunes, during the Permian era, around 250-300 million years ago. The stone was in much demand for bright-coloured buildings and was often used for public buildings and churches. Buildings known to have been constructed from the stone in the Victorian period include the Burns Monument in Kilmarnock (1879), St Vincent Place, Glasgow (1885), MacKechnie Institute, Girvan (1888), Hyndland Parish Church, Glasgow (1887), St Columba's Parish Church, Largs (1892), and many other buildings.

The quarries were originally managed by a Mr Lambie, but he failed to make much of a success of them and they were closed. At a later date, around 1850, they were leased by James Gibson, builder, Auchinleck, but on his death they were taken on by Marcus Bain.

In 1861 a steam crane was installed at the works by William Gibson. This was one of the first such cranes to be used in local quarries, being built by the Ayr engineering firm of Messrs. J. and A. Taylor. On Saturday 20 April 1867 a second steam crane was installed at Ballochmyle Quarry for lifting blocks of sandstone. The new crane allowed larger blocks of sandstone to be handled more easily, and was capable of raising stones in excess of 10 tons in weight. Again the crane was built by Taylor of Ayr. On the first day a demonstration run was arranged, after which William Gibson gave a treat to the workers, nick-naming the crane the 'Monarch of the Rocks'. The older crane was relocated for lifting stone from the finishing yard onto the waggons for delivery to customers.

Marcus Bain was the son of Robert Bain. Robert Bain came to the Cumnock area from the Highlands in the 1840s when the Glasgow & South Western Railway was being built. He liked the area and locals so much that he decided to settle here, becoming a spirit merchant in Glaisnock Street. Marcus was his eldest son, born on 10 March 1849. Marcus was educated at the Free Church School in Cumnock, followed by a period of employment with Hamilton Rose, a solicitor, based in Cumnock's Lugar Street. He then moved to Glasgow, followed by Rosewell, near Edinburgh, where he was employed by Archibald Hood, coalmaster, as cashier. Hood also owned the Ballochmyle Collieries in Auchinleck and Sorn parishes and Marcus was sent there to become cashier.

In the mid nineteenth century Bain moved to work at the Haughyett, or Ballochmyle Quarry, at that time leased by James Gibson. The quarry was still just a smallish concern, supplying stone for local building requirements. However, Marcus Bain realised the quarry's potential, and soon began developing it. On the death of James Gibson, he took over the quarry himself.

Marcus Bain was married to Marion Gibson (1852-1886) and then to Aggie Morton (1869-1949). In 1889 Marcus Bain was elected the councillor representing Mauchline on Ayr County Council. The manager in the quarry was Neil Niven (1821-1891). His son, Rev Samuel Niven, was for twenty-four years minister at the Free Church, Bannockburn, Stirlingshire. Rev Niven emigrated to Harrison, Idaho, United States, and died in 1901 aged 54.

By 1894 the quarry had reached a depth of two hundred feet, and several saw frames were in daily use for cutting the solid stone into usable blocks. At that time the quarry employed around 200 men. The freestone quarry near to the Ballochmyle Viaduct was under the charge of William Smith, who died around 1897.

Barskimming Quarry was established on land at Mosshead in 1891, part of Barskimming estate. The quarry was originally leased by Baird & Stevenson of Glasgow, who quarried sandstone and took most of it to Glasgow where many city tenements and other buildings were constructed from it.

On 3 December 1896 James Davidson was killed in the quarry at the age of 33. He was interred at Stair kirkyard.

The Boswell Quarry was established in the mid nineteenth century near to the Ballochmyle Viaduct, on the lands of Willoxton, working sandstone on the estate of the Boswells of Auchinleck. In 1873 this quarry was leased by George Reid, builder in Catrine, but it proved to be unprofitable and it was abandoned in 1881.

In addition to Ballochmyle and Barskimming, sandstone was quarried at other locations. A small sandstone quarry existed at Haughhead, but was been closed by 1850. Another small sandstone quarry was located near to the mouth of the Kingencleugh Burn. It was abandoned by 1850.

In 1860 a small sandstone quarry was still in operation at Killoch, adjacent to Killoch Mains, on the south side of the Killoch Burn.

The quarry at Deaconbank, at the north end of the parish, remained operational during the nineteenth century. In 1860 the Ordnance Survey map shows it working the rock by the side of the Cessnock Water, and the quarriers' homes, Quarry Houses, built above the quarry to the east.

A number of small quarries existed across the parish, and probably were only opened up by farmers and landowners when they required building stone to erect new steadings or houses, or were found to contain stone that was not so good for building purposes.

Whinstone was extracted in a number of places in the parish. One small quarry existed north-west of West Hillhead. It was disused by 1850.

Freestone is a term used to describe stone that was quarried which could be cut in any direction, usually sandstone or limestone. Small freestone quarries were located in the parish at Barskimming, by the side of the River Ayr, near where the small burn from the Kipple Moss meets the river. It appears to have been working in 1856.

The extraction of sand from the ground was carried on in a fairly small scale at places across the parish. A disused sand pit is shown on the 1860 map to the north-west of Lawersbridgend.

Using local clay, at one time there was a small tileworks at Damhead, on the south side of the River Ayr, opposite Kingencleugh. This tilework was abandoned by 1899. Another tilework existed at Barneight, in 1851 the manager being Alexander Woodburn, who employed twelve labourers at the time.

Saw mills operated on a small scale at various places in the parish. At Killoch a saw mill was in operation in 1856. In the late nineteenth century Ballochmyle Sawmill was operated by George Wilson.

David Hillhouse operated as a timber merchant in Mauchline. He died on 23 October 1892 aged 79. At Auchmillan a saw mill was established in the 1870s by James Wilson, a cabinetmaker and joiner. Other joineries existed at Crosshands (in 1899 run by William Smith).

A number of long-established businesses started up in the nineteenth century. Of these, one of the longest lasting was Thomas Findlay & Sons Ltd, which was established in 1879. The firm, which specialised in building work and high class joinery, also worked on farms and byre work.

There were a few small building firms in the village at the turn of the century. Mention is made of John Campbell, mason, and David Lees, wright, who carried out building projects, among these being the new school and gaol in Cumnock in 1804.

Stonemasons who had their own businesses in Mauchline include Hugh Lire, which operated in 1837. It may have been his brother or another relation, Matthew Lire, who was a plasterer in the village. By 1867 the stonemasons working in the village were James Gibson and MacCulloch & Campbell.

The construction industry required nails for joining wooden materials, and in Mauchline in 1837 we have records of two nail manufactories. These were operated by James Brown and John Mason.

The manufacture of land drainage tiles was carried on at a tileworks at Barneight during the nineteenth century. The works, which are shown as being operational on the Ordnance Survey maps of 1856, were located by the side of the Barneight Burn, with two separate clay pits, one on each side of the stream. In the late nineteenth century the works were managed by D. White. A second tileworks was located at Damhead, at the north western extremity of the parish, within Carnell estate. The tileworks were located south of Damhead farm, by the side of the Garroch Burn, and the 1860 Ordnance Survey map indicates it in use at that time, with a sizeable kiln.

The manufacture of curling stones became more specialised in the nineteenth century, these stones being regarded by 1895 as being of a 'world-class' standard. Thomas Kay made his first curling stones at his home, which was originally located at Hayhill, near to Coylton. He was assisted by his two sons, Thomas and Andrew. They later moved to the Haugh, taking over the old mill and converting it into their stone works.

During the late nineteenth century Mauchline also had a factory producing chairs and cabinets. This was owned by Messrs. H. & A. Alexander, who had previously worked in the box factories.

A worsted and woollen spinning mill was in existence in the late nineteenth century. At the start of the nineteenth century, John MacGaan was a local agent for the sale of woven cloth. He commissioned local weavers to produce the cloth, which he transported to larger dealers in Glasgow.

In Mauchline the manufacture and distribution of coal gas commenced in the early nineteenth century. The gas works was located at Burngrange Lane, just off the High Street. In 1867 the manager was Robert Lambie (1822-1897). He was succeeded by Robert Pollock.

COMMERCE
The annual fairs and markets in Mauchline gradually diminished in size as the century wore on, and by the late nineteenth century the weekly fairs at Ayr and Kilmarnock had all but killed off any such trade in the community.

In 1815 Mauchline Savings Bank was established to let small investors to deposit funds in a safe place, and to allow them to earn interest on their money. By 1837, according to the *New Statistical Account*, 'the deposits of investors mostly from the labouring classes amount to £900, the sums annually invested about £140, while nearly as much is withdrawn.' The bank appears to have survived for around twenty years, for the minute book of the Mauchline Races noted that it was dissolved in December 1834.

A branch of the Commercial Bank was established in the village in May 1834, no doubt the reason that the Parish Bank, or Savings Bank, was closed. Initially the Mauchline branch was a sub-branch of the Kilmarnock bank, which had opened fifteen years before. The location of the Commercial Bank in Mauchline is not known at this time, but by 1858 it is known to have been located in Earl Grey Street. In the early part of the nineteenth century the local agent was John Strathdee (1798-1865), a Writer to the Signet. He was also an agent for the Insurance Company of Scotland, which insured against fire, and the Edinburgh Assurance Company, which insured lives. He served for a number of years in the committee of Mauchline Races, and as President on occasion. He died on 20 October 1865 and was buried in the kirkyard.

The next bank agent was William MacMillan (1834-1915). He started in the lawyer's office at an early age and became agent of the bank soon after. He also served as factor to Netherplace estate and was a senior director of the gas light company. He died on 8 May 1915 at his home of Williamfield. During MacMillan's time as manager, the Commercial Bank had become so successful that its link with Kilmarnock was severed, and it became a full branch in its own right.

A branch office of the Union Bank existed in Mauchline around this time. In 1841 William Campbell of Netherplace became one of ten partners in the reconstituted Hunters & Company Bank, based in Ayr. Due to his influence, there may have been a branch office or agency established in Mauchline. In 1843 Hunters Bank was taken over by the Union Bank of Scotland.

Mauchline was in the nineteenth century a postal town, where money orders could be granted or paid. According to the Post Roads map of Scotland, dated 1813, a 'foot runner' made his way from Kilmarnock through Mauchline to Cumnock and on to Thornhill and Moniaive. The service took place six times per week. In 1828 David MacRae was appointed as the official Mauchline Carrier, taking parcels and letters from Mauchline to Glasgow and back. He had given security of £100 to cover any claims against loss or damage. He also distributed letters south to Ochiltree and Cumnock.

A later post map of 1838, the 'Circulation of Letters in Scotland', indicated that Mauchline was now served by a ride or gig, one of which came to the village from Kilmarnock, the other from Ayr, which continued on through Muirkirk to Douglas Mill, meeting the London to Glasgow mail coach. In the first half of the nineteenth century the post master in the town was Hugh Wilson. Letters from Edinburgh, Glasgow, Kilmarnock and Ayr arrived at Mauchline Post Office every morning at 6 o'clock. Letters from England came by way of Douglas, arriving every afternoon at three o'clock. Letters were despatched from Mauchline every morning at 6 o'clock or at 3 o'clock in the afternoon. Parcels of various sorts could be sent by the use of various carriers in local towns, such as Andrew MacCulloch, who was based at the Commercial Inn in Kilmarnock, or David Lambie, who based himself at the Wheatsheaf Inn there, and who were available to deliver parcels to Mauchline. In the village, John MacGaan was a distributor of stamps, based at the Stamp Office at the Cross.

The post office appears to have been moved around the village quite considerably in the nineteenth century. At the beginning of the century it was located in the Cowgate, followed by Hugh Wilson's apothecary in mid-century. It was then moved to the Economical Society's shop (forerunner of the co-operative), under Bruce Taylor. For a time the post office was located at 33 Loudoun Street, now A. L. Kennedy Prime Cuts butchers. It was then moved to New Road, occupying a couple of premises, under the charge of David Miller (1836-1882), followed by his daughter, Miss Maggie MacLure Miller.

By 1895 the post office had money order, telegraph, and savings bank departments. Carriers were available to transport goods to Glasgow on Tuesdays and Fridays, to Kilmarnock and Catrine on the same days, and to Catrine or Ayr on Tuesdays. George Mitchell (1841-1923), was the post-runner from Mauchline to Catrine and Sorn in the late nineteenth century.

A second post office was located at the clachan of Crosshands, in operation in 1860.

There were three writers, or solicitors, in Mauchline in the early part of the nineteenth century. These were Alexander Hamilton, who resided in Mauchline Castle, William Murdoch and John Strathdee. By 1867 there appears to have been only one firm of writers in the village, Messrs Strathdee and Meikle.

A number of small shops with associated premises existed in various places in the village. From early records and other sources, the following commercial businesses are known to have existed.

The National Commercial Directory published in 1837 gives a good account of the various commercial businesses that operated in Mauchline at that time. There were two bakers in the village – William Ferguson (1788-1863) and John Miller. Thomas Meikle worked as a blacksmith. Of joiners in 1837, we have records of Robert Goudie, David Lees, William Lees, and James MacGill. Hugh Wilson operated a drug store in 1837. Of butchers we know of Thomas MacClelland in 1837. Robert Nisbet had a grocery in the village. Andrew MacGaan was an ironmonger.

Thirty years later, in 1867, we have mention of the following small shopkeepers: Elizabeth Miller, Robert Nisbet, Agnes Wallace and John Wallace.

Shoes continued to be made on a small scale. In 1837 we have records of James Garvan, James Gibb, Robert Nisbet, William Weir and Thomas Wilson having shoe-making premises. James MacGaan, shoemaker, died in Mauchline on 18 February 1883 aged 72. John Weir, shoemaker, died in 1885 aged 71.

Clothing was available from the following merchants in 1837 – John Goldie, draper, Euphemia Paton, milliner and dressmaker, John Mason, dressmaker and milliner. John MacGaan (1788-1841) was 'for many years Cloth Merchant in Mauchline,' according to his gravestone. James Logan (admitted a burgess and freeman of Ayr on 3 June 1835), John Lambie, Margaret Lambie, William Lambie, James Logan, and John Montgomery had tailoring businesses in 1837.

In 1867 the tailors listed in *Slater's Directory* were James Gibson, John Hood, James Lambie (also a clothier), James Logan and William Sharp.

Other premises in 1837 included Joseph Caldwell's saddlery. By 1867 the saddler in the village was Henry Doak. Other shops in 1837 included those operated by William Alexander, James Gibb, James Hood, Matthew Lamont, William MacGaan, Janet Morton, Andrew Richard and Hugh Wallace. In 1837 Montgomerie Fergusson was a watch and clock-maker in the village. In 1867 we have reference to John Green, who had a gun-making business in the village.

During the Victorian era a number of businesses in the village were formed which were to survive for many years. Among these was James Murdoch Jamieson, grocer, which was founded around 1885. James Jamieson died in 1923, but the business continued. In 1808 the William Ferguson established a family bread and biscuit maker. His nephew was William Ferguson Blair, who was born at Ednam in Berwickshire in 1842. His parents died when he was five years old and he was brought back to Mauchline and brought up by his grandparents. He took over the bakery and rebuilt the premises in Loudoun Street in 1900. He died on 27 December 1927. The business was still in operation in 1936 when the partners were James Blair (born 1873) and Robert Drummond Blair (1876-1957).

The co-operative movement was championed by Hugh Gibb (27 May 1812-7 March 1895). Gibb was 'a life-long ardent social reformer and a zealous worker in the co-operative cause,' according to the memorial that was erected over his grave in Mauchline cemetery by the Ayrshire Co-operative Conference Association. Mauchline Co-operative Society was founded in 1863. In 1866 they built a new shop building on the site of Johnnie Doo's inn at the corner of Loudoun Street with the Cowgate.

In the nineteenth century there were a number inns and hotels in the parish for the supply of board, lodgings and refreshments. The Whitefoord Arms, located at the corner of the Cowgate with Loudoun Street was renamed the King's Arms Inn and then the Cross Keys Inn. The Cross Keys was in the early part of the century under the management of John Reid. In 1837 the host was William Calderwood. This inn was often referred to as 'Johnnie Doo's'.

The Black Bull Inn also existed, being located in Earl Grey Street, the host being David Lindsay (1784-1866) in the 1830s-1850s. By 1899 it was William Walker.

In Poosie Nansie's the landlord in the first half of the nineteenth century was Richard Gibson. By 1888 the landlord was James A. Logan.

5.24 Poosie Nansie's Inn, around 1900 *(Author's Collection)*

The landlord of the Loudoun Hotel in the first half of the nineteenth century was William Lees. In the 1840s the inn only had one storey and was thatched, the landlord being Thomas MacLelland. In the early 1850s the landlord was Andrew Muir, who remained in charge until his death in January 1883, aged 77. He was born in Ochiltree, becoming a farmer with his brother at Burnton, but leaving that business behind to take over the Loudoun Hotel. By 1899 the hotel keeper was John MacIntyre, but the inn still remained the property of Netherplace estate.

At the Market Inn overlooking the Loan Green, the owner at the end of the nineteenth century was Mrs Isabella MacLennan (nee Brown), the inn being leased to Alexander Walker, innkeeper. Prior to the MacLennans, the inn was under the control of William Reid.

The Sun Inn was demolished around 1820 to allow the construction of the New Road through Mauchline. The inn stood on the south side of the Cross, where Earl Grey Street now joins the Cross. This inn was at the time occupied by John Miller as landlord. He was the father of two of the Mauchline Belles referred to by Burns.

The Ballochmyle Inn was leased by James Gibb, then Helen Gibb (nee Taylor) in 1899. She was the mother of John Taylor Gibb, who wrote a history of Mauchline in 1911.

In 1899 other inns or public houses included that at the cross, tenanted by Mary Mair or Logan, widow. In the Townhead, or High Street as it became, was another, operated by Hugh Train and Mrs Jessie Porter, or Train, his wife. At the Star Inn the host in 1837 was Andrew Young. The Thistle Inn was operated by Jane Nisbet.

Other inns that formerly existed included those located at the corner of the Knowe (operated by Andrew Young), in the old Post office (operated by Robert Nisbet), at the corner of Castle Street (operated by William Ronald), and two at the Cross, operated respectively by Hugh Wallace and John Crawford. There was one in Earl Grey Street, later converted into Mrs Brownlee's shop. There was an inn at Crosshands, and also one at the Haugh.

In addition to proper inns, there were a number of other sellers of alcohol and spirits in the village. In 1837 these included James Lockhead, Hugh MacClelland, Thomas MacClelland, William MacGaan, Matthew Muir, Jean Nisbet, Robert Nisbet, William Ronald, James Sharp, Hugh Smith and Hugh Stirling.

AGRICULTURE

In the first half of the nineteenth century most of the farmhouses on Ballochmyle estate, which at that time covered around two-fifths of the parish, were rebuilt. The new houses erected were in general two storeys in height, complete with slated roofs. In addition, office buildings were added. The farms were often re-allocated, some of the old steadings being abandoned around this time, and new fields created, bounded by hawthorn hedges. Typical of these was the old farmhouse at East Mossgiel, which had its thatched roof removed in 1858, the walls increased in height by one foot and a new thatched roof returned. At the same time the windows were increased in height by one foot. In 1870 the house was rebuilt once more, the thatch removed, the walls increased to form a second storey, and the roof replaced, but covered with slate this time. In 1883 a new cheese house was added onto the western wing.

During the nineteenth century a number of smaller farms were abandoned, their lands being conjoined to neighbouring farms to create larger holdings. Farms lost during the nineteenth century include Fallhead, which was in ruins by 1860, Willockstone, which was demolished and the name transferred to Barlosh farm, and Roadinghead of Auchinleck, in ruins by 1860. In 1837 the average rental of the farms was 26 shillings per acre, which was regarded as being quite high at the time, preventing many farmers from improving their holdings.

Much of this work was carried out in the 1840s, for there exists in the Alexander family archive a plan book showing the improvements made of the estate at that time. The improvements were made according to advice from Alexander E.

Nicholson, land surveyor, Ayr, and Robert Nicholson, Kingencleugh.

The *New Statistical Account* of 1837 gives a table showing the value of produce grown or worked on the farms of the parish. The produce of a variety of grain types, for feeding humans or animals, amounted to £6,865 10s 0d. The value of various crops, such as potatoes, turnips, cabbages, carrots etc., was calculated to be £2,172 5s 4d. Hay, either meadow or cultivated, was valued at £1,953 0s 0d. Pasture land, used for grazing by cattle or oxen, rated at £3 per cow, totalled in value £3,600 0s 0d. It was reckoned that the value from gardens and orchards amounted to £250 0s 0d. There was £500 worth of thinnings or felling of trees in the parish, including timber from copses. From quarries £300 worth of material or road-metalling was obtained. A further £150 worth of miscellaneous produce was enumerated. In total, the 'total yearly value of raw produce raised' came to £15,790 15s 4d. In addition to this, £3,656 worth of dairy produce was produced each year, as well as £800 worth of young cattle.

5.25 East Mossgiel farm *(Author's Collection)*

At the turn of the nineteenth century, the local farmers, encouraged by the landowners, changed the style of agriculture practised in the parish. The old ways of growing bere, barley and oats was abandoned, and the cultivation of wheat became the target of the farmer. This was copied from farms on the east coast of Scotland, where the better soil and warmer weather was more conducive to the crop. However, according to the *New Statistical Account*, 'the system had not been many years pursued, before it was discovered that the soil and climate of this neighbourhood were decidedly unfavourable to its profitable continuance.' At the time when 'war prices' were obtainable for the wheat, the crop was continued with, but when 'peace' prices arrived for wheat, the income was not enough to give the farmers sufficient income.

In 1847-50 Loch Brown, or Loch Broom, was drained by the landowner. On old charters this loch was styled 'Duveloch', which perhaps is a derivation of the Gaelic *Dubh Loch*, which actually means black or dark loch. The loch was noted for its wild ducks, geese and occasional swans. The loch had only been a few feet in depth, and it was a fairly simple task to dig a channel and let the water drain away. The land revealed under the sixty-acre loch was quickly cultivated and soon was growing crops. Among the Alexander archives are various legal papers concerning the draining of the loch, as well as a plan of 1849 by the surveyor J. Sturrock, showing the lands as apportioned between the farms.

Unfortunate accidents could occur on the farm to labourers employed there. In August 1809 a farm servant, who was working in a hayfield on a farm near Mauchline, was struck by a bolt of lightning during a thunderstorm which left him dead.

TRANSPORT

Roads continued to be constructed in the early part of the nineteenth century, creating almost the full road network that exists across the parish to this day. After the establishment of the turnpike roads of the eighteenth century, estates and farmers built minor roads across their property, linking their houses with the parish roads. Many of these were to become the minor roads of today.

In the early part of the nineteenth century only one major new roadway was planned, though it was never to come to fruition. William Johnson's map of Ayrshire was published in 1828, and on it there is delineated the 'Proposed line of Road from Cumnock to Glasgow'. The route shown passes through Mauchline parish, but misses the village by a few miles. From Cumnock it would have made its way through Auchinleck before taking a route further east of the present A76. The road would have passed by the steading of Meikle Heateth then north-west past Little Heateth and Kenstey to Whiteflat. The road would then have crossed the River Ayr near the foot of the Burn o' Need. Now in Mauchline parish, the road would have passed along the foot of the Brae of Ballochmyle, curving round to join the Sorn road at Grassyards. Making its way along the northern edge of Mauchline Hill, the road would have passed by Fowler, west of Barwheys to Friendlesshead. After turning to a more northerly route, the road would have reached Low Holehouse before leaving the parish and heading by way of Bruntwood and Sornhill before dropping down to Newmilns. The road would have then went by way of the Glen Water and Eaglesham to Glasgow. What prevented construction of the road is not known, perhaps the cost was prohibitive or landowners prevented it from being built through their property.

In 1848 the Glasgow, Paisley, Kilmarnock & Ayr Railway Company opened their new line south from Kilmarnock towards Dumfries as far as Auchinleck. Mauchline Station on this line was opened on 9 August 1848. Within a short time, in 1850, the company became part of the Glasgow and South Western Railway. The double track passed through the platforms on which were two station buildings, one on either side, each having a projecting canopy held aloft by cast iron supports, and a steel footbridge connecting the two. The station was popular as a stopping off point for visitors on the Burns trail, and initially it was the terminus for carriers taking goods to and from the Catrine cotton works of James Findlay. In 1887 the station was renamed 'Mauchline for Catrine', but the name was shortened to Mauchline once again in 1903, when a station was opened in Catrine itself.

The station was located 700 yards or so away from the village, accessed from either Barskimming Road or the new Station Road, built to link the station with the roads for Catrine and Cumnock. Station Road was 500 yards in length, running gently downhill from the Catrine road-end to the station.

Stationmasters at Mauchline include John MacLean (1796-1861), who served for eleven years, and Francis Logan in the 1860s.

The four-and-a-half mile stretch of line between Mauchline and Auchinleck required one of railway's greatest industrial engineering feats – the construction of the Ballochmyle Viaduct. The industrial engineers, Messrs. Grainger and Miller of Edinburgh, were responsible for the design – Thomas Grainger and John Miller. It is reckoned that it was the latter who had principal responsibility for designing the bridge. He was born in Ayr on 26 July 1805 and died in 1883.

This massive bridge spans the gorge of the River Ayr, to the south of Kingencleugh and west of Howford. The first piece of masonry laid occurred on 10 January 1846. The official foundation stone, which weighs ten tons, was laid on 5

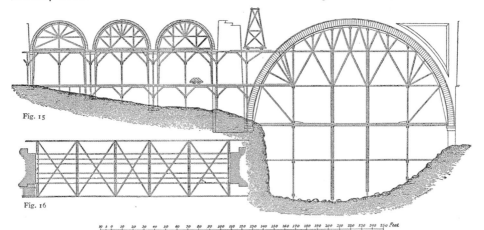

Centring of Ballochmyle Viaduct, L.M.S. Railway

5.26 Timber frame for Ballochmyle Viaduct (*Author's Collection*)

THE FOUNDATION STONE OF THIS VIADUCT,

on the Line of the

Cumnock Branch of the Glasgow, Paisley, Kilmarnock & Ayr Railway,

was laid according to the ancient usages of Masonry,

ON THE FIFTH DAY OF SEPTEMBER,

IN THE YEAR OF OUR LORD ONE THOUSAND, EIGHT HUNDRED & FORTY SIX,

IN THE TENTH YEAR OF THE REIGN OF

HER MAJESTY QUEEN VICTORIA,

AND IN THE YEAR OF MASONRY FIVE THOUSAND, EIGHT HUNDRED AND FORTY SIX.

Officers of Mother Kilwinning Lodge.

George Fullarton Esq.r of Fullarton, M.W.G.M & P.G.M.
George Johnstone Esq.r of Redburn, M.W.D.M.
John Wyllie Esq.r Kilwinning, Senior Grand Warden.
James Small Esq.r Kilwinning, Junior Grand Warden.
James Blair Esq.r Kilwinning, Secretary.
Robert Dickie Esq.r Kilwinning, Treasurer.
Rev.d D.r Arch.d Campbell, Chaplain.
Bryce Conn, Tyler.

Railway Directors.

JAMES M^cCALL ESQ^R *CHAIRMAN.*

JAMES CAMPBELL ESQ^R	W. G. MITCHELL ESQ^R
JOHN HENDERSON ESQ^R	JOHN MILLER ESQ^R
GEORGE STIRLING ESQ^R	R. DOUGLAS ALSTON ESQ^R
ARCH^D SMITH ESQ^R	HUGH MILLER ESQ^R
THOMAS D. DOUGLAS ESQ^R	WILLIAM BROOKS ESQ^R

Secretary.	Manager.
J. F. SMITH ESQ^R	WILLIAM JOHNSTONE ESQ^R
Engineer.	Resident Engineer.
JOHN MILLER ESQ^R	WILLIAM M^cCANDLISH ESQ^R
Contractors.	Manager of Works.
MESS^{RS} ROSS & MITCHELL.	MR JOHN FULTON.

ENG^D BY ALLAN & FERGUSON,
GLASGOW.

5.27 Foundation Plaque of Ballochmyle Viaduct (*Author's Collection*)

September 1846, according to the rights of masonry, by George Fullarton of Fullarton, Grand Master of Kilwinning and Provincial Grand Master of Ayrshire, and work commenced on constructing a massive sandstone viaduct, the central arch of which was to be the longest masonry arch in the world.

On the day that the foundation stone was laid, dignitaries met at the George Hotel in Kilmarnock before being conveyed to Mauchline. At the foundations of the viaduct two platforms were constructed for the party, and the foundation stone was lifted by a crane and laid in place. Below it a zinc box was placed containing various artefacts – copies of the *Kilmarnock Herald, Kilmarnock Journal, Ayr Observer, Ayr Advertiser, Glasgow Herald, Citizen, North British Advertiser, North British Railway and Shipping Gazette, Reformers' Gazette* and copies of the Acts of Parliament relating to the construction of the railway. The box also contained an impression of a zinc plate with details of the laying of the foundation stones, a programme of the day's proceedings, a ticket of invitation, and one each of all gold and silver coins of the realm. When the foundation stone had been laid and the ceremony was finished, the principle party of 300 returned to Kilmarnock where a banquet was served at the George Hotel.

At the laying of the foundation stone, between 6,000 and 10,000 spectators were present, the good weather bringing people from all over to witness the event. The procession gathered in a field on the north side of the village, before setting out to the bridge.

Trains carrying members of numerous masonic lodges were run to Kilmarnock, from where carriages took the visitors to the gorge. In Mauchline the crowds were considerable, the reporter for the *Ayr Advertiser* noting that:

> Here all was gaiety, animation, and enthusiasm; the numerous trades and masonic bodies, with bands of music, flags, and the various insignia of their craft, were mustering; crowds of pedestrians, in holiday attire, were pouring in from the surrounding villages; while vehicles of every description, from the dashing landau to the slow but safe country spring-cart, crowded the streets, every face beaming with happiness and joy…
>
> The procession moved from the place of rendezvous to the scene of operations about one o'clock. It extended to about a mile in length, and consisted of 26 masonic lodges, with 12 bands of music, accompanied with banners and all the other splendid trappings and insignia proper to the 'brethren of the mystic tie.' From the importance attached to the occasion, the inhabitants of Catrine had resolved to celebrate it by a holiday, and business having there accordingly been suspended, the villagers turned out to the number 700 to 800, marshalled in the Mill Square, and joined the procession. Among

these were 300 females, whose fancy dresses and decorations, and fair countenances, had a very pleasing effect as they moved along. The whole line of march, from the town to the Bridge, was thronged with a concourse of people. Arrived at the site, the various sections of the procession took up their allotted stations…

The application of the square, the plumb, and the level to the stone, having been gone through with the accustomed formalities, the Grand Master gave three knocks upon the stone, pronouncing the masonic benediction in these words:- 'May the Grand Architect of the Universe grant a blessing on this foundation-stone which we have now laid, and, by his Providence, enable us to finish this great undertaking.' Having concluded this portion of the ceremony, three tumultuous cheers, that made the welkin ring, were given by the assembled multitude, which were followed by a salute of twenty-one guns from the battery erected for the occasion, as if warning the rural deities who had long reigned undisturbed in the solitudes of the woods, that they must now retire before the march of science and civilization…

Wine and oil having been poured over the stone, and the cornucopia containing ears of corn emptied of its contents, the Rev Dr A Campbell of Kilwinning offered up a prayer, at once solemn and appropriate, for the Sovereign, the success of the undertaking, the people, etc.

On the day of the official opening a commemorative engraving was presented to a number of those present as official guests. This indicates that the ceremony was more of a Masonic event than a railway celebration:

The
Foundation Stone of this Viaduct
on the line of the
Cumnock Branch of the Glasgow, Paisley, Kilmarnock & Ayr Railway
was laid according to the ancient usages of Masonry
on the fifth day of September
in the Year of Our Lord One Thousand, Eight Hundred & Forty Six,
in the tenth year of the reign of
Her Majesty Queen Victoria,
and in the year of Masonry Five Thousand, Eight Hundred and Forty Six.

Officers of Mother Kilwinning Lodge.
George Fullarton Esqr. of Fullarton MWGM & PGM
George Johnstone Esqr. of Redburn MWDM

John Wyllie Esqr. Kilwinning, Senior Grand Warden
James Small Esqr. Kilwinning, Junior Grand Warden
James Blair Esqr. Kilwinning, Secretary
Robert Dickie Esqr. Kilwinning, Treasurer
Revd. Dr. Archd. Campbell, Chaplain
Bryce Conn, Tyler

Railway Directors
James McCall Esqr, Chairman
James Campbell Esqr. W.G. Mitchell Esqr.
John Henderson Esqr. John Miller Esqr.
George Stirling Esqr. R. Douglas Alston Esqr.
Archd. Smith Esqr. Hugh Miller Esqr.
Thomas D. Douglas Esqr. William Brooks Esqr.

Secretary	Manager
J.F. Smith Esqr.	William Johnstone Esqr.
Engineer	Resident Engineer
John Miller Esqr.	William McCandlish Esqr.
Contractors	Manager of Works
Messrs. Ross & Mitchell	Mr. John Fulton

The main arch is semi-circular in shape, and has a span from side to side of 180 feet. From the bed of the River Ayr to the crown of the arch is 160 feet, to the level of rails – 165 feet. There are three lesser arches to either side of the principal arch, each of these having a span of fifty feet.

The construction of this massive arch required scaffolding of some size and strength, constructed from Baltic pine. There were 1,200 logs of 14 inches in diameter used in the construction of the scaffold alone. At one level the scaffolding was wider than the proposed width of the viaduct, and along this rails were affixed, supporting a travelling crane, which could be used to carry and lift the massive sandstone blocks used in the construction of the bridge.

The stone for the bridge was quarried locally, although the main hard bluish stones forming the outside ring of the arch came from a quarry near to Dundee. This stone was transported by ship from Troon harbour, from where the blocks were hauled to Ballochmyle on what were called 'jankers'. The construction of the bridge was technically advanced for its time. The main piers are not solid, there being vertical inspection shafts within the piers.

The construction work employed 400 labourers and masons, under the direction of John Fulton, manager of works. Many of the labourers employed in the building work were Irish, and a number of them are known to have erected temporary huts for themselves nearby using stones, turf and timber. The main crane was powered by an eight-horse power steam engine.

The keystone of the bridge was inserted on 8 April 1847 by William Alexander, just seven months after the foundation stone, and the final stone was put in place on 12 March 1848. On the parapet of the bridge is an unfinished inscription – *THE LAST STONE OF THIS STRUCTURE WAS LAID ON THE … DAY OF …* – though why it was never completed is unknown.

Although the viaduct was completed, it had to stand for around eighteen months until the remaining bridges on the Kilmarnock-Auchinleck line were completed. It was reckoned that the bridge cost £100,000 to construct.

It has often been reported that the viaduct was erected without any major accidents or fatalities, but this appears to be untrue. An Irish labourer, Barney Burns, was killed on Friday 17 September 1847 when he tried to jump onto one of the stone trucks. A mason's labourer, the rules stated that he should not have done this, but he fell from the truck onto the rails. The waggon passed over his head, killing him instantly. Another workman, far luckier, fell from the scaffolding during the construction and landed in the river, 160 feet below. The water broke his fall, and he was rescued uninjured.

On 1 September 1870 a branch line from Mauchline to Ayr was opened, with stations at St Quivox, Annbank and Tarbolton, the last-named being over one mile distant from the village.

In 1897 a siding at Garrochburn was created which was used as a goods station for local farmers.

5.28 Ballochmyle Viaduct around 1900 *(Author's Collection)*

A number of accidents occurred on the railway, such as on 31 July 1874 when a collision of wagons took place at Mauchline station. Slightly earlier that year, in February 1874, the son of Francis Logan, stationmaster, was killed on the railway.

In the latter part of the nineteenth century there were plans for a further railway through the parish. The Muirkirk, Mauchline and Dalmellington Railway would have passed from east to west through the district, passing Sorn and reaching Mauchline. The bill for this railway was passed by parliament in 1895, but the railway was never constructed. The cost of the railway was estimated to have been £521,880. The scheme was abandoned in 1900, and by 1903, with the line undeveloped, the remaining partners in the scheme were trying to reclaim their deposits from parliament.

5.29 Painting of Ballochmyle Viaduct *(Private Collection)*

LEISURE

The Glasgow Mauchline Society was founded on 10 February 1888 by John Leiper Gemmill (1857-1934) at a public meeting in the Alexandra Hotel in Glasgow. The first president was Hamilton Marr of Govan. Gemmill was born at Muirside in Kilmarnock parish, but was educated at Mauchline Public School, followed by Kilmarnock Academy. He then went on to study at Glasgow University before setting up in business in the city.

It was proposed that a memorial should be erected at Mossgiel in memory of Robert Burns, and that it should be erected in time for the centenary of his death in 1896. It was decided that the monument should not only commemorate Burns, but also be more practical and benevolent. Accordingly a monument with convalescent homes was planned. The Society was responsible for raising funds with which to erect the National Burns Memorial and Cottage Homes.

An architectural competition was organised and a variety of architects submitted entries. Among these was one by the Glasgow architect, William F. McGibbon (1856-1923) which included a two-storey tower, with glazed cupola, and cottages of a Flemish style, with curvilinear gables. The winning entry was by another architect based in Glasgow, William Fraser (1867-1922), who produced a neo-baronial style tower with adjoining cottages. The first sod of the tower foundations was cut on 4 July 1896 by J. Leiper Gemmill, and he was presented with a miniature silver spade to commemorate the event. The foundation stone was laid on 23 July 1896 with full Masonic honours by Hugh R. Wallace of Busbie and Cloncaird, Provincial Grand Master of Ayrshire. It was estimated that over 10,000 people attended on that day. A banquet took place in the afternoon within the grounds of Netherplace House, chaired by J. Leiper Gemmill. Present were Annie Burns and Margaret Burns Hutchinson, grand-daughter and great grand-daughter of the poet. The cost of the tower and homes was in the region of £2,500. The Glasgow Mauchline Society contributed £3,000 towards the project, the surplus funds being used to start an endowment for future maintenance. It was hoped that £5,000 would be raised for this, and at the time the memorial was opened £4,410

5.30 Burns Monument around 1900 (*Author's Collection*)

had been raised. J. Leiper Gemmill, who founded the Glasgow Mauchline Society, died on 22 March 1934.

The official opening took place on Saturday 7 May 1898. Newmilns Brass Band played, the Ayrshire Yeomanry paraded and a massive crowd turned out to witness the opening. A march from Mauchline to Mossgiel took place, and speeches were delivered by the treasurer of the Cottage Homes, Thomas Killin, the President of the Glasgow Mauchline Society, Marcus Bain, and John G. A. Baird of Wellwood MP. The tower had cost £1,515 2s 11d to build. Constructed of Ballochmyle sandstone, the tower stands 67 feet in height. The first five cottages had been occupied since November 1897. One of the first tenants was the widow of a great-grandson of Burns himself.

In 1886 the Jolly Beggars Burns Club of Mauchline was established to promote the works of Robert Burns. The club became federated to the Burns Federation, as club number 28. In the years up to the turn of the century the president was James Young of Haughyett, the secretary being Hugh Mair of Hillhead. The club met in Poosie Nansie's Inn.

Mauchline Races continued to be held into the nineteenth century, on the last Thursday of April. The route followed by the horses was from Mauchline along Kilmarnock Road and left onto Tarbolton Road. Old Ordnance Survey maps state 'Mauchline Races Held Here' on Tarbolton Road. Originally the race appears to have been 80 yards in length, but it was later increased to 100 yards.

On 8 May 1809 a meeting of the merchants and inhabitants of the village took place concerning the races. The meeting passed a resolution, which stated that:

> The principal inhabitants of the town [sic] of Mauchline considering that the races which has been accustomed to be held there the third Thursday of April, O. S., every year is of great advantage to the town, and considering also that great inconvenience has arisen from the want of a proper arrangement for the management of the business thereof, have entered into the following resolutions:
> 1. That they shall meet twice every year, the first meeting to be held upon the first Monday of April, and the second upon the Monday immediately succeeding to the race.
> 2. That at the second meeting of every year they shall elect a Presses whose office shall be to preside at all meetings, and to give the necessary order for the calling the same. He shall likewise sign the minute of every meet.
> 3. That after the Presses is elected he shall choose some person to be clerk during his time that he is in office, whose business it shall be to engross in a book kept for the purpose, a minute of every meeting and any other thing which the meeting shall think proper

to record. That any person refusing to accept of any office after being elected shall pay a fine the extent of which a majority of the meeting shall determine.

At a meeting held on 28 May, Dr Dugald Hamilton was elected as Presses; he nominated James MacKerrow, merchant, as clerk. The second meeting was arranged to take place in the home of Hugh MacClelland, carrier. It was decided that Robert Paterson, Thomas MacClelland, and Alexander Beattie should be the judges for the race meeting, and that the starting hour should be two o' clock precisely. The committee was allocated 'quarters' of the village to collect funds for the prizes, and when they reconvened a total of £7 16s 7d had been raised. At the first race after the reconstituted meeting, the first prize was £4, second place getting £1 10s.

In 1811 it was agreed that first prize should not be more than four guineas in cash, the second prize to be determined by the judges. From 1811 until 1821 there appears to have been no racing due to a dispute which seems to have taken place. The minutes were blank, and the next entry occurred in 1821. A race took place that year, and first prize was £3 3s 0d.

In 1826 the race did not take place, for no horses came forward to take part. The poor prize fund was blamed, as well as perhaps a lack of publicity. It was determined that on the following year the first prize should be raised to five sovereigns, and that advertisements would be placed in the *Ayr Observer and Courier*, the *Glasgow Herald*, and that hand bills would be distributed. This race went ahead, with first place getting £5, second ten shillings and third 7 shillings and sixpence. In 1828 the race again suffered from a lack of entries, only one horse and rider turning up. It was agreed to pay the jockey £1 for his trouble.

With the prize fund not being required in 1828, and with a growing balance held in the parish bank, it was proposed that £12 of the £21 funds should be used for the purpose of procuring lamps for the village. This was agreed, and a sub-committee was formed to see this through. The race of 1829 has the winners recorded – first was Mr Alexander, getting £5, second place went to Mr Aitken, who got 7s 6d, and third was Mr Mills, who received the same amount.

In 1834 extra funds raised by the race committee were used to improve the roads in the Cowgate and the Back Street. The minute book records that, 'It was proposed and seconded, and unanimously agreed to, that a sum of 50 shillings Sterling should be given to the proprietors in the Cowgate; fifty shillings to the proprietors in the Back Street, from William Ronald's round to Matthew Muir's, and 50 shillings to the proprietors from John Campbell's to Mr Finnie's house on the Burn, on the condition of the raising the causeway in the streets, and macadamising the same in a sufficient and substantial manner. The proprietors in the Cowgate covering the siver at Calderwood's and carrying the repair from Calderwood's corner to the junction of the Catrine Road. The proprietors of the Back Street, carrying the repair from the corner of Mr Ronald's house, to the junction at Matthew Muir's, and the other from John Campbell's to the bridge. It being expressly understood that the sum given from the funds to the public's subscription and no aid is to be asked by the proprietors from the public.' The committee would ensure that the work was carried out properly. In 1835 it was noted that £2 10s had been paid for the repair of the Cowgate, a similar sum for the Back Street, and 15 shillings for the repair of Greenhead Road.

In 1838 the race committee disbursed more funds to purchase a further ten lamps for the village. These, like the other lamps already erected, were gas lamps, the coal-gas used in them being piped from the gas works. The cost of the lamps plus erection was £12 9s 6d, the burners cost £1 10s 0d and the gas cost was £2 5s 0d.

Only one horse was entered in 1846, so the owner, James Crawford, was awarded £1. As a contrast, in 1849, 'owing to the number and superiority of the horses that came forward, and having made a good race, and for the encouragement to others in future years they though proper to augment the prizes , first to £5.' Also that year it was noted 'The great falling off in the number attending our race of former years being spoke of athletic sports being mentioned intend thereof as an inducement to a greater attention of the public. The following persons were elected as a provisional committee with power given to call a meeting of the inhabitants and to have the alteration carried into effect should it meet with approbation.' This committee did not proceed with the proposed athletic sports at this time.

The minute book of the race committee from 1850 to 1905 has gone missing, and we can only assume that the race was carried on, horses permitting, as in previous years.

A library was established in Mauchline by the first half of the nineteenth century. In 1837 it was noted that the books in the library were not numerous, but that new volumes were added to it annually. Membership of the library cost five shillings, with three shillings payable annually. In addition to this library, in the first half of the nineteenth century, there was a religious tract and book society.

The Temperance Hall was erected in New Road, between the first of the new houses on the east side and the Mauchline Burn, around 1870. The public library was relocated here, having around two thousand books available to lend. Temperance, or abstinence from alcohol, was a popular trait in the nineteenth century. Mauchline Total Abstinence Society was formed in 1840 and survived for a number of years.

The growth in popularity of football spread across Scotland in the late nineteenth century, and Mauchline men were keen to get involved. Mauchline Football Club was founded in 1873, playing in the field at Clelland Park, owned by Ballochmyle estate. The team used the Loudoun Arms Hotel hall for their changing room, and they played in blue and white stripes (jersey and socks) with white shorts.

The club appears to have become very successful, and by 1877 the *Kilmarnock Standard* noted in a draw between Mauchline and Kilmarnock Portland F. C. that 'Mauchline [is] one of the best clubs in Ayrshire.' Similarly, in 1878, the paper noted that 'the career of Mauchline is well-known. For the last two years they have been the terror of the county, and in their cup ties they have beaten all-comers in a most decided manner.' The club played in various local cups, as well as in fundraising games, such as that held in 1877 to raise funds for those suffering as a result of an explosion at Blantyre's Dixon's No. 3 Pit, where over 200 men and boys were killed.

In 1877 the first Ayrshire Cup, purchased at a cost of £150, was played for, the competition being between twenty clubs. The first game Mauchline played in the event was against Burnfoothill Ramblers, winning 16-nil. Mauchline beat all other teams and reached the final against Kilmarnock Portland. Mauchline won by four goals to two. The team comprised R. Davidson (goal-keeper), Hugh Wilson, John Smith, H. Train, A. Mair, W. Wilson, J. Howie, W. MacIlvean, W. Tannock, A. MacIlvean and J. MacMinn.

Mauchline also played in the Scottish Cup, and managed to beat a number of larger teams. The competition against Kilmarnock seems to have been fierce, and a number of battles erupted between them. In 1876-77 they beat Kilmarnock 2-1 at Rugby Park, resulting in an objection to Mauchline's winning goal. The referee upheld this objection, but the Scottish Football Association overturned the rule and awarded the tie to Mauchline. In the 1879-80 cup tie against Kilmarnock Mauchline were to win 6-2. In 1880-81, in front of a crowd of 3,000, Mauchline beat Kilmarnock 2-1, but again Kilmarnock objected, claiming that the game had not lasted the full 90 minutes. Their complaint was upheld, and a replay was ordered. The match was drawn three goals each, but in the following game Mauchline beat Killie 3-0. In 1881 Kilmarnock put Mauchline out of the cup in the first round, beating them 2-0, the first time that the Mauchline team had been beaten in the first round of the cup. The best Mauchline ever did in the Scottish cup was to reach the last eight, but after 1891, when the cup structure was reorganised, the team was no longer eligible.

Support for the Mauchline team was considerable during the glory years of the 1870s and 1880s, several thousand spectators turning out to watch them. By 1886 things had started to take a turn for the worse and the club did not do so well in subsequent competitions. Although the club had played against other senior clubs, such as Queen's Park and Glasgow Rangers, by 1897 the team had to drop out of senior football, joining instead the ranks of the junior football teams. As Mauchline Thistle Football Club, they played in the junior football cup.

It was in 1879, at a game against Mauchline, that Lugar Boswell Thistle F. C. introduced the famous 5-3-2-1 formation, previously teams usually playing in the 8-1-1-1 formation or 6-2-2-1 formation.

Some of the Mauchline players were selected to play for their country. One of the most notable was Dr John Smith, of Springfield, who played against England on six occasions – 1877, 1879, 1880, 1881, 1883, 1884, scoring on various occasions. He also played against Wales in 1877, 1879, 1881 and 1883. Smith is also credited with introducing football to the University of Edinburgh, for the Scottish Football Association annual for 1878-79 noted that, 'J. S. Smith, of Mauchline, is a very reliable forward, with rare speed, and a good dodger, passing judiciously. We have every reason to thank Mr Smith for having introduced the Association games to Edinburgh University.'

Hugh Wilson, who was 'a good and clever forward', played for Scotland against Wales in 1885.

The sport of curling became very popular in the nineteenth century. Mauchline Curling Society was founded and held its first annual general meeting on 20 November1812. At first the curlers met in different locations, but in 1812 one acre of ground was offered to the curlers at Greenhead farm, where a loch could be created. Following a meeting held in the school on 17 February 1812 it was agreed to rent the acre at £3 6s 6d for the year. A new loch was created, known as the North Loch, or Nor' Loch. This was located along what became known as Loch Road and it had four unequal straight sides. By 2 December 1812 the club had 90 members. The first president was David Muir, The cost of constructing the loch meant that the club remained in debt until 1817.

On 2 January 1821 the club was reconstituted following an offer from Campbell of Netherplace to lease the loch for seven years at 16s per annum. This was accepted, and in 1888 a new curling house was erected alongside the loch. In 1871 the Curling Society was reconstituted as the Mauchline General Curling Club.

The club was divided into five subsidiary clubs, each one seemingly covering an area of the town. These were known as Netherplace Curling Club, Mauchline Senior Curling Club (affiliated to Grand Caledonian Curling Club in 1838, but left in 1880), Thistle Curling Club, Burns Curling Club and Town Curling Club.

In the mid-1800s there appears to have been major rivalry between Sorn and Mauchline clubs, resulting in a major dispute. According to the minutes, in 1860 there was an attempt at a friendly match between the clubs, but 'the wound was made deeper by the unreasonableness of some in power in said parish of Sorn'. On 23 January 1871, after 29 years, a truce was arranged by Colonel Alexander of Ballochmyle and Mr Somervell of Sorn. A match was arranged, food and drink supplied, and a bonspiel with 80 players a side resulted in the difficulty being forgotten, though Sorn won by 67 shots. In February 1873 Claud Alexander of Ballochmyle presented Mauchline General Curling Club with the 'Silver Ice Stone', a silver curling-stone shaped trophy.

A second curling pond was located at Netherplace House, known as Netherplace Loch. Rectangular in shape, this pond was situated on the west side of drive from South Lodge to Netherplace House and was surrounded by woodland.

Within Ballochmyle House policies were a further two curling ponds. One of these, the larger of the two, was located adjoining the northern drive into the estate. The second was positioned alongside the wood across the road from the sawmill. Both were rectangular in plan, indicative of being man-made.

Archery was a fairly popular sport across Scotland in the nineteenth century. In Mauchline the shooting of arrows at targets, in some cases dressed as parrots, or papingoes, seems to have been followed by some men of the district. The Eglinton Tournament of 1839, when the Earl of Eglinton held a massive mediaeval festival at Eglinton Castle in Kilwinning, had a major archery competition as part of its activities. A team from Mauchline, known as the Ballochmyle Archeresses, took part on that occasion. The interest in archery grew for a period after the famous tournament, and a regular meeting was held at Ballochmyle House, home at the time of Sir Claud Alexander.

Quoiting was played by the lower classes in the villages of Ayrshire. A pitch of clay was made at various locations in the area, and circular rings of iron were thrown at a pin, similar to a target in curling. In Mauchline the quoiting ground appears to have been established adjoining the Loan in 1808, in part of a field known as Burngrange Park. Although mainly played by the less well-off, the sport was encouraged by the local gentry, for in 1840 a silver quoit was presented by Claud Alexander of Ballochmyle as a prize. This remained the principal prize for the remainder of the century and into the next. The first winner of the quoit was Alex Smith of Mauchline. In 1842 a game of quoits was played in the nearby parish of Craigie, the winning team being awarded the Ballochmyle Silver Quoit. On that occasion Claud Alexander also paid for the players and umpires to dine that night. Although he visited the meal, it was reported that the laird of Ballochmyle did not dine with them. The Silver Quoit was to be won by Robert Kirkland of Mauchline on no less than twelve times between 1849 and 1873, a record that was to stand for many years.

The quoiting competition failed for a few years, but in 1882 it was revived, and played annually thereafter. The only Mauchline player to win it in the new games in the nineteenth century was Hugh Train, who won it in 1891.

In 1860 'Old' Tom Morris (1821-1908) came to Mauchline to try out an experiment with golf clubs and balls. He stood in the quarry beneath the Ballochmyle Viaduct and, using a stick that was elevated horizontally, he attempted to hit golf balls over the bridge. Although he was able to hit the balls to the pathway, four hundred feet above the level of where he stood, he was unable to hit balls over the viaduct. However, his ability to hit the old gutta ball such a height was regarded as a great feat.

Early in 1867 the first steps were made in the formation of Mauchline Bowling Club. The club was formed in August that year, and a site for a bowling green was acquired. At the time the Glasgow and South Western Railway was being constructed by Messrs Mitchell & Ireland, and Mr Ireland, engineer of the firm, helped the club with the levelling of the green and other tasks. The green was laid over a rock, meaning that it often became too dry. At the time fifty £1 shares were subscribed, and by the time the green as opened in 1868 a total of £118 had been raised. The first president of the club was Gavin Hamilton (who served from 1868-1874), grandson of Burns' contemporary, Gavin Hamilton. Other long-serving presidents from the nineteenth century were David MacQueen (nine years) and John hay (eight years). When the club was founded, the ladies presented a silver jack for annual competition. The club grew over the years, the clubhouse being erected in 1899 by Thomas Findlay & Sons at a cost of around £30, the funds raised by a bazaar.

In the mid nineteenth century Mauchline Cricket Club was formed, but it seems not to have lasted for very long.

In the early to mid-nineteenth century the St Mungo Lodge of Freemasons existed in the village. How long this lodge survived is not known.

The masonic lodge in Mauchline was re-established in 1869 when the Lodge St David (Tarbolton) Number 133 was re-established in the village. Originally Lodge Tarbolton Kilwinning was chartered on 17 May 1771, under the Kilwinning jurisdiction, but some members felt that they should have a lodge under the Grand Lodge of Scotland, so formed a separate lodge on 5 February 1773, known as Lodge St David Tarbolton, Number 174. The original lodge joined the Grand Lodge as Lodge St James, Number 178, in 1774. The two lodges were small, and soon realised that strength was in numbers, so on 25 June 1781 merged as Lodge St David Tarbolton, Number 174.

Within a short time, on 4 July 1781, Robert Burns was initiated as a member, paying a fee of 12s 6d. The master at the time was Joseph Norman, and Burns was passed and raised on 1 October 1781. The lodge had some difficulties and in June 1782 was broken. Burns remained a brother of Lodge St James, becoming Depute Master on 27 July 1784.

Lodge St David became dormant in 1843, the minute books passing into private hands. However, the Charter was recovered by the Provincial Grand Master and retained by the Grand Lodge of Scotland. When the lodge was re-opened in Mauchline, in 1879, the principal instigator was Thomas Harvie (1845-1917), solicitor, of Dunloy, Barskimming Road.

SONS OF THE PARISH

In the parish kirkyard the wife of George Julian Harney, one of the greatest Chartist activists, was buried, and a memorial was erected over her grave. George Julian Harney was born on 17 February 1817 at Deptford in south-east London, the son of a seaman, George Harney, and Sarah Southcott. At the age of eleven he entered the Boy's Naval School at Greenwich but left to become a shop-boy for Henry Hetherington, who edited the *Poor Man's Guardian*. The newspaper was unstamped, and Harney was imprisoned three times for selling it. Harney became a strong radical, and was one of the founders of the republican East London Democratic Association in January 1837. In 1839 he toured Britain promoting a 'Grand National Holiday', or general strike, to be held on 12 August that year. In his speeches he said:

5.31 Julian Harney's gravestone *(Dane Love)*

We demand Universal Suffrage, because we believe the universal suffrage will bring universal happiness. Time was when every Englishman had a musket in his cottage, and along with it hung a flitch of bacon; now there was no flitch of bacon for there was no musket; let the musket be restored and the flitch of bacon would soon follow. You will get nothing from your tyrants but what you can take, and you can take nothing unless you are properly prepared to do so. In the words of a good man, then, I say 'Arm for peace, arm for liberty, arm for justice, arm for the rights of all, and the tyrants will no longer laugh at your petitions'. Remember that.

Harney was arrested with others for making seditious speeches and the strike was cancelled. At his trial he was acquitted. George Harney then moved to Ayrshire, where he married Mary Cameron on 14 September 1840 in Mauchline. He was to return south the following year and organised strikes in Sheffield. Following his arrest he was convicted of sedition, but this was reversed following an appeal. Harney then became a journalist with the Chartist *Northern Star*, becoming its editor in 1845. Harney's interest in international suffrage resulted in him meeting with notable men such as Karl Marx and Friedrich Engels. George Harney became a keen proponent of socialism and had to resign his position with the *Northern Star*. He was one of the first people in Britain to become a Marxist, and first to publish the 'Communist Manifesto' in English. He then set up his own newspaper, the *Red Republican*. In 1848 he stood as the Chartist Candidate in the election against Lord Palmerston, the Foreign Secretary, for the seat of Tiverton in Devon. Although Harney won on the show of hands, Lord Palmerston demanded a poll, and Harney decided to retire from standing. George Harney established a number of other periodicals, the *Red Republican* being financially disastrous, but these were short lived. He then worked for the *Northern Tribune* and the *Jersey Independent*.

Harney's wife, Mary, appears to have died around 1853 and was buried in the kirkyard at Mauchline.

In May 1863 Harney emigrated to the United States, where he worked as a clerk in the Massachusetts State House for the next fourteen years. He returned to England after his retiral and contributed articles to the *Newcastle Chronicle*. He died on 9 December 1897 at Richmond, after suffering poor health for a number of years. He was married twice, his second wife, Marie LeSuer, widow of James Metivier, being a teacher at Boston, Massachusetts.

Adam Brown Todd was born at Craighall farm on 6 February 1822, the fourteenth child of a small tenant farmer. Craighall stood on the northern side of Glover's Hill, between the farms of Barwheys and Boghead (of which it became part). It no longer exists. Todd's father, Matthew (1768-1850), had taken on the lease at Whitsunday 1795. He was a contemporary of Robert Burns, and knew him. His mother, Mary Gibb (1779-1861), was the daughter of James Gibb of Auchmillan. The Todds moved to Barrshouse, in the parish of Sorn, in 1826. A. B. Todd was to become a journalist, writing for the *Cumnock Express*, as well as a minor poet, four volumes of his verse being published. He was also the author of a couple of books on the Covenanters, which were popular in their day. These were *Homes, Haunts and Battlefields of the Covenanters*, published in 1886 and 1888, and *Covenanting Pilgrimages and Studies*, published in 1911. He was also active in erecting memorials to the Covenanters, the monument in Cumnock to Rev Alexander Peden, being a notable example. He died on Sunday 31 January 1915 aged 92. He was buried in Cumnock New Cemetery, where a tall sandstone headstone marks his grave.

5.32 Adam Brown Todd *(Author's Collection)*

A few Mauchline characters' names are still known from the nineteenth century. One of these was 'Blind Archie' who was a noted fiddler. He often travelled across Ayrshire playing his fiddle at various events, and from his takings was able to keep himself. He was also a noted bird fancier, and though blind, it was said that he could tell the colour of a bird's feathers just by touching them, and thus work out what type of bird it was. Blind Archie lived in Loudoun Street, and he had a small room at the back of his house in which he kept as a small aviary.

Another local character was 'Auld Jockie', or John Clark Senior. He died at the age of ninety years early in the twentieth century, but for much of the nineteenth century he was known in the village for being the bellman.

CHAPTER SIX

A TIME OF WARS

VILLAGE LIFE

The Census of 1901 stated that the population of Mauchline village had grown to 1,767. The parish population in 1901 was 2,572. Another census took place in 1911, at which time the population of the parish had fallen to 2,441. By 1936 the village population was estimated at 2,000. There was no Census in 1941 due to the war.

		Parish	*Village*
1901	-	2,572	1,767
1911	-	2,441	
1921	-	2,357	
1931	-	2,484	

The census threw up various other pieces of information, such as in 1931 the average number of occupants per room in each house in the parish was 1.13, which was the lowest, and thus best, in the old Cumnock and Doon Valley area.

The parish council was under the chairmanship of Mr Young in 1902, the Inspector being James Allan. By 1916 the chairman was Lt Col W. K. Hamilton-Campbell DSO. He was followed by John Gilbert. The council met monthly in the Council Chambers, located in Earl Grey Street in a building owned by John Findlay, joiner, Horwood Place.

The Parish Council was responsible for poor relief in the district. In 1918 the council received grants of £5 7s 6d for poor law and medical relief; £38 9s 10d for pauper lunatics; and their proportion of agricultural rates grant was £62 0s 6d. John Fisher, Inspector of Poor for the parish from 1908-1911, moved on to a similar position at Maybole. Elliot Gray was appointed Parish Clerk and Inspector of the Poor in April 1919. He also served as session clerk and treasurer of the parish church.

The local councillor who sat on Ayr County Council at the turn of the century was still Marcus Bain, who lived at Woodside, a large villa in Station Road. Bain played a prominent part in the life of the town, being a Justice of the Peace and chairman of the School Board. He was also a leading light in the committee which established the Glenafton Sanatorium at New Cumnock, which opened in June 1906.

6.1 Earl Grey Street in 1904 *(Author's Collection)*

The Ayrshire Constabulary had a base in Mauchline, the police station at the turn of the twentieth century being located on the north side of Loudoun Street at number 24. Various police constables were based in the village. Among these were Constable Morrison, transferred from Cumnock in 1912, and Constable Alexander MacLean, promoted to sergeant at Galston in 1921. He was replaced by Constable James Burnett, transferred from Glenbuck. The police station was later relocated to Burngrange Lane.

In 1901 the local police compiled crime statistics, and it was noted that in Mauchline the number of offences recorded to the end of December 1901 was 22. In the following year this had dropped to 17.

Similarly, the registrar filed returns, such as the fact that by the year end of 15 May 1916 there had been 47 interments in the cemetery.

Developments in transport and roadways were being made at the turn of the century, and some of the road surfaces in the village were to be covered with tarmacadam. The Cross was one of the first places where this took place, the old cobbled area being covered around 1908.

The Mossgiel Tunnel underwent major renovations in 1924-26. Hundreds of workers came to the area to work on the tunnel, requiring the construction of temporary wooden houses for them. One of these had 85 beds within it. In addition, there was a joiner's shop, blacksmith's shop, and other facilities. An electricity cable was supplied from Kilmarnock to the camp, the first real use of mains power in the area.

Electricity became more generally available in the village soon after, and some of the better-off households converted their lighting to it. The supply to the village from Kilmarnock Power Station arrived in 1926, en route to Auchinleck and Cumnock. In October 1926 the first 34 electric streetlights were erected in the village, greatly adding to the safety of the inhabitants, and over the following years they eventually replaced the original gas lamp standards. By the winter of 1926-27 thirty houses were connected to the supply for the first time. Electric lighting was installed in some streets in February 1927, and when the war memorial was erected street lamps were placed around it. In 1943 the Jean Armour Burns Houses in Castle Street were converted to electric lighting.

For many years a lot of Mauchline village was supplied from an old artesian well located at the upper end of the Loan Green. With an increasing population and growing industry, the supply soon became insufficient, so in 1901-02 Ayr County Council bored an artesian well to supply water to the village. Plans for this were drawn up by W. R. Copland, Glasgow. This water was stored in a vaulted brick chamber off Burngrange Lane. The well supplied water until 1912, when it was found to be insufficient for the demand.

In 1908 new pipes were laid to supply water to the Loudoun Spout. To pay for these a public concert was held on 6 November 1908.

In 1930 the public water supply was improved considerably when the village was connected to the Loch Bradan supply, instigated by Ayrshire County Council. A main pipe was laid from Burns' Monument down the street as far as the Cross, from where a pipe led up to the tank on the hill top.

In 1935-6 the Mauchline water scheme was joined on to the newly-created Afton Reservoir, which was constructed in Glen Afton, south of New Cumnock. This allowed water from the Afton to be piped into Mauchline, supplemented when required by water taken from the larger Loch Bradan scheme. At the northern end of the village, at West Hillhead farm, a covered water storage tank was constructed, storing water for use in the community. This was later to become disused when a greater head of water was supplied from both Afton and Loch Bradan reservoirs.

In 1908 a new local newspaper was published from the press of J. Dickie at the Cross. The *Mauchline & Catrine News and Advertiser* was a four-page newspaper, the first issue being produced on Saturday 11 July 1908. Selling at a halfpenny, the front page contained a number of advertisements for local businesses, such as J. MacPherson, drapery and hardware, the Cross, John Lyall, watchmaker and jeweller of Earl Grey Street, Robert Yuille & Sons, slaters and plumbers. The two inside pages did not contain any local news, being a copy of a national paper, with a story series, national news and cartoons. The back page had local news and comments, some of the news coming from Cumnock, Ochiltree and elsewhere. The newspaper appears to have only lasted a few months before ceasing publication.

In 1909 a *Guide to Mauchline, Catrine, Sorn & Surrounding Districts* was published by J. Dickie & Co. of Ye Burns' Press.

In October 1924 proposals were made to have the houses in the village numbered for the first time.

On 4 April 1930 a bill was passed which extended Mauchline's special water district, special drainage district, and special lighting and scavenging district. The act defined the extent of the village at that time. In 1934 the special scavenging and drainage district was extended to match the special lighting district.

In 1910 five new homes were added to those erected at Burns Monument, bringing the number up to ten in total. These were known as The Dick Terrace, having been paid for by the trustees of James Dick of Glasgow. In February 1923 proposals were made for more cottages to be erected at a cost of £6,000. Numerous fund-raising events were arranged to raise money to build the cottages and endow them, such as a large fete held in the grounds of Ballochmyle House in July 1924. In July 1931 another five cottages (numbers 12-16) were opened at the monument. Erected of red sandstone, the cottage included one with a plaque stating simply Bulloch, a condition of the donor of funds towards the cost. The first sod was cut by Mrs Annie Burns Gowring. The cottages were opened on 18 July 1931 by George Ian Burns Gowring, great, great grandson of the poet. A further two cottages were opened on 26 June 1938. In total 20 of the houses are occupied by deserving old folks, selected from different areas. They pay neither rent nor taxes, and are also paid an annual allowance.

6.2 Burns Memorial Homes *(Dane Love)*

6.3 Burns' House and Castle Street *(Author's Collection)*

The houses and monument were operated by the National Burns Memorial and Cottage Homes, by which name the Glasgow Mauchline Society was called as from 1932. In 1933 the Duke and Duchess of York became patrons of the society, followed by Princess Alice, Duchess of Gloucester.

In 1902 the Glasgow Rosebery Burns Club decided that they would like to erect a marble tablet on Burns' House in Castle Street, as no memorial marked the building. Accordingly, J. & G. Mossman Ltd. of Glasgow were commissioned to produce the memorial, and this was unveiled on 28 June 1902 by Rev James Higgins of Tarbolton.

Burns' House was still in private ownership at this time, the property of a Miss Miller, who let it out to tenants. A few relics of Burns were apparently still in existence, and tenants were often asked to show these off to inquiring visitors. As time passed the house became empty, and began to deteriorate considerably. In 1911 a local society made approaches to buy the building, but proceedings came to nought. In 1915 the owner of the house placed it on the open market, and this came to the attention of various Burns Clubs.

The Glasgow Association of Burns Clubs and Kindred Societies organised a meeting and invited delegates from various clubs. One who attended the meeting was Charles R. Cowie JP, President of Partick Burns Club in Glasgow, and he subsequently paid a visit to the house. After inspecting the property and visiting the National Memorial, he generously put up the money with which to buy the house and carry out some necessary repairs. On Saturday 5 June 1915 the house was informally opened by the association, H. MacColl being the president at the time. On Saturday 28 August 1915 the house was officially opened to the public. A service of dedication was held in the church hall, attended by 400 guests, followed by a service at the house. The museum was officially under the ownership of the Glasgow and District Burns Clubs Association.

Restoration work commenced, and Burns and Jean Armour's bedroom was returned to its original appearance. The adjoining room was fitted out as a museum of Burns' relics. Also purchased were Dr John MacKenzie's House (where work began in November 1916 on the double-storey thatched building by the mason Mungo MacKie), and Auld Nanse Tinnock's. The architect, Ninian MacWhannell FRIBA, was responsible for overseeing the work. When it opened, the museum cost two pence to visit. To guide visitors to the museum, a signpost was erected on Kilmarnock Road at the Back Causey.

The Glasgow and District Burns Association used the other properties to provide accommodation for deserving old aged pensioners. Accordingly, nine old ladies were given rooms in the house, where they lived rent-free and rate free, and were also given a small pension. The endowment fund was started with a donation of £25 from Lord Rosebery. Dr John Mackenzie's house had suffered in a fire, but with another donation from Charles Cowie, it was acquired and once the war was over, restoration work (again under the guidance of Ninian MacWhannell) commenced in 1919. Water and gas were introduced to the house for the first time, and four ladies were given the tenancy of the apartments. This allowed the Burns House Museum to be extended, being formally opened on 12 April 1919 by Mrs Cowie. Following a service in the church, Mrs Cowie was presented with a box made from the rafters of the old house. At the same time a memorial tablet to Gavin Hamilton was unveiled in the kirkyard by Major Carswell of Partick Burns Club, the work of sculptor William Vickers. This bore the inscription, *The burial place of Gavin Hamilton. Born November 1751, died 5th February 1805. A patron and friend of Burns. A poor man's friend in need, a gentleman in word and deed. Erected by Partick Burns Club 1919.*

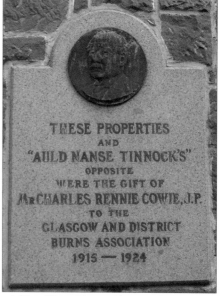

6.4 Burns' House Museum Plaque to Charles Cowie
(Dane Love)

Nanse Tinnock's house was also acquired by the association, bought by Charles Rennie Cowie. On 24 May 1924 the house, which stands across the street from Burns' House, was opened as a home for four female occupants. The house was opened by Mrs C. R. Cowie.

At the same time a red granite slab with a round bas-relief of Cowie was built into the wall of Burns' House, bearing the inscription, *These properties and 'Auld Nanse Tinnock's' opposite were the gift of Mr Charles Rennie Cowie JP to the Glasgow and District Burns Association, 1915-1924*. The bas-relief in bronze was the work of George Henry Paulin (1888-1962). The plaque was unveiled by J. Jeffrey Hunter, secretary of Glasgow and District Burns Association. The Rosebery Burns Club tablet, which formerly occupied the same spot, was relocated within Burns' House, and was unveiled by Councillor J. Kennedy of Glasgow.

Various building developments took place in the village in the Edwardian years, and up to the First World War, when most work ceased. Campbell Place was erected at the western end of Loudoun Street. At the time the old single-storey cottages were demolished and new sandstone buildings erected on the same site. When this took place, the gardens behind the houses were halved in length, previously the feus measuring around 300 feet in length from the road. The land removed from the gardens in Loudoun Street was added to the policies of Netherplace, and was planted with trees. In May 1905 1 Loudoun Street was sold for £450 at auction to Lt Col W. K. Hamilton-Campbell of Netherplace.

At the corner of Cumnock Road with Glebe Avenue, Dr John Reid built a large villa for himself, named Haplan. On his death, the villa was sold to William George Jamieson Pollock.

The Co-operative society continued to develop some properties, building the Glebe Villas (four semi-detached houses) in Cumnock Road.

At the railway station, the stationmaster, John O'Hagan, who lived in the station house, left the position in 1914. He was replaced by James Richmond (1914-1920), whose son, Andrew, was drowned in the First World War. John Reid was stationmaster from 1920-25, followed by William MacInnes. James Kirkland, the railway inspector at Mauchline, retired in 1917. On 26 June 1915 George Young, the Bridge Guard employed at Ballochmyle Viaduct for the duration of the war, was killed as he walked back along the line from Mauchline station to his billet. On 4 March 1920 Edward John Farrow, goods guard at the station, was accidentally killed when he was run over by a train at the age of 42.

Village life went on after the Great War. In 1928 the local registrar recorded a total of 29 deaths, 49 births and 11 marriages.

In July 1927 the thatched roof on Burns' House was removed and the roof replaced in slate. At that time part of the ash rafters was removed and the wood was converted into small gifts by W. and A. Smith's boxworks. One of the items made was a chairman's mallet and plaque, presented to London Burns Club in 1933.

Developments in the village took place in the late 1920s and early 1930s. On Sorn Road, Anthorn, the last villa on the left hand side on leaving the village, was built in 1924 for Dr Andrew Smith Hannay MB ChB. This was to be the first house in Mauchline to be erected by the double-brick and cavity method. Dr Hannay was born on 30 June 1888 and graduated in medicine from Glasgow University on 27 April 1911. He did not remain in Mauchline for very long, moving to London where he continued to practise. The house was owned by Dr Alexander William MacGregor by 1927, followed by Dr Thomas Bliss and Dr David Kemp. Dr Kemp remained living in the house for many years, until around 1976.

Ayr County Council commenced building houses in the village after the First World War. The first of these were sixteen houses erected in Barskimming Road (opposite Brown Terrace) in 1926-27. The county council erected 32 houses off Kilmarnock Road in 1930, built of brick and coated with rough cast. In February 1931, new streetlights were erected in Kilmarnock Road. The scheme of houses off Kilmarnock Road was proposed to be of 240 houses, and by April 1938 23 of these were occupied. In 1940, numbers 52-66 Beechwood Road were still under the course of erection. Similarly, the council also built houses in Barskimming Road, such as 1-6 The Bungalows and 1-16 Park Terrace.

As developments were taking place, an opportunity was taken to demolish many of the older sub-standard houses in the area. In the late 1930s most of the old houses at the Haugh were demolished, the residents being rehoused in Mauchline. By 1940 the six houses in High Celland Park were uninhabitable and they too came down. The cottages built on Glenlee, named Wilson Place, Leafield, were also becoming empty by the war, in 1940 only the first three still occupied, at the time owned by James Campbell & Son, owner of the adjoining smithy.

In 1927 A. C. Riddell, joiner, of Cowgate, gifted the parish council a piece of ground on his property at the top of the Tanfield to improve access.

The Housing (Scotland) Act of 1930 allowed for councils to purchase and demolish older buildings in communities that were past their best, in order to stimulate development. The Mauchline Parish Clearance Areas were thus defined by the Public Health and Diseases of Animals Committee of Ayr County Council on 7 February 1935, resulting in 34 houses of sub-standard quality to be flattened. It was at this time that Mauchline House, or Place, was demolished. In its closing years it was occupied by MacShane's Chip Shop and a bookmaker. The Mauchline House grouping of eleven houses comprised of those within Mauchline House, as well as in the Bellman's Lane, and in High Street as far as the old gateway.

At the Loan a row of five houses at the eastern end were demolished, and in Loudoun Street four small houses were pulled down. In Castle Street four houses located within the large building adjoining Grey's Bridge were demolished, and at the Knowe a further ten houses, located on both sides of the roadway leading from Kilmarnock Road to Castle Street.

The Loudoun Spout, in front of the Loudoun Arms Hotel, stopped flowing mysteriously in August 1937. Investigations discovered that this was due to a burst pipe and soon the normal flow of water resumed.

In July 1939 there were proposals to widen the High Street as part of the developments which planned a new police station. However, the plans did not materialise due to the outbreak of war.

Mauchline Parish Council had formed a fire brigade for the village, the captain in 1916 being James Reid. The fire brigade was eventually disbanded in November 1927 due to a lack of use. It had only been called out to a fire once in the previous five years. It was decided that the village could readily be served from Kilmarnock or Ayr, and the parish council sold the local fire-fighting apparatus. The first fire station had been in a garage in Kilmarnock Road, owned by George MacMillan.

In 1939 a new sewerage scheme for Mauchline was designed and approved by Ayr County Council. This scheme was to cost £11,000 and work was expected to start soon after April 1939.

Mauchline Funeral Society was still in existence in the new century, and by 1919 had £403 in funds. President at the time was James Campbell.

Poosie Nansie's Inn was stilled thatched in 1941 – William Murdoch of Bridgend, Mauchline, fell to his death from the roof on 11 October 1941 whilst thatching it.

The Lousie Tree, which stood by the side of Tarbolton Road, almost opposite Mossgiel farm, was cut down sometime between the two wars. The wood from this tree, which had a long local tradition of being the place where locals met to have a blether, is said to have been taken to the boxworks, where it had been the intention to convert it into souvenirs. However, it is said that the tree never made it, being burned when the rest of the factory was destroyed by fire.

Another notable tree that was lost was the ancient beech tree that grew at the northern end of New Road. It blew over in a gale in November 1926. It just missed the Old Toll Cottage, but did some damage to the new houses adjoining.

A few events in the district caused some interest among the locals over the years. In May 1917 the body of David Geddes was discovered in the Old Quarry near to Haughyett farm by some boys who were looking for rabbits. A native of Dalmellington, he had been missing for three months until his partially decomposed body was discovered. Similarly, accidental deaths caused grief in the area. On 20 April 1918 Thomas Dunlop, aged 5, was killed when he fell off of a van he was hanging onto and was run over by the threshing mill it was pulling. This took place in Earl Grey Street. Similarly, in 1919, Hector Walker died of burns at Martinshill, near Syke farm. A fire at Mossbog farm killed an old worker on 28 March 1922. On 1 September 1922, James Hodge, farmer at Friendlesshead, was found drowned in a pool following his return home from Mauchline. A young girl named Jenny Hogg drowned at the Haugh Bridge in March 1923.

On 23 June 1923 the body of James Brown (aged 52) was found in Crosshands Wood. He had been missing from his Peebles Street home in Ayr for a week. On 6

August 1926 William Tannock, a boy of ten years, was drowned in the reservoir at Catrine Road, whilst playing with friends. The reservoir, which was six feet in depth, had been constructed to fill engines at Mauchline railway station with water. In the same year, on 24 August 1926, David MacTurk, aged 11, on holiday from Clydebank, was drowned in the River Ayr near to Haugh.

The depression of the 1920s, when many strikes took place in the local pits and other businesses, resulted in a number of people being unemployed. Although not as badly affected as other local parishes, where coal-mining was a larger employer, the problems were still felt in Mauchline. In 1921 it was noted that there were thirty unemployed men in the village, and they were given work by repairing the old clay road that linked Mauchline Hilltop with Hillhead.

On a more uplifting note, Sir Harry and Lady Lauder paid a surprise visit to Mauchline on 10 September 1926. He was driving with Mr Thomson of Govan, who was friendly with Archibald Riddell of Mauchline, and they called at his joinery in the Cowgate to meet him. Sir Harry apparently introduced his wife as 'Bonnie Annie', and after a short blether he sang one of his songs. They then moved on to visit Poosie Nansie's and the old kirkyard.

FIRST WORLD WAR

On 4 August 1914 Great Britain declared war against Germany. The Great War had started, and was to last for a further four years, in time becoming known as the First World War. Mauchline was tied up with the struggle, and many men from the parish served in the army.

As part of the national defence network of servicemen, Mauchline Volunteer Company was founded in 1917.

Many soldiers from other lands passed through Mauchline, and various groups were stationed in the district. At one time Canadian soldiers were camped nearby, and prior to being sent to fight on Flanders fields were addressed in the church hall by Rev Dr Joseph Mitchell. Many of the Canadian soldiers were employed in cutting down trees which were used as part of the war effort, for example, in January 1917 the wood at Crosshands was cleared for its timber. The Canadian soldiers were based in Mauchline, taking over the Temperance Hall.

The Young Men's Christian Association took over Mr W. F. Blair's rooms in Loudoun Street and converted them into a hut for use by the soldiers billeted in the district.

Three men who worked at Highhouse Colliery, Auchinleck, were regular fishermen in the Ballochmyle glen. They were called up to serve in the Great War in 1914, and their last meeting together prior to joining the army took place at a spot known as 'The Fisher's Tryst', near to where a small burn joins the River Ayr. The men agreed that they would meet at the same spot once the war was over. However, two of the soldiers were killed in action, and the surviving member of the three returned to the tryst and carved the names of his friends on the vertical sandstone cliff. The inscription includes their names, regiment, army number and where they were killed. In addition, representations of their fishing hooks are carved on the cliff. One inscription reads *In memory of Pte Daivd [sic] Strickland R.S.F. who fel [sic] at Hulloch, Feb 27 1916 in Great War. J.L.* Strickland was born in Sorn and lived in Auchinleck. He enlisted in the 7th Battalion, Royal Scots Fusiliers at Bramshott in Hampshire with service number 17456. He was killed in action in Flanders in France. A second inscription reads, *In memory, Pte G. Rowan, Gordon Highlanders, who fell on 23 Nov at Cambrai 1917. J.L.* George Rowan was born in Prestonpans, Midlothian, and enlisted in the 6th Battalion, Gordon Highlanders at Perth, service number S/41186. He was killed in Flanders. A third inscription is *In memory, Donald Stuart Livingstone, who died at Inghs 1926. J.L.*

6.5 Fisher's Tryst carving *(Dane Love)*

In September 1916 Private Thomas M. Bole, 5th Cameron Highlanders, was awarded the Military Medal for his bravery at the Battle of the Somme. He was the first soldier from Mauchline to receive an honour for his part in the war. He was later to suffer within a German prisoner of war camp. Sergeant Robert Orr was awarded the Military Medal and in 1917 was awarded a Bar to the medal for his bravery. He served with the Royal Scots Fusiliers. The third Mauchline soldier to be awarded the Military Medal was Gunner Thomas MacMillan, RFA. He was given the medal for gallant behaviour. Lance Corporal John Harper, RSF, was awarded the Military Medal in 1917 for gallantry in the field at Salonica front. Captain James Bell of Clelland Park was awarded the Military Cross for his gallantry in the field in 1917. He served with the North Staffordshire Regiment. Private Allan Ramsay of the Argyll & Sutherland Highlanders was awarded the Military Medal for gallantry in the field in 1917. Private John Baird, Gordon Highlanders, was awarded the Military Medal in 1918 for his conspicuous bravery.

To support the sons from the parish in battle, the people of Mauchline regularly had a collection of goods that could be sent to the front. For example, in September 1916, 80 pairs of socks, 9 flannel shirts, 8 pairs of bed-socks, 4 waistcoats, 1 sweater, 100 insect-proof shirts, 22 scarves, 15 pairs of mittens and 4 helmets were sent to soldiers. This sort of collection was repeated for most of the war years. Mauchline woman Mrs W. Templeton (1853-1936), set a record by knitting 277 pairs of socks for the soldiers during the duration of the war, for which she had been presented with a badge by the Mauchline Red Cross Party.

6.6 Fisher's Tryst names *(Dane Love)*

Various flag days were held in the village, often by children under the guidance of James Campbell MA. Numerous fund-raising groups and committees were formed during the war to raise funds for the effort. In 1918 the cinemotor, a travelling exhibition, visited Mauchline to show examples of war pictures. On 15 June the Mauchline War Savings Association was formed and opened for business.

In 1917 a national allotment programme was started with the aim of growing more food for the country. As with most local communities, Mauchline designated an area of ground which was divided into smaller allotments, which were let out to residents. In February 1917 a second field, located between the railway station and the road, was divided into small plots for this purpose.

The minister of the parish kirk, Rev Dr Mitchell, decided to allow part of his glebe to be used as garden plots and invited applications. The land used was located close to the existing school gardens. In 1917 the occupiers of the allotments formed an association.

In a similar manner, some of the local lairds used their policies for food production for the first time. At Ballochmyle House the tenant, Mrs Crookston, arranged for the grass parks around the mansion to be ploughed for potatoes, the first time in thirty years that these areas of grass had come under the plough.

The First World War took place from 1914 until 1918, and hundreds of men from the area served with the troops or navy against the Germans. Many families lost more than one son, there being a number of cases where brothers died within months of each other. Within the old kirkyard is a memorial erected to the memory of John Cunningham and his family. He served in the 27th Foot and fought at Toulouse, Orthes, Nivelle, Pyrenees, Vittoria, Salamanca and Badajoz. He died in Mauchline in 1868, aged 81 years. On it is a warning of the results of war – it lists the members of his family who were killed in the Great War, namely, Sapper Robert Cunningham, RE; Sergeant Duncan Cunningham, NZEF; James Cunningham, 31st Division QMGUS, Army; Private James Cunningham, 15th Gordon Highlanders; Private Robert Cunningham, 5th Royal Scots; Private Robert Murphy, Royal Scots Fusiliers, Thomas Ritchie, Royal Engineers; and Private William Ritchie, Highland Light Infantry.

Mauchline parish lost a number of men, amongst these being:

- 2nd Lieutenant Allan Muir Aird, King's Royal Rifle Corps, died 21 October 1918 aged 28. Born in Glasgow, he was the son of Alexander and Janet Aird of Braemore, Mauchline. He is buried in the Harlebeke New British Cemetery.
- 2nd Lieutenant George Allan, 3rd/19th London Regiment, was accidentally killed at Winchester on 14 March 1916 at the age of 31. He was the son of George Allan and he is buried in Mauchline Cemetery.
- Alexander Barrie
- Private William Barrie, No. 331593, 9th Battalion (Glasgow), Highland Light Infantry, was killed in action on 15 July 1916, aged 18. He is commemorated on the Thriepval Memorial.
- Sergeant Alexander Baxter, Canadian Expeditionary Forces, was killed at Vimy Ridge in France on 9 April 1917 at the age of 26. He was brought up in Mauchline but had emigrated to Canada. A keen sportsman, he was one of the members influential in forming the Mauchline Harriers' Club. He had trained in the bank and emigrated to Canada where he continued the profession, before becoming an estate agent.
- Private Archibald Baxter was the brother of the above, serving with the Royal Naval Volunteer Reserve – Drake Battalion. He originally enlisted with the Royal Scots Fusiliers in August 1914 before transferring to the Navy. He died of wounds in France on 24 April

1917 and was buried in the Aubigny Communal Cemetery. He had the distinction of being the first man in Mauchline to sign up for the forces at the outbreak of war.

- Private David Bell, 8th Battalion Royal Scots Fusiliers, was born in Mauchline, educated in Ayr and signed up in New Prestwick. His regimental number was 35904. He was killed in the Balkans on 19 September 1918.
- Private George Blair, of the 1st Battalion Seaforth Highlanders, was killed in Mesopotamia on 22 February 1917 aged 23. He was the son of William Ferguson Blair and Marion Blair, 39 Loudoun Street. Educated at Kilmarnock Academy, he found work in the Glenfield works there. He is commemorated on the Basra memorial.
- John G. Blair was killed in action in France on 11 November 1916 at the age of 37. He served with the 47th Battalion, Canadian Infantry (Western Ontario Regiment). His grave is located in the Adanac Military Cemetery at Miraumont. He was the brother of the above George Blair.
- Samuel Bole
- Private Andrew Brown, Royal Scots Fusiliers, was born near Fenwick, the son of John Brown, but moved to Grassmillees, Mauchline, in 1910. He was educated at Kilmarnock Academy before joining his father as a farmer. He was fighting at Hailete, France, when he was killed on his first morning 'going over the top', 25 October 1918, just before the Armistice. He was just 21 and was buried in the Ingoyghem Military Cemetery. His Service No. was 61018.
- John Cairns
- Gunner George Caldow, No. 176128, C Battery, Royal Field Artillery, 52nd Brigade. Killed on 25 October 1917 and buried in The Huts Cemetery.
- Lance Corporal James W. B. Chalmers, 17th Highland Light Infantry, who died of wounds received in France, 5 May 1917, aged 20. He was the son of James and Agnes Chalmers, Ballochmyle. He was educated in Mauchline, followed by Kilmarnock Academy, leaving to become a booking clerk at Annbank Station. At first he served with the Ayrshire Yeomanry, moving to serve in France in 1916. He received a wound to the head from shrapnel and was brought back to Britain where he died in a military hospital in Bristol one week later. He is buried in Mauchline Cemetery.
- William Cochrane
- Private Thomas Conner was killed in action in France on 31 July 1917. He served with the 12th Battalion, Highland Light Infantry. He was the

son of Mary Conner and the late Bernard Conner of Burnside, Mauchline.

- Private George Chesney Wield Corson, No. 315081, Royal Highlanders, Black Watch, 13th (Scottish Horse) Battalion, died of wounds in France on 10 November 1918 (the day before the Armistice was signed), aged 24. His grave is located at the St Sever Cemetery, Rouen. He was the son of William and Emilie Margaret Martin Corson, born in Australia, but moved to live with his sister and aunt at the Haugh.
- Private Alexander Crawford, 6th/7th Royal Scots Fusiliers, No. 40051, died of wounds on 9 November 1916. He is buried at Ste. Marie Cemetery, Le Havre.
- Lance Sergeant Duncan Cunningham, No. 10/1460, 3rd Battalion, Wellington Regiment, New Zealand Expeditionary Forces, was killed on 22 June 1917. He is interred at the Trois Arbres Cemetery, Steenwerck.
- Private John Cunningham. He is not listed on Mauchline War Memorial.
- Corporal Robert Dickson, No. 15540, of the 1st Battalion Royal Scots Fusiliers, was killed in France on 6 June 1915. He was the son of Robert H. and Hannah Dickson, 8 Brougham Street, Greenock. He is commemorated on the Ypres (Menin Gate) War Memorial and on a gravestone in Mauchline Cemetery.
- Private Robert Edgar, No. 11356, 1st Battalion, King's Own Scottish Borderers, killed in action on 1 July 1916. A native of Dumfries, Edgar was employed as a lamp-boy at Mauchline railway station. He is commemorated on the Thiepval memorial.
- Sergeant Charles John Gibson, No. 12152, was killed in France on 29 September 1915 at the age of 24. He served with the 6th Battalion, Royal Scots Fusiliers. He is commemorated on the Loos War Memorial.
- Private Samuel Gibson was killed at the Dardanelles on 25 April 1915 at the age of 26. Serving with the 1st Battalion King's Own Scottish Borderers, he is commemorated on the Helles War Memorial. He was the son of John and Agnes Gibson, Clelland Park, Mauchline, and had signed up to the army in 1912. It was noted that he was a 'well-known Mauchline pedestrian'.
- Private John Gordon, No. 7078, 1st/5th Royal Scots Fusiliers, killed by a piece of shrapnel at Dardanelles, 12 July 1915, aged 27. He is commemorated on the Helles War Memorial. He was the son of William Gordon, Bridgend of Montgarswood, Sorn. There is a military

gravestone in his memory within Sorn kirkyard.

- James Graham
- Private John Hair, 1st/6th Battalion, Highland Light Infantry, No. 37488. He died on 24 November 1917 and is buried in Jerusalem War Cemetery. He was the son of Robert and Margaret Hair, Barskimming Mill, and husband of Agnes Swaney, Leith, Edinburgh.
- Private William Hammond, 1st Battalion, King's Own Scottish Borderers, No. 202781, was killed 19 August 1918. The husband of Jennie Hammond, he lived in Loudoun Street. He is buried in the Le Grand Hasaid Military Cemetery, Morbecquw.
- Gunner William Harper, Royal Garrison Artillery, 13th Mountain Gun Battery, died of pneumonia in Egypt, 13 January 1919. His service number was 170828 and he is buried in the Alexandria (Hadra) War Memorial Cemetery.
- Private Andrew Howie, No. 34920, 6th/7th Battalion, Royal Scots Fusiliers, died of wounds on 23 March 1918 at the age of 34. He was buried in Doullens, France. He was the husband of Flora Howie, Bilboa, Mauchline, and son of John and Lilias MacCartney Howie, Mauchline.
- Private James Howie, No. TR/2/20792, served with the Training Reserve, 77th Battalion Labour Corps. He was killed on 16 September 1917 and is buried in Nine Elms British Cemetery. He was the son of John and Mary Lambie Howie, Gasworks Row, Mauchline.
- Private Robert Howie, No. 47726, 12th Battalion, Royal Scots, was killed in action in France on 17 October 1918 aged 27. He is buried in the Harlebeke New British Cemetery.
- Private William C. Jamieson, 9th Battalion, Royal Scots, No. 4365, killed 18 August 1916, son of James F. Jamieson, Rodenloft, Stair. He is commemorated on the Ploegsteert War Memorial. He is also commemorated on the war memorial lychgate at Kinclaven Parish Church, Perthshire.
- Lance Corporal Andrew Drennan Kay, 2nd Battalion, Black Watch (Royal Highlanders), No. 5/10652, died of wounds received at Amara, Mesopotamia, on 25 May 1917 at the age of 21. He was the son of Thomas Kay of Burnside House.
- Private Hugh Dickie Lambie, King's Own Scottish Borderers, 1st/5th Battalion, died on 18 October 1918 at the age of 18. He is buried at the Harlebeke New British Cemetery. He was the son of Robert and Margaret Lambie, Loudoun Street.
- Private Robert Lambie, 10th Battalion, Cameronians (Scottish Rifles), Lanarkshire Yeomanry, killed in action on 24 June 1917 aged 27. No.

41119, he is buried in Brandhoek Military Cemetery.

- Private Alexander Learmont, 56th Battalion Australian Infantry, was killed at the Battle of the Somme in France on 1 November 1916 at the age of 29. He is commemorated on the Villers Brelonneux Memorial. He was the son of Thomas Learmont, baker, of Loudoun Street and was educated in Mauchline and Kilmarnock Academy. On leaving he became a clerk in the Clydesdale Bank, but was soon promoted to the National Bank of India in London. He emigrated to Australia and became a farmer in New South Wales.

- Private James Love, Royal Marine Light Infantry, was killed in action in France on 26 October 1917. He had previously worked as a lawyer's clerk with J. D. MacMillan at the Commercial Bank. He was the son of Peter and Catherine Murdoch Love, Knowe, Mauchline. He is commemorated on the Tyne Cot Memorial.

- Private William Alexander Lyell of the Haugh served with the 10th/11th Battalion Highland Light Infantry. He was to die of wounds received in action, at Etaples Hospital in France on 14 April 1917, aged 30. He is buried in Etaples Military Cemetery.

- Sergeant James S. MacCartney Jun., RAVC, died on active service 11 November 1918. He was married to Isabella MacKie (1882-1911).

- Lance Corporal Richard Ritchie MacCrae, 7th Battalion, Black Watch (Royal Highlanders), died 5 May 1917 aged 31. No. 292665. He was the younger son of the late Andrew and Ann Brown MacCrae, Earl Grey Street. He was married to Matilda May MacLean MacCrae, and lived at 487 Sauchiehall Street. He is buried in Etaples Military Cemetery.

- Lance Sergeant Alexander MacCurdie, son of James MacCurdie of Burngrange House, was killed at Peronne, France, on 24 April 1917, aged 22. Just prior to his death he had been recommended for the Distinguished Conduct Medal. His Military Number was S/8960. He was serving with the 14th Battalion Argyll and Sutherland Highlanders. He is commemorated on the Fifteen Ravine British Cemetery, Villers-Plouich. The son of James and Mary MacCurdie, he was a noted footballer, playing at one time with Kilmarnock F.C. He was educated at Kilmarnock Academy and Glasgow University.

- Gunner William Bone MacDonald, No. 935995, Royal Field Artillery. Killed on 31 March 1917, aged 19. Buried in the Savy British Cemetery, he was the brother of James MacDonald, The Knowe, Mauchline.

- Private Andrew MacIlvean, D Company, 6th Battalion, King's Own Scottish Borderers. Regimental Number 15154, he was killed on 10 April 1918, aged 37, and is buried in La Clytte Military Cemetery. He was the son of the late Andrew and Annie MacIlvean, Mauchline.

- Gunner William Nicol Burns MacIlvean, Royal Garrison Artillery, died 21 October 1918 aged 39. Regimental Number 188051, he is buried at Busigny Communal Cemetery. He was the son of William Nichol Burns and Mary MacIlvean, Mauchline, and husband of Margaret MacIlvean. They had moved to live at 106 Trevor Terrace, North Shields.
- Private Matthew C. MacIntosh, 10th Company, Machine Gun Corps, died 1 July 1916 aged 26. He is buried in the Serre Road Cemetery. He was the son of Mrs Marion MacLeod MacIntosh, Townfoot, Dunlop.
- James MacKay
- Private George MacKerrow, No. 2899, 17th Battalion, Highland Light Infantry, was killed on 1 July 1916, aged 28. He is commemorated on the Thiepval Memorial.
- Private John G. MacKerrow, 6th Battalion, Royal Scots Fusiliers, was killed on 10 February 1916 aged 37. Number 14703, he is buried in Lancashire Cottage Cemetery. He was the son of A. H. MacKerrow, Loudoun Street, Mauchline.
- Rifleman Charles R. MacKie, No. 373001, 1st/8th Battalion, London Regiment (Post Office Rifles). He is listed on the Thiepval Memorial.
- Sergeant James MacKie, 103 Squadron, Royal Air Force, No. 401121, was killed in France on 8 October 1918, aged 24. He was the son of David R. MacKie, 4 Jeffrey Street, Riccarton, Kilmarnock, and was buried in the Grevillers British Cemetery.
- James MacLatchie
- Robert MacLintock
- Gunner David MacMillan served with the 94th Brigade, Royal Field Artillery. No. 167375. He was killed at the age of 31 on 27 November 1918. Buried in Mauchline Cemetery, he was married to Margaret MacMillan, 5 Millbrae Terrace, Thankerton, Lanarkshire.
- Gunner Archibald D. MacPhee, 9th Brigade, Royal Field Artillery, died in Omara, Mesopotamia, on 9 May 1917. No. 125625, he is buried in Baghdad (North Gate) War Cemetery.
- Gunner Harry (Henry Charles) Mathieson, No. L/6859, C Battery, 59th Battalion, Royal Field Artillery, was killed on 26 July 1916, aged 25. He was the son of Edith Louisa Mathieson, 36 Roseburn Street, Edinburgh. He was killed by a shell whilst riding on his horse through a French village. He was buried at the Dive Copse British Cemetery at Sailly-le-Sec. Prior to signing up he was employed as a gardener at Ballochmyle House and had become well known in Catrine.

- Lance Corporal Hugh Hay Miller, of the 1st Battalion, Scots Guards, was killed near Ypres on 1 May 1916 aged 22. No. 13302. Buried in the Potijze Chateau Wood Cemetery, he was the son of the late Hugh and Joan Miller, San Fernando, Trinidad, who had emigrated from Mauchline. He joined the Scots Guards in 1915. He was killed by Germans in a listening post - he had served in the same place the two previous nights, and did not require to do a third, but had volunteered.
- 2nd Lieutenant John Miller MC, 10th Battalion, Highland Light Infantry, killed in France, 1 August 1917 aged 25. He is buried at Tyne Cot Cemetery but also commemorated in Mauchline Cemetery. He was the son of James and Janet Miller, Stairhill farm.
- Private George Bruce Mitchell, No. S/14460, 7th Battalion, Gordon Highlanders, killed in France, 13 September 1918, aged 19. Buried at Leuze Communal Cemetery.
- Private John Murchie, 2nd Battalion, Royal Scots Fusiliers, No. 9494. Killed on 12 March 1915, aged 27. He was the son of John and Mary Murchie, Main Street, Ochiltree and is commemorated on the Le Touret Memorial.
- Gunner Robert MacIlvean Murdoch, No. 209205, A Battery, Royal Field Artillery, killed 27 November 1918, aged 20. He was the son of James and Martha Murdoch, Mauchline and is buried at Valenciennes (St Roch) Communal Cemetery.
- Private Thomas Murdoch, No. 240383, 1st/5th Royal Scots Fusiliers, killed by shell-fire on 26 August 1918. He is listed on the Vis-en-artois War Memorial.
- Trooper William Galt Paton, Life Guards – Household Battalion, No. 1943. He was killed on 20 May 1917 at the age of 20 years. Commemorated on the Arras Memorial; he was the son of Robert and Mary Paton, 23 Riverbank Street, Newmilns.
- Edward Potts
- Private David Reid, Service Number 238047, 8th Battalion, Seaforth Highlanders, was killed on 23 April 1917, aged 19. He was the son of Elizabeth Reid, Newton, Catrine, and the late Lewis Reid. Buried at Faubourg D'amiens Cemetery, Arras.
- Lance Sergeant James Reid of the 1st/5th Royal Scots Fusiliers, died of wounds at Abbeyville Hospital in France on 7 September 1918 aged 29. His military number was 240438. He lived at the Loan and had previously been awarded the Military Cross for bravery. He is buried in the Abbeville Communal Cemetery extension. He was the son of John and Jane Reid, Albert Place, Mauchline.

- Private Robert Reid, No. 8405, 1st/5th Battalion, Royal Scots Fusiliers, was killed at the Dardanelles on 12 July 1915 aged 19. He is listed on the Helles Memorial.
- Ordinary Seaman Andrew Gemmell Richmond, Royal Navy, from HMS *Nereus* (or HMS *Vivid*), was drowned at sea on 4 September 1918 at the age of 19. His service number was J/74682. He was the son of James Richmond, Mount Pleasant, Annan Road, Dumfries.
- Private Hugh Ritchie, No. 29952, 6th/7th Battalion, Royal Scots Fusiliers, was killed on 2 August 1917 aged 28. He was the son of Mr & Mrs Hugh Ritchie, Cowgate, and husband of Margaret Ritchie, St Cuthbert's Street, Catrine. He is listed on the Ypres (Menin Gate) War Memorial.
- Sergeant Louis Somervell Robertson, Wellington Mounted Rifles, New Zealand Expeditionary Forces, A Squadron, was killed at Gallipoli on 9 June 1915 at the age of 30. His Service Number was 11/454. He was the son of Edward Robertson, schoolmaster at Sorn, and Margaret Heron Robertson, of 3 High Street, Mauchline. Born in Sorn, he served in the South African War and was later to adopt New Zealand nationality. He is buried in the Walker's Ridge Cemetery, but a memorial stone in Mauchline Cemetery also commemorates him. He is not listed on Mauchline War Memorial.
- David Stewart
- Private Donald Stewart, 1st/7th Battalion, Gordon Highlanders, No. 203008. He died of wounds on 12 April 1918, aged 37. Born in Durness, Sutherland, to Donald and Catherine Stewart, of Laid, Durness, he was married to Grace Oliver, proprietrix of the Black Bull Hotel, Mauchline. He is buried at Vielle-Chapelle New Military Cemetery, Lacouture, France. He is also commemorated on the war memorial at Durness.
- Private Henry Reid Telfer of the 12th (Ayrshire and Lanarkshire Yeomanry) Battalion, Royals Scots Fusiliers, was killed in France on 22 September 1918 at the age of 46. Service Number 29259, he was the son of John Telfer, 11 Bank Street, Paisley, and husband of Janet Brown Telfer, High Street, Mauchline. He is buried in the Trois Arbres Cemetery, Steenwerck.
- Lance Corporal Robert Templeton, 2nd Battalion, Gordon Highlanders, third son of Robert and Agnes Templeton of Willoxton, was killed in Italy on 4 May 1918, aged 25. Number S/40899, he is buried in Magnaboschi British Cemetery.
- Able Seaman Alexander Vance, Mercantile Marine, SS *Cyrene* (Sunderland), killed 5 April 1918 aged 24. He was the adopted son of

Hugh and Mary Anne Vance, Drumley Cottage, Annbank Station (or Mossblown). He was born at Busbie, near Glasgow, and is commemorated on the Tower Hill memorial.

- Private James Vance, No. 11758, 6th Battalion, Royal Scots Fusiliers, was killed in action in France on 29 September 1915 aged 24. He was born in Glasgow, the son of Margaret Vance, Albert Terrace, Mauchline and the late George Vance. He was educated in Kilmarnock and signed up in Mauchline. He is commemorated on the Loos memorial.
- James Wallace
- Gunner James M. Watson, No. 663073, D Battery, Royal Field Artillery, was killed in action on 4 May 1917 at the age of 27. He was interred at Anzin, St Aubin British Cemetery in France. Watson was the son of James Watson, Glebe Villas, Mauchline.
- Trooper Robert Watson, Service No. 1919, Life Guards, Household Battalion, was killed in action on 9 May 1917 at the age of 26 years. He was the son of the late John Watson and Mrs J. Watson (Stepmother), 25 Kirkwynd, Maybole. He is buried in the Wancourt British Cemetery.
- Lance Corporal John Wilson, No. 43963, 11th Battalion, Royal Scots, was killed in action on 8 July 1918, aged 21. He was the son of David and Elizabeth Wilson, Mauchline.
- Sergeant Robert Winder, 12th (Ayrshire and Lanarkshire Yeomanry), Royal Scots Fusiliers, died 20 September 1918 aged 25. His service number was 295055. He was the son of Mrs Cameron, formerly Winder, of Barskimming farm, Mauchline, and the late Adam Winder. He is interred in the Trois Arbres Cemetery, Steenwerck.
- Gunner John Wyllie, RGA, 261st Siege Battery, was killed in France on 7 December 1917. Service No. 152103. He is buried in the Vaulx Australian Field Ambulance Cemetery.

The end of the Great War, or First World War as it later became known, was marked with celebrations in the village. On 11 November half a dozen low-flying aeroplanes flew over the village by chance, adding to the atmosphere. On the following day, Tuesday 12 November, a combined service of thanksgiving was held in the parish church.

On 30 May 1919 at a special service in the church hall, watches were presented to the soldiers of the parish who had won distinction during the war. Winning the Military Medal were John Baird, Robert Bell, Thomas Bole, Hugh Drummond, John Harper, Henry Lyle, David Morton, Donald MacDonald, Thomas MacMillan, and Allan Ramsay. Awarded with the Military Cross were James Baird, Thomas

6.7 War Memorial *(Dane Love)*

Gilliland, James Reid (who had been killed), and Thomas Woodburn. Gaining the Croix de Guerre were John Aitken and John Clark.

Soon plans were being made to commemorate those who had paid the ultimate sacrifice for their country, and fundraising for a war memorial began. A public meeting was held in the Temperance Hall in February 1919 to arrange a memorial, Robert MacCrone of Auchinleck House presiding. The Rev Dr Mitchell proposed a reading room and institute, and MacCrone proposed a bronze memorial located at The Cross. However, after fundraising for a number of years, the war memorial proposals withered for a time, and it was not until 1924 that the first new set of discussions commenced, a public meeting being held on Friday 27 June in the Temperance Hall. With funds raised, a further meeting took place on 9 January 1925 to discuss a site – either the one chosen at the end of Catrine Road, or else at the kirkyard gate. The Catrine Road site was offered free by Major Campbell of Auchmannoch and Avisyard and it was pursued. This spot was known as the Breaking Stones, or Braking Stones, as road-metalling was originally stored there. A further fund-raising 'carnival' dance was held in the Temperance Hall on 26 March 1926 to augment the funds. Numerous other events continued to raise funds, right up to a few weeks before the memorial was unveiled.

The memorial was unveiled on the Friday afternoon of 20 May 1927 by Sir Hugh M. Trenchard, Baronet, GCB, DSO, Air Chief Marshal of the Royal Air Force. Built of Ballochmyle sandstone, the war memorial had cost £904 8s to construct, after which the custody of it was passed to the Parish Council. It has a base 9½ feet tall, on which are bronze plaques listing the fallen, topped by an Ionic pillar surmounted by an Italian vase, totalling 31½ feet. The architect responsible for the design was Alexander Caldwell Thomson (1873-1925), who died before it was unveiled. On the day that the memorial was unveiled the event was chaired by Major R. J. Dunlop of Barskimming, who had been the chairman of the War Memorial Committee.

Other memorials were erected elsewhere in the parish. Within the parish church a brass plaque was erected that listed seventy-three members of the church who had died for their country. The plaque was unveiled on 25 July 1920 by Rev Dr MacLean of the Old Abbey Church, Paisley.

In the Walker U. F. Church the war memorial tablet was unveiled on 26 December 1920. It lists the thirteen men of the congregation who lost their lives in the war.

LANDOWNERS

Eliza, Lady Alexander of Ballochmyle, outlived her husband by 28 years, dying on 16 July 1927. Her son, Sir Claud, had only owned the estates for one year at the turn of the century, inheriting them in 1899. He was Sir Claud Alexander, 2nd Baronet. Born on 24 February 1867, he was educated at Eton, followed by New College,

Oxford, from where he graduated with a BA in 1899. He served in the 3rd Battalion of the Royal Scots Fusiliers for a number of years, attaining the rank of lieutenant. He served as a Justice of the Peace for Ayrshire. Claud had married Lady Diana Montgomerie, youngest daughter of the Earl of Eglinton and Winton, on 14 December 1889, but they were divorced five years later. She died on 27 October 1914. However, from this marriage two sons were born. The first, Arnulph Claud, was born on 6 September 1891 but died four months later, on 6 January 1892. The second son, Wilfred Archibald Alexander, was born on 6 October 1892. Claud married a second time, on 28 January 1896, to Rachel Belasyse Holden, youngest daughter of Rev Henry Holden DD. She died on 1 February 1944. By her he had three children, two sons, Claud Alexander, born 4 June 1897, died 1976, and Boyd Alexander, born 3 December 1902, died unmarried on 25 March 1984, and a daughter, Wilhelmina Alexander, born 18 May 1907, died unmarried on 31 August 1986. As well as living at Ballochmyle House, the Alexanders spent some time at Fay Gate Wood in Sussex. Sir Claud Alexander, 2nd Baronet, died on 18 March 1945.

From the death of Sir Claud in 1899, Ballochmyle House was let out to a variety of tenants – up until November 1919 it was occupied by Mr and Mrs Crookston.

In 1919 the house was leased by Sir Archibald MacInnes Shaw DSO MP, who had previously rented Glaisnock House in Old Cumnock parish. He was the son of

6.8 Sir Claud Alexander as a boy with Eliza Alexander *(Ballochmyle Archives)*

James Shaw, iron-founder in Maryhill, Glasgow, and was born in 1862. Following an education at Glasgow Academy, he joined the family firm. He continued his studies in later life, however, graduating from St Andrews University in 1911 with a Doctor of Laws degree. He was for a time Colonel of the 1st Lanarkshire R.G.A., and Hon. Colonel of the 4th Lowland (Howitzer) Brigade, R.F.A. (V.D.). He became the head of the iron-founding firm of Shaw and MacInnes, Maryhill. He served for a time as Lord Provost of Glasgow, as well as a Justice of the Peace and Deputy Lieutenant for Glasgow and Lanarkshire. He was also chairman of Broxburn Oil

6.9 Sir Claud Alexander *(Ballochmyle Archives)*

Company. In 1902 he was elected as Bailie of the River and Firth of Clyde. He was president of the Glasgow Territorial Force and was Associate and Lord Lieutenant of Glasgow from 1908-11. In 1911 he received the Coronation Medal. He also received the orders of Sacred Treasure of Japan and of St Olaf of Norway. Sir Archibald was married in 1891 to Rosina Elisabeth Douglas Fraser, daughter of Archibald Fraser, merchant in Glasgow. He was knighted in 1911.

Wilfred Archibald Alexander was outlived by his father, and so did not inherit Ballochmyle. He worked for the Consular Service in China. He married Mary Prudence Acheson on 17 November 1919, daughter of Guy Francis Hamilton Acheson, Commissioner of Customs in China. They had three children, Claud, who became the third Baronet, Mary Primrose Alexander (1921-1988), who married Lieutenant-Colonel John Edward Margesson in 1947, and Penelope Mary Acheson Alexander (1924-), who married Sir Francis David Somerville Head, 5th Baronet, on 25 January 1967. Wilfred Alexander died on 26 March 1927. On his death the family moved back from China to England. Mary Prudence Alexander died on 25 July 1960.

The baronetcy was inherited by Sir Claud Alexander, 3rd Baronet. He was born on 6 January 1927 in Peking. Back in England he was educated at Sherborne School in Dorset, followed by Corpus Christi College, Cambridge University, where he

6.10 Wilfred Alexander *(Ballochmyle Archives)*

qualified as a Bachelor of Arts in natural sciences and physics in 1948.

Kingencleugh was still let out, being occupied for 41 years by Miss Margaret Thomson of Glasgow, until her death in 1919 at the age of 83. She was buried in Glasgow Necropolis. Her sister, Miss Mary Thomson was the last of the family to occupy the house, dying on 28 January 1926. She was described as being a generous lady, taking part in many affairs of the parish, especially with the Nursing Association and the Abbey U. F. Church. She, too, was buried in Glasgow.

At Netherplace the mansion was still tenanted by James Baird Thorneycroft JP DL (1851-1918). He was appointed a Deputy Lieutenant of Ayrshire on 12 April 1901. Thorneycroft was a director with James Baird, but he spent some time developing rifles. A number of patents were filed by him, including British Patents numbered 13,073 and 14,622, the latter filed in 1901. The first one was an *Original Patent Application for Improvements in Rifles and Other Small Arms*. The Thorneycroft Rifle, as it became known, was similar to the Godsal rifle, and was specially developed for use by cavalry. The bolt and block had a wooden shroud, and in the wrist of the butt there was a magazine which could contain five rounds. Thorneycroft moved to Hillhouse, in Dundonald parish, in 1908, and from then he moved between the two properties. Eventually in 1912 he gave up the tenancy of Netherplace, the sale of his Daimler car, furniture, carpets and other items being held at Netherplace on 24 May that year. He died on 15 December 1918.

During Thorneycroft's tenancy in 1904, the Ayr architect, Allan Stevenson, was employed to carry out some minor alterations and additions to the house. This comprised a new bathroom between the east wings, and a rebuilt north wing to contain a servant's hall and additional bedrooms. Earlier plans were drawn up in April 1902 for additions to loose boxes in the grounds. Thorneycroft's widow, Annie Chalmers Nicoll, died on 19 March 1934 in London and was buried alongside him in Troon cemetery.

Netherplace was to become the home of the Hamilton-Campbells once more, Lieutenant Colonel William Kentigern Hamilton-Campbell bringing his family to live there in 1912.

6.11 Netherplace House, from the air, 1928 *(Stroma Leith)*

Lieutenant Colonel William Kentigern Hamilton-Campbell DSO JP DL CC TD was born at Carnell Castle on 30 September 1865 and was educated at Sedbergh Grammar School in Yorkshire. He served in the Boer War in South Africa from 1900-02 with the 6th Battalion of the Imperial Yeomanry. At first he was a captain in the 17th Company, then as a Major and second in command of the Battalion, and finally as a Lieutenant Colonel Commandant. He was awarded the DSO in 1902 and was mentioned in despatches. After retiring from the army, he was appointed Honorary Lieutenant Colonel and Lieutenant Colonel Commandant in the Ayrshire Yeomanry (TD). He was also appointed a Justice of the Peace and Depute Lieutenant for Ayrshire. In 1908 he was elected as a county councillor, representing Mauchline. He was chairman of Mauchline Parish Council for many years. In politics he was a supporter of the Conservative party, an Imperialist and a 'Tariff Reformer'. A keen huntsman, he enjoyed shooting. Hamilton-Campbell was also a skilled curler, being part of the winning rink that competed at the International Curling Bonspiel at Celerina in Switzerland in 1908. He was married at Monkton Parish Church on 15 October 1908 to Edith Angus, daughter of Robert L. Angus of Ladykirk. They lived at Greystones, a townhouse in Ayr, for a time, bringing up three children. He served in the military, with the cavalry in India. He went to serve in the Great War, being commander of the Ayrshire Yeomanry, until he became too ill and retired. He died at Netherplace on Thursday 22 November 1917 aged 52 after a few weeks of ill-health, having contracted tuberculosis in Africa. He left £48,214

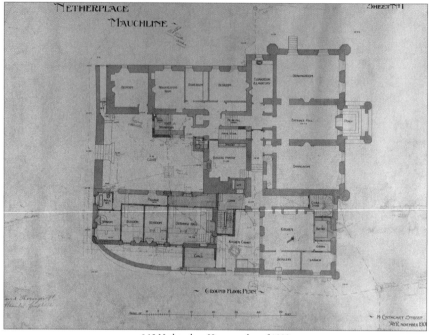

6.12 Netherplace House – plan of 1902
(Darley Hay Architects reference Accession 1223, held at Ayrshire Archives)

8s 11d in his will. His wife, Edith, died on 4 February 1935 at the age of 58.

In 1900 a poem was written by a soldier under Hamilton-Campbell's command in the 17th Company of the Imperial Yeomanry, fighting at the time in Bloemfontein. The verses were published in the *Ayr Advertiser* of 27 September 1900:

> Have you heard of Captain Campbell, he's the Laird of Netherplace?
> He's the truest-hearted mortal of all the human race,
> He's adored by all who know him, and right well he may be so,
> For he's every inch a soldier, not afraid to face the foe.
>
> He's at present in South Africa fighting nobly for his Queen,
> He'll do it as a soldier should, and that will yet be seen,
> There's a lot of lads behind him who all love their Captain well,
> If he only gave the order, we would follow him to h-ll!

He's a man, and that is something that we all can say with pride,
Then who would think of turning from such a Captain's side,
If you want to see some fighting, just say 'Campbell, yon's the place,'
Then you may bet your bottom dollar, first man in is Netherplace.

Followed by his lads in kharki, by young 'Graham' and 'Boulton' true,
With 'Jim Bell' and sturdy 'Boswell', we will make the Boers blue,
And if by chance we meet some bullets, on that point we've nought to fear,
Is not Dr Naismith coming, curing all who are in rear?

As the snow melts in the sunshine, so the Boers will melt away,
They will find that we mean business; they've had time enough to play,
Now then Ayrshire, Lanark, Scotland, welcome us from o'er the sea,
We have fought for Queen and country – risked our lives for love of thee.

William's second daughter, Edith Julia, was born on 24 December 1910 and died in infancy on 9 February 1914.

William Hamilton-Campbell's son, Mungo Charles Hamilton-Campbell DSO MC TD DL JP, was born in 1912 and came of age in 1933 to great celebrations. On Tuesday 15 June 1937 he married Every Muriel Kay Finlayson (born 5 April 1917), daughter of C. K. Finlayson of Merchiston House, Johnstone, at Paisley Abbey. On the previous evening a huge bonfire was lit by the tenantry at Laurieland farm. They had a daughter, Edith, but she died in infancy on 1 October 1939. He served in the Second World War in North Africa and at Monte Cassion on Italy. He took over command of the Ayrshire Yeomanry in December 1944 and remained in command until it was disbanded after the war. He was awarded the Military Cross and Distinguished Service Order. He was a

6.13 William Kentigern Hamilton-Campbell of Netherplace
(Stroma Leith)

Justice of the Peace, and Depute Lieutenant of Ayrshire. His career was as a stockbroker. Mungo Hamilton-Campbell died on 9 July 1953 at the age of 41, and was buried in Mauchline cemetery. Two other daughters survived – Stroma and Tara.

Although Mauchline Castle was still owned by the Earl of Loudoun, it was let to various tenants, one of them at the start of the twentieth century being Alfred Arthur Greenwood Hales. Born at Kent Town, Adelaide, Australia on 21 July 1860, he was always interested in writing, his first published story appearing at the age of sixteen. He found employment as a reporter with various newspapers, but eventually founded his own, the 'Coolgardie Mining Review'. He was something of a character in Australia, trying his hand enthusiastically at many things, including standing for parliament in 1897. In 1899 he became a war correspondent for the *Daily News,* sending back reports of the Boer War in South Africa. At the battle of Maggersfontein General Wauchope was killed and Hales was later to send back an account of 'The Burial of General Wauchope'. This was so well written that it became a popular recitation piece thereafter. Hales was also captured by the Boers, and remained in prison until the end of hostilities.

A. G. Hales, as he styled himself in print, wrote over fifty books, many of them novels which became best-sellers in Britain. His first was *The Wanderings of a Simple Child*, published in 1890. He wrote a series of McGlusky adventures (around twenty) between 1902 and 1935, accounts of a tough, adventurous Scot who travelled the world 'with a Bible in one hand and a brick in the other'. These had titles like *McGlusky the Sea Rover* (1935) and *McGlusky o' the Legion* (1932). These sold over two million copies in total. He also wrote a number of biographies, historical novels, poems, ballads and plays.

Hales was twice married, firstly on 15 May 1886 to Emmeline Pritchard (died 1911) and secondly, in 1920, to Jean Reid, a Scot. Hales was known as 'Smiler', probably more in sarcasm. He died on 29 December 1936 at Herne Bay, Kent, where he was buried.

In 1912 the parapet stones at Mauchline Castle were taken down, it being thought that the weight of the parapet was too much for the walls to support. Another tenant was Harry Lewis Bowyer, excise officer, who died in April 1920. His widow, Laura Bowyer, remained for a time thereafter.

Still the property of the Earl of Loudoun, by 1925 the castle was tenanted by Lieutenant Colonel Alexander Cecil Adair OBE. Born on 10 October 1872 at Taunton in Somerset, son of Major Henry Atkinson Adair (1839-1919) of the 52nd Light Infantry, and Charlotte Martha Hamilton (1846-1929), he was educated at St Edward's School, followed by Christ Church, Oxford. He was married in 1907 to Gwendoline Flora Mary (1883-1958), daughter of W.W. Wynne. They had one son, Lieut. Walter Alexander Adair RN, born in 1911. Alexander Adair served with the 3rd Battalion of the Cheshire Regiment in 1900, West India Regiment (1900-11), being appointed adjutant from 1907-10 and Adjutant in the 4th Battalion East Yorkshire Regiment (1911-13) before being appointed as Captain in the Royal Scots Fusiliers in 1913. He served during the First World War and was wounded at Ypres. He retired in 1922 and in the following year he was appointed the secretary of the Territorial Army Association of the County of Ayr. From 1934-5 he served in the county council and was to take on numerous positions with charities in the county, such as treasurer with the Ayrshire branch of the Soldiers', Sailors' and Airmen's Families Association, British Red Cross Society and Ayr Society for Social Service. He edited the Journal of the *Royals Scots Fusiliers*, and was the Honorary Secretary of the Regimental Committee. He died on 5 May 1948.

By the Second World War Mauchline Castle was the property of the Heritable Securities & Mortgage Investment Association Ltd. of Edinburgh. There were a number of short tenancies, for example, in 1939 the tenant was the Hon. Matthew Arthur, and in 1940 the tenant was Ludovic M. Stuart.

Ownership of land changed considerably after the First World War. In the county many large estates were broken up, and in Mauchline parish the change was no different. In fact Barskimming estate began to be broken up in 1914, and this continued after the war had ended. In 1915 Barskimming House and the farm of Highaird was purchased by Robert Jack Dunlop, brother of Sir Thomas Dunlop, 1st Baronet, Lord Provost of Glasgow, and second son of Thomas Dunlop, ship-owner and grain merchant in Glasgow. R. J. Dunlop was born on 8 April 1857 and became a partner in the firm of Messrs Thomas Dunlop & Sons, as well as serving as President of the Council of Chamber of Shipping. He was married on 21 September 1882 to Mary Louise MacKenzie (died 20 February 1929). He married a second time, to Mary Hastie (died 7 July 1956), widow of James Craig Gatheral. R. J. Dunlop was appointed County Councillor for Mauchline area in January 1920. By his two wives he had five daughters, Louise (married Archibald MacKenzie); Robina Jack (married Andrew Ross Scott); Anne Jack (married William Galbraith); Alexandra (married Thomas Purdie) and Janet (married Thomas MacGuffie). R. J. Dunlop died on 11 September 1938.

Although owned by the Dunlops, Barskimming was still occupied by the Misses Anderson, who remained there for almost forty years. In 1919 they vacated the mansion and moved to Drumley House, near Annbank.

From 1942 Barskimming House was used as a Roman Catholic institution for Brothers of the Christian School. Known as St Mungo's Approved School, 88 boys were lodged and educated there.

Rodinghead House was purchased by the Findlay-Hamiltons of Carnell Castle and it was let for a number of years. Up to 1918 Rodinghead was the home of Augustus Bernard Tellefsen Cayzer, third son of Sir Charles Cayzer, 1st Baronet of Gartmore. Born on 21 January 1876, he was a Lieutenant in the Royal Navy and was married in 1904 to Ina Stancomb (died 25 September 1935), daughter of William

Stancomb of Blount's Court, Potterne, Wiltshire. They had two children, William Nicholas Cayzer (born 1910) and Ina Heather Cayzer (born 1907). A company director and chairman, especially in shipping lines, he was created a baronet on 17 January 1921. On his death on 28 February 1943, he was succeeded by his son, Sir Nicholas, as second baronet, who was created Lord Cayzer in 1981. Lord Cayzer died in 1999, whereupon both the baronetcy and barony became extinct.

George D. Findlay-Hamilton of Carnell sold Rodinghead House to Lord Glenarthur in March 1921, who bought it for his son, Hon. James Cecil Arthur, who had previously lived at Treesbank House, in Riccarton parish, near Kilmarnock. Cecil Arthur was born on 2 June 1883 and was educated at Eton and at Christ Church, Oxford. He served as a lieutenant in the 4th Battalion Princess Louise's (Argyll and Sutherland Highlanders). He was married in 1907 to Evelyn March-Phillipps, elder daughter of Henry March-Phillipps of Fairby, Tiverton in Devon. They had two children, Matthew, born in 1909, and Pamela Helen, born in 1908.

The Arthurs latterly let Rodinghead. Tenants for a short period were the MacCorquodale family, including Alistair MacCorquodale (1925-2009). He ran in the Olympics of 1948, coming 4th in the 100m. He also took part in the 4x100m relay, gaining a silver medal. At the time he was claimed to be the fastest white man in the world. He gave up running thereafter and concentrated on playing cricket, but over his life he was regarded as being a good all-rounder.

Cecil Arthur retained Rodinghead House until August 1928, when he placed it up for auction. The upset price was £10,000, and the house was sold with Rodinghead farm and 130 acres of land. The purchaser was Commander Russell Broom (1890-1964) who came from Campbeltown where he was involved in the whisky industry during its heyday. He, however, had a personal distaste of whisky. He married Averil Mary Boyd Auld (of Craigend House in Troon) in 1929. The Brooms remained at Rodinghead for 36 years. During the Second World War Commander Broom held a senior position in the Royal Observer Corps.

CHURCHES

Membership of the parish church at the turn of the century continued to remain strong, the number of communicants being 729 in 1908. The membership tailed off gradually before rising again, falling to 713 in 1913 and 655 in 1918, 676 in 1923, 695 in 1928 and 707 in 1930.

In 1903 a new set of stained glass windows were inserted in the parish church commemorating Major General Claud Alexander, Baronet. Located on the western wall, these windows tell the story of Jesus and the centurion.

In 1911 plans for a new pipe organ were made, and by 1912 this had been carried through. A donation in 1915 was used to pay for a bronze plaque listing the ministers who had served in the church.

Rev Joseph Mitchell B.D. continued in the pulpit of the parish church. He served as clerk to the Presbytery from 1901 until 1930. It was in 1916 that Rev Mitchell was awarded an honorary Doctorate of Divinity for his work in the wider Church of Scotland.

Dr Mitchell's first wife, Helen Honeyman Litster, eldest daughter of George Litster of Bridge of Allan, whom he married on 15 April 1896, died on 25 June 1921 and Dr Mitchell remarried to Jean Walker JP, eldest daughter of William Brown Robertson of Dundee, on 31 October 1924. By his first wife he had a son, Joseph Litster Mitchell, born on 10 April 1898 and died in 1962.

Dr Mitchell wrote a number of works, including *The Present Ecclesiastical Situation: Proposals for a Reconstructed National Church*, published in Ayr in 1904. He also contributed a number of articles to Hastings' *Dictionary of Christ and the Gospels, and to the Review of Theology and Philosophy.*

Dr Mitchell was a supporter of the union of the United Free Church with the Church of Scotland, which occurred on 1 October 1929. He, with Very Rev Dr John White of the Barony Church, Glasgow, were the two main proponents of the union, driving the merger between the two branches of the church. Just prior to the union, he was selected as Moderator of the General Assembly on May 1929 to guide the church through the process. The session in Mauchline were proud of their minister, and recorded 'the honour which had been conferred on him and on the church and parish of Mauchline… [They] unanimously resolved to record in the Minutes the Session's high appreciation of the fact that the great services rendered by Dr Mitchell to the Church as a whole, and the very active interest taken by him in the movement towards Church Union, soon to be consummated, had thus been fittingly recognised.'

During the final years of Doctor Mitchell's ministry the parish church celebrated the centenary of the building in August 1929. At the time considerable restoration and renovation work was carried out. A new heating system was installed at a cost of £237 8s 2d. At the west end of the church an extension was added below the Alexander windows, to include a vestry and toilet. This extension cost £336 11s 7d. The 1912 organ was also overhauled at a cost of £51 2s 0d.

Dr Mitchell demitted his office on 1 October 1930 after having served in Mauchline Parish Church for forty years. He did not enjoy his retirement for very long, for he died at Bridge of Allan on 18 March 1931. A brass plaque was erected by the congregation in his memory within the parish church in 1933. In 1952 Dr Mitchell's widow donated a brass plaque listing the ministers of the church in Mauchline from 1890.

At the union of the United Free with the Church of Scotland, the parish church adopted the name of Mauchline Old Church.

In the Parish Church Rev. Alasdair Robert Ellis MacInnes was inducted in 1928 as an assistant to Rev Dr Mitchell. He was born on 4 October 1897 at Tayvallich in

Argyll, the son of Rev Alexander MacInnes and Margaret Ellis. Educated at Dingwall Academy and Edinburgh University, he was licensed by the United Free Presbytery of Bathgate in 1926, and served as assistant at Larbert and Buenos Aires. From Mauchline, he was translated to Cadder Parish Church, near Bishopbriggs, in 1929. He demitted in 1941. In 1946 he was admitted as minister of Rodney Street Church, Liverpool, where he remained for three years.

On 5 March 1931 Rev. David Edward Easson MA BD PhD was translated to the Old Church from Carrington Church in Midlothian. Easson was born at Wormit in Fife on 2 August 1897. He was educated at Dundee Harris Academy from 1909 until 1914. Easson was interested in Scottish history and wrote extensively on the subject. Some of his researches were to win awards, such as the Hume Brown Prize in Scottish History in 1938. From 1936-9 he was an examiner in ecclesiastical history for the University of St Andrews. Easson published a number of books prior to the war, including *Charters of the Abbey of Inchcolm* (of which he was co-editor, published in 1938), and 'Foundation Charters of the Collegiate Church of Dunbar', published in the *Miscellany of the Scottish History Society*, Vol VI, published in 1939.

ABBEY U. F. CHURCH

In 1900 a national union of the Free Church of Scotland and the United Presbyterian Church took place. This resulted in Mauchline having two congregations of the same denomination of the United Free Church of Scotland, and it was decided to name the churches the Walker Memorial U. F. Church and the Abbey U. F. Church.

At the turn of the century the minister in the Abbey U. F. Church was still Rev. William Binnie MA. He was a noted preacher, and often had representatives from other churches arriving to hear him preach. He refused a call to South Australia in 1897. He moved to Ayr St Andrew's U. F. Church in 1904 after having served Mauchline for thirteen years. He died in 1924.

The next minister appointed was Rev Alexander Reid Taylor MA, who was ordained and inducted on 28 October 1904. He was to remain in Mauchline for ten years, before accepting a call to Kinross West U. F. Church on 1 September 1914. He later moved to Aberdeen.

In February 1915 Rev David Foulis LitA was inducted at the Abbey Church. He had been admitted by the General Assembly in May 1914. He was born in 1875 at Penicuik and served with the Y.M.C.A. during the war in France. As a youth he worked in the ironmongery trade in Edinburgh. Prior to coming to Mauchline, he had been a minister at Amble, Northumberland, and at Kirkwall in Orkney. He served in Mauchline until 1925, accepting a call to Invertiel U. F. Church at Kirkcaldy in Fife, when the Abbey Church was closed. Rev David Foulis died at Invertiel on 8 February 1927.

WALKER MEMORIAL U. F. CHURCH

The old United Presbyterian Church was renamed the Walker Memorial Church after the union with the Free Church in 1900. The congregation was still served by the Rev Wilson Baird at this time. He continued for a number of years, passing the fifty year mark in 1925. Rev. Wilson Baird of the North Church retired to allow the union of the Walker and Abbey churches on 4 September 1925 and died on 13 June 1932 aged 85. He was buried in Mauchline cemetery.

The United Free Church nationally was streamlining its church estate, especially in communities with two congregations. Meetings were held simultaneously at the Walker Memorial and Abbey churches on 28 November 1924 to discuss the union, and a joint meeting was held on 13 December which ratified the agreement. The churches in Mauchline were united on 6 September 1925, following an agreement made on 23 January 1925. The former Abbey U.F. Church was closed for worship, and the united congregation met in the Walker Memorial Church. The church was given the new name of Mauchline United Free Church. At this time the communion tokens of 1799 that had been used by the Walker Memorial Church were removed from use and were presented to former members of the Walker Church as keepsakes. At the time of the union, the church did not have a minister and the interim moderator was the Rev Dr George Johnstone Jaffrey of Kilmarnock. He was a noted spiritual minister, later becoming Moderator of the Church of Scotland in 1952.

The united Mauchline U. F. Church retained both buildings for some time. The Walker Memorial building was to remain as the place of worship, the former Abbey church being used for the Sunday school, bible class, board meetings and week-night services.

Following the union of the two U. F. churches the first minister inducted was Rev. George Alfred Charlton MA, who took up post on 23 December 1925. Charlton was born in Edinburgh on 22 February 1889, the son of Rev Alfred Henry Charlton (minister at Kilwinning) and Mary Helen Gillam. He was educated at Kilwinning Public School, Ardrossan Academy, Harris Academy, Dundee, and the University of St Andrews, from where he graduated with a Master of Arts degree in 1912. He then attended Glasgow College. During the First World War Rev Charlton served with the forces in France and Belgium, from 1915-19. On the resumption of peace, Rev Charlton returned home and was licensed by the Presbytery of Dundee in April 1919. His first charge was at Largo in Fife, where he was ordained and inducted on 2 October 1919.

After the Union of the Church of Scotland with the United Free Church in 1929, the churches in Mauchline were renamed Mauchline Old (the present parish church) and Mauchline North (the former Mauchline United Free, or Walker Memorial Church). It was the Rev G. A. Charlton that had suggested that the Name Mauchline North be used for the church. The Abbey Church building was sold in the 1930s and the Walker Memorial Manse at Greenhead was sold in the 1930s.

Rev Charlton was married on 2 June 1925 to Margaret Wilson (1895-1982), just before coming to Mauchline. They had a son, Gillam Charlton (1929-1984).

The Brethren group in Mauchline seems to have folded in 1903.

SONS OF THE PARISH

Professor James Fairlie Gemmill was born in Mauchline in 1867. Educated at the public school, followed by Kilmarnock Academy, he studied for his degree at Glasgow University, graduating with honours in 1894. In 1900 he gained a Doctorate of Medicine with honours, and in 1910 became a Doctor of Science. He started lecturing at Glasgow Provincial Training College. In 1919 he was appointed as Professor of Natural History at University College Dundee. He was also involved with the Millport Marine Station on Great Cumbrae, as well as numerous other societies associated with zoology and biology. He wrote *Natural History in Poetry of Robert Burns* and The *Teratology of Fishes* (1912), in addition to numerous articles for learned journals. He was found drowned in the River Tay at Dundee on Wednesday 10 February 1926, adjacent to the Esplanade, several hundred yards west of the Tay Bridge. He was never married, and was buried in Dundee's Western Cemetery on 13 February.

Alexander Galt DSc FRSE was born in Mauchline in 1854, the second son of Alexander Galt. He was educated at Kilmarnock Academy followed by Glasgow Church of Scotland Training College and Glasgow University. There he became the Kelvin Scholar. Galt was for a time Keeper of the Technological Department of the Royal Scottish Museum in Edinburgh and became Official Assistant to Lord Kelvin in Glasgow for a period. Galt wrote a number of papers on physics and physical chemistry which were published in various journals.

Not a son of the parish directly, but one who lived for a number of years at Haughbank House, was Guy McCrone, author and theatre manager. Guy Fulton McCrone was born in 1898, the son of Robert McCrone, manager of the Ballochmyle Creamery. He was born at Birkenhead in England but moved to Glasgow, and was educated at Glasgow Academy. He then studied modern languages at Pembroke College in Cambridge, followed by a course in singing at Vienna. When fund-raising bazaars were being held at Ballochmyle House in aid of the Broomhill and Lanfine Homes in 1922 he organised the concerts in the library. He was one of three founders (with James Bridie and Dr Tom Honeyman) of the Citizen's Theatre in Glasgow in 1943, being its first managing director. He was more noted for his novels, many of which were based on historical Glasgow events and families. These include *Antimacassar City*, *The Philistines* and *The Puritans*, the three novels being collected as a trilogy called Wax Fruit, which is still in print. Other novels include *Aunt Bel, The Hayburn Family, Charlotte and Dr. James, Red Plush – the Moorhouse Family, The Striped Umbrella*, and *An Independent*

Young Man. Guy McCrone retired to the Lake District and died at Windermere in May 1977.

Cuthbert Nairn was born at High (or East) Welton farm on 21 June 1864. He was to marry a daughter of Hugh Miller of Grassmillees and had at least one son (Bryce Nairn, who became the British Consul General in Morocco) and a daughter. In 1889 he and his sister Jessie Nairn went to Morocco where they served as medical missionaries. They were the first two members of the (Glasgow) Southern Morocco Mission to go from Scotland to Morocco. Cuthbert served in the country until 1944 when he was stabbed in his own dispensary by a fanatical Muslim. There were many thousands at his funeral on the following day, which took place at the European cemetery in Marrakech. Jessie Nairn was married to John Richmond (1862-20 February 1945), another missionary in Morocco, and she died on 10 June 1954 in Cumnock.

Not a son of the parish, but resident in Mauchline in his final years, was Robert Samson Ingram, a prolific local architect. He was born in 1840, the son of James Ingram, himself a noted architect, who had his practice in Kilmarnock. James was born in Catrine and was responsible for numerous buildings in Ayrshire, notably the Town House in Irvine, the Corn Exchange (now the Palace Theatre) in Kilmarnock, and St Marnock's Church in the same town. More locally he designed New Cumnock Parish Church, Catrine West Church (now a house), and Glaisnock House.

Robert Ingram entered his father's office where he served his apprenticeship, followed by a time in London where he extended his experience. He returned to Scotland where he became a partner in his father's practice, remaining the sole partner when his father died in 1870. He continued to work alone until 1906 when he was joined by D. M. Brown. Ingram lived for a time in Auchinleck, in a cottage on Barony Road. He later moved to Mauchline where he lived at The Grove

Ingram designed numerous schools, churches, institutes, houses and monuments throughout the west of Scotland. He had contracts with a number of school boards, the Roman Catholic education committees, and with William Baird & Company, the latter giving him commissions for public buildings within mining communities owned by the company. Among Ingram's more notable works are the Grange Church (Kilmarnock), Barrhill Parish Church, Hurlford Parish Church, Gartsherrie Parish Church, Glenbuck Parish Church, Cumnock Town Hall, Baird Institute (Cumnock), A. M. Brown Institute (Catrine), Dick Institute (Kilmarnock), Kilmarnock Academy, the old Public School in Cumnock, Burns Monument (Kilmarnock) and the Peden Monument (Cumnock).

Ingram died at The Grove, Mauchline, on 6 October 1915. He was buried in the High Kirkyard in Kilmarnock. He was survived by his wife, Frances Hay Torrance, leaving £357 14s 6d in his will.

EDUCATION

At Mauchline Public School the inspector was delighted with the education given to the pupils at the turn of the century. In 1901 his report noted that 'On the elementary side this is quite a model school, a school of which the Board have just reason to be proud … there is hardly a place of weakness anywhere… the advanced department is doing capital work up to a certain point but in existing circumstances it has hardly a chance of it full development. The headmaster has far too much to do.' The headmaster, James Marshall, left the school in 1902 after having served at the school for sixteen years. He died on 11 August 1921 aged 61 years and is buried in the new cemetery.

A new headmaster was appointed in August 1902 – James Campbell MA, who was brought up in Cumnock. At the time the school had over four hundred on the roll – 214 boys and 211 girls. On 7 July 1903 the Marcus Bain Silver Medal was presented to the school for the best pupil. It was won by Agnes L. Young. Seven years later she became a teacher at the school, but left in 1926 on the occasion of her marriage. When she died in 1969 she bequeathed the medal back to the school.

At the start of the twentieth century the Stewart Trust Fund awarded six bursaries of £5 to pupils at the school. The fund also paid for the majority of pupils' class books, as well as giving the school board £40 annually.

In 1910 a new cookery room was provided at the school. The architect was to be Mr MacGaan (of Janefield, Ayr), who had been architect to the board for many years, but he was unwell and subsequently died in 1910. Instead, Messrs Ingram and Brown of Kilmarnock were engaged. On 15 May 1918 the local parish School Boards were abolished, and the school came under the control of Ayrshire Education Authority. Campbell served at the school for 26 years until 1928, when he retired. He was to serve as a justice of the peace and died in 1944.

At the school he was replaced by Mr Walter Amos Rawson MA on 19 November 1928. At the time the roll had fallen to 324 pupils, 168 boys and 156 girls. In 1929 Rev Dr Mitchell announced to the pupils that he was going to present a gold medal for the dux.

In September 1930 the roll of the school was 365 pupils, with a regular attendance of 95%. By September 1931 the roll had increased to 382. The school had become too small for all the pupils, and in May 1931 a new £10,000 extension was started. A new gymnasium at the back of the school was opened on 3 October 1932, as well as an extension which provided ten classrooms, practical subjects room, as well as rooms for post-primary instruction.

On 26 May 1931 Mrs Dunlop of Barskimming offered the Barskimming Medal for dux of the school. It was presented for the first time on 1 July that year by Rev Dr Easson to Donald A. Ramsay. The medal appears to have been re-presented in 1933 by Robert Jack Dunlop of Barskimming, when it was won by Thomas R. Cowan. The medal continued to be presented by him until his death in 1938, after which it was endowed by Mrs Dunlop in her husband's memory. It appears to have been awarded continuously until 1971, the last person to receive it being Elizabeth Irving.

The school log books give brief details of various reasons that the school was closed, from serious weather, illness, or on 21 September 1932 when the pupils were given a half day holiday to mark Sir Walter Scott's centenary. On the following week, 26 September, the new high pressure heating system was installed, 'with excellent results'. Each April, the school was closed to allow the pupils to attend Mauchline Races. This appears to have been the tradition up to the outbreak of the Second World War

Mr Rawson had been suffering from ill-health for a period of time and in 1932 resigned his position because of this. The Inspector's report referred to him with glowing colours: 'Mr Rawson, the late headmaster, whose resignation owing to prolonged ill-health is much regretted, had not only proved himself a competent and sympathetic head, but had won for himself the warm affection and regard of the community in which his lot was cast.' Walter Rawson died in May 1934. On the day of his funeral, 31 May, the school held a one minute silence.

The next headmaster was Thomas A. White, who took up his post on 25 April 1933. In the meantime Mr J. S. Selbie had been acting headmaster. The roll continued to increase, in October 1933 reaching 400. The Inspector's report of 15 December 1934 noted that 'in both classes seen the work that was seen gave clear evidence of sound instruction in all the main subjects … the lower class did a test on arithmetic with good success … senior 3 made quite creditable appearance in the written test in arithmetic and in the subject examined orally … the reconstructed and extended premises are now in full use.'

Improvements were being made all the time, and in January 1935 a new radiogram was introduced, allowing the pupils to listen to broadcasts, as well as a projector, which could show pictures. These were purchased following a fund-raising concert. In 1936 there were seven primary and 3 post-primary classes in the school, a total enrolment of 388.

In the 1930s the subject of gardening was introduced to the school as part of the education of the pupils, and the ground to the rear of the building was converted for that purpose. Inspectors from Auchincruive Agricultural College came to the school on a regular basis, to see how the gardens were progressing. In 1935 they reported that 'throughout the season the garden has been kept in excellent condition. Flowers, fruit, and vegetables in variety have been cultivated most successfully. Twenty-four individual plots created a good deal of competition amongst the scholars … an outstanding example of the value of gardening.'

On 22 January 1936 the pupils and staff of the school attended the hall to listen on their radiogram of the proclamation of King Edward VIII.

The outbreak of the Second World War caused major disruption at the school, and on 31 August 1939 the school was 'closed this afternoon for evacuation of children, which takes place tomorrow.' This appears to have been extended, for it was not until 11 September that the school resumed. On that day the roll was 428 Mauchline pupils, plus 207 evacuees from Glasgow and other places. A temporary reorganisation of classes had to take place to accommodate the extra pupils. As time passed, the evacuated Roman Catholic pupils were relocated to the town hall, and the infant evacuees were absorbed into the Mauchline classes.

On 6 September 1943 word was received, following R. J. Dunlop of Barskimming's death, that the dux prize was being endowed by £75. Other events in the life of the school brought a change to the regular lessons taught, such as on 6 October 1944 when the pupils were taken to the town hall to hear 'Miss Bertha Waddell's Children's Theatre'. On 6 March 1944 Mr A. L. Barr, from the Scottish Band of Hope Union, came to the school to talk to the older pupils of the benefits of temperance. On 26 January 1940 a record low temperature of 0°F (-18°C) was recorded in the school garden.

In the Inspector's report of 1946 he recorded that the 'school garden was devoted throughout the war to food production. 23 cwts of vegetables were produced and disposed of, mainly to the county kitchen for school meals. A stock of poultry was introduced early in the war. In March 1941 there were 23 laying pullets. Beekeeping was also undertaken…'

At Crosshands Public School the building remained the property of the Duke of Portland, but it was leased to Ayrshire Education Authority. The teacher in 1902 was Miss Mitchell, who retired in 1911. In 1909 the school had 21 pupils on the roll, but over half of these were from outwith the parish. This caused much trouble for the board of Mauchline, for they felt it was unfair that they had to pay for a school which had most of its pupils coming from other parishes. In addition, in 1909 the Duke of Portland stopped paying his annual subscription of £5 towards the cost of the school. The board wrote to his factor asking that this would continue, but he replied that the payment was at the personal pleasure of the Duke, and he no longer wished to continue. Discussion took place on closing the school, but it was discovered that the cost of transporting the pupils to Mauchline would cost more, so it was allowed to remain open. A Combination School, with Tarbolton, Craigie and Galston parishes, was proposed in 1911, but this came to nought. Instead, the school board pursued the other parishes for payment to cover their parishioners.

Barbara MacDonald was appointed as the teacher at Crosshands in 1911 and she remained through the 1920s. She was paid a salary of £70 in 1911, rising to £75 soon after, including her free house adjoining the school. The school came under threat of closure again, but survived, the chance of new mines being sunk in the vicinity, and the possibility of new miners' houses being erected. Nevertheless, the Duke of Portland wished to sell the property in 1921 (when he was selling off much of his surrounding estate) and it was purchased by the Ayrshire Education Authority. Agnes B. Laughland was the teacher in 1940. Mrs Barbara M. Elliot was appointed as the sole teacher in June 1942.

The school board continued to operate the parish schools. The chairman, Marcus Bain, resigned in 1909 after having served for 23 years. The clerk for many years was William MacMillan.

INDUSTRY

At the turn of the century Ballochmyle quarries were still operated by Marcus Bain, who employed between 200-300 men. Stone from the quarry was in demand for building work across the country, and notable buildings erected with the stone includes Annbank Parish Church, Mossblown (1903), Henderson Church, Kilmarnock (1907), Stepps Parish Church, Lanarkshire (1900), King's Theatre, Kilmarnock (1904) and hundreds if not thousands of other public buildings and houses. Around 1901 Bain also took on the lease of the Gatelawbridge sandstone quarry near to Thornhill in Dumfriesshire. This quarry was noted in history as being tenanted by Robert Paterson (1715-1801), the 'Old Mortality' of Sir Walter Scott, who spent much of his life restoring the memorials to the Covenanters.

Marcus Bain built a number of houses in Mauchline, both for his workers but also for other tenants. A row of nine houses in Haugh Road was erected by him.

Marcus Bain died on 14 October 1910 and was buried in Mauchline cemetery. His obituarist in the *Cumnock Chronicle* noted the many offices in public life that he held, but also remarked that he was a man of plain speaking - 'there was, it must be said, a brusquerie about his manner which did not make for popularity in its common sense.'

Following the death of Bain, the quarry continued, but demand for stone fell as the cost of preparing it became prohibitive, especially when compared to the cheaper bricks. There were 200 workers in the quarry in 1914, and between the wars around 70. During the Second World War there was only four men employed in the quarry.

In August 1919 work in the quarry resumed, after being closed for five years due to the war. By June 1920 stone was being produced once more, staff were being taken on, and several wagons of stone were being sent by rail daily.

The Barskimming Quarry was closed in November 1916, although it had practically ceased production of stone since the outbreak of the First World War, due to a lack of demand for building stone. The quarry was owned by Messrs Baird & Stevenson. The firm withdrew plant from the quarry over a period of months. The engines, boilers and rails were removed. A few years earlier the fine-planing plant had been installed, but this, too, was removed. By April 1917 it was noted in the local newspaper that the quarries 'are now closed until further notice and the workmen have all found employment elsewhere.'

In May 1927 the Ballochmyle Brick Company was founded.

Work continued in W. and A. Smith's boxworks. The company sold part of the former Wilson & Amphlet factory in Barskimming Road in 1907 and on 18 and 25 February 1911 sold the remainder to Andrew Kay, who relocated their curling stone factory there.

At Smith's boxworks in Kilmarnock Road, a fire broke out on 15 November 1933 and the strong breeze fanned the flames so much that the building was gutted. Two of the three buildings facing onto the main road were so badly gutted that they were demolished. At the time of the fire the firm was running down. It struggled on for a few years but in 1937 went into voluntary liquidation. William Smith died on 13 July 1949.

Smith's boxworks was taken over by five men, Robert Wood Wyllie (curling-stone manufacturer), Alexander Anderson (joiner, Catrine), James Murdoch Jamieson (grocer), William Wilson Jr. (clerk) and John MacKenzie of the Loudoun Arms. The new firm was named W. & A. Smith (1937) Ltd, established on 22 March 1937. The firm only seems to have survived for a few years, stopping production during the Second World War. During hostilities, the workshops were partially used to store potatoes and milk powder.

The boxes produced by Smith and other manufacturers became collectable in later years, and have gained the generic name of 'Mauchline Ware'. The Mauchline Ware Collectors Club was founded in 1986. On 26 April 1997 the club erected a bronze plaque on the wall of Smith's former showroom in Kilmarnock Road, at the time an ironmongery operated by Iain Cowan, to commemorate the business. Unveiled by Councillor Eric Jackson, this plaque reads:

> Until 1939 this was the site of W. & A. Smith's Boxworks. For over 100 years 'Mauchline Ware' was made here and sent to all corners of the world. This building was the showroom and offices. This plaque was presented by the Mauchline Ware Collectors Club 1997.

In the Cowgate Andrew Pollock's agricultural machinery works continued to manufacture various items used on the farms. He was later joined by his sons, Andrew and William, and the firm was later renamed A. & W. Pollock. Still an expanding business, the firm moved to a new factory in Station Road in 1917, the premises being built from 1915-16. Pollock was one of only four manufacturers of carts in Scotland in any scale. In 1910 a new tattie digger was designed, continuing to be manufactured until the 1960s.

Mauchline Colliery was sunk to the north of the village by Caprington and Auchlochan Collieries Ltd. The owner and director of the company lived in the village at Beechgrove House. Work preparing for the colliery had been ongoing for a number of years, the cutting for the railway being halted due to the war, and not re-started until March 1922. In March 1923 sinking operations for the pit commenced. The first 'kettleful' of coal was raised in Sunday 5 April 1925. However, in May 1925 the pit was closed, and a start was made of dismantling the plant. The manager was Alexander MacCall, who lived at Laurel View, Loudoun Street.

6.14 A & W Pollock letterhead *(Jimmy McGhee)*

During the strike the pit was abandoned, but work recommenced in sinking it in the early months of 1927. In August 1927 a new seam 5 feet 10 inches thick was discovered forty fathoms below the seam that was currently being worked.

In 1933 there were 132 workers at the pit. In 1934 Caprington & Auchlochan went into liquidation and the pit was bought by Bairds and Dalmellington Co. Ltd. Bairds considerably extended the colliery and the new pit was reopened in 1938.

The pit was sunk into the coal seams which were around 150 fathoms below the ground. The pit was located north of a major fault line, for south of this the coal was around 500-600 fathoms below the ground. There were two shafts at the pit, numbered One and Two, each with winding gear on a surface horrals. The shafts were both 890 feet deep. Number One shaft was the downcast shaft, the other one being the upcast shaft, through which foul air was drawn from the pit. The shafts had two double deck cages, each deck of which could hold two hutches of coal, or eight men. When the hutches full of coal reached the surface they were pushed off by means of a compressed air ram. The hutches were then transported to the screening plant by means of a small gauge railway.

As part of the Coal Industry Social Welfare Organisation, pit-head baths were erected at Mauchline Colliery. Work commenced in January 1939 and they were officially opened on 6 July 1939 by R. L. Angus of Ladykirk. These had 42 showers and were erected at a cost of £13,148. The architect was John Henry Forshaw. At the same time as the baths were erected a new pit canteen was added, at a cost of £800. In 1945 there were 800 workers at the mine.

A number of fatalities occurred in the mine - on 18 October 1931 William Reid was killed at the pit. On 30 August 1939 William Grant was killed at the pit. He was twenty years old.

A new pit was also sunk at Friendlesshead in 1927. By June that year the first block of coal, weighing around eight hundredweight, was lifted from the mine and was sent to the manager's house where it was exhibited. The manager went to the miner's working place, congratulated him and gave him ten shillings.

Many men from Mauchline parish found work in the new Barony Colliery which was opened in Auchinleck parish in 1912. A number of locals were to die there, including James Blair, who died of injuries sustained on 29 June 1927.

In February 1936 work commenced on building a new creamery in the Bent field for the Scottish Milk Marketing Board. Mauchline Creamery was designed by the architect Alexander Mair (1883-1944) of Kilmarnock, the plans being proposed in 1935. Mair was also responsible for designing the milk powder factory, which was erected at the same time. The new creamery was modern in its appearance, and parts of it were designed in an architectural style that has become associated with the 1930s – white concrete blocks with horizontal windows.

The milk powder factory was the first such to produce milk powder successfully on a commercial scale. It produced dried milk which was supplied to the services during the Second World War. It used 10,000 gallons of milk each day.

At the Haugh the Ballochmyle Creamery Company produced margarine. The owner of the works was Robert McCrone, a pioneer of margarine production. The works had been rebuilt from 1899-1910 in a distinctive style of architecture. The

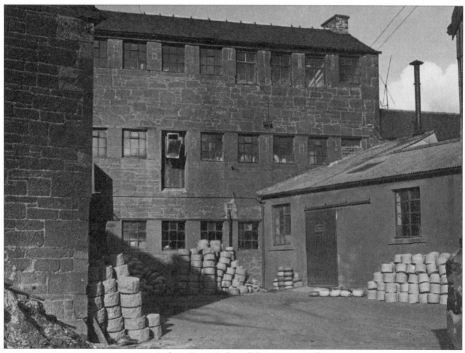

6.15 Andrew Kay & Co.'s workshop *(James Wyllie)*

creamery manager at one time was John Cadas (later to move to Rowallan Creamery, Kilmarnock), the engineer being George Wallace, who lived in the Woolmill House. The creamery produced two types of margarine – 'Blue Bell', which was sold to the domestic customer, and 'Seafoam' which was supplied to bakeries. A local tradition claims that the popular 'Blue Band' margarine received its name from the fact that the tilework within the factory had a strip of blue tiles on an otherwise white wall. In the mid-1920s the creamery was sold to Jurgens. In 1925 the manager was D. O. Clarkson, who entertained the fifty employees at his home of Moorfield.

Robert McCrone lived at Haughbank House and served locally as a Justice of the Peace. In January 1915 he was appointed as a county councillor for Mauchline. In 1918 he moved into Auchinleck House, leasing it from Lord Talbot de Malahide. He moved out of the house at Whitsunday 1923, but J. D. Boswell reckoned that he had not maintained the property to a sufficient standard during his tenancy and in January 1925 a legal court case took place, Boswell suing for £957 worth of articles removed from the house. McCrone was by this time living at Dinwiddie, near Hollybush.

Andrew Kay & Co. continued to manufacture curling stones at the Haugh, one of the finest being 'Kay's Excelsior', which weighed forty pounds. In 1907 the firm was using six varieties of stone, three of them being fine-grained Ailsa Craig granites. The three other stones were Crawfordjohn dolerite (which had large black crystals of augite), and dolerites from Burnock and Tincornhill (New Cumnock) quarries. In 1920 stones were offered in seven granites – Crawfordjohn (95 shillings per pair), Red Hone Ailsa, Blue Hone Ailsa, Ailsa Craig (58 shillings), Burnock Water, Tinkernhill (sic), and Carsphairn (cheapest at 50 shillings per pair). Many stones were exported around the world, one of the largest markets in 1935 being Canada. Many medals for quality were received by Kay's from various trade exhibitions, including Chicago's World Fair and the Toronto Industrial Exhibition.

Andrew Kay & Co moved into Mauchline, taking over the old boxworks, known as the Victoria Works, that had been occupied by Davidson, Wilson & Amphlet, located behind Wilson Place. The site was purchased in 1911, but in 1913

6.16 Andrew Kay & Co., letterhead from 1913 *(James Wyllie)*

advertisements still indicated that the firm was based at the Haugh. Andrew's son, also Andrew, kept the business going, his other son, Thomas, setting up a separate business of his own. This was located at Burnside House, a spot that was formerly known as 'Castle Daffin'. Thomas Kay's works survived until the 1920s, closing once Thomas had died and his son, also Thomas, was badly gassed in the First World War. On 19 July 1927 Mrs Catherine Kirk or Kay, heritable proprietrix of the factory, passed it to her brother-in-law, James Wyllie.

6.17 A worker in Andrew Kay & Co., 1925 *(James Wyllie)*

At the Haugh the Woollen Mill continued to produce wool until it suffered in a fire early in the twentieth century. It was not rebuilt after this time, instead standing in ruins before it was eventually demolished.

Other industries existed in the village on a small scale. In the first part of the twentieth century Mauchline Hosiery existed. On the railways, and at the station, between 30-40 men were employed in 1950, carrying on maintenance and signalling on the line.

Mauchline Gas Light Company continued to produce town gas for the community from the turn of the century up to and including the Second World War. In July 1908 the price of gas was reduced by five pence per 1,000 cubic feet to

4 shillings and 2 pence. At the start of the twentieth century the manager was Robert Pollock. In May 1926 the Gas-Light Company was sold as a going concern to Messrs Robert Pollock & Sons.

Many of the smaller smithies were closed, as demand for horse-shoeing and machinery manufacture diminished. At Crosshands the smithy operated by Thomas Elliot was by 1940 converted into a garage, with repair facilities and a petrol pump. By 1953 it was run by W. B. Aitchison.

Joineries existed in various places on different scales. In January 1918 A. C. Riddell & Co opened a new business in Earl Grey Street as cabinetmakers, joiners, upholsterers and undertakers. A joinery also existed at Crosshands in the early years of the twentieth century, operated by William Candlish.

COMMERCE

Mauchline Co-operative Society Ltd. grew in the early years of the century. In 1917 sales were £700 for the second quarter of the year. President of the society at the time was Alexander Cumming. He was followed by John Hood. In 1920 there were plans to rebuild the Mitchell Place property into shops, but this did not proceed at that time. New and updated shops were erected at Mitchell Place in 1927, designed by W. F. Valentine. In 1920 the annual sales had totalled £14,491.

Soon after the First World War the old Cross Keys Inn (or Whitefoord Arms) was acquired by the society and subsequently demolished to allow the erection of a new shop. The new double-storey sandstone building contained a grocery and drapery. A plaque was erected on the gable commemorating the old inn it replaced. The co-operative also owned the Jean Armour Restaurant at 39 Loudoun Street and operated it for weddings and other social functions.

In 1928 an old building located between the churchyard and the entrance to Mauchline Castle was acquired by the Co-op and subsequently demolished to allow the erection of new premises, which were opened in 1929. This comprised of two shops facing Loudoun Street, the drapery and grocery. Behind these, built at the back of the plot, was the co-op bakery. At the society's annual general meeting in

6.18 Mauchline Co-operative Society letterhead *(Author's Collection)*

1930 it was recorded that there were 689 members and that the business had share capital of £24,368 12s 9d. The president for many years was James MacIntyre.

At the post office in New Road, next to the Temperance Hall, Maggie MacLure Miller was the postmistress at the turn of the century. In 1905 a new post office was erected in Loudoun Street, at the corner with Barskimming Road, being opened on 23 May. The property was owned by Netherplace estate, as was much of Loudoun Street at that time. The post office building in New Road was converted into a fish restaurant and ice cream business by S. M. Bryden in 1908. Later post masters were William MacDonald, Miss Ribbeck (to 1920), Andrew J. W. Lyell (1920-1923) and Norman MacCrimmon (from 1923).

Old businesses in operation from 1900 until the Second World War included Miss MacMinn, newsagent and tobacconist, at the Cross. M. H. Lyall had a china merchant and confectionery in Loudoun Street (1935). Henry Ullrich had a bakery and tea rooms at 4-6 New Road. George Allan & Sons operated a butcher's shop in Loudoun Street. In Earl Grey Street was James Brownlee, grocer.

In 1933 Mrs R. J. Dunlop of Barskimming opened the Mutual Service Club at the Cross and it was hoped to use some of the premises as small workshops.

Agents for the Commercial Bank of Scotland were the solicitor firm of J. D. & S. MacMillan. In 1902 John Davidson MacMillan returned to Mauchline from elsewhere to open up in business with his father, who was to retire in 1911. In 1940 John Davidson MacMillan's son, J. D. S., joined the business, eventually taking over. In August 1943 John Davidson MacMillan died aged 70, at his home of Ardmillan in Cumnock Road. He had been associated with many local organisations.

The Commercial Bank in the village had become so popular that the directors agreed that the premises were 'old and small' and decided to look for a new building. In 1912 the house next door came on the market, and the bank purchased it. The building was extended and remodelled into new banking premises and opened in 1913.

William Gilmour Pearson sold lemonade in green bottles, on which the words 'W. G. Pearson Mauchline' were moulded in capital letters. His aerated water factory was located at the Loan and comprised two buildings – a Beer House and a Lemonade House. The latter had a gas engine, two machines capable of filling six bottles at a time, a soda machine, washer, syrup machine and corking machine. The firm was later known as Pearson & Smith, producers of 'Ballochmyle Mineral Waters'. Pearson died in 1915 and the factory was put on the market.

With the arrival of the motor car, new businesses sprang up to service the needs of both them and their passengers. In Mauchline William Baird established himself as a motor agent and hirer, offering petrol, oils, tyres and other accessories. He had open and closed cars for hire. Around 1912 William Murray (d. 1927) opened a new garage in Cowgate with his sons.

There remained a number of inns in the village, supplying drink and refreshments to locals and visitors. The Loudoun Arms Inn was under the control of John Reid (of the Craighead Inn, Cumnock) from 1905 and, on his death, by Mrs Reid (1912). It then passed to William C. MacKenzie by 1917 and John MacKenzie by 1937. By the Second World War the hotel was still the property of Netherplace estate, but was tenanted by Charles and Catherine Gray.

The Black Bull Hotel was still occupied by William Walker, but on his retiral it was taken on by Private Donald Stewart and his wife, Grace Murchie, daughter of Mrs Murchie of the Burns Tavern in Tarbolton. Donald Stewart was previously the butler with Mr Arthur at Montgomery Castle, Tarbolton, before taking on the hostelry. He signed up with the Argyll & Sutherland Highlanders at the start of the Great War but was killed in France on 12 April 1918. His widow, Grace Stewart, continued to operate it for some time, retiring in 1944.

At Poosie Nansies, William Gibson was the landlord in the 1920s, followed by Daniel Blair Hamilton in the 1930s and 1940s.

The Ballochmyle Inn's hosts over the first half of the twentieth century included John S. Buchanan (from the First World War until the 1920s) and William George (by the Second World War).

The Market Inn remained the property of Isabella MacLennan (nee Brown), widow of Andrew MacLennan. In 1916 the inn was placed on the market, offered with a small field opposite it that was used for quoiting, and the inn came with the privilege of pasturing on the green or Loan. It was a two storey building with attic - still thatched. It does not appear to have been sold at this time, and Mrs MacLennan let the property to Alexander Walker who continued to operate it for a couple of years. In 1918 Quintin MacLennan, a surgeon in Glasgow, and trustee of the late Andrew MacLennan, applied to have the license transferred to him, only to have it refused. In 1921 the inn was owned by H. W. Morton, of the picture house, but was leased and managed by H. Fraser. In April that year the inn went on fire. It was later closed and converted into a cottage.

The Thistle Inn had been occupied by Jane Nisbet, but by 1918 was operated by Mr H. Train.

The telephone arrived in Mauchline in the early twentieth century. The first telephone in the village was installed in the parish council office. Only the well-off and business owners had telephone lines in the early days, and the following is a list of some of the earliest numbers:

13	Ballochmyle Creamery Company
15	William Baird, motor agent and hirer.
15	Loudoun Arms Hotel
21	A. & W. Pollock

AGRICULTURE

At the start of the century most of the farms remained the property of local estates, farmers leasing them for varying lengths of time. In 1918 and shortly afterwards, some of the farms on the Duke of Portland's estate, at the north end of the parish, were placed on the market and in many cases were purchased by the sitting tenants.

In 1922 the Scottish Board of Agriculture acquired Grassmillees farm and divided it into fifteen smallholdings, varying in size from 5 to 12 acres. Typical of these was one that was 3.589 acres in extent, for which the fixed rent payable was £5. The compensation paid to Ballochmyle estate for the lands in 1922 was £2,347. Small-holdings numbered 7-15 were the property of Ballochmyle estate.

Similarly, in 1931 the Scottish Board of Agriculture acquired Mosshead farm and divided it into ten smallholdings. The first tenancies on these smallholdings were offered to ex-servicemen, returning after the First World War.

In 1924 there was a notable outbreak of foot-and-mouth disease in the district. This appeared at the southern end of the parish, affecting Haughhead and Haughyett farms, where the cattle were all slaughtered.

HEALTH

General Practitioners who operated in Mauchline at the turn of the twentieth century included Dr Pollock, who lived at Box Villa. In 1904 he sold up and emigrated.

Mauchline Nursing Association continued to operate in the new century. In 1916 it was noted that Nurse Thomson had attended 249 patients in the year, for which she made 2,419 visits. The president of the association at that time was Lady Eliza Alexander, who resided in London.

A new Factories Act of 1937 required the appointment of examining surgeons for each parish. The first in Mauchline was Dr Thomas Percy Bliss of Anthorn, Sorn Road, who resigned in 1939 after which Dr David T. Kemp MB, also of Anthorn, took over.

Dr John Reid MBCM was for almost forty years a much loved and highly esteemed doctor in the village. Born in Auchinleck, he was educated in medicine and surgery at Glasgow University. Practising in Mauchline from 1882 until his retiral in April 1921, he died at his home of Haplan, Cumnock Road, on 15 October 1929. He was succeeded in the practice by Dr MacFarlane, son of the schoolmaster of Craigie school.

In 1939 the Emergency Medical Services acquired Ballochmyle House and immediate policies and constructed a hospital there, one of seven established in Scotland. Proposals for this were first mooted in 1938, but the missives were not competed until October 1939. Work on the temporary wards started in that month. By the autumn of 1940 a number of temporary wards had been erected, increasing to 33 wards by 1942. Staff accommodation was also provided.

The hospital was constructed on the pavilion plan, which was typical of Emergency Medical Services hospitals. At the start there were two blocks of eight wards plus a third block in which were the administrative office, kitchen, laboratory and pharmacy.

The first patients were admitted to the hospital in 1940, some of these being survivors of a U-boat attack in the North Atlantic Ocean. The first actual patient was an eighteen year old soldier, a private in the Argyll and Sutherland Highlanders, who was admitted on 20 October 1940 to have his tonsils removed. The first civilian patient was a ward-maid who worked in the hospital. She was admitted on 6 November 1940 for an appendicectomy.

The first major incident which required the services of the hospital was the Clydebank Blitz, which occurred in March 1941. So many were the casualties of the bombing raid that not only ambulances, but trucks, buses and vans brought the wounded to the hospital. Soon after, in May 1941, the same story was repeated when Greenock suffered a blitz, many of the casualties being burned.

In December 1940 a new Plastic Surgery and Jaw Injuries unit was opened at Ballochmyle. This was operated under the guidance of Sir Harold Gillies until 1943 when Mr Tough took control. This unit was later transferred to Canniesburn Hospital in Glasgow in 1967.

Two newer wards were opened in 1941, as was the isolation unit.

The hospital treated service personnel to start with, including those who served with the Free French and Polish forces. From 1942 many service personnel were brought to the hospital for treatment from the front in the Middle East and Mediterranean. In April 1943 the hospital dealt with 297 patients being admitted in one day.

In June 1944 a large number of invasion casualties were brought to the hospital for treatment. These had been injured at the D-Day landings in Normandy. In the period to May 1945 six thousand patients were admitted. During the height of the German attacks on London, several hundred civilians were evacuated to the hospital from the London area. At the time the hospital was operating at its maximum capacity – 1,200 patients.

The first hospital train to arrive in Ayrshire terminated at Mauchline Station in July 1944. A number of servicemen who had been injured on active service in France were transported from the station to the new Ballochmyle Hospital by local hospital and ambulance personnel, plus many volunteers. Within one hour, all of the patients had been taken from the station to the hospital and most were allocated beds.

The hospital also treated prisoners of war who were held in the local camps at Kingencleugh and Pennylands (near Auchinleck). These prisoners were mainly Italians or Germans.

The number of patients at the hospital rose to about 1,000 in 1945 due to the number of inpatients who were brought from London as a result of the flying-bombs. This was to be the peak for numbers at the hospital, but with the resumption of peace the numbers started to drop off and the hospital remained for the treatment of civilians.

A unit at the hospital was established to offer plastic surgery to the face and jaw areas. The expertise gained was such that the hospital was selected as a training school for officers of the Royal Army Dental Corps.

Ballochmyle House was part of the hospital, and it was originally used as residential accommodation for the medical, nursing, administrative and technical staff. Within a year a new nurses' accommodation block was erected, and the house was abandoned. A second nurses' block was opened in 1941, nick-named 'Siberia' by its occupants from its cold condition, being heated only by three coal stoves located in the corridor.

LEISURE

Mauchline Races continued to be a popular leisure attraction in the parish. Secretary of the committee in 1905 was William Pearson. In April 1914 the race meeting was held at 2 o'clock in the afternoon, with three different races - open gallop, open handicap trot, and trot confined to Mauchline parish. There was £21 10s worth of prize money that year.

During the First World War the horse races were cancelled, but the day was still marked in the parish as a gala day. On the night prior to race day in 1917 (Thursday 27 April), for example, the bellman walked around the village informing the residents that the foot-races would still be held, starting at 2.30pm for the infants, with races later in the day for older children and men and women. In that year there was a large turnout of competitors, keen to win the prizes on offer of money, cutlery, clothing, sugar and potatoes. On race day the shows set up on the Loan Green.

Mauchline Races resumed after the war, and continued to be held for a number of years. In April 1919 they were held in the Mountfield, Netherplace. There were only two horse entries for the open gallop, but more for the walk, trot and gallop race. However attendance at the races had been falling and in March 1929 a meeting was held in the Thistle Inn to determine whether they should continue. It was agreed that they should, and the races went on for a number of years thereafter. In May 1931, for example, twenty horses took part in the races held at Bogwood Field. In 1932 over 600 people attended, twelve horses taking part in the open trot and five in the open gallop. There was only a small turnout in May 1933 but by 1936 there were 400 spectators. In 1938 greyhound racing was introduced for the first time, in that year there being races for 43 dogs in addition to five horses.

By the time of the First World War Mauchline Fair had dwindled in importance. In May 1918 it was noted that it was now just a holiday for farmers. In that year many of them came to the village and held a competition at the bowling green, farmers versus town residents.

Mauchline Sports were held in the Clelland Park, in 1906 the events included a wrestling contest, place kick, 220 yards race, 440 yards race and penny pitching. The sports were organised by Mauchline Thistle F. C.

In September 1925 the first proposals were made for acquiring the Beechgrove Park for conversion into a recreation ground.

The interest in football continued in the new century. Mauchline Thistle F. C. was the new junior team that was established in 1897 once the senior football time had succumbed at the end of the nineteenth century. In 1905 the team appears to have merged with Catrine Football Club, retaining the Thistle name. The team played well in local matches but closed down at the outbreak of the First World War. Prior to that, however, the team had struggled for players, it being noted in August 1907 there was a local effort to raise enough players to form a team. When peace resumed, the club reformed, but as the 1930s approached they found themselves struggling to survive, and eventually the club folded altogether.

At the turn of the century Mauchline Thistle organised a five-a-side tournament, with various teams playing at Clelland Park. Among these were Mauchline Tramps, Mauchline Willowbank, Mauchline Thistle and Mauchline Gala Five.

After the cessation of the First World War, the Cumnock and Mauchline Junior Football Association was established, but there was no team from Mauchline within it. They were later to join. A new league, named the Kilmarnock and District Junior League, started up soon after, and Mauchline played in it – most teams being from the villages around Kilmarnock.

The Mauchline and District Cup was presented in the early years of the twentieth century. This was fiercely competed for up to the Second World War.

Mauchline Greenlea Football Club played at juvenile level from the early 1900s up to the Second World War. When Mauchline Thistle F. C. folded, local support gravitated towards the Greenlea club, which continued until the Second World War, playing on West Connel Park. Other teams included Mauchline Swifts Football Club, which existed in the 1930s. A new football club was founded in 1930, known as Ballochmyle LMS Football Club, the team members were made up from employees of the railway, hence the name.

A number of the Mauchline players went on to senior teams elsewhere in Scotland. Amongst these were James 'Tibby' Bell, who played for Kilmarnock, Dumbarton and Celtic. Andrew Reid (d. 1926) played for Kilmarnock in 1901, Isaac Reid played for Dundee. John 'Corrie' Reid played for Rangers. Dougie Reid played for Stockport and Portsmouth. Frank Reid played for Huddersfield. Willie 'Bronk' Reid played for Hibernian. Symon Currie played for Kilmarnock. James Cowan played for Kilmarnock.

Curling remained popular in the parish, though Mauchline Senior Curling Club was wound up on 11 March 1924. Another club was Mauchline Netherplace Curling Club. This club won the Eglinton Jug, the highest trophy for the sport in Ayrshire, in season 1925-6, beating Cumnock's Glenmuir Water Curling Club by 13 for 8. The men in the rink were George Black, Thomas Harvey, John Findlay (skip) and William Mair. This same rink almost won the trophy again in 1929-30, meeting Ayr and Alloway Curling Club in the semi-final but losing out.

Interest in outdoor curling had more or less stopped by the start of the 1930s. In 1933 it was noted that Mauchline Loch had been abandoned, but curling was still played on a small scale on Netherplace Loch and on Mr J. MacMillan's private pond at Williamfield in Sorn Road.

Mauchline General Curling Club was reconstituted in 1936 when the remaining subsidiary clubs in the village were closed and merged. The new club was named Mauchline Curling Club. In the 1940s membership of the club reached its peak.

One of the more noted local curlers of the 1940s was William Smith. He reached the final of the British Open Championship and other important competitions.

Bowling was played on a number of local greens. Mauchline Bowling Club celebrated its fiftieth anniversary with a fete on 21 July 1917.

On 1 August 1941 a new bowling green was opened at Burns Memorial Homes by James Harper, district councillor. On that occasion he brought with him two old bowls from the old Mauchline clubhouse, which had been out of commission for almost fifty years.

The sport of quoiting was still popular at the turn of the century, and Mauchline Quoiting Club arranged an annual tournament for local clubs to enter, in 1908 there being 32 entrants. The competition usually took place on the first Saturday of August. The Ballochmyle Silver Quoit was still being played for in the new century, there being a massive entry for the 75th annual competition, which took place at Mauchline in August 1915. Such was the entry that the finals had to take place a few weeks later, being won by James Orr of Springside. The winner of the Ballochmyle Quoit was regarded as being the 21 yard champion of Ayrshire. By 1916 Tom Bone, the famous quoiter from Glenbuck, had won the Silver Quoit fourteen times, his first in 1890. Around 1920 the club became the owners of their quoiting ground. In 1922 the Quoiting Club was reconstituted, the President at that time being William White. A. G. Hales, who resided in Mauchline Castle, presented the club with a new challenge shield. The quoiting ground was located at the side of the Loan Green, next to the school, and was still in operation in 1940.

Mauchline Harriers running club was founded in 1907 and survived until the First World War. In 1920 the club was restarted, having its own hut with hot and cold showers (the old engine house, Burnside), and survived until 1938. In 1922 there were 100 members, often taking part in cross-country races. A. G. Hales presented a shield to the Harriers in 1924 for competition. The club was reformed after the Second World War.

There were a number of other organisations in the village formed by groups who had similar interests. Cricket was played on a small scale, for example in 1908 the Netherplace XI team played in Mauchline. Mauchline Homing Club existed in the early years of the twentieth century.

Mauchline Tennis Club was formed in 1923 and new tennis courts were opened on Saturday 18 August that year by Mrs Hamilton-Campbell of Netherplace. These were built at the expense of the new club, and prior to them being ready, Mrs Hamilton-Campbell had allowed the members to use the tennis courts at Netherplace. The new clubhouse was opened on 9 July 1926 by Rev Dr Mitchell.

Beechgrove Park was opened to the public on Saturday 25 June 1932 by R. J. Dunlop of Barskimming. The opening service was presided over by John Nicol of Mauchline District Council. The new park greatly enhanced the leisure facilities in the village, having a football pitch, swings, seesaws, may-pole, seats and a fountain located in its 4¼ acres.

In the new scheme of houses off Kilmarnock Road, the county council passed 1.56 acres of land in the middle of the scheme to the district council in May 1940 for use as a play park.

Mauchline Reading and Recreation Room was established in an upper room of the new post office in Loudoun Street in 1905. The club had a billiard room, summer ice and carpet bowling room, and a snug reading room. At the time annual membership was 2 shillings and sixpence; non-members paying one penny per visit. It had 78 members in 1916. Their income for that year was £90, plus £18 for concerts, of which £46 had been raised from billiards and £6 from summer-ice. The president at the time was Rev Joseph Mitchell DD.

Mauchline Public Library's membership fell considerably in 1929 due to the establishment of a free library in the village.

The fashion for the cinema, or picture houses as they were known in the early days in the district, reached Mauchline in 1920. At the Loan a timber picture house was built that year by John Lawrence, who lived in the house next door. It could seat 400 and showed films on Mondays, Wednesdays and Saturdays. Adults paid eight pence or five pence for a seat, children three pence for the three o'clock Saturday matinees. The new picture house was opened on 1 October 1920. By 1925 the cinema was acquired by Herbert W. Morton of Cumnock, who also operated the picture houses in Auchinleck followed by Cumnock. This small cinema remained in operation by Lawrence until 1940.

In 1940 the Abbey Church was purchased and converted into a cinema by John Lawrence, and it operated as such until 1963. It was later taken over by Thomas

Findlay & Sons, building contractors. The old timber cinema at the Loan was in 1940 taken over by Cadzinc Galvanising Co. Ltd., which operated it as a small factory for a few years.

The Masonic Lodge St. David (Tarbolton) Mauchline No. 133 continued to operate in the new century, its meeting place moving from hall to hall, such as within the Loudoun Arms. Unfortunately the original wooden chest that contained many historical possessions was destroyed in a fire in the later 1920s or early 1930s, but the original charter was saved.

At the Annual Burns Dinner of Lodge St David in 1923, held in the Loudoun Arms, the suggestion was made that Mauchline should have a new Burns club, the old Mauchline Jolly Beggars' Club being defunct. This was proceeded with, and Mauchline Burns Club was founded on 8 February 1923. On that day sixteen men of the district met in the Lesser Temperance Hall in New Road with the intention of forming a Burns Club. James MacIntyre had called the meeting, and he presided over it. In his opening speech, he noted that Burns had written much of his best work in Mauchline, and he felt that it was only right that the village should have a Burns club of its own, in order to promote the work of the bard, and encourage the protection of places associated with him. The club was officially inaugurated on 17 May 1923 in the Temperance Hall. Sir Archibald MacInnes Shaw was the first Honorary President, and James MacIntyre was the first President. The club's first secretary was John Taylor Gibb FSA Scot, author of *The Land o' Burns - Mauchline Town and District*, published in 1911. Gibb lived at 9 High Street, operated a photographic business in the village, and died on 14 April 1948 at the age of 84 years. He is buried in the new cemetery.

Stephen Cosh (d. 1940) was the next president. In 1940 another literary president was appointed in J. Kevan MacDowall FSA Scot, who worked as a lawyer in Glasgow. He was a noted Burnsian, but also the author of *The Carrick Gallovidian*, published in 1947. He remained president until 1946, only missing two meetings, despite having to travel from Glasgow during the war years. He was also President of the Burns Federation 1952-3. Other presidents included James Dunlop (who was club secretary for over twenty years), William MacFarlane, Rev J. C. Rennie and Hugh Rowe.

The Burns Club held annual Burns Suppers, starting in 1924. Both that supper and the one held the following year were broadcast on the radio by the BBC, something that was quite unique for the time.

The club also commenced work on protecting Burns artefacts, and from 1927 contributed one guinea towards the cost of cutting the grass around the parish church, in order that visitors could find the graves of those associated with Burns. They had in 1926 been given permission by the church to erect small wooden plaques at the graves of Burns' contemporaries and erect a plan of the kirkyard for the use of visitors. The plan was prepared by James Pollock, a local surveyor. The funds for the plaque and name-plates were provided by J. Stirrat, a native of Irvine who lived in the United States.

The Temperance Hall in New Street had a large hall with accommodation for 500. For a number of years a public library was located in its lesser hall, having 2,000 books. There existed reading and recreation rooms in the hall, where a regular whist drive in 1910 between married and single men often attracted forty players. On the same evening music was played on a gramophone, brought to the halls by D. Murray specifically for the night.

Abstinence was a popular trait at the turn of the century, and in Mauchline the Covenanter's Tent of Rechabites existed in 1916. A branch of the British Women's Temperance Association existed, Mrs Lambie being president in 1917.

At the start of the twentieth century a field at Bogwood farm was laid out as a golf course and this was officially opened on Saturday 22 May 1909 at 3:00pm by Lieut. Col. William Kentigern Hamilton-Campbell DSO. The first ball on the course was hit by Miss Hamilton-Campbell. Following this, an exhibition game was demonstrated by J. H. Irons and F. W. Kennedy of Pollok Golf Club, ex-holders of the *Evening Times* trophy. Bogwood proved to be a successful course for a number of years, but eventually it was closed at the outbreak of the First World War.

A few years elapsed before interest in golf in the district grew, until on 2 February 1937 a public meeting was held in the Temperance Hall to discuss an offer of land made by Ballochmyle Estate for a golf course. R. D. Blair presided over a

6.19 Opening of new clubhouse, Ballochmyle Golf Club *(Ballochmyle Gold Club)*

meeting of around fifty. The annual rental was £80 (though Sir Claud gave a reduction of £20 for the first year) and a nineteen year lease was offered for 60 acres. A nine-hole course was laid out, and membership cost £1 10s. By 23 February there were 166 prospective members. On 6 March 1937 the committee walked round the proposed course, Mr Monie showing the intended holes. It was decided that this was too long, and that a new plan for 14 holes should be pursued. On Saturday 26 June 1937 Mrs R. J. Dunlop of Barskimming opened the new golf course and clubhouse at Ballochmyle. Her husband, R. J. Dunlop of Barskimming was the club's first president, and the first captain was Thomas Anderson White MA, headmaster of Mauchline School. The course was officially opened on Wednesday 15 June 1938, when Mr MacInally, Scottish Amateur Champion, with three others gave a demonstration game. The clubhouse measured 24 feet by 12 feet and cost £38 5s. On 10 March 1938 it was agreed that golf could be played on a Sunday. Early trophies were the MacCosh Silver Salver, presented in 1937, the Ballantyne Silver Cup, presented in 1937, and the Stewart Silver Cup, presented in 1938.

During the war, it was agreed to allow club members serving with the forces to play on the course free of charge. The war affected the course in other ways, however, for in March 1941 twelve acres of the course (11th and 12th fairways) were ploughed for the war effort. This part of the course was subsequently farmed for the remainder of the war. With peace a possibility in the near future, it was agreed in November 1944 to reconstruct the course with eighteen holes, and this was approved at the annual business meeting in February 1945.

For children, a number of youth organisations existed. Mauchline Boy Scouts appears to have been formed in 1913 and met at first in an attic room of Charles D. Ross's mill in Barskimming Road. By 1919 they were under the command of Scoutmaster Alexander MacLean. They rented the old pumping station as their hall and had various camps to local places, such as to Sorn in 1923. This group appears to have folded soon after.

Mauchline Scouts, or 32nd Ayrshire Troop, was founded following a meeting in the Loudoun Arms Hotel on 27 January 1928, the first donation of £2 being presented by R. J. Dunlop of Barskimming, who was appointed as President. At first they met in the Lesser Temperance Hall and soon had organised a 'Mermaid' concert to raise funds. They moved into the church hall, followed by the Co-op hall, and from 1934 until 1939 the Scouts met in the school gymnasium, thereafter in the Mission Hall in Mansefield Road. Membership in 1937 was 50 boys. In 1939 proposals for a Scout Hall in Castle Street were made, but these came to nought due to the war. Instead, the Rovers cultivated the ground for the production of vegetables. In 1939 a large fete was held in Netherplace grounds to raise funds for the hall, in the presence of Lord Rowallan. At the time the scoutmaster was George Ferguson. Scoutmasters were Mr Selby (from 1928), D. B. Hamilton (1935-1937), William Abbott (1937-1938), Alexander Gibson Alexander Findlay (1938-1939), then George Ferguson (from 1939). The Cub Scouts were formed in 1935. Mauchline Scouts were closed in May 1942 and the lease of the hut in Castle Street was given up.

For girls, a group of Guides was formed in 1924. On 2 May that year a public meeting was held in the school where Miss Wilson spoke about the movement. Eighteen girls soon enrolled, Miss Campbell, Carment, being appointed as the first captain. The District Commissioner for a period was Gwendoline Adair of Mauchline Castle.

Mauchline Women's Rural Institute was founded in 1923, following a suggestion by James MacIntyre of the Co-op. The first meeting was a great success, with 89 women turning up and Mrs Evelyn Arthur of Rodinghead being appointed as President and the schoolteacher, Miss J. D. Hyslop, as secretary. Membership remained strong thereafter, with numbers reaching a high of 200 in the late 1930s and 1940s. The women took part in numerous local competitions, entering baking and craft competitions at Ayr County Show and Kilmarnock Cheese Show. A choir was formed, as was a dramatic society. The latter organised a number of fund-raising shows, one of which was to raise money during the Second World War to provide much-needed fire-fighting equipment for the village.

The Mauchline Horticultural Society held annual flower shows up until 1914, when they stopped due to the war. In December 1924 the society was re-organised, James Campbell MA being the president.

In 1933 Mauchline Horticultural and Agricultural Society was founded, organising an annual show at which cattle, farm animals and local produce were displayed and judged. This was held on the first Saturday in September. It latterly became a flower and produce show.

Mauchline Young Farmer's Club was founded at a meeting held in the public school on Monday 1 March 1943, at the suggestion of R. C. Baird, T. A. White and John Marr of Friendlesshead.

Other groups which existed in the first half of the twentieth century included Mauchline Musical Association, which held an annual concert in February. The 1924 concert raised money to provide public seating for the village.

Travelling groups often stopped in Mauchline on their way through Scotland, such as Bostock and Wombwell's No. 1 Royal Menagerie, which visited on 28 August 1908.

SECOND WORLD WAR

Almost immediately after the outbreak of war with Germany was announced in September 1939, hundreds of evacuees from Glasgow and Clydeside were sent to Mauchline. Many of the local mansions took in children, often with their mothers, including Ballochmyle, Barskimming, Mauchline Castle, and Stairaird. However, not all evacuees were pleased with their lot, and one mother demanded that she should get lodgings with one room for each of her four children, plus a fifth for herself. Although she was accommodated in the district, it was not on her terms! A local Welfare Committee was formed in October 1939 to deal with all matters concerning the billeting of evacuees. The chairman was county councillor, William Bushell, and his officers were R. C. Baird and A. B. Cannon.

A local troop of Home Guard was formed to assist with the war effort, and to prepare for any eventuality. Initially the Local Defence Volunteers, formed in the summer of 1940, it soon became known as the Mauchline Company of the 5th Battalion Ayrshire Home Guard. The officer in charge was Major George Dunn, of the Grove, manager at Mauchline Pit, with Major Marcus Bain as Group Commander. Another Group Commander was Major David Ross of Gilmilnscroft, whose estate was often used for camps and training purposes. In 1944 the Officer in Charge was Lieutenant Hamilton. The Home Guard met in their own premises located in the 'Tattie Howker's Howff' at High Clelland Park.

In July 1944 Mauchline Home Guard was camping at Barskimming, during which training exercises were taking place. During that time, on Sunday 23 July, a bomb in a weapon failed to leave and exploded, killing Corporal John MacFadyen Halliday (aged 32 years), and injuring three others. Halliday's grave is located in Mauchline cemetery. He had the only military funeral to be held in Mauchline, and the Home Guard was allowed to fire a volley of shots over the burial.

For youngsters a flight of the Air Training Corps was formed in March 1941 by T. A. White, headmaster.

At Ballochmyle golf course it was decided in 1941 to cultivate 12 acres of the fairways for the war effort, oats being planted and subsequently sold, and potatoes planted for a time. Similarly, much of the ground was let for grazing, but twelve holes were retained for play. Military manoeuvres took place over part of the course at one time, and a claim for damage was submitted to the War Office.

Szer. W. Dawidowski died on 1 April 1946 at the age of 21. He was a member of the Polish forces. Sp. Karol Jan Dilling (1898-1949) was a lieutenant of the Polish armed forces. He came to Ayrshire but never returned to his homeland and family. On his death he was buried in Mauchline cemetery.

Land at Kingencleugh was also requisitioned for war use in 1943. There, immediately west of the house, Camp 112: Kingencleugh was established. This was to be an Italian prisoner of war camp, housing 500 prisoners. It was later converted to a German Working Camp, used to house prisoners of war. These men were taken daily from the camp to work on local farms.

Support for the war effort was considerable in the parish for the duration of the hostilities. Billets had to be found for evacuees who were sent to Mauchline from larger conurbations where there was a higher possibility of attack by bombing raids. The initial rush of evacuees was soon to be replaced by the children returning home, the threat of bombing being seen as less likely.

The locals not on active service abroad all did their bit to make the life of the soldiers, airmen and seamen more comfortable. Knitting was carried out by various groups, and the local Rural Institute used wool gifted by farmers from northern Ayrshire to produce almost 700 pairs of socks, over 250 pairs of gloves and over 150 other items. The same sort of knitting was produced by other organisations in the village.

Another contribution to the war effort was the gathering of sphagnum moss, which was used for dressing wounds. Local children collected rosehips from the hedgerows, considerable amounts of these being used for making rosehip syrup, which was high in vitamin C. The Women's Rural Institute also grew vegetables and gathered fruit to be sent to those in need.

A Welcome Home Fund was set up in Mauchline, the money being used to fete those returning from action and to support them as they returned to civilian life.

The list of those killed in the Second World War with associations to the parish includes the following:

- Lieutenant Reginald John Coombes of the Pioneer Corps was killed on 22 June 1943 aged 53. Service No. 46051. He was the son of Frederick John and Caroline Coombes, Torquay, and husband of Ellen May Coombes. He is buried in Mauchline cemetery, grave number 1822.
- Sergeant William Crawford. No. 3135167, 6th Battalion, Royal Scots Fusiliers, was killed on 16 September 1944, aged 32. He was the son of William and Marion Kerr Crawford and husband of Marion Crawford, Cumnock. He is interred at the Kasterlee war cemetery.
- Sergeant John Wilson Dalgliesh BSc (Hons), a pilot with the RAF Volunteer Reserve, was killed on 15 February 1942 at the age of 23. His service number was 1005336. He was the son of David and Janet Little Dalgliesh, Mauchline.
- Fusilier William Ferguson was killed in action on 18 February 1943 at the age of 22. His service number was 3131344 and he served with the Royal Inniskillen Fusiliers, 1st Battalion. He was the son of Mr and Mrs James Ferguson, Mauchline, and is commemorated on the Rangoon memorial.
- Corporal John MacFadzean Halliday, Home Guard, 5th Ayr Battalion, died 23 July 1944 aged 32. He was the son of Archibald and Rosine MacMichael Halliday (nee Reid), Mauchline, and was married to Lily Scott. He is buried in Mauchline cemetery, Grave No. 1549.
- Driver George Alexander Hay, Royal Army Service Corps, born in Ayr on 31 May 1919, was killed in action near Dunkirk on 28 May 1940. His service number was T/100853. He was the son of John and

Agnes Hay, Ayr, and is commemorated on the Dunkirk war memorial.

- Driver James Scott Jamieson, Royal Army Service Corps, died 19 September 1944 aged 32. Service No. T/107248. Buried in the Sangro River War Cemetery, he was the son of William John and Margaret Jamieson. He was married to Hannah Wilson, and they lived in Catrine.
- Andrew K. MacBride
- Able Seaman Lewis MacDonald was killed on SS *St Malo* on 22 June 1941. He was 24 years of age. He served with the Canadian Merchant Navy and was the son of Joseph and Elizabeth MacDonald, Burges, Newfoundland, Canada. He is buried in Mauchline cemetery, grave number 1823.
- Sergeant George MacCulloch MacGavin, an Air Gunner with the Royal Air Force Volunteer Reserve, No. 1305505, was killed on 5 May 1941 at the age of 21. He is buried in Mauchline cemetery. He was the son of George MacCulloch MacGavin and Janet Elliot MacGavin of Stewarton.
- Captain Archibald MacLellan, RAMC, West Yorkshire Regiment (Prince of Wales' Own). Died 14 March 1943, aged 42. Service Number 159919. He was the son of Mr & Mrs Neil MacLellan, Paisley. He was married to Florence Mary MacLellan of Ayr. He was a graduate (BSc and MB ChB). He is commemorated on the Rangoon War Memorial.
- Gunner William MacFarlane MacVey, Royal Artillery, 151 (The Ayrshire Yeomanry) Field Regiment, died 5 August 1944 aged 25. His service number was 326491. He was the son of Francis and Margaret MacVey, and husband of Annie Gavin MacVey, Mauchline. He is buried in the Tilly-sur-seulles War Cemetery.
- Rifleman Lindsay Maxwell of the 13th Battalion, Cameronians (Scottish Rifles) was killed on 20 February 1941. His service number was 3242005. His grave is in Mauchline cemetery, plot number 1824.
- Aircraftman 1st Class Samuel Murphy served with the Royal Air Force and was killed on 27 August 1943 at the age of 20. His service number was 1571082. He was the son of William Dougall and Agnes Campbell Murphy, Mauchline. He was a dux medallist at Mauchline Public School. His grave is in Mauchline cemetery, lair number 1581.
- Fusilier James S. Ramsay, Service Number 14633670, 6th Battalion, Royal Scots Fusiliers, killed on 28 September 1944, aged 19. He was the son of William Ramsay, Mauchline, and is interred at Valkenswaard War Cemetery.
- Lance Corporal George Rankin, Gordon Highlanders, 2nd Battalion,

died on 6 January 1944, aged 33, as a prisoner of war in Thailand. His service number was 2879991. He was the son of Thomas Young and Helen Parker Rankin, husband of Agnes Maxwell Rankin, and is interred at the Kanchanaburi War Cemetery.

- Corporal Adam Cumming Reid, Royal Air Force Volunteer Reserve, killed on 3 July 1943, aged 30. His service number was 1111187. He was the son of Adam and Mary Reid and husband of Annie Reid, Dreghorn. He is buried in Campbeltown's Kilkerran Cemetery, Argyll.
- Corporal Thomas M. Reid, son of William and Agnes Reid, Mauchline, died of wounds in Italy on 17 February 1944, aged 25. He served with the Royal Scots Fusiliers, No. 3132575, and is interred in the Minterno War Cemetery.
- Fusilier Douglas Seaton, No. 3134419, 2nd Battalion Royal Scots Fusiliers, was killed on 4 June 1942, aged 28. He was the son of James and Jane Seaton, Hurlford. He is buried at the Diego Suarez War Cemetery.
- Private Thomas F. Simpson, Service No. K/53601, Seaforth Highlanders of Canada, killed 21 July 1943, aged 32. He was the son of John and Jean Fowler Simpson, and husband of Jessie Simpson. He is buried in the Agira Canadian War Cemetery, Sicily, Italy.
- John Walker
- George Wallace
- Driver James Paton Wightman, No. T/157774, Royal Artillery Service Corps, killed on 6 February 1941, aged 23. He was the son of Joseph and Margaret Paton Wightman, Markinch, Fife. He is buried in Appleby Cemetery.
- James Williamson
- Private Samuel James Wilson, No. 14625730, 1st Battalion, Gordon Highlander, killed on 11 July 1944 aged 21. He was the son of Anne Tait, Mauchline. He is buried at La Delivranole War Cemetery, Douvres.

CHAPTER SEVEN

1945 - PRESENT

VILLAGE LIFE

The population of the village continued to grow rapidly after the Second World War. By 1950 the village population was around 3,400. In 1951 the parish population was 4,164. The population was as follows over the next few years:

		Parish	*Village*
1951	-	4,164	3,400
1961	-	4,451	
1971	-		
1981	-		
1991	-		3,931
2001	-		4,105
2011	-		

In 1950 there were 890 houses in Mauchline, of which 216 were the property of Ayr County Council. At the time there was some overcrowding in the village, with 200 families needing to share a home with others.

A few proposals were made to try to alleviate the overcrowding in the village. One of these was to take over the former Kingencleugh Prisoner of War camp and erect new houses there. However, by 1950 this scheme had not taken place, the old camp buildings being used to house 'displaced persons' from central Europe.

In January 1946 Ayr County Council commenced installing electricity in all of its council schemes, including Mauchline. By February 1946 eighty of the council houses had electric ovens installed.

The Jean Armour Burns Houses were erected from 1957 onward on part of Mossgiel farm. The first ten houses cost £20,000 which included a common room. They were operated by the Glasgow and District Burns Association. The first houses were opened on Saturday 20 June 1959 by Mrs Myer Galpern, Lady Provost of Glasgow. The tenants live in the houses rent free, and receive a small pension from the association. These new houses became the homes of the tenants of Burns' House in Castle Street, allowing proposals to develop it as a museum to commence. Nanse Tinnock's was also let by the association to the local council for use as an old men's cabin.

The association always wanted to add a further ten houses to the scheme, but funds didn't materialise quick enough to allow this to take place when they wanted. In 1977 a legacy of almost £35,000 allowed the association to renovate the existing properties and to erect a house for a caretaker. The cost of these works was around £56,000, and the property was formally opened on 20 September 1980 by John Hamilton.

The housing scheme at Mary Morrison Avenue and Hamilton Avenue was constructed in the 1950s. The proposal was for a scheme of 600 houses, complete with a new primary school and two nursery schools. None of these schools ever came about, and development took place slower. The first houses were constructed in Welton Road and Lochlea Avenue. The first phase comprised of 76 houses, built by the Scottish Special Housing Association from 1949-50. The second phase followed, creating Mary Morrison Drive, Ballochmyle Avenue, Mossgiel Avenue, and Loanhill Avenue. The third phase saw the construction of the link of Hamilton Avenue with Catrine Road, as well as Alexander Terrace and Auld Avenue. Most of the new streets, apart from Loanhead Avenue, were named after Burns associations.

Since the Second World War a number of private housing developments have been erected in Mauchline. One of the earlier larger estates was the Netherplace development, comprising Clarinda Crescent, Southpark Avenue, Eastpark Avenue and Netherwalk. This was built by MacTaggart and Mickel from 1961-4. The same firm extended westwards in 2008-11, adding to Westpark Avenue and in 2008 creating a new access from Ayr Road, opposite Arran View. This new development comprised 56 houses. The original development of the 1960s saw much of the site of Netherplace House being built upon, the exact location of it now behind the garden of 19 Netherwalk. The lands around Netherplace House gardens were built upon by individual owners, creating homes in comparatively large gardens. These include Wellwood, erected in 1983.

Select Scottish Homes Ltd erected a number of private houses in the village from 1972-73.

The Arran View development, which comprises Connel Crescent, Whiteford Place and Rawson Crescent, was built in 1985 by John Lynch. Donaldson Crescent was built in 1979, located off Hamilton Avenue.

The 'Cornriggs' development of Southfield Avenue, Gregory Street and Fernlea Avenue was built in 1991-95 by John Lynch (Builders) Ltd. of Ayr. This estate has 61 houses in it, designed by MacLean Gibson Partnership of Ayr. Adjoining it, the 'Burns Meadow' development, consisting of 49 homes, was built by Miller Homes in 2008-9.

King's Homes of Cumnock developed the Burnsland Nursery lands, creating Grassmillees Way in 1999-2002. Other small private developments often included only two or three houses, such as Pollock's Way – 10 houses in 2000; Burngrange Lane, three houses and alterations to the old house in 2004; and 28 Loudoun Street – three houses erected in 2007.

In 1980 the British government introduced the 'right to buy' scheme for council house tenants, after which many of Mauchline's council houses were sold off to their occupants. To compensate for the lack of social housing available thereafter, Shire Housing Association was founded in 2001, and in 2002 was able to erect 24 new houses, flats and bungalows in the village on the site of Horwood Place. The new development was named Curling Stone Place, the association's first new-build homes.

Social housing in the late twentieth century comprised small developments of mainly flatted dwellings. Fourteen such houses were built at Robert Burns Place in 1996 by Link Homes, opened on Wednesday 11 December 1996 by Provost Robert Stirling.

Within the parish, a large private development was created on Ballochmyle estate, on land formerly occupied by the hospital. Northkirk Ltd purchased the site for £175,000 in 2000. The old wards were demolished and the site cleared, the property then being passed on in 2006 for £9.2 million to Ardgowan Homes, which commenced building large luxurious houses on the grounds. These typically had five bedrooms, triple garages, and in some cases indoor swimming pools. Ballochmyle House was also restored as large luxury flats, work commencing in November 2006.

Ellisland Court sheltered housing complex was erected off Loch Road in 1975, with eighteen separate houses for elderly people. The houses were erected by Cumnock and Doon Valley District Council and the unit was opened by Councillor James Paterson, Chairman of the Housing Committee, on 15 December 1975. Following refurbishment, the houses were re-opened by East Ayrshire Councillor Kathy Morrice on 24 February 2009.

The core of the village, around the Cross and immediate area, was designated a Conservation Area in 1992 by Cumnock & Doon Valley District Council. This designation restricted development to existing buildings within the area, and prevented unsympathetic development of new buildings. As part of a national 'listing' of important buildings for their architectural or historical interest, one Grade A, or top historical building was designated, namely Mauchline Castle. In addition, eight separate Category B buildings were listed for the secondary importance. These were Mauchline Parish Church and graveyard; Gavin Hamilton's House; 3 High Street (John Richmond's house); 2 and 4 Castle Street (Burns' House); Auld Nanse Tinnock's, Castle Street; Poosie Nansie's Inn, and the block of shops and flats from 1-17 Loudoun Street. In addition, the sandstone Summer

House at the top end of the garden of Springfield House was listed.

At the centre of the Conservation area stood the former Post Office and yard, at the corner of High Street with The Cross. The building was demolished and the post office relocated. In its place a new library was erected, with flats to the east. A public consultation took place on the design of the building, resulting in a more traditional structure, with fake arched pend forming the library entrance, and red sandstone dressings to blend with the adjacent buildings. The new library was opened in 1996.

The railway station was subject to the Beeching cuts of the 1960s, and was closed on 6 December 1965. Proposals for the closing of the station had been made by the British Railways Board in 1963, when all passenger stations between Kilmarnock and Dumfries would have been closed. Since that time there have been many campaigns to have it reopened, but at the time of writing this has still to bear fruition, despite various surveys having been carried out to determine how feasible this would be.

On 14 June 1965 the railway from Dumfries west to Portpatrick was closed, so the London to Stranraer trains, bound for Ireland, were re-routed up Nithsdale to Mauchline before being sent along the Mauchline-Ayr link before returning south to Stranraer.

At Mauchline Station the Number 1 signal box was demolished in 1976. The station buildings themselves were removed in 1977 and the railway lines altered at that time.

On 5 May 1975 the line from Mauchline to Ayr was closed to passenger trains. There were proposals to close the line altogether, but it remained in use. The line was eventually closed, but was restored and opened once more to freight trains, in particular those carrying coal.

The increasing use of the private car and the lack of transportation by rail placed extra demands on the poor roads of the parish. Various widening improvements were made, but the most significant improvement was the construction of the Howford Bridge.

The massive concrete structure of the Howford Bridge was commenced in June 1960. Two large concrete arches were erected across the gorge, each having a span of 300 feet. Rising from the arches were concrete pillars supporting a concrete road deck. When it was built, the arches were the largest concrete arches in Scotland, and the second longest single-arch reinforced concrete bridge in Britain. Construction required the use of a crane with a jib 150 feet long. The engineers of the bridge were Messrs F. A. MacDonald & Partners. The bridge was opened to the public on 6 July 1962, but the official opening did not take place until 28 September 1962, when Rt Hon Michael Noble MP, the Secretary of State for Scotland, was invited to perform the ceremony.

A fire station was established in Barskimming Road in 1948, when the South Western Area Fire Brigade was established to replace the old National Fire Service. This station comprised of a 'fire shed', which was formerly a brick munitions shed with corrugated roof, located within the council highways department yard. Within this the fire engine was kept. There was one leading firemen and nine firemen in the village, operating as retained, or temporary firemen. In 1957 the fire brigade was reorganised, The South Western Fire Area Administration Scheme Order being passed. At that time Mauchline had one sub officer, one leading fireman and eight firemen.

A new fire station was erected in Kilmarnock Road and opened in December 1963. It was built on the site of the old boxworks owned by Smiths. Officers in charge included Sub Officers A. Howie (to 1987) and Willie White (to 2002). The fire station was supplied by one fire tender. The fire brigade attended various fires and other emergencies across the district. On one occasion in the later 1940s a house was burned down, leaving two sisters homeless. The locals raised over £150 to aid them in furnishing a new home.

The Police Station, which had formerly been located in small huts, was erected in 1958 and opened in 1959. Located in Sorn Road, it was built by the county council as part of the Mary Morrison scheme of houses. The police station remained in use until 2006 when it was closed. Police services were thereafter controlled from the police station in Cumnock.

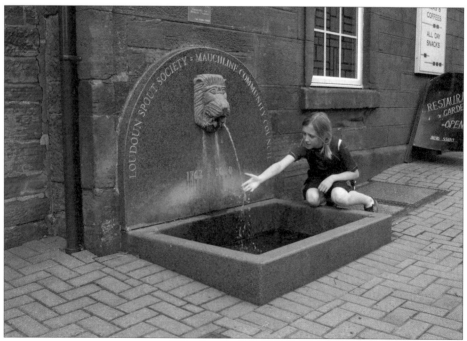

7.1 Loudoun Spout *(Dane Love)*

7.2 Burns House Museum *(Dane Love)*

A number of exhibitions and festivals have been organised in the village over the years. In January 1955, to mark the Festival Year, the Burns Club had an exhibition on the life and activities of Mauchline and its people, past and present. Although the weather was abysmal, several thousand people turned up to view it.

For a week from 12-19 September 1959 The Mauchline Exhibition took place in the Old Church Halls. Organised by the Mauchline Burns Club, this was an exhibition of relics of bygone days as well as of present industry and was arranged to mark the bi-centenary of Burns' birthday. The theme was 'What Mauchline makes, makes Mauchline', and thirteen trade stands displayed examples of work and produce that was made locally. These exhibitors were Robert Dale & Sons, of Burnsland Nursery (established prior to 1930), which specialised in growing trees, shrubs and hardy rose bushes, the site now occupied by Burnsland Crescent; James Wilson, building contractor, Arran View; W. & A. Auld, Ballochmyle Hatchery – owned by George C. Houston and producing 27,000 eggs per week and pullets for sale, located at Southfield, Cumnock Road;

7.3 Smith's Boxworks plaque *(Dane Love)*

255

Mauchline Burns Club; National Coal Board; South of Scotland Electricity Board, which had its office at Beechgrove House in Mauchline; James Campbell & Co. (proprietor D. A. MacBain), which ran the Mauchline Forge and Engineering Works in Barskimming Road; M. Wiseman & Co. Ltd., of Mauchline Optical Works; Thomas Findlay & Sons Ltd, established in 1879; William Whitelaw of 'Ye Burns Press' in Mauchline, which had been established around 1850 by H. S. Nisbet; Andrew Kay & Co. (Curling Stones) Ltd.; the Scottish Milk Marketing Board, from Mauchline Creamery, and George Henderson, agricultural and general engineer, of Catrine Road.

A resident of the village, Mohammed Shafiq, was killed in a car accident in 1999 at the age of 42. A memorial plaque commemorating him was erected in the Games Hall. In the Barskimming Road cemetery is a gravestone to Janos Achim, a homeless Hungarian, who died in emigration on June 1951, aged 61.

The Burns House was redeveloped from 1967-69 and was officially opened on 6 June 1969 by Sir Claud Hagart-Alexander of Ballochmyle. The museum was created by the collaboration of four main organisations – The Burns Federation, The Glasgow Association of Burns Clubs, the National Burns Memorial and Cottage Homes and Mauchline Burns Club. Work had started on Nanse Tinnock's house, which had been converted into a meeting room for the elderly gentlemen of

7.4 Howford Bridge under construction *(Author's Collection)*

Mauchline. The original Burns House and Dr MacKenzie's were redeveloped and formed into a museum and caretaker's house. The lower floor was occupied by a 'folk museum' detailing the history of Mauchline, the upper floor dedicated to Burns relics. The first caretaker was Kathie Kyle.

Burns House Museum was in need of considerable renovations and work on rebuilding it commenced in the 1990s. The renovated museum was reopened on St Andrew's Day, 1996, by Sir Claud Hagart-Alexander Bt DL JP, Vice-Lord Lieutenant of Ayrshire and Arran.

On 27 February 2003 Burns House Museum was sold by Burns House (Mauchline) Tryst Ltd to East Ayrshire Council. This allowed the museum to be reopened to the public. Soon after, on 12 April 2003 the Glasgow and District Burns Association and Mauchline Burns Club jointly passed their collections on loan to the council for display in the museum.

LANDOWNERS

The Galbraiths at Barskimming established a company named Barskimming Estates Ltd. in June 1946 to oversee the running of the farms and forestry on the estate. The mansion, located across the bridge in the parish of Stair, was still occupied by the Roman Catholic fathers, who operated it as St Mungo's Approved School. The school was closed in 1956 and the mansion was returned to the family in 1957.

Ballochmyle estate remained in the ownership of the Alexander family. Sir Claud succeeded to his grandmother's estate and so on 15 December 1948 he was recognised by the Lord Lyon King of Arms as having the surname Hagart-Alexander. He received a new grant of arms incorporating the Alexander, Hagart and MacCaul arms at the same time. Sir Claud Alexander took up employment with a variety of institutions, starting with the Cavendish Laboratory. He then moved to RAE Farnborough where he was involved in radar. It was Sir Claud who discovered that the islet of Rockall, in the north Atlantic Ocean, had been mapped in the wrong position. He then found employment with Ferranti in Edinburgh, where he published a number of scientific papers in 1956. He became a Member of the Institute of Management Consultants in 1980. Sir Claud was later to work for ICI at Ardeer in Ayrshire, and this was when he decided to have Kingencleugh House restored. In 1957 he engaged Mervyn Noad of Glasgow as the architect. Noad restored the house to its Georgian roots and added a new entrance porch on the north-east or entrance front. On the small gable of this porch he added a sculpted elephant, taken from the Alexander crest. A former stable wing to the south-east of the entrance front was converted into a row of outbuildings.

On 16 April 1959 Sir Claud married Hilda Etain Acheson, second daughter of Miles Malcolm Acheson of Ganges, British Columbia, and they had four children – Helenora, Anna Joanna, Claud and Boyd. Sir Claud became involved in many local and national groups. In Mauchline he was a patron of the Scouts, Boys'

Brigade, Mauchline Horticultural and Agricultural Society, Burns Memorial Homes and Mauchline Burns Club. He was a keen supporter of Burns House Museum, and was instrumental in ensuring its on-going existence. In a wider field Sir Claud was an Honorary Sheriff of South Strathclyde, Dumfries and Galloway (1997), Deputy Lord Lieutenant of Ayrshire and Arran (1973), Vice Lieutenant of Ayrshire and Arran (1983-98), Justice of the Peace (1985) and chairman of the Justices' Committee. He was a member of St Ninian's Church in Prestwick. Nationally he was a joint patron, with the Duke of Kent, of the ME Society. It was of this disease that he died on 23 January 2006, aged 79.

Sir Claud Hagart-Alexander was succeeded in the baronetcy by his eldest son, Sir Claud Hagart-Alexander, 4th Baronet. Born on 5 November 1963, Claud was educated at Trinity College, Glenalmond, followed by Glasgow University, from where he graduated with a BSc. In 1994 he was married to Elaine Susan Park, only daughter of Vincent Park, Manitoba, Canada. They have a son and heir, Claud Miles Hagart-Alexander, born on 28 September 1998. Sir Claud, 4th Baronet, lives in Redwood City, California.

7.5 Sir Claud and Lady Etain Hagart Alexander
(Ballochmyle Archives)

Netherplace House was not to survive long after the war. The owner, Mungo Hamilton-Campbell, had been a member of the Ayrshire Yeomanry. In peacetime, he was invited to unveil the war memorial erected in Tarbolton in 1948.

Mungo Hamilton-Campbell died suddenly in 1953 at the age of 41. The estate became too much of a burden on the surviving family, and it was sold the following year to Sir Claud Alexander of Ballochmyle. It had been his intention to renovate the house and live in it, but on entering the building a ceiling collapsed. Within a short time the house and its immediate policies were sold on to the Glasgow house builders, MacTaggart and Mickel. The house was demolished in 1956 and on its site new private bungalows were erected. The Trustees of Mungo C. Hamilton-Campbell still owned property in the village, especially houses in Loudoun Street, into the late 1960s.

Mungo Hamilton-Campbell's widow, Every, was remarried to Lt Col Alexander H. RoosmaleCocq MC (1911-2005). With her two daughters, Stroma Vereker Hamilton-Campbell and Tara Every Hamilton-Campbell, they moved away, severing their links with Mauchline. On 24 June 2000 to mark the many years the Campbells and Hamilton-Campbells owned Netherplace, a small inscribed stone was affixed to the former gateway leading from Loudoun Street to the grounds. This was inscribed, *Netherplace, Home of the Campbells 1620-1954*. It was unveiled by Tara Hamilton-Campbell.

The last of the Hamilton-Campbells are probably the two daughters of Mungo Hamilton-Campbell, Stroma and Tara. Stroma Vereker Hamilton-Campbell was born on 24 June 1941 and was educated at a private boarding school, Downham in Hertfordshire (1953-57). She spent most of her working life in commercial and aerial photography, running Leith Air Ltd, latterly Leith Photography, with her business partner, Bill Leith and one other. She had her own pilot's license for 25 years, keeping a plane at Elstree. The company was closed in 1998. She was married to Bill Leith in 2009, but he died that year. She lives in London.

Tara Every Hamilton-Campbell was born on 21 May 1943 and was educated privately and at Hartfield School in Ayr. She was married to Col. Robert Alistair MacTaggart, Largs, in 1965, but later divorced. They have two children, Charlie (born 1967) and Ila Venetia MacTaggart (born 1970). Ila was married on 22 July 2000 to Sir James Henry Fleetwood Fuller, 4th Baronet, by whom she has two children, Archie (born 2001) and Harry (born 2003).

7.6 Kingencleugh House in 2012 *(Dane Love)*

Rodinghead House was still owned by Commander Russell Broom after the war. At Agadir, Morocco, his wife suffered serious head injuries during an earthquake in the 1950s and was unable to lead a normal life thereafter. Russell Broom died in 1964 at the age of 74. He was a lover of angling and had taken a heart attack whilst playing a salmon in a loch near to Spean Bridge.

In 1964 Rodinghead House and its immediate grounds were sold to William Kenneth James Weir, later 3rd Viscount Weir. By this time the house had no estate attached to it. William Weir was born on 9 November 1933, the son of James Kenneth Weir, 2nd Viscount Weir (1905-1975), and Dorothy Isabel Lucy Crowdy (died 1972). He was educated at Eton and Trinity College, Cambridge. He became chairman of Weir Group in 1983, as

7.7 Mungo Hamilton-Campbell of Netherplace *(Stroma Leith)*

well as a director and chairman of a number of other businesses, including the British Steel Corporation. He was a member of the Queen's Bodyguard for Scotland, Royal Company of Archers, from 1967.

William Weir was married on 5 April 1964 to Diana Lucy MacDougall, by whom he had two children – James William Hartland Weir (born 6 June 1965, and heir of the viscountcy), and Lorna Elizabeth Weir (born

7.8 Rt. Hon. 3rd Viscount Weir *(Dane Love)*

17 May 1967). The marriage to Diana was dissolved by divorce in 1974 and Weir remarried on 6 November 1976 to Jacqueline Mary, elder daughter of Baron Louis de Chollet, of Switzerland. He was divorced in 1989 and in the same year he married for a third time to Marina Sevastopoulo by whom he has a third child, Andrew Alexander Marc Weir, born in 1989.

Beechgrove House was purchased by the South of Scotland Electricity Board and used as an office and showroom. The SSEB later sold the house and it was converted back into a private dwelling. Its grounds were also developed for housing, creating Grove Park.

Mauchline Castle was occupied by a variety of people after the war. In 1966 it was occupied by Lady Jean Hubble. In 1969 it was occupied by Dr Alex Stewart, who worked at Ballochmyle Hospital but who was noted as being a missionary doctor abroad. The castle was owned by John and Alison Holliday in 1991. The Holliday family remain in possession at the time of writing.

CHURCHES

In the Old Church Rev David Easson was still the minister after the war. The church had a membership of 721 in 1947.

Rev Easson's output of writings continued, with Charters of the Abbey of Coupar Angus and *Gavin Dunbar, Chancellor of Scotland and Archbishop of Glasgow* both being published in 1947. On 30 September 1947 Easson demitted his charge and took up the post of Lecturer in Church History at the University of Leeds. He was also an examiner in Ecclesiastical History at Aberdeen University from 1954-7. He was married on 23 August 1952 to Mary Breckenridge (born 1905, daughter of William MacInnes and Margaret Breckenridge). In 1955 he was awarded an honorary Doctorate in Divinity from the University of St Andrews. After leaving Mauchline he was to publish a book on the *Mediaeval Religious Houses* of Scotland in 1957 and to contribute many articles on church history to various journals. Rev Easson died on 2 November 1957.

Within the church a plaque was erected in 1946 in memory of John Ferrier Hamilton-Campbell, who had died in Australia in 1944. It was gifted by his sister, Miss May Hamilton-Campbell. Another donation of £400 in 1944 was gifted by John and Thomas Gemmell of Hillhead farm in memory of their grandfather and father. It was intended that this was to be used to buy individual communion cups, but wartime restrictions prevented this occurring until 1948, when 432 glasses were purchased.

Another donation to the church had been made in 1942 by Mrs Mary Dunlop. She gifted £650 for the extension and redecoration of the church hall, but again wartime restrictions prevented the work from progressing. The additions to the hall were eventually built and opened on 6 February 1953, the new room named the Dunlop Hall in memory of the benefactor.

At the Parish Church Rev James Cruikshank Glennie MA was inducted on 12 May 1948. Born on 27 October 1909 at Bucksburn in Aberdeenshire, son of David Glennie and Helen Ritchie Cruikshank, he was to be educated at Aberdeen. At first he attended Bucksburn Public School from 1914-20, followed by Aberdeen Rosemount School in 1921. He attended Robert Gordon's College from 1921-7, from where he moved to Aberdeen University until 1934. He graduated as Master of Arts, with First Class Honours in Classics. In 1933 he was the student assistant at Aberdeen Mannofield Church for a year. He was licensed by Aberdeen Presbytery on 19 September 1934 and ordained for F.M. service by the Presbytery of Aberdeen. Rev Glennie served in Rajputana (now Rajasthan in India) from 1934-45. He had married Jean Galt on 24 October 1936 (born 30 August 1910, daughter of William P. Lochrie and Catherine MacFarlane, and died 5 May 1964) by whom he had a son, Hamish David MacFarlane Glennie, born 22 June 1942, who was to marry Anne Hodge. During his time in India he was Hon. Chaplain to the Forces at RAF Jodhpur from 1942-4. At the end of the war he was inducted to Kilmarnock Glencairn Church on 19 July 1945. Three years later, aged 38, he was translated to Mauchline Old Church. Rev Glennie edited *Religion of a Common Man* by R. Prentor, published in London in 1950. In 1962 he was elected as Moderator of Ayr Presbytery. He retired from the pulpit at Mauchline on 31 December 1975.

During Rev Glennie's ministry, the membership fluctuated, rising to 766 in 1949, 904 in 1959, 987 in 1962, 922 in 1967, 808 in 1972 and 771 in 1975.

The parish church was suffering from dry rot, and from 1956-7 it had to be extensively repaired. At this time the side galleries were removed, the choir gallery, which had been rather high, was brought down to floor level, and the pulpit was repositioned nearer to the south wall, the double-stairway removed. The organ was overhauled and the console repositioned. A new heating system was introduced, and new lighting was installed. On the wall a wrought-iron Celtic cross was affixed, donated by James A. Campbell. Once the work was completed a special rededication service was held on 3 November 1957.

With the retiral of Rev Glennie from the church, the presbytery decided that it was time for the North and Old parish churches in Mauchline to unite. At the same time Rev Stewart was retiring from the North Church charge due to ill-health, leaving room for a new minister to take charge of the newly-named Mauchline Parish Church. The official date for the union was 14 January 1976.

From 1976 until 1990 the parish minister was Rev Dr Charles Smith Morrice. A son of the manse, Charles Morrice was born at Leitholm in Berwickshire, the son of Rev William Morrice and Mary Gorman. He was educated at Peterhead in Aberdeenshire followed by Aberdeen University, where he obtained his Master of Arts degree, Bachelor of Divinity and Doctorate of Philosophy. Part of his doctorate was completed at the Pacific School of Religion in Berkeley, California. The first post he held was as minister of Newarthill, in Lanarkshire, where he served from

1959-71. He then moved to Buenos Aires, Argentina, where he served at the Scots Presbyterian Kirk of St Andrew, translating sermons from English into Spanish.

In 1975, mainly because of his children's education, he returned to Scotland and was inducted as minister at the parish church in Mauchline on Wednesday 23 June 1976. He had married Margaret Sutherland, in 1958, and they had three children – Michael, Kenneth and Elizabeth.

On 27 May 1979 a memorial plaque was erected within the parish church in memory of the various other ministers of the two churches in the parish. This lists the eleven ministers who served in the former Walker and Abbey churches. In this year the congregation of Mauchline Parish Church numbered 1,239.

Dr Morrice left Mauchline in 1990 when he moved to Limuru, Kenya, where he taught Greek and New Testament theology at St Paul's University in the city. In 1997 he retired to Linlithgow in West Lothian, where he continued to serve the church in other ways. He died on 26 February 2010 after a short illness at St John's Hospital, Livingston.

During the ministry of Dr Morrice, the church was again refurbished in 1979, at which time a new organ was installed. This was a Willis model, built in 1888 for Strathbungo Parish Church in Glasgow. The cost of the installation was covered by a bequest from the Rev Allan Stewart, last minister of Mauchline North Church.

On 14 March 1991 Rev Alan B. Telfer BA BD was inducted to the parish church. At the time it was decided to change the manse, the old manse being too large for modern needs. Accordingly the old manse was sold in November 1992 and Rev Telfer and his family moved into the new manse, located in Westside Gardens, in May 1993.

Alan Telfer was born in Glasgow on 14 February 1956, the son of Walter Telfer and Ismay Barclay. He was educated at Giffnock Primary School, Woodfarm Junior High School and Eastwood High School (all Glasgow). From 1973-75 he worked in Glasgow Stock Exchange. From 1975-79 he studied at Paisley College of Technology, graduating with a Bachelor of Arts in Social Science and CQSW. He then moved to Glasgow University, studying from 1979-1982 and qualifying with a Bachelor of Divinity degree. He served a probationary year from 1982-83 at Dundee St Mary's Parish Church, and was ordained on 30 August to Falkirk St James Parish Church. He remained there for eight years, before moving to Mauchline. Rev Alan Telfer was married on 23 June 1983 to Marjory Crawford, by whom he has three children, Andrew (b. 1984), Peter (b. 1987) and Fiona (b. 1992). Rev Alan Telfer served as the Moderator of the Presbytery of Ayr from 2006-7.

A new extension to the church hall was erected in 2002, the site of the building works being deemed important enough to carry out an archaeological dig prior to work commencing.

Rev Alan Telfer remained in Mauchline for nineteen years before moving to Strathaven's Avondale Old Church and Drumclog Parish Church on 16 March 2010.

The vacancy allowed the Presbytery of Ayr to link Mauchline Parish Church with that of Sorn, the latter breaking its previous link with Muirkirk Parish Church. The new linkage was created on 31 August 2010, the two congregations to share the same minister.

On 22 June 2011 Rev David Alastair Albon was translated to Mauchline Parish Church from West Calder and Polbeth Harwood Parish Church. Born on 9 March 1958 at Peterborough, the son of Geoffrey Albon and Beryl Kingston, he was educated at Thorpe County Primary School and Jack Hunt Secondary School, both Peterborough, followed by the International Bible Training Institute at Burges Hill in Sussex, qualifying with a Diploma (with Honours) in Biblical and Theological Studies. He was ordained in 1991 at Dublin St Mark's Assembly of God Pentecostal Church. He continued studying with the International Correspondence Institute of Brussels, receiving a Bachelor of Arts degree in Biblical and Theological Studies. Further studies at Trinity College, Dublin and Regent College, Vancouver, resulted in a second degree – Master of Christian Studies. In 1999 Rev Albon attended St Andrews University and acted as Assistant Minister at St Leonard's Church linked with Cameron from 2001-2. He was admitted to the Church of Scotland in 2002, serving in St Bryce Church, Kirkcaldy. On 6 January 2004 he was inducted to West Calder and Polbeth Harwood Parish Church, West Lothian, where he served until translating to Mauchline and Sorn. David Albon was married on 6 July 1985 to Katie Coughlin and they have two children, Timothy Geoffrey (born 25 June 1987) and Andrew Joseph (born 2 March 1990).

The church, at the time of David Albon's induction, had a membership of 480 communicants plus a further sixteen adherents. The church continues to run a Boys' Brigade Company, which celebrated its fiftieth anniversary in 2011, a Guild, Men's Club, Bible study groups, Youth Group and choir, with a Holiday Club during the summer.

At the North Church Rev Charlton continued as minister. He was later to require a leg amputation, but he still managed to get around in a wheelchair. He died on 6 September 1952. During his ministry, the roll in 1950 was 438 members, with an average of 230 attending communion services.

The pulpit was filled by Rev Allan Stewart in 1953. He was born on 20 December 1910 at Renton in Dunbartonshire, the son of Rev Donald Stewart and his wife Elizabeth. After an education at Dumbarton Academy (1917-20) and at Aberfeldy Breadalbane Academy (1920-9), he attended Glasgow University from 1945-50. He was licensed by the Presbytery of Ayr on 4 April 1950. For four years he was the assistant minister at Glasgow Camphill Queen's Park Church from 1949-53, before being ordained and inducted to Mauchline North Church on 8 April 1953. Suffering from a nervous and psychological complaint, Rev Stewart demitted the charge on 30 September 1975, allowing the union of the Old Parish Church with the North Church.

When, on 14 January 1976, the North Parish Church was united with the Old Parish Church, the North Church was closed and the building remained standing until 1983 when it was demolished. It was used occasionally, such as when the parish church had its chancel restored. A house was later built on the site. Two old stones from the building were saved and relocated to Mauchline kirkyard – the Burgher Kirk stone of 1796, donated by a Catrine widow, and the 1884 date stone of the Walker Memorial Kirk.

After the Second World War the local group of the Ayrshire Christian Union continued to meet in the mission hall, located in the converted parochial school at the end of Mansefield Road. In the 1960s the hall was owned by Hugh Miller of North Berwick, but leased to trustees who ran the hall.

EDUCATION

At the public school, Thomas A. White relinquished his duties as headmaster on 29 June 1945, following his appointment as headmaster of Troon Primary School. After the summer holidays, Andrew C. MacPherson MA was appointed on 27 August 1945. The school was closed on 24 September 1945 to celebrate Victory in Europe (V.E.) Day. On the following year, on 20 August 1946, the school at Crosshands was closed by Ayr County Council and the seventeen pupils who were enrolled there were transferred to Mauchline, bringing the roll to around 440. In the same year, the number of pupils at the school meant that it couldn't house them all, so a new two-room hut was erected. School meals had been introduced and around 130 pupils were given these, within the domestic science room and the corridors!

The Inspector's report in 1946 notes that there were 129 infants attending school, 241 primary pupils and 67 of secondary age. A meeting was held in January 1947 regarding the need for a dining hall, which was agreed to be built in the lower part of the garden.

In 1949 the national school leaving age was raised to fifteen, resulting in the numbers attending the public school increasing considerably, from 476 in January 1948 to 541 in 1949. The public school could not cope with the numbers attending and so the former parochial school at the corner of Welton and Mansefield roads was pressed into service. In addition, huts were erected in the school playground. With the erection of a new HORSA hut in April 1949 those pupils who had been taught in the old Mission Hall were returned to the school. On 28 November 1950 the headmaster recorded in the Log Book that 'Today the Mission Hall was vacated. Conditions there in regard to position, heating, lighting and ventilation have proved so unsatisfactory and so prejudicial to the progress of the class, that its use is no longer to be contemplated. The class occupying the hall, P VVV, has been transferred to the new hut-classroom, causing, unfortunately, more congestion on the Secondary department, where two of the five classes have no regular class-room, and are now floating.'

In February 1950 the roll was 563, of which 100 were in the junior secondary classes. Pupils wishing to take languages had to travel to Cumnock Academy. A second hut was being erected and a dining hall had been built. Plans for additional toilets were also being made. For classroom use a new film projector and 40 film strips had been purchased. A new staffroom was provided in 1957.

A few teachers from Mauchline were to move on to become headmasters of their own school. Among these were David W. Parker, who became headmaster at Sorn Public School in 1951, John Weir who became head of Glaisnock School, Cumnock, in 1952, and John D. Pollock, who became headmaster at Kilmaurs Junior Secondary School in 1960.

Andrew MacPherson retired as headmaster on 26 August 1964, being replaced by Alexander C. H. Brown MA, who had previously worked at James Hamilton High School in Kilmarnock. He remained only for one year, being replaced in 1965 by Matthew Borland, who served in the school for ten years.

Douglas H. Davidson was appointed headmaster of the primary school in January 1975. He had previously worked at Kirkmichael Primary School. A new detached extension was opened in 1974. Davidson also only remained at the school for one year and was replaced in 1976 by Fiona Wright. She remained until 1982. In February 1983 Catherine W. Davidson was appointed as the new head teacher. She retired in 1996.

To mark the centenary of the school building, on 2 June 1989 Councillor James Jennings JP, Convenor of Strathclyde Regional Council, presented a plaque to the school. A nursery class was added to the school in August 1996. The roll of the school in 2002 was 406, at which time it had a capacity for 453 pupils. The nursery class took thirty pupils in the morning and the same in the afternoon.

In 1996 Moira Crocker was appointed as head teacher at the school. She remained for thirteen years before retiring in 2009.

Mauchline Primary School was rebuilt in 2006-8. The school was decanted on 27 March 2006 and the pupils transferred to either Auchinleck Primary, Greenmill Primary in Cumnock, or Auchinleck Academy for just over one year whilst the old building was refurbished and a new wing was added. This contained a new gymnasium, assembly hall, administration facilities, nursery class and other rooms. The extension was designed by SMC Parr, architects, and the work was carried out by Barr Construction. At the same time the two memorial stones to the Covenanters were relocated in a new entrance portal to the school. The pupils returned to the new school in October 2007 and it was formally reopened on 25 January 2008 by Adam Ingram MSP, Minister for Children and Early Years at the Scottish Parliament. To mark the return a memorial quaich was presented to the school.

Mrs Lynne McLean was appointed the new head teacher in 2010. She was a graduate of Craigie College of Education, Ayr, in 1986. She worked in various Ayrshire primary schools – Heathfield Primary (Ayr) from 1986, John Galt Primary

(Irvine) from 1987, Silverwood Primary (Kilmarnock) from 1988, and Darvel Primary from 1993, being promoted to Depute Head Teacher at the latter school. In 2006 she was appointed acting head teacher at Newmilns Primary, followed by Darvel Primary in 2008 and Barshare Primary, Cumnock in 2009.

INDUSTRY

Work in the Ballochmyle Quarry resumed after the Second World War, but nowhere on so large a scale as before. Only small quantities of stone were taken from the quarry adjacent to the railway line. To try to make things easier for masons, the quarry master started making standard sized stones, and with cutting prices managed to continue for a few years. However, demand for stone was limited. In 1950 there were around one dozen men working in the quarry.

In the 1960s, Richard, Lord Beeching carried out a major pruning of the British railway system. As part of his famous 'cuts' the station at Mauchline was closed to passengers on 6 December 1965.

Mauchline Gas Works were closed in December 1945, the village having been mostly converted to electricity. However, the works had to be restarted in March 1946 and operated for a time thereafter. The supply of gas was nationalised in 1949 and with a new gas main being laid from Kilmarnock to Cumnock in 1958 the works were closed.

The site of the gas works was taken over by Messrs Ramsay and Jackson, an agricultural contracting and engineering company. The firm was established soon after William Ramsay married Isabella Kay in 1922 and commenced contract work with mobile threshing and baling machines, driven by steam traction engines. William Ramsay died in 1932 and James Jackson was brought in as a manager. In 1942 Isabella Ramsay married Jackson, establishing the name Ramsay & Jackson. The firm developed as agents for various agricultural machinery manufacturers as well as repair and service engineers and fabricators. In 2000 the firm moved from Burnside to a new building erected on a five acre site at the former Mauchline Colliery. The new building comprised workshop, offices and stores. This was doubled in size in 2008.

Mauchline Colliery continued to employ many local men after the war, and attracted others from as far as Galston, Hurlford and Kilmarnock. Still owned by Bairds and Dalmellington Ltd., the company was taken over when the coal mines were nationalised in 1947. In 1948 there were 820 men working at the pit, producing an average of 250,000 tons per annum, or 1,000 tons per day. The mine was worked by the longwall and stoop and room methods. There were five screens for dry coal, and a Baum type, or Norton, washer. The baths could wash 756 men, and a canteen supplied packed meals. The pit was powered by steam and electricity, produced on-site.

7.9 Mauchline Colliery, looking south towards Hillhead *(Author's Collection)*

In 1950 there were 800 men employed in the pit. At the time, over one quarter of a million tons of coal was produced. The peak year of production was 1958.

Tragedies continued to take place on a fairly regular basis. George Paterson, aged 17 years, was killed in June 1946 when he was run over by some hutches. On 1 March 1950 Alexander Gibson Hamilton, a colliery machineman, was killed in an accident in which he suffered multiple injuries.

In December 1953 the workers at the pit threatened to go on strike when the coal board forced the colliery fireman, William Farrell, to take a holiday. Mr Farrell had a family of eleven and had not taken a holiday for the previous twelve years. He refused to give in to what he termed such a dictatorial demand, and the workers threatened to strike in his support. However, Mr Farrell relented and started a fortnight holiday before the end of the year.

A number of disputes did occur at the pit, for example in May 1953 when an unofficial strike affected 850 men at the pit. Again, in December 1957, when 382 men were left idle over a dispute over two clippers who had asked for assistance. The under manager informed them that they would receive this assistance if they completed more than 360 hutches. The clippers walked out, followed by 39 men on their shift, and then the whole workforce the following day.

Mauchline Colliery was closed on 26 August 1966, the remaining miners still employed at the time (numbering 860) being transferred to the Barony Colliery in

Auchinleck parish. Some of the surface buildings were retained for a time for screening coal from other mines, such as Sorn mine, which itself closed in 1983. The complex at Mauchline was finally closed in 1969 and the buildings demolished, leaving the pit bing to indicate its whereabouts. The conical bing itself was partially flattened, reducing its dominance in the landscape. The preparation plant was closed in 1974.

Many miners continued to live in Mauchline and work in mines outwith the parish. In 1984-5 there was a lengthy strike by miners, over possible pit closures. The strike started in March, the local pits becoming idle. The strike continued for many months, but by Christmas finances were becoming severe and a number of miners returned to work before the strike was over. Fifteen of Mauchline's miners returned before Christmas, lured by the promise of bonuses, holiday pay and having no tax to pay in the remainder of the tax year. At the time of the strike there were 118 miners based in Mauchline. During the dispute the community centre was used as a strike centre, the local committee receiving £60-70 per week from the Ayrshire branch of the National Union of Mineworkers. Miners' wives and others organised fund-raising events, such as bingo, raffles and discos. At a later date, the reminiscences of those miners' wives in Mauchline who endured the strike were collected into a booklet, *A Very Hard Year*, published by the Workers' Educational Association.

The firm of Andrew Kay & Co., makers of 'Kay's Excelsior' curling stones, weighing forty pounds, continued to operate in the village at their Victoria Works. Originally all granite used in the stones was quarried on Ailsa Craig, over an eight-month period, and the export of stones took them all around the world, but in particular to Canada. In 1950 there were sixteen men employed at the factory, producing around 1,500 to 2,000 stones each year. Eighty per cent of these were exported.

In 1955 shipments of granite from the Ailsa Craig stopped, granite from North Wales being used instead. In 1961 quarrying for stone on the island commenced once more. At that time Ailsa Craig Quarrying Company employed four quarries who dug out the granite. This was to be used in the manufacture of 2,000 curling stones per annum, shipments from the island being made once a month on a vessel owned by Gem Line Ltd of Glasgow. After the death of Charles Wyllie in 1958, the firm was managed by Mrs Ellen Mary Wyllie (died 1971) and family.

In 1993 the directors of the company, which was renamed Kay Bonspiel International Ltd, were James Wyllie (grandson of Andrew Kay), Michael Hughes and Hiroshi Kobayashi. By this time Welsh granite was no longer used, the whole stone being made from Ailsa Craig granites.

In 2012 the firm had five full-time and two part-time makers of curling stones employed at the factory, plus two office and administration staff, producing between 600 and 700 stones. In addition, they also repair older stones and make small ornamental curling stones, used as souvenirs, making up around one half of their turnover. The stone used is taken from Ailsa Craig, loose boulders lifted irregularly, such as in 2002 when 2,000 tons of granite was transported from the islet. Stones sold for £350 each in 2012, being exported world-wide. Still owned by the Wyllie family, in 2012 the owners were James Wyllie, Russell Wyllie and Donald McRae.

The agricultural engineers, A. & W. Pollock, continued to make agricultural machinery at their works in Station Road. In 1950 the firm employed twenty people, manufacturing their own machinery as well as assembling components imported from America. The maximum number of employees reached 34. In 1958 John Pollock (William's son) joined the business.

In 1963 the firm developed the byre-cleaner, making 1,950 units in the following years. In 1973 the firm celebrated the 500th unit it had made and exported to Japan, a number that would rise to 1,000. In 1979 the automatic cubicle house cleaner was developed, selling 2,200 units by 2012. In 1981 the firm became John Pollock (Mauchline) Ltd. and it continued to manufacture agricultural equipment from its Station Road factory. In 1998 the family-owned firm was sold to Jimmy and Effie McGhee, Jimmy having worked for the business for the previous thirty-one years. The Burnside works was closed, and the company moved to the former Lugar works site on 1 June 1998, where it had room to expand. New implements were developed, from bale handling machinery to cow brushes and scrapers.

W. & A. Auld operated the Ballochmyle hatchery, breeding chickens and cockerels for sale in the post-war years.

7.10 Pollock's Byre Scraper *(Jimmy McGhee)*

Mauchline Creamery continued to make cheese after the war. Adjoining it was the milk powder factory, but it struggled to get sufficient milk for the demand, so converted into a factory producing ice cream powder. In 1950 the factory, which had around 30 employees, produced approximately five tons of powder each day.

In October 1957 the creamery, owned by the Scottish Milk Marketing Board, produced the largest Dunlop cheese in the world, weighing over ½ ton. This was to be the star attraction at the Scottish Dairy Show in Glasgow that year. The creamery then produced another four cheeses of a similar size, two of which went on display at a trade show in London. At the time the manager was Joseph Thomson, a native of Kirkcudbright.

In 1972 the factory was upgraded, when a new cheese tower and 'Cheddarmaster' were installed. In 1975 a pre-packing facility was commenced.

Cheese production ceased in August 1991 when the company relocated all cheese production to the Galloway Creamery at Stranraer. The cheese plant was sold in 1996 and the buildings demolished in 1997-98.

The factory remained as a processing centre owned by Scottish Milk Products, packing cheese produced elsewhere. Known as the Scottish Cheese Packing Centre, only fourteen employees were kept on by the new owner, but demand for cheese grew and gradually the number of employees increased to 25. On 22 August 1997 the electronically guided forklift truck collided with storage racking, causing it to collapse with the loss of 1,500 tonnes of cheese (valued at between £3 and £5 million) and damage to the building. Work at the plant was suspended for some time.

The factory was later bought by Lactalis, a French based company. Lactalis announced in April 2007 that it was cutting the number of jobs at the factory by 37, existing contracts being transferred to a creamery at Stranraer. In August 2007 First Milk announced that the remaining 43 jobs would go by the end of the year, and the processing factory would be closed. The remainder of the packing work being carried out at Mauchline was to be transferred to a factory in north Wales, Mauchline being deemed uncompetitive. Eventually, in June 2008 First Milk decided that the remaining distribution jobs at the plant would go, and that the factory would close completely, which occurred on 1 August 2008.

The Ballochmyle Creamery was closed on 30 May 1946. The building was taken over by Max Wiseman & Co. Ltd, headquartered in London and with factories across the United Kingdom, including Strathleven in Dunbartonshire. Wiseman converted it into a plastic factory that specialised in the manufacture of spectacle frames, bifocal lenses and sunglasses. With the advent of the National Health Service in 1948, demand for glass increased considerably, and Wisemen produced glass for the NHS. Soon after it opened the factory employed 400 girls. In 1948 there were 450 workers at the factory, between 50-60 working in the bifocal department. A strike in March 1949 resulted in 250 workers downing their tools.

The factory was mechanised in 1973. In April 1981 UK Wiseman Ltd paid off 35 of their 186 workers at their optical plant. Factory Manager, Tom Dickson, blamed a falling demand for mass-produced frames, and the job-losses were in the frame-making section. At the same time, some of the frame production was also moved to Northern Ireland.

The factory was taken over by UK Optical. In February 1985 the firm announced plans to create 80 new jobs at the factory, and a new extension was added, however, by the end of the year things had taken a turn for the worse and 22 employees had to be made redundant. This had come about due to plummeting sales, down from 18,000 pairs of glasses per week to around 5,000. In 1987 UK Opticals Co. ceased trading and the factory was closed.

7.11 Billy Ramsay at Ramsay & Jackson's Burngrange yard *(Ramsay & Jackson)*

Thomas Findlay & Co. continued in business after the war, one of the village's older companies. In 1950 the firm employed around 200 men, carrying out joinery work, general building work and agricultural building work. In January 1978 the firm went into administration, but was purchased by Melville Dundas & Whitsun. This company was later taken over by Lilley Construction, but it too went under, and part of the business was sold to Robison & Davidson. It survived until the late 1980s, but again suffered financially and was totally closed down.

At the old boxworks in Kilmarnock Road, Alexander Anderson, joiner of Catrine, built a small factory in the 1950s where he produced a novel steel and timber girder which was sold to the building trade. Supplies of material and post-war restrictions meant that the business did not survive for very long.

In Haugh Road a saw mill was established in 1948 by John Neil. In 1959 it was taken over by Sam MacBlain and family, producing fencing and other timber. The firm still operates at the time of writing. Down at the Haugh the old woollen mill was demolished in 1967.

At Auchmillan, the long-established firm of James Wilson & Son continued to operate a joinery business. The founder, James Wilson, was succeeded by his son, James, who was a joiner and cartwright. When he died in 1957 the firm became a limited company. It continued to be run by Robert Wilson, and then by the fourth generation, James D. Wilson. Specialising in renovation, restoration and alteration work, the firm employed around twenty staff in the 1940s, dropping to around ten in 2012.

At the station yard a small industrial estate was established, with units, or small factories. In 1989 one of these was leased by Donald Kay, who had borrowed £150 to start up Burns Crystal. This business specialises in engraving crystal ornaments, creating gifts and decorative souvenirs.

The old grain mill off Barskimming Road, owned by Charles D. Ross of Barskimming Mill was later converted into a workshop for Diamond Concrete Drilling Company Ltd., founded in 1974.

Small scale production of spring water commenced in the 1990s following the rediscovery of the council's artesian well in Burngrange Lane. This had been forgotten about until Andrew and David Cooper built two houses in the lane and unearthed the well head. The water was tested and found to be extremely pure, and the brothers recognised that with a rising demand for bottled waters they could set up a business. Accordingly, Burnswell Spring (Mauchline) Ltd was established and water from the well was bottled in either still or carbonated varieties. The four-inch bore produces 30 million litres of water per annum.

COMMERCE

The Post Office in Loudoun Street, at the corner of Barskimming Road, was still operating until the new Post Office building at the Cross was opened on 23 May 1965. Built on the site of Mauchline House, the new premises were located in a square brick building which was to be thereafter vilified as being of a very poor architectural style, not in keeping with its surroundings. The post office was closed in the spring of 1992 and relocated to the old post office building at the corner of Loudoun Street with Barskimming Road. Postmasters in the village were Mr T. F. Officer (in the 1950s), Mr MacCall, followed by John C. Kavanagh (1982-1998) and Jim Robertson (from July 1998).

The Commercial Bank of Scotland in Mauchline became the National and Commercial Bank of Scotland in 1959 when the bank merged nationally with the National Bank of Scotland. Again, in 1969, the bank was taken over by the Royal

Bank of Scotland. The bank branch in Mauchline was extended and refurbished in 1988.

The Bank of Scotland purchased the property consisting of 27-31 Loudoun Street in March 1950 for £2,000. After some internal work, the branch was opened on 11 December 1950, the first manager being Archibald MacEwan. The branch became a sub-branch of Cumnock in 1975. The branch was closed completely in 1997-98.

7.12 Bank of Scotland, Loudoun Street, 1950 *(Courtesy of Lloyds Banking plc Archives)*

The *Third Statistical Account* noted that in 1950 there were six grocers, three bakers, two chemists, two coal merchants, two newsagents, one ironmonger, one electrician, one jeweller, one printer and stationer, one saddler and one fruiterer in the village.

Many old businesses continued to serve the village after the war, but as time passes, so too do the owners and over the years many businesses have either changed hands or closed. Some of the older businesses in existence in the 1950s and 1960s included William Bee, chemist and photographic supplies, E. Bowie, chemist, James M. Jamieson, licensed grocer in Loudoun Street, D. & E. Paton, stationers at The Cross, High Street Dairy, owned by Hugh Spittal, Robert Anderson, potato merchant and haulage contractor, Andrew Wilson, newsagent,

Castle Cafe (owned by A. Vanni), Lyall's Stores, Robert Pirrie, grocery, Young Brothers, successor to Thomas Learmont, bakers, R. L. Mackay, watchmaker and jeweller, John Scott, boot and shoe merchant, Robert Johnston, coal agent, Station, Whitton's butchers, and Connell's (proprietor William Riddell), ladies' and gent's outfitters.

The co-operative society continued to flourish after the war, there being five branch shops across the village. There were one thousand local members. Eventually the Mauchline Co-operative Society joined the Scottish Co-operative Wholesale Society and the local name was lost. The SCWS opened a new branch in Mauchline on 29 November 1965.

A new shop with flats above it was erected in Kilmarnock Road in 2004. In 2008 the Ayrshire Cancer Support charity shop in Kilmarnock Road was burned down, but it was rebuilt and opened once more in April 2009.

The inns in the village continued to serve the regulars, as well as passing trade. Poosie Nansie's Inn was owned by Thomas MacInally until April 1950, when it was bought by William & Diane Blake, the Blakes retaining possession for 45 years until Bill Blake retired on 15 March 1995.

The Black Bull Hotel was owned by William Cheshire in the 1950s. It was then acquired by the Scottish & Newcastle brewery chain, and managed by licensees, including Joe Nutt, John MacGill, Alex Vallance and Harry Farrell. It returned to private ownership under Hugh Flanagan, and quickly passed through owners such as Martin MacCallum, Dick Grant, Tom MacFarlane and Robert Kyle, who stripped the rendering from the walls to expose the natural stonework. Two maisonettes were formed from the hotel accommodation in 2001. It was acquired by Belhaven and the licensee was Karen Murdoch.

The Ballochmyle Inn was owned by Mrs George in the 1950s. Around 1960 the building suffered a fire, after which the bar was rebuilt, the upper storey being removed at this time. Like the Black Bull, it passed through a number of hands, namely Cathy Gibson, David Davidson, Daniel Sinclair, William Trimble, Paul Norman, Tom MacFarlane (managed by Margaret Aitken) then Libby Lyle from 2005. In 2010 it was renamed as 'The Myle', its local, and seemingly trendier, name.

The Loudoun Arms was owned by Mr Cobban until 1957, when it was sold. It passed through a number of hands from that time, operated by Bill Blake, David Brown (in the 1960s), Allan Barr, Joe Stewart, Mike Burnham, Jim and June Farmer, Messrs Clark, Brighton, Les Taylor and John Higgin. It was taken over by Robert Kyle and following a refit it reopened as the Fairburn Hotel. It was sold to Mike and Aoirig Carry in 2008.

With the increasing number of cars on the road, new businesses were created to supply the needs of motorists. The Burnside Garage Company was formed and operated by five partners for a number of years, having a workshop at New Road and a petrol station at the Central Garage in Cumnock Road.

AGRICULTURE

Shortly after the Second World War there were 46 farms operating as such in Mauchline parish. The size of these varied from 70 to 270 acres, most of it good quality land. Of these farms, thirty were owned by the farmers themselves, the estates selling off property after the Second World War. Of those which remained in other hands, twelve of the farms were the property of Ballochmyle estate, one to Netherplace, one to Barskimming and one to Auchinleck estate. A further farm was the property of the National Coal Board. Rentals were approximately 20 to 30 shillings per acre, and leases were usually held for fourteen years.

Most of the farms had a dairy at this time, all but two herds of cattle being Tuberculin tested. The average dairy herd was 38 cattle, all of the Ayrshire variety apart from one, which had a Friesian herd. Half of the milk produced in the parish was sent to the creamery at Riccarton, near Kilmarnock. The remainder was sent to dairies in Glasgow.

Breeding of Ayrshire cattle was a major income for many Mauchline farmers. A bull from Bargower farm was sold in 1949 for what was at the time a record price of 9,000 guineas.

Most farms were now run by the farmer and his family, there being little demand for additional labour. Only on larger farms were ploughmen or dairymen employed, in most cases living in Mauchline. In the late 1940s eight agricultural workers' houses were built in the village.

Sorn Parish Agricultural Society's annual show was moved from Burnpark at Catrine to the Holm Field at Kingencleugh. The show continued to be popular, attracting farmers from around the county.

In 1944 Mauchline Tractor Ploughing Association was founded by some local farmers who had become mechanised. This association held a number of ploughing matches over the following years, the 14th being held in February 1958.

In the latter part of the twentieth century, and into the twenty-first century, farmers had to diversify in order to make a living. Many farmers started up new businesses, often associated with country produce, but in many cases farms were abandoned as such, and the steadings converted into residential houses.

The manufacture of ice cream was pursued by at least two farms in the parish. At Syke farm William and Jo Templeton made home-made ice-cream from milk produced by their cattle. They established an ice-cream parlour and coffee shop at the former Catrine House site in October 2007, catering for passing trade as well as locals.

At Killoch farm, in the north of the parish, Hugh Woodburn also produces ice-cream, selling it through various outlets across Scotland and into the north of England. Known as 'Woody's White and Wild' luxury dairy ice cream, it is made in a variety of flavours using milk from what is reckoned to be the oldest Ayrshire cattle herd in the county. The firm is known as Ayrshire Glen.

HEALTH

At Ballochmyle Hospital the new School of Nursing was established in 1947. The first intake took place on 1 February, when 55 students enrolled. Most of the nurses taught at the school were locals, but some were brought from around the world, including far flung places such as St Helena, the Seychelle islands, Mauritius, Pakistan, India, West Indies and Malaysia. This training facility was closed in 1970.

7.13 Ballochmyle Hospital *(Author's Collection)*

In April 1947 a new Polish Unit was established at the hospital to treat Polish resettlement and repatriation casualties, many of whom were living in local camps, such as Kingencleugh. As the numbers of Poles diminished, and those remaining improved their English, the unit was closed in January 1962.

The National Health Service was established on 5 July 1948, at which time it was decided to keep Ballochmyle Hospital for the treatment of patients in the district. The Western Regional Hospital Board took control of the hospital, which was under the Board of Management for Southern Ayrshire Hospitals. At the time new facilities were added to the hospital, such as day rooms. A new out-patient department was also set up to deal with minor injuries and treatment. A reallocation of wards and departments took place at the same time, with some wards closing and new clinics established. The number of beds in each ward was also reduced from 40 to 26.

In 1950 the hospital had 350 beds, averaging 300 occupied at one time. At the hospital 24 doctors were employed plus 103 nurses. In addition, the hospital employed a further 270 in manual and domestic works, plus 55 in administration or technical jobs.

By 1959 the number of wards had dropped to fifteen, with around 300 beds in total. Geriatric care was introduced in December 1957, some of the wards converted for this purpose. Additional wards were added in 1967. The outpatient department also treated around 37,000 people per annum at that time, with about 5,000 new patients each year. The wards at that time treated surgical, medical, plastic (including faciomaxillary and dental), gynaecological, urological, ear, nose and throat, eye and geriatric patients. The outpatient department treated the same ailments in addition to psychiatry, skin diseases and chest diseases. In addition, there were laboratories, physiotherapy departments, X-ray and electrocardiographic departments. In 1959 there were 40 doctors working at the hospital, with a nursing staff of 200 and a further 200 employees in ancillary occupations.

Improvements and changes continued to take place. In 1957 the main access along the West Drive was replaced by the new roadway. The West Drive was closed completely in 1959. Sixty acres of woodland were transferred to the ownership of the Forestry Commission in 1964. Ballochmyle Hospital was threatened with closure in 1961, just one of many times this threat was to occur in subsequent years.

In 1967 there was a proposal to convert Ballochmyle Hospital into a maternity hospital, but this was abandoned. At the time, however, the plastic surgery unit was closed and the facility moved to Canniesburn Hospital in Glasgow.

Ballochmyle House was abandoned by the health board in 1969 when it was discovered that the building was riddled with dry rot. The hospital staff were moved out, re-housed in temporary mobile homes on the front lawn. Through time many of the lower windows in the house were bricked up to prevent access. In the same year Jacob's Ladder, the long flight of steps that linked Ballochmyle House with the lower ground at Catrine, was destroyed on the orders of the South Ayrshire Hospital Board of Management. Ballochmyle House remained a problem for the health board, and they applied for permission to demolish the building in 1975 and 1977, but on both occasions this was refused. In 1987 a further attempt by the health board to gain permission to demolish the house was refused, and in 1989 they eventually relented and placed the house on the market.

In 1974 the National Health Service was reorganised, Ballochmyle coming under the control of the Ayrshire and Arran Health Board (South Ayrshire District). In April 1992 the hospital transferred with others in the area to the South Ayrshire Hospitals NHS Trust.

New hospitals were being erected across Ayrshire, nearer to the larger centres of population, meaning that the future of Ballochmyle as a hospital was limited. In 1982 the laboratory service was transferred to Crosshouse Hospital, but the pharmacy was developed to supply other hospitals. As the new hospital opened at Crosshouse in 1983, some units were transferred there. The accident and emergency department was also relocated to Ayr County Hospital. Other departments were gradually relocated, such as the Ear, Nose and Throat service, and the

Ophthalmology unit, moved to Heathfield in 1974. Nevertheless, in 1987-9 further improvements and redevelopment work took place, at a cost of £1.5 million.

From 1991 the hospital was gradually run down, with units being transferred to the new Ayr Hospital, opened in 1991, or the refurbished Biggart Hospital in Prestwick. Local health services were relocated to the new East Ayrshire Community Hospital, erected in Ayr Road, Cumnock, which opened in August 2000. With the opening of this hospital, Ballochmyle was eventually closed.

Much of the redundant equipment was collected by the world renowned plastic surgeon, Jack Mustarde MBE, and transferred to Ghana, where a new 70-bed plastic surgery hospital was being constructed, the first of its kind in Africa.

Following the closure of Ballochmyle Hospital, the whole site of 100 acres was sold by the health trust in 2001 to Northkirk Homes for £175,000, who commenced demolition of the remaining hospital wards. At the same time the mansion house was stripped to the bare stonework, and the roof removed. Once the site was cleared the estate was sold on to Ardgowan Homes for £9.2 million, who commenced building upmarket houses on the grounds in 2006.

A doctors' practice had existed in Mauchline for many years. In the 1960s a clinic was erected adjoining the library at the Loan by Ayr County Council health department. Dr Donald A. Rawson served the village for many years as a General Practitioner until his retiral in 1990. In 1997 the doctors in Mauchline merged with those in Catrine to form the Ballochmyle Medical Group. They continued to operate from two surgeries, one in Mauchline and the other in Catrine. In May 2004 a new surgery, known as Loan Green Surgery, was opened at the top of the High Street. This was a traditional styled building. In 2009 the doctors in the practice were Dr David Richardson, Dr Katharine Morrison, Dr Walter Campbell, Dr Joyce May, Dr Elizabeth McMillan, Dr Amit Sharma and Dr Conrad Harvey. In addition to doctors, the practices employ a number of health specialists and other staff.

LEISURE

After the war Mauchline Races died a death. In the year 1946 no races were held, but the traditional day was still a public holiday.

The former reading and recreation rooms attached to the Post Office were taken over by the British Legion in January 1948 and they were converted to a British Legion Club.

The Masonic order continued to operate in Mauchline. Lodge St David No. 133 (Tarbolton) Mauchline Masonic Lodge acquired the former recreation room over the post office at the corner of Loudoun Street and Barskimming Road, and converted it into a new masonic temple. This was officially dedicated on Saturday 10 October 1959 by Brother T. Muir Wilson JP, Provincial Grand Master. The lodge celebrated their fiftieth anniversary in the temple in 2009.

The Cinema in the former Abbey Church continued to offer films until 1963 when it closed, the owner/manager being Robert Lawrence. A firm known as Abbey Cinema Ltd. was registered in August 1946 with the Lawrence family of Mauchline as owners. After closure, Thomas Findlay & Sons, builders, used the building as a workshop and store.

Robert Lawrence of Mauchline also owned the Doon Cinema in Dalmellington from 1966, which reopened in January that year after being closed for three years due to falling attendances.

The *Third Statistical Account* gives a list of various organisations that existed in Mauchline in 1950. These included the Women's Rural Institute, two church guilds, the Co-operative Women's Guild, the Eastern Star (Mossgiel Chapter No. 402), and various other education classes, drama groups and discussion groups. Mauchline Angling Club fished the River Ayr near to the Haugh. Mauchline Musical Society was reformed in 1920 and survived until at least 1950, when it had 42 members.

Mauchline Burns Club continued to flourish after the war, meeting successively in the Loudoun Arms, Poosie Nansie's Inn, Jean Armour Restaurant, Kilmarnock Supporters Club, and back at the Loudoun Arms, or Fairburn Hotel, as it was renamed. Over the years notable speakers have addressed the club, such as Dr Tom Honeyman, Douglas Gifford, the Earl of Rosebery, Lord Weir, Jack House, William MacIlvanney and Edwin Morgan.

Presidents of the club continued to be local men of standing, such as Rev J. C. Glennie (1959-60) and Dr John Strawhorn (1996-98). Strawhorn was a noted resident in the village for many years. Born in Darvel in 1922, he moved to Mauchline in 1961, where he brought up his two sons, John and David. He worked as a teacher, at first at Cumnock Academy, and latterly at Ayr Academy, where he became Assistant Rector, until he retired in 1982. Strawhorn was a noted historian, his first major work being the compilation of the Ayrshire volume of the *Third Statistical Account of Scotland* in 1951. He was awarded a Doctorate on the back of his work for this volume. Other works followed regularly thereafter, including *Ayrshire at the Time of Burns* (1959), *A New History of Cumnock* (1966), *Ayrshire, the Story of a County* (1975), *The History of Irvine* (1985), *The History of Ayr* (1989) and *The History of Prestwick* (1994). Dr Strawhorn was a keen Burnsian, being an active member of Mauchline Burns Club, and he was a regular contributor to the *Burns Chronicle*. He also had much knowledge of James Boswell, and was appointed to the advisory committee of Yale University, which was publishing Boswell's journals. He was a founder member of the Ayrshire Archaeological and Natural History Society in 1947, being president from 1973-7. He died on 7 August 1997.

In 1959, to mark the bicentenary of the birth of Robert Burns, the guest speaker at the annual Burns Supper of Mauchline Burns Club was the renowned Burnsian, Dr David Daiches. In 1978 the club had 81 members, dropping to around 60 in

1986. In 1978 they had two Burns Suppers, a second one being organised so that it could be filmed by BBC television for broadcasting.

The Burns Club has taken part in the wider preservation of Mauchline's history, as well as in promoting the heritage of Burns. Burns House in Castle Street had become abandoned and was subject to vandalism in the late 1950s. The club, under the guidance of its committee, saved the building, raising funds in order to restore it and display artefacts from Burns' time, as well as general local history.

In 1986 a booklet, *Mauchline in Times Past*, was published by the club, a popular photographic history of the town. In 2000 the club assisted with the restoration of the Loudoun Spout. The flow of water had been diminishing, and renovation work to the pipes was carried out. Once the flow was returned a new granite front was added to the Loudoun Arms Hotel, bearing an inscription commemorating the renovation. The rejuvenated spout was unveiled by Stroma Leith, nee Hamilton-Campbell, on 24 June 2000, along with Fred Dibnah, television personality.

On 3 March 1996, as part of the celebrations commemorating the bicentenary of the birth of Robert Burns, a horse-drawn ploughing match was held at East Mossgiel farm. Sixteen pairs of horses took part in the competition, described as probably the last chance to witness a large gathering of such horse-drawn ploughs in action. The day was immensely successful and it was claimed that 10,000 people turned up to watch the ploughing. A number of other stalls with exhibitions of old country life also entertained the crowds. After the event a round cairn with memorial plaque was erected by the side of the road at Mossgiel.

In 2001 Mauchline Burns Club decided to organise a Holy Fair, much as it had been in Burns' time. A street market with stalls, entertainment and participants in period costume was arranged, being most successful. This Holy Fair was repeated the following year and has grown to become a significant annual event.

Mauchline Burns Club was instrumental in arranging the erection of a statue of Jean Armour, Burns' wife, at Mauchline Cross. Some of the funding was provided by Score Environment Limited. The statue was sculpted by Ruaraig MacIver. The bronze figure was then cast by Beltane Studio in Peebles. It depicts Jean as a young lady of 23 years. The statue was unveiled on 30 November 2002 by Lady Hagart-Alexander of Ballochmyle. The figure of Jean Armour is five feet ten inches in height and stands on a sandstone plinth in front of the library. On the day that the statue was unveiled, the great great great grand-daughter of Jean Armour, Mrs Lavinia Drew, was present.

Still keen to make their mark in the world, the club decided in 2009 that they would like to attempt to break the world record for making the largest haggis ever. Accordingly, plans were made for the gigantic haggis to be cooked at the Holy Fair that year. The haggis weighed in at 560kg, a weight that was confirmed by the Guinness World Records organisation as the largest ever made.

On Wednesday 30 November 2011 the Burns Club officially dedicated the new plaques that they had erected on buildings with an association with Robert Burns. A total of twenty plaques were erected on various buildings throughout the village.

The Mauchline branch of the Women's Rural Institute continued to thrive after the war was over, holding competitions, meetings, shows and fund-raising activities. In 1973 their founder member and first secretary, Miss J. D. Hyslop, donated a trophy for annual competition. She was honoured in 1981 when her name was added to the national 'Roll of Honour' for her contribution to rural life.

In 1955, when a number of other local communities received grants from the Coal Industry Social Welfare Organisation (CISWO) towards the erection of new community centres, Mauchline applied for the same. However, its application was turned down and instead it was proposed to make alterations to the Temperance Hall in order to allow it to function as a new centre.

The Public Hall, or Temperance Hall, was demolished in 1965 as the building was by this time unsafe. To replace the facilities, Mauchline Community Centre was eventually erected in 1972, officially opened on 31 March that year by James Sillars MP. The hall floor comprised of timber taken from the former North Church. The large hall was augmented in 1993 when the Cooper Trust Suite was added alongside. This was officially opened by Thomas Farrell, Regional Councillor, on 29 June. The Cooper Trust was established following the sale of the Failford properties owned by the Coopers, funds being used in Mauchline and Tarbolton.

A new Games Hall was erected by the side of Kilmarnock Road in 1979 by Cumnock and Doon Valley District Council. The hall, which contains a large games hall suitable for badminton, tennis or indoor football and smaller gymnasium, was built of concrete blocks and steel frame. The hall was opened to the public in February 1980.

Mauchline Horticultural and Agricultural Society continued to run after the war, having their annual show in September. The show was given up in 1965, but was revived at a later date. Serving as president for 27 years (1984-2011) was Dr Keith Martin. In 2001 the club had 165 members. The seventieth annual show took place on 3 September 2011, president of the society at that time being G. Kerr.

A number of amateur football teams have played in Mauchline since the war. A juvenile football club survived the war, and continued to play on the public park for a time. Mauchline United played in the premier league of the Ayrshire amateur football clubs league in the twenty-first century. At Beechgrove Park a new pavilion was erected at a cost of £20,000 in 1982.

A number of sons of the parish went on to become notable football players across the country. Archie Glen was born at Coalburn in Lanarkshire on 16 April 1929 before moving to Mauchline. He played football with success as a youth. Just after the Second World War he was playing for Glenbuck Cherrypickers, followed by Annbank United. He was spotted at Annbank at the age of eighteen and was signed for Aberdeen Football Club in July 1947. He was restricted in his playing time, due to National Service, but during the early 1950s he changed position to wing half, followed by left half. He was described as being the 'equal of Willie Miller in defence.' Glen was regarded as one of the cornerstones of Aberdeen's successful run in the 1950s, being 'the thinking man's player'. In October 1955 he was selected for Scotland against Northern Ireland, and in April 1956 against England. These were his only two international caps. In April 1955 Glen acted as captain at Aberdeen, and his winning penalty against Clyde clinched the league championship for Aberdeen. Archie Glen continued to play for Aberdeen until 1960, but by then he was suffering from his age and injuries. He retired in 1961, though had prepared for this by gaining a BSc at Aberdeen University. He then worked for a decorating firm in Scotland's north-east. He died on 30 August 1998.

Archie's brother, Alexander (or Alec) Glen, a geologist employed by the National Coal Board, played for Kello Rovers, followed by Queen's Park (1955-1957) then Dundee.

The Mauchline and District Kilmarnock Supporters' Club was founded in 1965 by a number of local supporters of Kilmarnock Football Club. Over the years the club flourished, attracting members who supported other teams, or none at all. Premises were acquired in Earl Grey Street, where a successful social club was established, noted for its live entertainment.

The 1st Mauchline Company of the Boys' Brigade was founded in September 1961, under the guidance of the first captain, Donald McBain (served 1961-1965), a blacksmith in Barskimming Road. The first enrolment parade took place in November 1961, at which over forty boys attended, the company growing to have 60 boys. The colours were presented by Mrs Bell in memory of her brother who was killed in the war. The company, which is connected with the Parish Church, has had a number of captains over the years, including Andrew Wilson (1965-1968; 1970-1971), John Connelly (1968-1970), Russell A. Wyllie (1971-1992; 2009-present) and Hugh Brown (1992-2009). The company celebrated their fiftieth anniversary with a special enrolment service on 6 November 2011 and on Sunday 6 May 2012 a commemorative stained glass window was unveiled within the church, made by the Lighthouse Factory.

The Mauchline Scout Group was reformed in 1946 by James Fleming as the 34th Ayrshire (Mauchline) Scout Group (the old number of 32 having been allocated to Girvan) and proceeded to meet in the Cadet Hall in Loch Road from 1950 until 1953, when they moved to the Temperance Hall. The Scout colours were presented in 1958. They remained in the Temperance Hall for just a few months, until 1954, when they acquired an old wooden hut from Auchinleck church, which was placed in the Loudoun Arms car park. This was built with a small addition comprising of a Scouters' Room, store and toilet. The hall measured 40 feet by 24 feet. This land was sold to the county council in 1962, requiring the hall to be closed a few years later, when the car park was created. In 1967 the old quoiting ground at the Loan was purchased from the British Legion at a cost of £25, and a new Compton building measuring 100 feet by 30 feet was constructed. At the time there were 94 boys in all of the sections. The new hall was opened on 25 January 1969 by Alexander G. Findlay. The old timber hall was offered for sale. There were 28 Cubs and 23 Scouts in 1986 and a Beaver Colony was started that year. The Scouts continued to flourish, rebuilding their Scout hut next to the school in 2005. The concrete building was extended and a new brick skin and roof added to it. Group Scout Leaders were James Fleming (1950-1952), 'Scoutmaster' Stevens (1952-1954), J. Campbell (1954-1957), Ian Hall (1957-1958) George Lightbody (1958-1962), R. Gibb (1966-1967), J. R. Grant (1967-1969), Samuel Eaglesham (1969-1973), Ian D. Hall (1973-1976), Kenneth Haughan (1976-1991), Michael Carruthers (1992-2004) and David Hume (2004-   ).

The Guide movement for girls continued to remain popular, with Rainbows, Brownies and Guides for the different age groups. In 2012 one Rainbow unit, two Brownie units and one Guide unit operates.

The Cadet Hut located next to the old boxworks was used by the local Royal Scots Fusiliers 2nd Cadet Battalion.

Ballochmyle Golf Club continued to develop as the years passed, the clubhouse being extended and rebuilt. Soon after the war, plans were agreed to convert the course into eighteen holes, However, work on this progressed slowly, and it was not until 1947 that the eighteen-hole course was completed. In April 1959 the course was re-planned due to the loss of ground to the new Howford by-pass, but different land was acquired in 1961 and a new set of holes laid out, resulting in an increase in length from 5,100 yards to 5,621 yards.

7.14 Ballochmyle Golf Club, c. 1964 *(Ballochmyle Golf Club)*

7.15 Ballochmyle Golf Clubhouse in 2012 *(Gillian H. Love)*

7.16 Mauchline Bowling Club, winners of Eglinton Jug, 1960.
Seated extreme right on front row is John Fleming, noted bowling champion *(Mauchline Bowling Club)*

The sport of curling still had a following in Mauchline Curling Club. The club played an annual Christmas bonspiel against local rivals, Stair, often in Ayr ice rink, for the Gemmell Trophy.

Quoiting lost much of its appeal after the Second World War, and Mauchline Quoiting Club's membership dropped considerably. To try to improve things, the club introduced lighter quoits, as well as increased stakes in gambling. The club still had its quoiting rink near the school at the Loan Green, but it did not survive much into the 1950s. When the club folded the ground was passed over to the British Legion.

The bowling club continues to thrive in the post-war era. In 1960 they won the Eglinton Jug, beating other teams from Ayrshire and Glasgow. The club won this prestigious trophy once more in 2002. In 1967 the club celebrated its centenary, M. Allan as President, and L. Smith as Ladies' President at the time. Internationalists from the club include J. McWhirter, S. Grant, G. Hood, K. Milligan, and John ('Jock') Fleming, who won medals in the Commonwealth Games

Mauchline Pipe Band was formed in April 2007, under the leadership of Gordon Walker. A Grade 2 band, the pipers took part in competitions within weeks of their formation.

Among many other clubs and societies in the parish, the list includes Mauchline & District Accordion and Fiddle Club.

FARMS & SMALL LAIRDSHIPS

1900 – known dates
1899 – known dates, but not necessarily terminal
c. 1750 – approximate dates

Auchenbrain, North
100 acres in 1851.

1556-1567	Hugh Campbell of Killoch
1605-1652	George Campbell of Killoch
1652-	Earl of Stair
1663	Cessnock Estate
1695	George Campbell of Killoch
1798	Portland Estate – Alexander Mair
1841	Portland Estate – John Mair
1851-1888	Portland Estate – Agnes Mair (1835-1888)
1888-1908	Portland Estate – Mrs Ellen B. Mair (1832-1908)
1908-*1917*	Portland Estate – George Gibson (1848-1928)
1920-1927	Alexander Gibson
1974	David Wallace
2012	Robert D. Wallace

Auchenbrain, South
180 acres in 1851

1556-1567	Hugh Campbell of Killoch
1605-1652	George Campbell of Killoch
1652-	Earl of Stair
1665	Cessnock Estate
1798	Portland Estate - James Paton
1841	Portland Estate – Thomas Borland
1851	Portland Estate – James Wallace (1805-1868)
1887-1911	Portland Estate – Robert Wallace (1843-1911)
1917	Portland Estate – David Wallace
1920-1940	David Wallace (1887-1963)
1974	Robert Wallace
2012	Alastair Hutchison

Auchmillan
24 acres in 2012.

-1555	Melrose Abbey – James Gib
1555-	James Gib
-1661	James Gib
1661-	Mungo Gib
1680	John Gib
	John Gib (son)
1737-1775	Barskimming Estate – John Gib (-1775)
1775-1781	Barskimming Estate - James Gib (-1781)
1791	Barskimming Estate -
1841-1854	- James Marr
1887	- John Marr
-1903	John Marr (1829-1903)
2007	A. Murray
2012	Lynda Murray

Auchmillanhill

1796-1875	Hugh Marr (1780-1875)
1899-1905	David Marr (1831-1905)
1920-1929	Netherplace Estate – Hugh Hodge
1929-1947	Hugh Hodge (d. 1947)
1947-1948	Hugh Hodge (d. 1948)
1952	Alexander Hodge
1960-	Hugh Hodge & Sarah Hodge
1994-	Hugh Hodge
2012	George Innes

Bargour, Little
5 acres in 1851

1841-1851	Carnell Estate – William Wilson
1887-1901	Carnell Estate – James Wilson (1824-1901)
1901-*1903*	Carnell Estate – Mrs Wilson
1917-1920	Carnell Estate – James Sutherland
1927	James Sutherland
1940	Martha Donald Howie Manson
1974	Peter & Moyra Betts
-1995	Mrs Betts
1995-*2012*	William & Susan Hoggans

Bargower
Originally spelled Bargour; anciently known as Mains of Bargour; also as Meikle Bargour; 60 acres in 1851.

1545-1550	Charles Campbell
1634	Loudoun Estate – Andrew Gilchrist
1663	Loudoun Estate
c. 1775	Robert Wallace
-1799	Carnell Estate – Hector Paton
1799-	Rodinghead Estate –
1841-1851	Rodinghead Estate – John Wilson
-1858	- William Wilson (1770-1858)
1887	- John Nisbet
1899-1920	Carnell Estate – John Neill Drummond (1869-1938)
1927-1938	John Neill Drummond (1869-1938)
1938-	Robert Drummond
c. 1980	Caldwell
2012	Michael Cano

Barlosh
Renamed Willockston (qv).

Barneight
68 acres in 1851

1798	Portland Estate - John Wyllie
1839-1851	Portland Estate – John Mair
1887-1888	Portland Estate – George Mair (1817-1888)
1899-1917	Portland Estate – Hugh Mair (1867-1932)
1920-1932	Hugh Mair (1867-1932)
1932-1953	Jane G. Mair (1882-1953)
-1984	Hugh Mair (1918-1984)
	Alastair Woodburn of Killoch

Barneighthill
Hill of Barneight in 1800s; 70 acres in 1851.

1605-1613	George Campbell of Killoch
1634-1652	Hugh Campbell of Killoch
1652-	Earl of Stair
1663	Loudoun Estate
c. 1800	Portland Estate - Thomas Miller (1746-1814)
1841-1859	Portland Estate - Thomas Miller (1790-1859)
1887-1899	Portland Estate - James Young

1903	Portland Estate - James Hodge
1917-1919	Portland Estate – John Smith (1880-1935)
1920-1954	John Mitchell
1954-2006	Hugh Smith & Son – Hugh Smith
2006-*2012*	Hugh Smith & Son – Robert Smith (1956-)

Barskimming Home Farm (Mains)
119 acres in 1851.

1851	Barskimming Estate – Andrew Dale
1858	Barskimming Estate – Robert Young
1899	Barskimming Estate – Robert Young

Barwheys, East
Little Barwheys in 1851; 50 acres in 1851; now converted into two cottages.

1798	Portland Estate - Hugh Smith
1841-1851	Portland Estate - James Stevenson
1854	Portland Estate - James Morton
1927	Alexander Woodburn (1878-1948)
2012	John Caldwell of Ladyyard

Barwheys, West
West Barquheys to c. 1887; 101 acres in 1851.

1841-1854	Portland Estate - James Morton
1887	Portland Estate - James Wilson
1899-1903	Portland Estate - David & William Weir
1917	Portland Estate – Alexander Woodburn
1920-1940	Alexander Woodburn (1878-1948)
1974	William Smith Woodburn (1917-1992)
1994-2007	Alexander Woodburn (-2007)
2007-2011	Magaret Woodburn
2011-*2012*	Hugh Woodburn

Barwhillan
35 acres in 1851.

1798	- William Lambie
1841-1851	- William Lambie
1887	- William MacClure
1899-1903	Catrine House Estate – David MacClure
1917-1920	Catrine House Estate – Matthew Young
1927-1940	William Campbell

Bent
c. 1875   - William Weir

Bilboa
1798   - Henry Hann[?]
   -1832   - James MacCrone (1756-1832)
                        Andrew Paterson

Boghead
130 acres in 1851. Craighall included within farm.
1798   Portland Estate - James Smith
1841-1855   Portland Estate - John Stevenson (1782-1855)
   -1884   Portland Estate - James Stevenson (1804-1888)
1887   Portland Estate - James and John Stevenson
1899-1903   Portland Estate - John & Robert Stevenson
1917   Portland Estate – Robert Stevenson (1870-1933)
1920-1933   Robert Stevenson (1870-1933)
1940   Thomas Mitchell
1974-1985   David Mitchell
2003-2012   Peter William Latchford (1952-   )

Bogwood
1634   Loudoun Estate – Alexander Duncan
1663   Loudoun Estate -
1684   - John Mitchell
1815   Netherplace Estate – Robert Drummond
1841-1851   Netherplace Estate – Mungo Brown (overseer)
1887-1899   Netherplace Estate – Robert Drummond (1825-1899)
1903-1934   Netherplace Estate – David Hodge (1874-1934)
1934-   Netherplace Estate – David Hodge
1940-   Netherplace Estate – James Hodge (1903-1962)
   -1962   James Hodge (1903-1962)
1962-2008   James Hodge (1936-   )
2008-2012   Hugh Hodge & Alistair H. Hodge –
                 Hugh Hodge (1968-   )

Braehead
125 acres in 1851. Incorporated Willockshill (qv) in 1941.
   -1600   Andrew Mitchell (-1600)
1600-1643   Robert Mitchell (-1643)
1643-   James Mitchell

1672	John Mitchell
1692-1704	Robert Mitchell
1739-1756	Robert Mitchell
c. 1765-	Auchinleck Estate –
1782-1783	Auchinleck Estate – James Chalmers (-1783)
1783-1791	Auchinleck Estate – Andrew Arnot
1798-1841	Auchinleck Estate – Thomas Brown
1851	Auchinleck Estate – David Murdoch
1899-1920	Auchinleck Estate – David Bryson (-1935)
1940-1941	Grace Bryson – James C. Bryson (1900-1941)
1941-1972	James Weir (1903-1981)
1972-1995	James Alexander Weir (1947-1995)
1995-*2012*	James Weir (1976-)

Bridgehouse
Originally Nether Bargour; 70 aces in 1851.

1577-1615	William Wallace (-1615)
1615-*1623*	Robert Wallace
-1637	William Wallace (- 1637)
1637-	Hugh Wallace
1676	John Wallace
1798	- John Richmond
1841-1867	- John Wilson (1787-1867)
1887	- John Wilson
1899-1903	Carnell Estate – Alexander Renfrew
1917-1927	Carnell Estate – Janet & William Renfrew
1940	Carnell Estate – William Buchanan
1974	Carnell Estate – John Buchanan

Bridgend
80 acres in 1851.

1663	Loudoun Estate -
1851	- William Craig

Brigland
Latterly included Gorbals; 98 acres in 1851.

1798	- William Wyllie
-1841	- William Wyllie (1772-1841)
1841-1875	- Hugh Wyllie (1810-1875)
1887	- John Wyllie
1899	John Semple

1917	Thomas Semple of Colbeg – Robert Mitchell
1903	J & J Mair
1920	John Marr
1927	Hugh & Janet Marr
1940-1974	Hugh Marr (1894-1974)
1974	Alexander Barclay Marr
2007-2012	Hugh J. Marr

Craigend
1887	- Robert Hodge

Craighall
Latterly part of Boghead Farm.
1795-1826	Portland Estate - Matthew Todd (1768-1850)
-1865	Portland Estate - John Brackenridge (1794-1865)

Craighead [near Friendlesshead]
80 acres in 1851.
1841	Portland Estate - Mrs Young
-1851	Portland Estate - John Hodge (1768-1851)
1851-1872	Portland Estate - John Hodge (1790-1872)
1887-1909	Portland Estate – John Hodge (1840-1909)
1917	Portland Estate – John Hodge (1879-1957)
1920-1957	John Hodge (1879-1957)
1957-*1974*	James Goldie
2012	James Goldie

Craighead of Bargour
70 acres in 1851.
-1799	Carnell Estate –
1799-	Roadinghead Estate –
1841	- David Lindsay
1851	- John Lindsay
1887	- Hugh Drummond
1899-1912	Carnell Estate – Hugh Drummond (1836-1912)
1917-1920	Carnell Estate – Thomas Drummond
1927-1940	Thomas Drummond
1974	Thomas N. Drummond
1975-2012	John Frew

Dalsangan
45 acres in 1851.

1841	Portland Estate - Robert Morton
1851-1872	Portland Estate - Hugh Morton (1805-1872)
1887-1902	Portland Estate - Robert Morton (d. 1902)
1902-*1903*	Portland Estate - Jane Morton (-1949)
1917	Portland Estate – William Hodge
1920-c. 1955	William Hodge
c. 1957-1974	Mary Hodge
	Hugh Hodge of Auchmillan

Damhead (Bargower)

1899-1927	Carnell Estate – John Smith
1940	Carnell Estate – David Gray
1974	Carnell Estate – Bernard Boyce
2012	Carnell Estate – Andrew Webb

Damhead
40 acres in 1851. Became part of Willoxton farm c. 1955.

1841-1851	- William Taylor
1854	- William Walker (1806-1880)
1887	- Hector Walker & Robert Wallace
1899-1920	Auchinleck Estate – John Walker
1927	John Walker
1940	Mrs Margaret Walker
c. 1950	Wilson

Deaconhill

1887-1910	Carnell Estate – John Cuthbertson (1824-1910)
1910-*1920*	Carnell Estate – John Cuthbertson (1860-1942)
1927-1940	John Cuthbertson (1860-1942)
c. 1945-1974	Agnes F. Smith – William F. Smith
2011-2012	W. Fraser Smith

Drumfork
108 acres in 1851.

1577-1635	Mungo Reid (-1635)
1635-	Mungo Reid Jr
1673	Mungo Reid
1688	Rev Andrew Dalrymple, minister of Auchinleck
1757	Richard Reid

1798	- Robert Reid
1841-1851	- Andrew Bryson
1887	- Andrew Bryson
1899-1903	Auchinleck Estate - Matthew Bryson
1914-1917	- Bryson
1917-	- Bryson
1927-1940	Hugh Mair
1974-2000	William John Mair (1926-2011)
2000-	
2006-	

Dykefield
Meikle Dykefield in 1774. 70 acres in 1851.

1663	Loudoun Estate -
1774	Loudoun Estate – John Richie
1798	- Matthew Richmond (-1849)
1841	Ballochmyle Estate – Mark Richmond
1851-1854	Ballochmyle Estate - William Richmond
1887-1896	Ballochmyle Estate - William Richmond (1826-1896)
1896-1920	Ballochmyle Estate – James Richmond (-1920)
1940-1970	Ballochmyle Estate – Jessie Richmond
1974	Robert Smith
-2012	Gordon Smith

Fallhead
In ruins by 1860.

Fowler
Latterly included Smilegills; Foular in c. 1590; 130 acres in 1851.

1527	William Spottiswode
1555	James Spottiswode
1581	John Spottiswode
1584	John Spottiswode
c. 1590	William Spottiswode
1604	John Spottiswode
1634	Loudoun Estate – John Spottiswoode
1663	Loudoun Estate -
1798-1841	- John Vallance
1851-1874	Thomas Semple of Colbeg – John Mitchell (1819-1917)
1874-	Thomas Semple of Colbeg – Robert Mitchell
1920-1950	William Mitchell (d. 1954)

c. 1955	Robert Mitchell
	John Mitchell
2012	Robert Mitchell

Friendlesshead
90 acres in 1851. Now courtyard development. Ground sold to Barneighthill.

1777	Cessnock Estate - John Mitchell
1841-1871	Portland Estate - David Hodge (-1871)
1871-1903	Portland Estate – James Hodge (1839-1903)
1917-1920	Portland Estate – James Hodge (1884-1922)
1920-1922	James Hodge (1884-1922)
1927-1943	John Marr (1890-1949)
-c. 1965	John Marr
c. 1965-1974	John Murdoch

Garfield
88 acres in 1851.

1634	Loudoun Estate – James Millar
1788	- John Sillar (1767-1840)
1798	- David Sillars
1841-1903	- James Sillars
-1904	George Hunter of East Hillhead -
1917	late George Hunter of East Hillhead – John Mitchell
1920	Ralph Sillars
1927-1929	Robert Wallace Sillars & John Sillars
1940	Hugh Hodge (1876-1948)
1940-1947	Hugh Hodge (1915-1947)
1947-2007	Hugh Hodge (1942-)
2007-2012	Hugh Hodge (1967-)

Glenhall

1798	- William Morton

Grassmillees
Grassmailees to 1855; includes West Muirhouse; 150 acres in 1851; Split into three holdings in 1920.

1634	Loudoun Estate – James Reid
1663	Loudoun Estate
1841	- James Barr
1846-1851	Ballochmyle Estate – James Bone
1887-1903	Ballochmyle Estate – Hugh Miller

1910-*1920*	Ballochmyle Estate – John Brown	
-1922	Ballochmyle Estate –	
c. 1955	Ballochmyle Estate –	Gilliland
2011-2012	Ballochmyle Estate –	Gilliland

Grassyards
104 acres in 1851; 210 acres in 1861; 103 acres in 1881.

1798	Ballochmyle Estate – Andrew Paton
1841	Ballochmyle Estate – David Murdoch
1851	Ballochmyle Estate - Cuthbert Nairn (1802-1889)
1854-1889	Ballochmyle Estate – Cuthbert (1802-1889) & Robert Nairn (1839-1914)
1899-1903	Ballochmyle Estate – Robert Nairn (1839-1914)
1917-1927	Ballochmyle Estate – Elizabeth Nairn
1940-c. 1954	Ballochmyle Estate – Margaret & Janet Nairn
c. 1954-	Ballochmyle Estate – William Houston Jones
c. 1976-c. 1988	Prof. Ian Selman

Haugh

1569	Kingencleugh Estate –
1663	Loudoun Estate –
1846	Ballochmyle Estate –
1854	Ballochmyle Estate – James Hamilton
1887	Ballochmyle Estate – John Lithgow
1903	Ballochmyle Estate – William Lithgow
1935-c. 1957	Ballochmyle Estate – Archibald Morrison
c. 1957-1999	Ballochmyle Estate – William A. Morrison (d. 1999)
1999-2012	Ballochmyle Estate – Donald Morrison

Haughhead

1569	Kingencleugh Estate –
1785	- James Miller
1841	- James Stewart
1851	- Mary Smith
1903	Ballochmyle Estate – Mrs Reid
1924-1935	Ballochmyle Estate – Archibald Morrison
2012	Ballochmyle Estate – Colin Campbell

Haughholm

| *1569* | Kingencleugh Estate – |

1634	Loudoun Estate – James MacGawin
1663	Loudoun Estate
1841	- Andrew Ingram
-1887	Ballochmyle Estate – James Reid (1815-1887)
1899-1927	Ballochmyle Estate – Andrew & James Inglis
1940	Ballochmyle Estate – James Inglis

Haughyett
74 acres in 1851.

1798	- Thomas Niele
1846	Ballochmyle Estate –
1841-1854	Ballochmyle Estate - John Young
1887-1895	Ballochmyle Estate – James Young
1899-1903	Ballochmyle Estate – Hugh Young
1917-1927	Ballochmyle Estate – Thomas Gilliland
1940-1966	Ballochmyle Estate – Daniel Gilliland (-1966)
1966-2001	Ballochmyle Estate – Thomas Gilliland (1933-)
2001-*2012*	Ballochmyle Estate – Andrew Gilliland (1962-)

Highaird
83 acres in 1851.

1798	- George Campbell
1841-1851	- Matthew Campbell
c. 1865-1895	Barskimming Estate – William Wallace (1824-1895)
1899-1902	Barskimming Estate – Andrew Blackwood (1842-1902)
1902-*1903*	Barskimming Estate – John Blackwood
1915-	Barskimming Estate –
1917	Barskimming Estate – Alexander & John Blackwood
1974	Barskimming Estate –
2012	Barskimming Estate –

Hillhead, East
82 acres in 1851.

1796	Ralph Sillars
1841	- William Sellar
1851	- James Mair
1887	- James Mair
1895-1904	George Hunter (1852-1904) - Hugh Mair (1842-1916)
1904-	late George Hunter - Hugh Mair (1842-1916)
1917	late George Hunter – John Mitchell Jr
1920-1947	John Hunter

1947-	George Houston
1974	Dr William Dobson
2012	Neil James MacDonald

Hillhead, West
90 acres in 1851.

1796	- John Wallace
1841-1850	- Thomas Gemmell (1790-1850)
1850-*1851*	- Janet Gemmell
1866	- Cuthbert Gemmell
1887-1940	Netherplace Estate – Cuthbert Gemmell
1944	John & Thomas Gemmell
1966-1995	John T. Cunningham
1995-*2012*	Bryce Cunningham

Holehouse, High
172 acres in 1851.

1577-	Hugh Campbell of Killoch
1605-1652	George Campbell of Killoch
1652-	Earl of Stair
1663	Loudoun Estate
1695	George Campbell of Killoch
1798	Portland Estate - John Hillhouse
1841	Portland Estate - William Lindsay
1851	Portland Estate - Christopher Lindsay

Holehouse, Low
Laigh Hollows in 1851; 61 acres in 1851.

1577-	Hugh Campbell of Killoch
1605-1652	George Campbell of Killoch
1652-	Earl of Stair
1663	Loudoun Estate
1695	George Campbell of Killoch
1841-1851	Portland Estate - Robert Woodburn (1804-1874)
1887	Portland Estate - Robert & Alexander Woodburn
1899-1903	Portland Estate – Robert Woodburn
1917	Portland Estate – Andrew Woodburn
1920-1940	Andrew Woodburn
1953-1966	Robert Smith
1966-	Robert Campbell (1932-2012)
1974	William Campbell

Hollybush
Also known as Hollandbush; 70 acres in 1851.
1774	Loudoun Estate – Robert Wallace
1798	- Robert Clelland
1846	Ballochmyle Estate –
1841-1857	Ballochmyle Estate - James Murdoch (1790-1857)
1887	Ballochmyle Estate - John Harvie
1899-1903	Ballochmyle Estate - William Harvey
1917-1920	Ballochmyle Estate – William Bruce
1927	Ballochmyle Estate – Andrew Mackie
1940-c.1950	Ballochmyle Estate – Richard Mackie
c. 1964-2000	Robert Templeton
2012	Paul Bowman

Howford
1887	Ballochmyle Estate - Andrew MacCrae
1899	Ballochmyle Estate – William Walker

Killoch
85 acres in 1851.
1556	Hugh Campbell
1567	Hugh Campbell
1605	George Campbell
1634-1652	Hugh Campbell
1652-	Earl of Stair
1663	Loudoun Estate
1762	- John Smith
1791	Cessnock Estate –
1841-1862	Portland Estate - John Lindsay (1805-1862)
1887-1912	Portland Estate - William Lindsay (1847-1912)
1912-	Portland Estate – John Lindsay
1917	Portland Estate – Hugh Woodburn
1920-1947	Hugh Woodburn
1947-1989	A. Woodburn & Sons – Alistair Woodburn
1989-2011	A. Woodburn & Sons – Hugh Woodburn
2011-2012	A. Woodburn & Sons – Grant Woodburn

Killochhead
93 acres in 1851. 340 acres in 2012.
1758	Cessnock Estate - Alexander Dickie
1798	Portland Estate - James Dickie

c. 1840-1888	Portland Estate - Gavin Dickie (*c.* 1810-1888)
1887-1888	Portland Estate - Gavin Dickie (*c.* 1810-1888)
	& James Dickie
1899-1903	Portland Estate - Hugh Dickie
1903-*c. 1911*	Portland Estate – Gavin Dickie
1913-1917	Portland Estate – James Smith (d. *c.* 1965)
1920-1940	James Smith (d. *c.* 1965)
1965-c. 1982	David Smith (1919-1998)
c. 1982-2012	James Smith (1952-)

Killoch Mains
34 acres in 1851.

1841-1851	Portland Estate - Hugh Mair
1870	Portland Estate - William Jackson Lindsay (1805-1874)

Kingencleugh Mains
110 acres in 1851.

1569	Kingencleugh Estate –
1663	Loudoun Estate –
1803	- Hugh Stell
1846	Ballochmyle Estate –
1851-1855	Ballochmyle Estate – Robert Nicholson (1780-1855)
1855-1893	Ballochmyle Estate – John Young (1815-1893)
1893-1918	Ballochmyle Estate – Samuel Young (1852-1921)
1927-1940	Ballochmyle Estate – William Bruce
	Ballochmyle Estate – James Bruce
2012	Ballochmyle Estate – William Bruce

Knowehead
220 acres in 1851.

1774	Loudoun Estate – Andrew Hunter
1798	- John Gouldie
1846	Ballochmyle Estate –
1841-1854	Ballochmyle Estate - Robert Young
1872-1887	Ballochmyle Estate - James Marr
1899-1927	Ballochmyle Estate – Hugh Marr
1940-c. 1960	Bairds & Dalmellington – Hugh Marr
1974	Ian MacMillan
2011-2012	May MacMillan

Laurland

Originally known as Laurieland to 1920; 65 acres in 1851.

1617	- William Wilson
1841-1854	Netherplace Estate - Mathew Richmond
1887	Netherplace Estate - Matthew James Richmond (1828-1907)
1899-1907	Netherplace Estate - James Richmond (1828-1907)
1917-1955	Netherplace Estate – William Mair
1955-*2012*	Alastair W. Anderson

Lawersbridge

Smith since 17th century.

100 acres in 1851.

1798	Portland Estate - John Smith
1841	Portland Estate – William Smith
1909-1917	Portland Estate – William Smith (1855-1927)
1920-1927	William Smith (1855-1927)
1940	Mrs Annie Smith (1858-1941)
-1964	James Smith (1886-1964)
1964-*c. 2000*	David & Ann Smith
2011-2012	Crawford Smith

Lawersbridgend

1798	Hugh Hunter
1841	Portland Estate - John White
1899	Portland Estate - J. MacGill
-1998	David MacKerrow Smith (1923-1998)

Lochhill

140 acres in 1851. 153 acres in 2012.

1663	Loudoun Estate
1798	- William Murdoch
1825	- John Sillar
1841-1843	- William Templeton
1843-1850	Ballochmyle Estate – William Templeton (1778-1850)
1850-	Ballochmyle Estate – Mary Templeton
1854-1866	Ballochmyle Estate - James Mair
1887-1903	Ballochmyle Estate - James Mair
-1911	Ballochmyle Estate – James Mair (-1911)
1911-1958	Ballochmyle Estate – James Caldwell Taylor (1900-1974)
1958-1992	Ballochmyle Estate – James Edward Taylor (1943-)
1992-*2012*	Ballochmyle Estate – [James] Alistair Taylor (1969-)

Martinshill
100 acres in 1851.
1841   - Robert Mitchell
1851   - Nicholas Mitchell
1899   Auchinleck Estate – J. Ross
1917   Auchinleck Estate –
1920   Auchinleck Estate – became part of Syke farm.

Mauchline Mains
90 acres in 1851.
1663   Loudoun Estate -
1798   - Matthew Gray
    -1837   - Robert Wallace (1752-1837)
1841   - James Wallace
1846   Ballochmyle Estate –
1851-1854   Ballochmyle Estate - William Wallace
    -1868   Ballochmyle Estate - James Wallace (1805-1868)
1887-1903   Ballochmyle Estate – Mrs Agnes Borland (nee Findlay)
1917-1927   Ballochmyle Estate – William Ramsay
1940   Ballochmyle Estate – trustee of William Ramsay
c.1947-1974   Ballochmyle Estate – George Ramsay
2012   Ballochmyle Estate – George Ramsay

Merkland
1841   - William Hutton
1851   - Agnes Earl
1887-1921   Catrine House Estate – Matthew Young (1849-1921)
1940   now part of Barwhillan

Montgarswood, West
126 acres in 1851.
1544-1566   George Campbell
1612   John Campbell
1616-1658   James Campbell (-1658)
1658-1661   James Campbell
    -1781   Ballochmyle Estate – Andrew Fisher (1692-1781)
1781-1809   Ballochmyle Estate – William Fisher (1737-1809)
1841-1874   Ballochmyle Estate – John Mitchell (1789-1874)
1887   Ballochmyle Estate - James Gall
1899   Ballochmyle Estate – Agnes Simpson or Baird
1903-1922   Ballochmyle Estate – John Nairn

1927	Ballochmyle Estate – Robert Cunningham
1940	Ballochmyle Estate – Robert Cunningham & B. C. Cunningham
1974	Ballochmyle Estate – Bryce C. Cunningham
2011-2012	Ballochmyle Estate – James Johnstone

Mossgiel, East (Mid)
Anciently spelled 'Mossgaville'; 118 acres in 1784; 112 acres in 1851.

1527	Melrose Abbey Estate – William Hamilton of Macnairston
1617	- Annabella Wallace
-1642	Loudoun Estate – John Campbell (k. 1642)
1642-	Loudoun Estate – John Richmond
1774	Loudoun Estate – Andrew MacLelland
1783-1786	Loudoun Estate - Gavin Hamilton - Gilbert (1760-1827) & Robert Burns (1759-1796)
1786-1788	Ballochmyle Estate - Gavin Hamilton - Gilbert (1760-1827) & Robert Burns (1759-1796)
1788-1798	Ballochmyle Estate - Gilbert Burns (1760-1827)
1841-1887	Ballochmyle Estate - James Wyllie (1813-1882)
1899-1903	Ballochmyle Estate - Alexander Wyllie
1917	Ballochmyle Estate – Alexander Wyllie
1920-1927	Ballochmyle Estate – Alexander & William Wyllie
1940	Ballochmyle Estate – William Wyllie
1974	Ballochmyle Estate – William & Alexander M. Wyllie
1980-2011	Ballochmyle Estate – Alexander Wyllie (1923-2011)
2011-*2012*	Ballochmyle Estate – William Wyllie

Mossgiel, South
Laigh Mossgiel in 1841.

1798	- James Alexander
1846	Ballochmyle Estate –
1841-1854	Ballochmyle Estate - Thomas Brownlee
1887	Ballochmyle Estate - James Wyllie
1899-1917	Ballochmyle Estate – Alexander Wyllie
1920	Ballochmyle Estate – Alexander & William Wyllie
1927	In ruins – became part of East Mossgiel

Mossgiel, West
150 acres in 1851.

1798	- Andrew MacClelland
1841	- James Dunlop

1846	Ballochmyle Estate –
1851	Ballochmyle Estate – Thomas Brownlie
1887-1900	Ballochmyle Estate – John Brownlie (1828-1900)
1900-*1903*	Ballochmyle Estate – Mrs Brownlie
1917-c. 1950	Ballochmyle Estate – William Brownlie
c. 1950-1974	Ballochmyle Estate – Robert Cunningham
2008-2012	Ballochmyle Estate – Robert Bryce Cunningham

Mosshead
90 acres in 1851.

1841-1851	- John Crichton
-1855	- Robert Young (1808-1855)
1877-1903	Barskimming Estate - George Jamieson
1917	Barskimming Estate – William Jamieson
-1919	Barskimming Estate – George Jamieson (1845-1922)
1919-*1927*	Barskimming Estate – James Morton
	J. Brown & Sons

Muir
80 acres in 1851.

1841	- Mrs Murray
1851	- James Murray
1887	- James Taylor
1899-1903	Barskimming Estate - Hugh Mair
-1918	Thomas Speir (1851-1918)
1918-1920	Allan Speir
1939-1974	William Watson
	Andrew B. Watson
2012	William Watson

Roadinghead of Auchinleck
In ruins by 1860.

Rodinghead
150 acres in 1851. Included Springfield by 1919.

1841	- William Stevenson
1851	- Jean Stevenson
1866-1887	Carnell Estate – William Campbell (1836-1915)
1899-1921	Carnell Estate – James Hunter Smith
1925	Rodinghead Estate – Caprington & Auchlochan Collieries
1927	Rodinghead Estate - empty

Roughdyke
103 acres in 1851.

1837	Captain Campbell –
1841-1851	- Alexander Reid
1887	- Alexander Young
1899-1903	Portland Estate - Mrs Young
1917	Portland Estate – Helen Barclay
1920	Helen Young
1927	Helen Young – Alexander Young
1940-1969	Alexander Young (1895-1969)
1969-c. 2002	Robert Young
c. 2002-2012	Marion Young

Sawersbridge

1841	- William Smith

Springfield
From before 1919 part of Rodinghead farm.

-1882	- James MacFarlane (1812-1882)
1887	- James MacFarlane

Syke
Latterly included Martinshill and Cockmoss; 64 acres in 1851; 135 acres in 2005; 55 acres in 2010.

1798	- John Kay
1841-1851	- James Gibson
1887-1900	Auchinleck Estate – Thomas Lethardy (1824-1900)
1900-1903	Auchinleck Estate – George Lethardy
1917-1927	Auchinleck Estate – Thomas Templeton
1940	Auchinleck Estate – John & William Templeton
c. 1945-1963	William Templeton (1900-1976)
1963-2002	Robert William Templeton (1938-)
2002-2009	Robert William Templeton (1938-) & William Templeton (1974-)
2009-2012	Andrew Gemmell of Turnerhill

Turnerhill
Also included Roadinghead; 110 acres in 1851; 167 acres in 1924.

1681	- John Mitchell
1798	Auchinleck Estate - James Wallace
1841-1860	Auchinleck Estate - James Sloan (1778-1860)

1860-1892	Auchinleck Estate – James Sloan (1819-1892)
1899-*1903*	Auchinleck Estate – David Templeton
1917	Auchinleck Estate – late David Templeton
1927	Auchinleck Estate – Thomas Biggart
1940	Auchinleck Estate – Hugh Kerr
1955-1974	James Gemmell
2008-2012	Andrew Gemmell

Welton, East
High Welton in 1851; includes Welton Hill; 94 acres in 1851.

1663	Loudoun Estate -
c. 1770	- James Brydan Welston]
1841-1854	Ballochmyle Estate - William Crawford
1861-1899	Ballochmyle Estate - Bryce Kerr Nairn (1828-1910)
1903-1920	Ballochmyle Estate – Robert Paton
1927	Ballochmyle Estate – J. & A. Gilmour
1940-c. 1960	Ballochmyle Estate – Archibald Gilmour
1974-c. 2007	Ballochmyle Estate – John Gilmour (1936-2010)
c. 2007-2012	Ballochmyle Estate – James Johnstone

Welton, West
Includes Newlands; 60 acres in 1851.

1663	Loudoun Estate -
1798	- William Jamieson
1841	- Robert Morton
1846	Ballochmyle Estate –
1851-1854	Ballochmyle Estate – William Jamieson (1818-1881)
1887-1917	Ballochmyle Estate – George Ramsay
1927-1966	Ballochmyle Estate – George Ramsay
1966-2006	Ballochmyle Estate – Hugh & Thomas Spittal
2006-*2012*	Ballochmyle Estate – George Ramsay

Willockshill

-1604	James Reid
1604-	James Reid
1643	James Reid
c. 1690	Robert Millar
1774	Loudoun Estate – Quintin Dun & John Dun
1785-	Auchinleck Estate – (bought by James Boswell)
1841	Auchinleck Estate – James Hair
1887	Auchinleck Estate - David Wilson

1899	Auchinleck Estate – J. Herbertson
1899-1920	Auchinleck Estate – David Bryson
1941	became part of Braehead farm.

Willoxton

Willockstone to at least 1918; 76 acres in 1851. Replaced Barlosh (qv).

1569	Kingencleugh Estate – William Lauchlan
1663	Loudoun Estate
1783-1795	Auchinleck Estate – William Murdoch
1841-1851	Auchinleck Estate – John Reid
-1887	Auchinleck Estate – George Templeton (1807-1887)
1887-	Auchinleck Estate - Mrs Templeton
1899-1920	Auchinleck Estate – Robert Templeton (1875-1951)
1927	Robert Templeton (1875-1951)
1940	John Templeton
c. 1965-1974	James Templeton
	John Templeton

Woodlands

Wynd[s] (South and North)

80 acres in 1851.

1798	- James Wallace
1841-1847	Alexander Gebbie (1775-1847)
1851	Thomas Gebbie
1899	Portland Estate – Thomas Gebbie
1887-1903	Portland Estate – Thomas Gebbie
1917	Portland Estate – Robert Baird
1920	Robert Baird
1927-1974	John Baird (d. 1974)
1974-1992	Archibald, John and Roger Baird
1992-*2012*	Roger Baird

BIBLIOGRAPHY

Acts and Proceedings of the General Assemblies of the Kirk of Scotland from the year 1560, Bannatyne Club, Edinburgh, 1839.

Aiton, William, *General View of Agriculture in the County of Ayr*, Board of Agriculture, Glasgow, 1811.

Anderson, J., and Grant, F. J. (editors), *Protocol Book of Gavin Ros, 1512-32*, Scottish Record Society, Edinburgh, 1908.

Ayrshire: an Invitation to Industry, Ayrshire Development Council, Ayr, *c.* 1935.

Black, Mary Anne, *The Home Guard in Mauchline*, no date.

Blair, William F., *An Octogenarian's Reminiscences*, Kilmarnock Standard, Kilmarnock, 1922.

Bowen, Jane (editor), *Makers, Methods and Merchandise – a Mauchline Ware Handbook to Commemorate 25 years of the M. W. C. C.*, Belford Bowen Publishing, Belford, 2011.

Burke's Landed Gentry of Great Britain – The Kingdom of Scotland, Burke's Peerage, Wilmington, Delaware, 2001.

Burnett, John, *Riot, Revelry and Rout: Sport in Lowland Scotland before 1860*, Tuckwell Press, East Linton, 2000.

Cobbett, William, *Cobbett's Tour in Scotland … in the autumn of the year 1832*, London, 1833.

Debrett's Peerage and Baronetage, various volumes.

Dennison, E. Patricia; Gallagher, Dennis; and Ewart, Gordon. *Historic Mauchline: Archaeology and Development*, Council for British Archaeology and Historic Scotland, York and Edinburgh, 2006.

Dickson, Neil T. R., *Brethren in Scotland 1838-2000*, Paternoster, Milton Keynes, 2002.

Edgar, Rev Andrew, *Old Church Life in Scotland: Lectures on Kirk-Session and Presbytery Records*, Alexander Gardner, Paisley, 1885.

Ellis, Peter Beresford, & Mac a' Ghobhainn, Seumas, *The Scottish Insurrection of 1820*, Victor Gollancz, London, 1970.

Ewing, Rev. William (editor), *Annals of the Free Church of Scotland*, (2 vols.), T. & T. Clark, Edinburgh, 1914.

Forrest, Robert, *Mauchline Curling Club 1812-2012*, Mauchline Curling Club, Mauchline, 2012.

Gaskell, Ernest, *Renfrewshire and Ayrshire Leaders, Social and Political*, Queenhithe Publishing Co., London, n.d.

Gibb, John Taylor, *The Land of Burns: Mauchline, Town and District*, J. Taylor Gibb, Mauchline, 1911.

Gow, Bill, *The Swirl of the Pipes: a History of Water and Sewerage in Strathclyde*, Strathclyde Regional Council, Glasgow, 1996.

Haldane, A. R. B., *Three Centuries of Scottish Posts*, Edinburgh University Press, Edinburgh, 1971.

Hewison, Rev. James King, *The Covenanters* (2 vols.), John Smith, Glasgow, 1913.

Hood, John, *Old Mauchline and Tarbolton*, Stenlake Publishing, Catrine, 2001.

Johnston, G. Harvey, *The Heraldry of the Campbells*, Beinn Bhuidhe Holdings, Inveraray, 1977.

Knox, John, *History of the Reformation in Scotland*, ed. W. Croft Dickinson, 2 vols, Edinburgh, 1949.

Lamb, John A. (editor), *Fasti of the United Free Church of Scotland, 1900-1929*, Oliver & Boyd, Edinburgh, 1956.

Letters of John Graham of Claverhouse, edited by Andrew Murray Scott, in *Miscellany of the Scottish History Society*, Vol. 11, Scottish History Society, Edinburgh, 1990.

Levy, Catriona, *A Very Hard Year – 1984-5 Miners' Strike in Mauchline*, Workers' Educational Association, Glasgow.

Lindsay, Alistair, & Kennedy, Jean, *The Burgesses and Guild Brethren of Ayr 1647-1846*, Ayrshire Federation of Historical Societies, Drongan, 2002.

Lindsay, Maurice, *The Burns Encyclopedia*, Robert Hale, London, 1959.

MacClure, David, *Tolls and Tacksmen: Eighteenth Century Roads in the county of John Loudon MacAdam*, AANHS, Ayr, 1994.

MacGibbon, David, & Ross, Thomas, *The Castellated and Domestic Architecture of Scotland* (5 volumes), David Douglas, Edinburgh, 1887-1892.

MacIlvean, John Gardner, *The Birth of Football in the Burns Country*, MacIlvean, Cumnock, 1982.

Mackay, James A., *Burns: A Biography of Robert Burns*, Mainstream, Edinburgh, 1992.

MacKelvie, Rev Dr William, *Annals and Statistics of the United Presbyterian Church*, Oliphant & A. Eliot, Edinburgh, 1873.

MacKenzie, Rev Archibald, *William Adair and His Kirk*, Ayr Advertiser, Ayr, 1933.

Mair, James, *Cessnock: an Ayrshire estate in the Age of Improvement*, AANHS, Ayr, 1996.

National Commercial Directory of the Whole of Scotland, J. Pigot & Co., London, 1837.

Ordnance Gazetteer of Scotland, William MacKenzie, London, 1892.

Paterson, James, *History of the County of Ayr, with a Genealogical Account of the Families of Ayrshire*, (2 vols.) John Dick, Ayr, 1847 and 1852.

Protocol Book of Gavin Ros, 1512-32, eds J. Anderson and F. J. Grant, Scottish Record Society, 1908.

Rawson, Dr D. A., & MacNeill, D., *Ballochmyle Hospital, Mauchline, Golden Jubilee 1940-1990*, Ayrshire & Arran Health Board, 1990.

Register of the Privy Council of Scotland, (3rd Series, editor P. Hume Brown), Edinburgh, 1908-70)

Royal National Commercial Directory and Topography of Scotland, Isaac Slater, Manchester, 1867.

Sanderson, Margaret H. B., *The Mauchline Account Books of Melrose Abbey*, Ayrshire Archaeological and Natural History Society, Ayr, 1975.

Ayrshire and the Reformation, Tuckwell Press, East Linton, 1997.

Scott, Rev Dr Hew, *Fasti Ecclesiae Scoticanae*, Vol. 3 – Synod of Glasgow and Ayr, Oliver & Boyd, Edinburgh, 1920.

Smith, John, *Prehistoric Man in Ayrshire*, Elliot Stock, London, 1895.

Soldiers Died in the Great War, 1914-1919, Part 26: The Royal Scots Fusiliers, J. B. Hayward & Son, Polstead, Suffolk, 1988.

Steven, Helen J., *Historical Associations of Mauchline*, Dunlop & Drennan, Kilmarnock, 1897.

Stevenson, David, *The Battle of Mauchline Moor 1648*, Ayrshire Archaeological and Natural History Society, Ayr, 1973.

The Best of the Old, the Best of the New: A History of the S.W.R.I. Ayrshire Federation, 1921-2006, Ayrshire Federation of S.W.R.I., Ayr, 2005.

The Trial of Mungo Campbell, before the High Court of Justiciary in Scotland, for the Murder of Alexander, Earl of Eglintoun. From an Authentick copy, extracted from the Records of the Court, D. Wilson & G. Nicol, London, 1770.

Third Report of the Inspectors appointed under the provisions of the Act 5 & 6 Will. IV c 38, to visit the Different Prisons of Great Britain (II Northern and Eastern District), His Majesty's Stationery Office, London, 1838.

Thomson, Rev J. H., *The Martyr Graves of Scotland*, Oliphant, Anderson & Ferrier, Edinburgh, n.d.

Todd, Adam Brown, *The Poetical Works of A. B. Todd*, with Autobiography, Oliphant, Anderson & Ferrier, Edinburgh, 1906.

Trachtenberg, David & Keith, Thomas, *Mauchline Ware, a Collector's Guide*, Antique Collector's Club, Woodbridge, 2002.

Turner, Sir James, *Memoirs of His Life and Times, 1632-1670*, Constable, Edinburgh, 1829.

Wilson, James Pearson, *The Last Miller: the Cornmills of Ayrshire*, AANHS, Ayr, 2000.

Wilson, John G., *The Tartan Tree – Scotland, Burns, Mauchline and Me*, John G. Wilson of Kilwinnet, Lanark, 2011.

Wodrow, Rev Robert, *The History and Sufferings of the Church of Scotland*, (2 vols.), Blackie, Glasgow, 1832.

PERIODICALS

Ardrossan & Saltcoats Herald, 13 March 1891 – article on Mauchline boxworks.

Ayr Advertiser, 1803 - present.

Ayrshire Archaeological & Natural History Society Collections:
Fowler, James J., *The Presbytery of Ayr: its Schools and Schoolmasters 1642-1746*, Vol. 6 - 1958-60, 1961.

Ayrshire Post, 1880 - present.

British Medical Journal, 20 February 1926, p 352 (J. F. Gemmill).

Burns Chronicle:
Gibb, John Taylor, *More Mauchline Topography*, No. V, 1896.
Official Opening of Jean Armour Burns Houses, Third Series, Volume 9, 1960.
Burns House Museum, Third Series, Volume 19, 1970.
1978 issue.

Cumnock Chronicle, 1901 – present.

Discovery and Excavation in Scotland, Vol. 3 (Mauchline Parish Church Hall).

Glasgow Archaeological Journal:
Stevenson, J. B., *Cup-and-Ring Markings at Ballochmyle*, Ayrshire, Vol. 18, 1993.

Kilmarnock Standard, 1863 - present.

Mauchline & Catrine Advertiser and Tarbolton & Ochiltree Reporter, 1883.

Mauchline & Catrine News and Advertiser, 1908.

MAPS & PLANS

Johnson, William, *Northern Part of Ayrshire*, Edinburgh, 1828.

Plan of Estate of Netherplace, 1824.

Sturrock, J., *Plan of Loch Broom, as apportioned*, 1849, Ballochmyle Estate Archives, Kingencleugh.

Thomson, Alexander, *Ballochmyle Estate Plans*, 1847-8, Ballochmyle Estate Archives, Kingencleugh.

OTHER SOURCES

Ballochmyle Estate – family papers, etc. held at Kingencleugh.

Chartulary of the Earl of Loudoun to his vassals in Kylesmuir, covering the parish of Mauchline, 1773-1783, held by R. J. G. Shields DL, Parwich Hall, Derbyshire.

Minute Book of Ballochmyle Golf Club, 1937-1962, held at Ballochmyle Golf Club.

Plans of Ballochmyle House by Hew Montgomerie Wardrop, Edinburgh University Library.

Minutes of Mauchline Burgher Church, 1834-1890, held at Burns Monument Centre, Kilmarnock.

Managers' Minutes of Mauchline Burgher Church, 1826-1860, held at National Archives of Scotland, Edinburgh, record CH3/772.

Mauchline Kirk Session Minutes 1669-1985, held at Burns Monument Centre, Kilmarnock.

Mauchline Parish Council Minutes 1895-1928, held at Ayrshire Archives.

Mauchline Parochial Board Minutes 1888-1895, held at Ayrshire Archives.

Mauchline Public School Log Book, 1866-1903, held at Mauchline Primary School.

Mauchline Public School Log Book, 1903-1964, held at Mauchline Primary School.

Minutes of Mauchline Free Church, 1843-1925, held at National Archives of Scotland, Edinburgh, record CH3/771.

Minute Books and letter files of Mauchline Scout Committee, etc., held by Janette Paterson, Mauchline.

Minute Book of the Commissioners of Supply 1774, held at Ayrshire Archives.

Miller of Glenlee, Kirkcudbright, family papers, held at Department of Special Collections of Aberdeen University. Contains material concerning the Millers of Barskimming. Record Number MS 2769/I/28/1-3.

Netherplace, estate papers, held at Ayrshire Archives.

Rodinghead, estate papers of the Duke of Portland – letters from George Douglas to the Duke regarding tenancies, etc., held at Nottingham University.

INDEX

Figures in **bold** type refer to illustrations

Wilson Place, 119, 194
Wiseman, Max, and Co., 256, 271-2
Wishart, Rev George, 25, 31-2, **32**
Witches, 379
Wodrow of Viewfield, Robert, 131-3
Wodrow, Rev Robert, 26, 51, 131
Woodlands, 308
Woollen Mill, 50, 232, 273
Wyllie, Rev Thomas, 37-8, 40-1, 44-5
Wynds, 308

Ye Burns' Press, 190
Young Farmers' Club, 245
Young Men's Christian Association, 196
Young, Rev George, 39-40, 65
Young, Thomas (Covenanter) 50-4